Learning Lawyers' Skills

Learning Lawyers' Skills

Edited by

Neil Gold
Professor and Dean of the Faculty of Law,
University of Windsor, Ontario

Karl Mackie
Senior Lecturer in Law and Social Psychology, University of Nottingham
Director, Centre for Legal Studies, University of Nottingham

William Twining
Quain Professor of Jurisprudence, University College London
Chairman, Commonwealth Legal Education Association

Published in conjunction with
the Commonwealth Legal Education Association

Butterworths
London and Edinburgh
1989

United Kingdom   Butterworth & Co (Publishers) Ltd,
                         88 Kingsway, LONDON WC2B 6AB and 4 Hill Street,
                         EDINBURGH EH2 3JZ

Australia   Butterworths Pty Ltd, SYDNEY, MELBOURNE,
                         BRISBANE, ADELAIDE, PERTH, CANBERRA and
                         HOBART

Canada   Butterworths Canada Ltd, TORONTO and
                         VANCOUVER

Ireland   Butterworth (Ireland) Ltd, DUBLIN

Malaysia   Malayan Law Journal Sdn Bhd, KUALA LUMPUR

New Zealand   Butterworths of New Zealand Ltd, WELLINGTON and
                         AUCKLAND

Puerto Rico   Equity de Puerto Rico, Inc, HATO REY

Singapore   Butterworth & Co (Asia) Pte Ltd, SINGAPORE

USA   Butterworth Legal Publishers, AUSTIN, Texas;
                         BOSTON, Massachusetts; CLEARWATER, Florida
                         (D & S Publishers); ORFORD, New Hampshire
                         (Equity Publishing); ST PAUL, Minnesota; and
                         SEATTLE, Washington

Reprinted 1990

A CIP Catalogue record for this book is available from the British Library

ISBN 0 406 70060 5

Printed and bound by Thomson Litho Ltd, East Kilbride, Scotland

Preface

The Commonwealth Legal Education Association (CLEA) is a non-governmental voluntary organisation concerned with legal education at all levels, from law in schools to continuing legal education, in all Commonwealth jurisdictions. Among its objects are to disseminate information concerning legal education and research and 'to promote and conduct research in the field of legal education'. In recent years the Association has sponsored or assisted with studies and seminars on such varied topics as localisation of legal literature, legal education for non-lawyers, the training of magistrates and of law teachers, access to legal education and the legal profession and the teaching of Human Rights. The Association is particularly concerned to stimulate research and debate on neglected but problematic topics within its remit.

This book deals with such a topic. It is only relatively recently in the common law world that direct teaching of professional skills has been developed on a significant scale in courses and institutions that have been established specifically for this purpose. In December 1986 an inter-disciplinary conference on legal skills was held at the University of Nottingham, jointly sponsored by the Department of Adult Education of the University and the Centre for Socio-Legal Studies, Wolfson College, Oxford. Rather than produce a report of the proceedings, it was decided that it would be more valuable to collect together examples of materials actually used in teaching different skills, to set these in some general context, and to provide a basis for taking stock of the 'state of the art' with a view to disseminating ideas, to stimulating reflection and criticism and encouraging research and development in this important area of professional training. Accordingly, with the assistance of the recently formed Commonwealth Institute for Legal Education and Training (CILET), based at the University of Windsor, Ontario, relevant institutions and individuals throughout the Commonwealth were invited to submit examples of materials and teaching plans currently in use in their own jurisdictions. The contributors of materials selected for inclusion were invited to provide brief introductions explaining their context, purposes and uses. In addition, each of the editors has contributed an essay dealing with broader aspects of direct learning and teaching of professional skills. As with other CLEA projects the aim is not to produce a comprehensive survey, still less to make general prescriptions, but rather to provide a starting-point for informed local consideration of problems and issues in the very varied local circumstances that exist in different parts of the Commonwealth.

The teaching materials contained here follow many styles and formats, underscoring our belief that there is no one way to organise learning experiences of any kind, and most certainly, learning experiences to educate in the many acts of law practice.

Those readers who have worked the field before will find variations on themes they have already pursued. Some will find confirmation that the work they have done, sometimes in relative isolation, conforms largely with work done elsewhere. Others will find extensions and adaptations of notions they have already identified. Undoubtedly some will come across materials which they perceive to be at odds with their own work. Whatever the case, we hope that these materials will stimulate thought, critique, research, development and innovation.

The direct teaching of lawyers' skills is still very much an enterprise in its infancy. Only recently have we begun to identify the nature of legal work through needs, job, task and skills analyses. Just a generation ago most institutionally based legal training was limited to filling gaps in substantive law learning, introducing procedural law and detailing the elements of those transactions which it was predicted newly admitted practitioners were likely to conduct in their early years of practice. Now these materials are widely supplemented by teaching of skills and transactions central to lawyers' work – we have sought to add know-how to knowledge. The next generation will see further changes as we begin to understand better what lawyers do, how they do it and what distinguishes exemplary practice from its competent journeyman counterpart. When we know more and when our methods become more sophisticated we will be able to develop more effective, efficient, powerful and sure instruction.

The materials collected here represent just some of the full array of lawyers' skills. While there can be no one set of categories setting out what lawyers' skills include, the following list is illustrative: interviewing, counselling (advising), writing, drafting, negotiation, mediation, advocacy, planning, research, problem-solving, managing, investigation and fact-handling. One might add to this list the ability to acquire knowledge and understanding from disciplines outside of law which impinge upon legal work and legal knowledge, including, for example, medicine, psychology, accountancy, engineering, architecture, finance, literature, art and philosophy, to name but a few.

Some general intellectual skills lie at the heart of law work. Analysis, synthesis, evaluation, problem-solving and planning are central to lawyers' effectiveness. It goes almost without saying that one cannot draft, persuade, interrogate, advise or manage in law without first having intellectually manipulated the relevant materials. Materials relating to these skills are under-represented here. This is partly because very few examples were submitted to us, perhaps because these are widely perceived to belong to the academic rather than the professional stage of legal education and training. But there is a further reason: while it is clear that much cognitive skill work is done in the teaching programmes of the universities and professional training programmes around the Commonwealth, it is characteristically done indirectly, providing no specific instructional materials. The ultimate skill set, applicable to all persons no matter what their discipline, is the cluster of abilities which signify the capability to learn how to learn. For this, too, we have no direct teaching plans, though we believe the cumulative effect of effective instruction should be the acquisition of this capability. There is a challenge here to legal educators to develop materials which promote inquisitiveness, creativity and imagination. Linear thought must be complemented by analogous, metaphorical and other forms of thinking to pursue new solutions to new and old problems alike.

We have included three essays to accompany the collection of teaching plans. The first, 'Taking Skills Seriously', argues that the teaching, learning and assessment of individual professional skills is both under-theorised and under-researched. According to William Twining there is no coherent or articulated theory as to what constitutes basic lawyer skills nor to what extent these are really intellectual skills that can be abstracted or otherwise identified in a manner that would make it feasible for them to be taught, learned and thereafter systematically tested in educational institutions. Twining argues that work needs to be done to provide an informed, realistic and coherent picture of the role of lawyers in a given society and recognises that practical skills cannot be isolated from the ideological and ethical concerns which must be faced in teaching means.

Karl Mackie, a psychologist-lawyer, and the Convener of the Conference which stimulated this work, provides an analysis of the psychological and educational thinking on the subject of the teaching of lawyers' skills. Educational psychology and educational practice generally provide many insights into the ways and means to implement effective programming of the training in lawyers' skills. They provide a framework for thinking about lawyers' work and instruction suited to it. What is a skill? How do skills relate to transactions? What are the significant links?

In the closing essay, Neil Gold reviews briefly research activities to date and argues for the expansion of research and development activities both theoretical and empirical. Indeed, he seeks to chart a possible course for research and development activities in lawyers' skills and instruction in professional legal practice.

The materials selected and the skills outlines reproduced here derive from courses for students seeking admission to the Bar of England and Wales, applicants for admission as solicitors to the Supreme Court of the State of Victoria, Australia, applicants for admission to practice in the Province of British Columbia, Canada, those seeking qualifications for the Institute of Professional Legal Studies for admission to practice in New Zealand, students enrolled in the LLB course at the Kingston Polytechnic near London, United Kingdom and those enrolled in the fourth year of studies at Hong Kong University pursuing the post-graduate Certificate in Laws required prior to starting upon articles of clerkship prior to admission as solicitors in the Territory. While lawyers' skills courses are taught at the LLB level in the United Kingdom, Canada and to some extent in Australia and New Zealand, few of these courses have been reduced to the form of instruction that can be reproduced and gainfully used by others. Similarly, some experimentation has occurred in India, Malaysia, Zimbabwe, the West Indies and elsewhere in the Commonwealth. Regrettably, materials were not available for these or other courses. Perhaps the single most active jurisdiction in the development of lawyers' skills teaching is the United States of America. While many of the materials presented here and used in some Commonwealth jurisdictions draw on the American experience we have decided not to reproduce exclusively American materials though we recommend that those interested in finding out about the state of the art in the United States consult the *Legal Skills Source Book and Bibliography*, by Jeanine Watt, published for the Commonwealth Institute for Legal Education and Training by the College of Law, New South Wales, Sydney, Australia. We have also included 'Skills Guides' used in British Columbia for which versions have already been adapted to New Zealand practice. They provide examples of standards of performance and elements of skill sets in many areas of legal work.

This book is also closely related to another project connected with legal education and sponsored by CLEA. *Access to Legal Education and the Legal Profession: A Commonwealth Perspective*, edited by Rajeev Dhavan, Neil Kibble and William Twining, is published simultaneously by Butterworths as a companion volume. This contains a number of general papers and country studies which seek to provide information, clarify issues and suggest different ways of looking at and confronting problems of access. This is another rapidly changing area of legal education and training. Taken together, we hope these two volumes will stimulate interest and new insights into important aspects of legal education throughout the Commonwealth.

N G

K J M

W L T

September 1988

Acknowledgments

This volume represents the first effort of which we are aware to disseminate teaching materials used to teach legal practice and legal skills. Its original source is the Conference on Legal Skills presented by the Adult Education Department of Nottingham University and co-sponsored by the Centre of Socio-Legal Studies, Wolfson College, Oxford. Karl Mackie convened the conference and Sally Lloyd-Bostock and William Twining consulted on its development. The institutions which supported this novel venture will, we hope, take pride in the publication of this work.

Voy Stelmaszynski, a third year student of the Faculty of Law, University of Windsor, sorted out the many contributions which arose in compiling and editing this material. Ann Marie Hranka, secretary at the Faculty of Law, University of Windsor, maintained the various records and provided general support to both Mr Stelmaszynski and Professor Gold as they were putting the materials in order.

We wish also to thank the contributors who were patient and helpful in their responses, as we sought to finalise the materials for publication. Grateful acknowledgment to those individuals and institutes who granted permission to reproduce copyright material is made overleaf.

Finally, our gratitude to Butterworths for their foresight and insight in publishing a book which is new to the discipline of law and legal education.

N G

K J M

W L T

The authors and publishers also wish to thank the following for permission to reproduce certain copyright materials:

Christopher Allen
Terence Anderson
Susan Blake
Neville Carter
The Continuing Legal Education Society of British Columbia, Canada –
    Professional Legal Training Course
The Council of Legal Education, Inns of Court Law School, London, England
David Cruickshank
Mary Holmes
The Institute of Professional Legal Studies, Wellington, New Zealand
The Leo Cussen Institute, Melbourne, Australia
Mr F Lovett
Judith Maxwell
Stephen Nathanson
Andrew Pirie
David A Schum
William Twining
The University Press of America

Contents

List of contributors

William Twining
Quain Professor of Jurisprudence
Faculty of Laws, University College,
London, England

Karl J Mackie
Department of Adult Education
University of Nottingham,
Nottingham, England

Mary Holmes
Senior Lecturer in Law
Kingston Polytechnic
Kingston upon Thames, England

Judith Maxwell
Senior Lecturer in Law
Kingston Polytechnic
Kingston upon Thames, England

David Cruickshank
Professional Legal Training Course
Continuing Legal Education Society of British Columbia
Vancouver, Canada

Andrew Pirie
Professional Legal Training Course
Continuing Legal Education Society of British Columbia
Vancouver, Canada

Susan Blake
Inns of Court Law School
London, England

Stephen Nathanson
Faculty of Law, University of Hong Kong
Hong Kong

Christopher Allen
Inns of Court Law School
London, England

Neville Carter
National Director, New Zealand Institute of Professional Legal Studies
Wellington, New Zealand

Terence Anderson
School of Law, University of Miami
Florida, USA

Leo Cussen Institute for Continuing Legal Education
Melbourne, Australia

Neil Gold
Faculty of Law, University of Windsor
Windsor, Canada

Part 1

Background

1 Taking skills seriously*

William Twining

'The fox knows many things, but the hedgehog knows one big thing.'[1]

Tomorrow, in another place, I am due to present a foxy paper on legal education in England and Wales, calculated to start a few hares and to make some fur fly.[2] Today that role has been pre-empted by Robert Stevens;[3] so I propose to play the hedgehog and concentrate on a single theme: the direct teaching of professional skills.

My thesis is simple: what is involved in teaching, learning and assessing individual professional skills is under-theorised and under-researched. The result is that almost everyone involved in general debates about professional competency and professional training in the United States, the United Kingdom and the Commonwealth do not really know what they are talking about, because there is almost no systematic and developed body of knowledge on the subject, despite some individual studies, including admirable work sponsored by the American Bar Foundation, such as that of Zemans and Rosenblum.[4] Several years ago at the Council on Legal Education for Professional Responsibility (CLEPR) swansong in Key Biscayne, Florida, I listened fascinated as distinguished judges, deans and clinicians heatedly debated whether the leading law schools were failing in their responsibility to develop basic competence in intending lawyers. Two years ago in Hong Kong I participated in an even more heated argument, between leading lawyers in the Commonwealth, about the thesis, advanced by a leading Australian barrister, that all basic professional skills are ineffable, unteachable and only capable of being picked up by trial and error on live clients.[5] Among the most striking features of these debates were the following points: almost none of the protagonists had any competence in educational theory; there was little or no empirical evidence for most of the assertions that were made by any side; there seems to be no coherent or articulated theory as to what constitute basic lawyering skills nor as to how far these are intellectual skills that can be abstracted or otherwise identified in a manner that would make it possible and suitable for them to be taught, learned, or tested systematically in educational institutions. On the basis of these and similar experiences I have formed the impression, to paraphrase Holmes, that we have far too little theory about practical training rather than too much.

* This paper was presented at an American Bar Foundation symposium held in London in July 1985. It has also been published in the *Commonwealth Legal Education Association Newsletter*, No. 43, October 1985.

I wish further to hypothesise that this is potentially a very fruitful area for international co-operation, and for one good reason: if there are any 'basic legal skills' most of them probably involve the application in particular contexts of generic human skills especially skills of clear thinking. It is not just lawyers, but almost everyone, who in their practical affairs has to ask questions, diagnose problems, evaluate evidence, interpret, create and manipulate rules, negotiate, use and abuse statistics, construct and criticise arguments and so on. None of these are a lawyers' monopoly; what is peculiar about lawyering is probably more to do with how these skills are combined and the levels to which they need to be developed, than with the characteristics of the basic ingredients. Insofar as 'basic legal skills' involve work-handling, rule-handling, fact-handling, money-handling and people-handling...and some would add the processing of information, values, people and words...these are sufficiently general to be potentially transferable across geographical as well as occupational lines. This is largely a speculative thesis, for I have little evidence to support it. Like other legal educators in the amateur tradition of professional education I do not really *know* what I am talking about.

This thesis, or hypothesis, needs to be set in its historical context in both the United States and the Commonwealth. I presume that most of this audience is familiar with at least the highlights of the American story in its standard form: of, for example, Langdell's seminal shift from legal information, or know-what, to a peculiarly narrow and demanding form of know-how, that is 'case-law skills' perversely idealised in Kingsfield's favourite phrase, 'thinking like a lawyer', – as if these were the only relevant skills of analysis and synthesis. Or of the long-drawn out and varied reactions against Langdellism, spearheaded by Holmes and the early Realists, which involved, inter alia, a gradual recognition that the range of skills involved in being a competent legal practitioner, of one kind or another, was almost certainly much wider than just analysing and arguing about disputed questions of law in untypical courts. Most of you are also probably familiar with the Periclean Lasswell-MacDougal Plan of 1943,[6] and the rather less ambitious report of a committee chaired by Karl Llewellyn, in the following year, on 'The Place of Skills in Legal Education'.[7] You also probably know far more than I do about the details of what has been done since then in respect of particular skills and operations such as interviewing, negotiating, trial practice, appellate advocacy, drafting, office management, selecting and seducing jurors, winning clients, and influencing the powerful.

Obviously there is no time to comment on these in detail. To an outsider the scene seems to be extraordinarily rich, fragmented, and confusing and, at a general level, strikingly unsystematic. Let me make just one comment: it is perhaps symptomatic that two of the most ambitious attempts to develop coherent general theories in this area have been conspicuously ignored: I refer to Wigmore's *Science of Judicial Proof*[8] and Llewellyn's admittedly unfinished *Theory of the Crafts of Law*.[9] Even the better known, or notorious Lasswell-MacDougal plan[10] and Jerome Frank's pleas for taking facts seriously,[11] have been criticised largely in jurisprudential rather than educational terms. Given that we are meeting in his current headquarters and in close proximity to the only public house in the universe named after a jurist,[12] it is pertinent to observe that the British have also almost entirely ignored Jeremy Bentham's theory of evidence.[13] This is even more comprehensive than Wigmore's, though of less immediate utility for it would involve the wholesale abolition of all rules of evidence and a radical overhaul of most aspects of procedure and judicial organisation. For Bentham, most of the common law 'system' of adjective law and judicial organisation was based on wrong premises, sustained by the sinister interests of the legal profession; and, as he reminds me almost daily when I pass him in the cloisters, we have only gone about a third of the way to implementing his advice in the past 150 years. Of course, I register my dissent from much of what he says.

Let me turn briefly to the Commonwealth. Robert Stevens referred to the 'Lagos model', otherwise known as 'the Gower plan', which during the past 25 years has provided the main prototype for legal education and training in Australasia, the Caribbean, Ireland, Scotland, several countries in Anglo-phonic Africa and Asia, as well as in England and Wales. Although there are significant variations, legal education and training on this model is divided into a series of separate stages: academic, professional, apprenticeship and continuing (the last still primitive or non-existent in most of these jurisdictions). What is immediately relevant in this context is that the second or professional stage was originally envisaged as a full-time, intensive, direct training in professional skills. The stimulus came from a perceived need to find a substitute for apprenticeship in contexts where the conditions for apprenticeship did not exist, as in most African countries, or where the system of apprenticeship was under attack, as in England.

Over the past twenty years an international network of professional law schools and courses has grown up. They differ in many detailed ways, but the 'ideal type' has the following characteristics:

(a) the institution is largely or wholly under the control of the legal profession;
(b) it is constitutionally, sometimes physically, separate from university law faculties;
(c) the students are full-time and post-graduate;
(d) the curriculum is over-crowded (so, often is the building); it is obvious that one cannot *master* a skill by a quick scamper over too much ground in a crowded lecture hall;
(e) the costs of sustained direct training in professional skills, which is generally rather labour-intensive, have been under-estimated and the institution is significantly under-financed;
(f) it is mono-disciplinary rather than multidisciplinary. The courses have been planned, taught and monitored, if at all, by lawyers with minimal inputs from persons with expertise in such matters as job-analysis, educational theory and methods of testing competence;
(g) almost nothing is known about what difference these courses make to those who take them: What do they learn? How long does it last? Could it have been learned better or more economically by other means? Is it worth learning anyway? are largely unanswered questions. There is almost no research and no systematic theorising of the kind that is a necessary preliminary to such research. There is, in short, an almost complete vacuum in research and development.

Obviously it is not possible to carry this argument very far on this occasion. But, having pointed to a gap, let me end on a more constructive note in respect of three points:

First, we now have a rich and varied body of experience of attempts to develop direct teaching of some professional skills. It has evolved in a number of countries in the common law world over the past twenty or so years in a pragmatic and largely unco-ordinated fashion. What is needed now is reflection, co-ordination and systematisation; this I suggest would benefit from being institutionalised, international and interdisciplinary. Job analysis, skills analysis, the monitoring of educational programmes, the development of methods of testing competence and the setting of all these in the context of broader perspectives – of the experiences of other professions and of new perceptions of the legal profession, for example – are matters that require some assistance from non-lawyers.

Secondly, as a legal theorist, I perceive a pattern of convergence between some recent trends in jurisprudence and several specialised areas of professional training: for example, the work of Raiffa, Williams, Fisher and Ury[14] on negotiation is both abstract and intellectualised and yet highly practical: as Raiffa says: 'analysis . . . mostly simple analysis . . . can help' almost any negotiation.[15] Recent debates about probabilities and proof and other work in the theory of evidence have similar practical spinoffs. Ronald Dworkin's main concern is with what constitutes valid and cogent arguments about disputed questions of law; the fact that his own concerns are primarily philosophical does not mean that such ideas do not have potentially powerful practical implications and applications. Similar claims are made for the application of elementary techniques of microeconomic analysis to some branches of law. There is also a discernible trend within legal philosophy in the direction of suggesting that all lawyers' reasonings are no more than special applications and variations on a single model of practical reasoning. Perhaps Bacon was partly right:[16] maybe much of *formal* legal education, especially the skills aspects, should be *au fond* a training in logic or logics. But it needs to be suitably blended with *planned* experience. Insofar as this is so, there is considerable convergence between these ideas of skills training and a central strand of traditional liberal education.

Finally, as other theorists will be quick to point out, all of these concerns need to be related to informed, realistic and coherent pictures of the role of lawyers in a given society, the organisation of legal practice, and many other matters many of which are regularly contested. Nor can we responsibly treat instrumental training in practical skills in isolation from ideological and ethical concerns about ends as well as means. For as Karl Llewellyn reminded us often and eloquently: 'Technique without ideals is a menace; ideals without technique are a mess.'[17]

NOTES

1 Archilochus (Diehl, Frag. 103).
2 'The Paperchase in England and Wales: An Overview of Legal Education and Training', paper presented at ABA Conference, Section on Legal Education, London, July 1985.
3 Robert Stevens 'Legal Education: England and America', American Bar Foundation Symposium, London, July 1985.
4 Frances K Zemans and Victor G Rosenblum *The Making of a Public Profession* (ABF Chicago, 1981).
5 R Meagher QC 'How can you learn practice in theory?', Papers of the Seventh Commonwealth Law Conference, Hong Kong, September 1983, at pp 173–175.
6 H Lasswell and M McDougal 'Legal Education for Public Policy' 52 Yale LJ 255 (1943).
7 K Llewellyn 'The Place of Skills in Legal Education', reprinted in (1945) 45 Columbia L Rev 345.
8 J H Wigmore *The Science of Judicial Proof* (3rd edn, 1937).
9 See K N Llewellyn *Jurisprudence* (1962) 316–368. The fullest development of this theory is to be found in unpublished course materials, *Law in Our Society: A Horse-Sense Theory of the Institution of Law* (1950), extracts from which are printed in W Twining *Karl Llewellyn and the Realist Movement* (1973, 1985) pp 505–512.

10 Op cit, n 6.
11 J Frank *Courts on Trial* (1949); cf W Twining 'Taking Facts Seriously' 34 Jo Legal Educ 22 (1984).
12 The Jeremy Bentham, University Street, London WC1. University College is the headquarters of the Bentham Project.
13 J Bentham *Rationale of Judicial Evidence* (ed J S Mill, 1827); see further W Twining *Theories of Evidence: Bentham and Wigmore* (1985).
14 H Raiffa *The Art and Science of Negotiation* (1982); G R Williams *Legal Negotiation and Settlement* (1983); R Fisher and W Ury *Getting to YES: Negotiating Agreement Without Giving In* (1981). See also M Wheeler in 34 Jo Legal Educ 325 (1984).
15 Op cit, n 14.
16 Cited by Stevens, op cit, n 3.
17 K Llewellyn 'The Adventures of Rollo' (1952) 2 U of Chicago Law School Record 3, 23.

2   Lawyers' skills: educational skills

Karl Mackie

My concern in this chapter is to confront the question of legal skills education as a skilled activity in itself. What does one need to know and do to achieve a skilled performance in skills education? This question is answered, first, by an introduction to the concept of skill in the psychology of learning, and second, by outlining the issues in skills course design by means of a decision-making sequence for skills educators:

(1) Why should we plan a course using the terminology of 'skills'?
(2) How do we decide the skills to teach?
(3) How do we teach them?
(4) How do we assess learning?
(5) How do we evaluate course effectiveness?

The principles discussed under these headings may apply to areas of education other than skills but we shall see that a focus on 'skills' (including the use of this label for activities to which it is not normally applied in legal education) provides a particularly helpful means for educators to re-evaluate their current educational methods. While the discussion in the chapter deals with *course design*, the methods suggested also apply to decisions on teaching a *particular skills unit* within the overall design. The approach outlined attempts to provide one model of an 'ideal' or 'expert' level of performance in educational skills – most of us (including the materials selected for this volume) can only lay claim to degrees of approximation to such heights! However, a description of the varied techniques involved may help us identify where improvements or new efforts might be applied.

As in other forms of complex skilled behaviour, decision-making in each of the five areas is, to a greater or lesser extent, interdependent. The fact of complexity or interdependence in human skills leaves room for varied design approaches from the intuitive or holistic[1] to that of 'systematic instructional design'.[2] The latter is favoured in this chapter because of its ability to articulate the 'micro-skills' and thought processes of the course designer. Nevertheless, the underlying complexity in learning and teaching justifies a reference also to skills course design as an 'art' as much as a skill. Underlying both approaches, however, tends to be a preference for teaching-learning strategies which veer away from the traditional didactic style of legal education and towards the simple-minded (and oversimplified) prescription of one legal educator's army instructor – 'Practise bloody skills. Don't bloody talk about them.'[3] Why, how and what to practise, form the talk of this chapter.

The nature of a skill

The notion of skill suggests a learned competence, proficiency or expertise in an area. Initial interest amongst psychologists centred on the study of 'perceptual-motor' skills (such as typewriting or driving a car). The analysis of such skills provided a helpful analogy* by which 'skills' in more complex areas of human behaviour could be studied – intellectual skills (eg problem-solving, reasoning) and social or communication skills (eg interviewing, negotiating). The extension of the concept into such areas has also led to growing awareness amongst educators of the importance of skills-learning in professional disciplines.

While no single definition of a skill has won universal acceptance amongst educational psychologists,[4] one can list the main features which characterise 'skilled behaviour' as:

○ *goal-directed* – behaviour which is directed towards achieving a desired result (rather than being a product of chance or accident);

○ *learnt* – built up gradually by practice** rather than being reflexive or instinctive;

○ involves *co-ordinated activity that is responsive to the environment* – using one's perceptions of a situation to make appropriate choices of behaviour necessary to achieve the desired purpose (eg whether to reflect feelings in a client interview; whether to use open or closed questions). A skill therefore involves a *sequence of choices, actions and reactions*;

○ involves a *repertoire of micro-skills* – effective performance can generally be analysed into various elements or sub-routines (eg listening skills – showing attention and interest non-verbally, providing acknowledgments, restating client statements, reflecting feeling to demonstrate empathy);

○ the *transition from learning to accomplishment* is generally accompanied by a *shift to intuitive levels of response for micro-skill elements* – learning a skill such as driving a car initially tends to render the separate elements of the activity mechanical or artificial. However, with practice, elements of the skill, and co-ordination of those elements, tend to become almost 'automatic' and the 'player' can begin to concentrate on the more global activity (driving from here to there) or to single out other elements of a situation without disrupting performance (talking to other passengers). (This automaticity can later create difficulties if these actions need to change or have been learned in inappropriate ways – 'unlearning' habits accounts for many of the difficulties adults face in learning situations. They may for example have learned their listening skills in childhood in a manner that is inappropriate to a professional context, eg learned to interrupt others rather than to listen.)

---

* By emphasising that much behaviour was *learned* as opposed to attributable to predetermined genetic or personality factors, and by providing a framework for *analysing the processes* involved in this learning and behaviour.

** The emphasis on practice as the basis for skills leads some practitioners to feel (inappropriately) that the skills cannot be *taught*. In this connection, there is some interesting data in Zemans and Rosenblum[3] ch 6. The lawyers in their survey attributed their skills learning in many cases to experience rather than law school education. While the majority thought most skills could be taught effectively in law school and should be given more attention, for some skills only a minority thought they could effectively be taught there. Significantly, these were non-legal skills areas – getting along with other lawyers (only 16% thought this could be taught in law school), instilling others' confidence in you (17%), financial sense (32%), knowledge of other disciplines (32%), negotiating (35%), understanding the viewpoint of others to deal more effectively with them (42%), interviewing (48%).

Put more simply, 'the essential element of a skill is the ability to make and implement an effective sequence of choices so as to achieve a desired objective'.[5] Let us return therefore to the sequence of choices which the course designer may face in skills-education and training.

1 Why skills?

Given the relative recency of the lawyering skills movement in legal education, and the tendency of academic institutions to find the word 'skill' inappropriate, some justification for its use should be given. There are four important reasons to justify a reference to skills in course design.

(a) The concept draws attention to student *behaviour* rather than to tutor delivery ('to teach judicial precedent'), or vaguer 'inner' qualities such as 'understanding', 'awareness', 'appreciation', 'experiential learning'. What does 'understanding' mean? When is it demonstrated? Does it serve much purpose to say there is understanding without such demonstration? Such terminology is often used as a justification for teaching methods, the lecture in particular, where teaching objectives are otherwise unspecified or where, more often than not, the *teacher is practising the behaviour the student is supposed to adopt* (eg legal reasoning 'demonstrated' by a lecture – people who claim to teach legal reasoning may often be teaching *about* legal reasoning rather than how to reason, or they elide the distinction[6]). Of course even the lecture may be said to be an important teaching method for some skills in that it may achieve learning outcomes by providing a model to imitate, or by supplying new cognitive frameworks or the inspiration to learn. However, if such claimed learning is taking place, then it must become apparent by a behavioural activity (exam/essay/ student evaluation sheets) or we would be justified in doubting whether the claimed benefits had ensued.

(b) While the term emphasises the gap between a skilled performer and an unskilled one, it implies more clearly a notion of *practice* as a prerequisite to closing the gap. This in turn emphasises the activity nature of most learning, a factor that is underplayed in traditional academic contexts.

(c) The term draws attention to the place of *coaching* or guidance in closing the gap, of more personalised and detailed modes of teaching.*

(d) The terminology also draws attention to the fact of *patterns of response* in effective practice. There is implied some interaction between an actor and an environment, whereby processes of perception, judgment, decision-making and action need to harmonise for acceptable outcomes to take place. References to 'thinking', 'understanding', 'awareness', by contrast perpetuate a Western intellectual tradition that distances thought from action and compartmentalises intellectual endeavour.[7]

Despite these claims, one should also caution that 'skill' is not a precise term of art for a lawyering skills course designer. Rather it represents a convenient linguistic tool which implies a need to grapple with *a continuum of 'practical*

---

* Despite this, the emphasis on performance opens up the teaching-learning process to a greater degree of useful involvement by fellow students – see the frequent reference in the materials in this volume to the role of other students.

expertise', from fairly simple lawyer tasks which may be susceptible to certain ritualised techniques or procedures (eg some aspects of office systems management or ability to complete standard court forms) to more complex operations with less readily identifiable underlying techniques (eg judicial creativity). At either extreme, the word skill may be used loosely but its use may retain some of the benefits already described in contrast to alternatives.* Between the extremes come various lawyering acts – drafting, interviewing and counselling, negotiation, advocacy – where practical performance is widely recognised as important to individual effectiveness and where there is a range of known techniques that underlie such performance. In these areas the use of the terminology of skills is most readily accepted.

As yet we lack a commonly shared vocabulary to describe adequately the elements of a continuum of practical expertise. However, when we talk of a lawyer's 'skill', we are typically referring to a congerie of *techniques* (of varying complexity) directed to performing a particular *task* (or series of tasks, an *'operation'*) to an acceptable *level of performance* (ie 'skilfully').** Negotiating or interviewing are complex operations involving a series of tasks, within each of which identifiable techniques contribute to adequate or expert performance. 'Skills teaching' involves identifying the appropriate techniques within these tasks or operations and using appropriate educational methods to develop the ability of students to perform those required techniques to an acceptable level of performance. It is also worth noting at this point the common use by psychologists or educators of the term *'micro-skills'* to refer to more detailed techniques which can be identified by analysing the technique that forms one's starting point eg 'interviewing skills' can be sub-divided into the skills of attending, listening, questioning, counselling. In turn these techniques may themselves be seen as skills which can be further sub-divided into identifiable techniques or 'micro-skills' eg active and passive listening, which are further divisible themselves eg into 'summarising' and 'reflecting feeling' in the case of active listening, and so on.†

2 Which skills?

Decisions on course content require, first, some kind of 'needs' or course purposes analysis – what needs for skills training can we identify, given the purposes of our educational efforts? – and second, deriving from this analysis, some detailed learning objectives within the course which will specify to what extent we aim to meet those needs.

In broad terms one can describe this process in terms of the following stages:

(1) developing a picture of the social role of the lawyer as it relates to the education process – what do lawyers do? or (in a more critical context) what should lawyers do?;

---

 * At the latter end of the spectrum one sometimes finds resistance to the notion that the lawyer's 'art' or 'intuition' is capable of analysis or skills training through identification of relevant techniques. See, however, Anderson and Twining's chapter in this volume for an attempt to develop procedures in a relatively unexplored, yet central, area of such lawyer's art.
** I am indebted to William Twining for this example of a more rigorous conceptual structure with which to analyse practical expertise.
 † For examples of sub-division, see the *twenty* important elements of voice ('taken at random'!) mentioned in one of the Leo Cussen readings on advocacy; compare the micro-skills emphasised in the effective speaking section of the New Zealand materials on counselling. And for a useful example of micro-skills in listening, see the techniques listed in the interviewing materials, p 59(4).

(2) determining where educational objectives link in to these roles;*
(3) conducting an analysis of the job of the lawyer in terms of its relevant operations;
(4) making a task and skills analysis of each operation;
(5) using this detailed analysis to formulate learning objectives.

Some varied emphases within this overall framework are spelt out below.

Needs analysis

This is a stage which is often short-circuited by reliance on tradition or where there is a relatively vague mix of needs derived from: (a) educator (educational or professional institution) concerns; (b) assumptions about the capacities of student entrants; (c) anticipated post-student competence requirements (in professional practice, the vocational training stage, or 'life'). A skilled educational design should attempt to be more systematic in defining its rationale for inclusion of *both the skills content of the course as a whole and the 'micro-skills' emphasis within any particular skills area*. Consideration should be given to four different, not exclusive, methods of identifying course content at either of these levels:

(i) Deciding course content from the *nature of the educational institution or from the demands of the profession*. The social context of the institution (or department) will be relevant to the choice of skills selected as appropriate (and, of course, to the readiness with which skills education is seen as a valid concern). This is in part not strictly a category of needs analysis but an important political factor in the ease and manner in which skills educators can develop and justify a skills programme. Traditional academic institutions might find it easier, for example, to encompass courses within the law curriculum on legal reasoning skills than on human relations skills.

Aside from the political context, however, it is important to ask, first, what educational experiences current students are likely to have had, so that choices can be made between deepening or refining those skills experiences or emphasising new ones.[8] Second, to ask to what extent students are 'adults' or, perhaps more precisely, how much they bring occupational concerns into their learning motivation. There is some evidence for adults being more 'problem-centred' in their approach to learning.[9] They are therefore more likely to question skills-based approaches which are not 'integrated' with occupational concerns. Non-legal simulations which may work well with younger students may therefore need more careful justification in continuing education settings.**

(ii) Working out a course from the *nature of the subject*, eg the structure and content of negotiating theory and practice, the nature of legal argument in the law of contract. Within this overall framework, one then attempts to be more specific on the key skills that should be incorporated into each stage of the framework. The advantage and commonality of this approach is based on the

---

* There are of course long-standing debates on the question of how closely certain educational institutions ought to seek to be guided by the tasks of lawyers or the concerns of the legal profession. This chapter is not the place to respond to this except by asserting that most legal education contexts do teach 'legal skills' at some level, and by repeating our earlier assertion that using the terminology of skills may have beneficial effects however one seeks to describe the learning needs one is meeting.
** Compare the broad approach to communication skills adopted by the (longer) Kingston Polytechnic course with the more direct role-focus in other materials directed at professional training in this volume.

fact that it can be derived from a relatively familiar, simple and inexpensive process of desk research. (And it is worth noting that there is a long tradition going back to Aristotle's *Rhetoric* of philosophically based treatises on practical reasoning.) The approach tends, however, to lead to later incremental adjustment as it emerges that:

(a) some areas of skills knowledge have been tested primarily in settings other than law, therefore raising questions as to how appropriate the material might be (for example, negotiating texts are often based on industrial relations, commercial or laboratory studies);

(b) many areas of professional practice lack any substantial literature or are based more on tradition or anecdote than on research or theory, or suffer from a bewildering variety of types of material. For example, advocacy materials range from anecdotes (war stories) to materials with minimal analysis; from simple cookbooks to somewhat more substantial manuals; through to the books that are beginning to emerge from recent developments in the USA and Commonwealth (and illustrated in this book);

(c) this approach may become overly theoretical rather than emphasising the behavioural features of the skill. (Just as much of higher education tends to be content-based ie study of a 'discipline', rather than process-based – developing learning/reasoning/problem-solving/social analysis skills *through* a discipline.)

(iii) Assessing the gap between the 'average' student entrant and some level of skilled performance amongst 'average' practitioners ie *what will students be required to do in practice?* The most common area chosen would be the first few years of practice, eg pleadings or advice that a junior practitioner would draft.* The assessment of requirements would be based on some 'audit' of practice (often gleaned from knowledge amongst course tutors based on their own experience rather than from a systematic research survey). Usually there is an assumption that the gap is based on a 'blank slate' amongst student entrants rather than research as to the exact skill deficits.

(iv) Analysing '*master performers*' in practice and attempting to replicate some of their characteristics in the skills training programme. This entails a search for, and analysis of the characteristics of, those who are rated very highly by their colleagues within the profession/skill area. This is perhaps the least common explicit method, though often attempted on a smaller (and less effective) scale by way of examples of famous cross-examinations or bringing in leading practitioners to talk about their work.** (It is an approach used commonly, though not made explicit, in most academic teaching which relies on 'leading' texts (thinkers/appeal court judgments) in a subject area as a guide for students.)

In theory each of these techniques demands a fairly systematic research approach, though experience suggests that many courses make do with more rough-and-ready judgments on what skills content the course should contain. Thorough preparation of a course should involve, however, some attempt at adequate research back-up, drawing on several of these strands if possible.

---

* Explicitly referred to in the introduction to the Inns of Court materials – 'the sort of paperwork with which a newly-qualified barrister might be expected to deal'.
** For an unusual example of this approach, see the use of Martin Luther King's famous speech in the Leo Cussen voice materials.

From needs analysis to learning objectives

The results of the analyses above will give some indicators of the skills areas to be taught. A second stage should normally follow by way of an analysis of the *detailed learning objectives* of the course or skills area programme. These objectives should link back to the needs analysis, eg to specify the tasks and standards of performance which a junior practitioner could achieve. The stage is separate from the needs analysis since judgments will have to be made on *priorities* and *cost-effectiveness* of the response to the needs analysis. Needs will have been identified but can they and should they be met at this level of the educational process? Should some be left to continuing education, articles or pupillage, experience? And of those needs which merit attention from the course designer, which are the priority learning objectives within our educational programme?

There has been much debate about the role and value of setting 'objectives' in educational practice,[10] but there is little doubt that there is some value for designers in going through the *process* of attempting to set precise objectives.[11] Setting detailed objectives essentially requires hard thinking to make explicit what one is really about as an educator and whether or how it is achievable. A sophisticated approach might seek to spell out:

○ the terminal *behaviour expected* (eg to demonstrate reflective listening techniques in an interview, namely...);
○ the *conditions* under which learning is assessed (eg role play of an interview with a lay client; responses to a client statement script);
○ the *standard of performance* expected (eg 'satisfactory');
○ the *means of measurement* (eg observer/self/client ratings).[12]

In other words, criteria for learning should specify a product or 'output' of the learning programme (with sufficient specificity as to conditions and standards as to allow for relatively precise appraisal of the course outcomes) and not merely an input ('to teach negotiation') or process ('to examine interviewing') aim.* Nor should the output statement be so vague ('to make students aware of negotiating skills') as to add nothing to an input statement.

A useful short-hand classification system in setting objectives in a curriculum is to split the skills objectives into three types – those the student *must* learn, *should* learn, and *could* learn.

3 How do we teach them?

Decisions on appropriate learning and teaching methods require some knowledge of principles of learning and of educational methods and technology.

Principles of learning

The following principles can be used as useful guides to design decisions.

---

* For good examples of the 'objectives' method (though perhaps still short of Mager standards) see the Interviewing and Counselling programmes in our selection. Compare these with the other materials.

A Learning may involve different dimensions of human capacities

There is a variety of fairly complex taxonomies of learning to which one can refer in education.[13] A simple classification of *types of learning outcome* which can assist with thinking through the learning objectives of a skills curriculum might be:

○ *information acquisition* (eg ability to state the meaning of the 'T-funnel sequence' of questioning in interviewing);
○ *cognitive skills development* (eg ability to identify the legal issues raised by a set of new facts);
○ attitudes or *values creation* (eg readiness to adopt a stance in relation to a particular ethical question in negotiation);
○ *performance* or behavioural learning (eg ability to conduct a counselling session with a client to an acceptable level).

The classification is a matter of emphasis rather than absolutes. There is likely to be an overlap between the areas. Intellectual categories are rarely value-free, values are linked to information, and performance may also be influenced by values and knowledge. However, these sub-divisions of learning outcomes provide a useful starting point for decisions on learning objectives in a course. The emphasis in a skills course should suggest that *each one of these areas should ideally be susceptible to performance measures of some kind.* Can the student define, for example, the different characteristics of co-operative, competitive and principled negotiating? (information acquisition). Can he or she identify where an ethical issue may arise in a set of negotiating instructions? (cognitive outcome). Can he or she raise an ethical question 'effectively' in a mock negotiation situation? (performance). Does he or she rate this element highly in comparison with other values in the negotiation, such as 'winning' for the client? (attitude).*

It is worth a mention in this context that one of the discoveries many tutors make when they shift to the activity methods encouraged by a skills-based curriculum, is that the 'richness' of a subject is more readily apparent, ie that *the interrelatedness of performance, knowledge, cognitive skills and values becomes more apparent* where students engage in negotiating a case for a client than when the same legal area is the subject of merely 'intellectual' lectures/tutorials. (In particular ethical dilemmas are exposed more sharply.**)

B Student motivation is a key element in stimulating learning

This common-sense principle suggests the need to make the skills material *meaningful* and interesting to the student – why it is relevant to include it within the course, how it relates to student needs and objectives as well as the course designer's. The emphasis on activity methods in skills education may be an advantage in motivating students but can backfire if the students fail to see any real purpose or relevance in the learning activity. Similarly, exercises on 'micro-skills' in particular (eg being sensitive to client needs) should be linked back to the overall skill and their importance demonstrated. This heading also

* Compare these four outcomes against the objectives described in the interviewing and counselling materials – which of the four learning dimensions apparently dominate? Is there any difference in emphasis compared to the other materials where objectives are less explicit?
** This is well illustrated, for example, in the simple Yes/No negotiating game in the New Zealand negotiating materials (found in other versions of negotiating materials as the Red/Blue game or the 'Prisoner's Dilemma').

explains why there is often a cycle of experience in skills teaching whereby skills in the abstract are initially taught, then later there is a need felt to 'integrate' them to the subject area. This will be particularly the case in levels of education where students have very specific occupational concerns.

While there is some evidence that the nature of the effects of *criticism and praise* depend in part on the personality of the learner, it is a safe assumption to make that most learners benefit more from praise than criticism (though its effect may be lost if undeserved or indiscriminate), particularly in areas (such as social skills) where they may already be very sensitive.* Skills tutors should seek to employ methods which can provide support or encouragement for what is valuable in skilled performance as well as what needs to be remedied. This can be achieved by various means – student group support systems, assessment checklists which ask observers to identify the strong points in a student's activity before making 'suggestions for improvement', student self-assessment. It means also setting skills tasks where students can obtain an early *sense of achievement* to give them the confidence to tackle more difficult skills elements.

Finally it is worth noting that courses should take account of an *'energising'* factor in determining choice of method and sequencing of items, ie can one identify stages in a course where student motivation is likely to diminish? If so, it may be worth making appropriate adjustments to programmes in these areas by way of, for example, inclusion of new material or outside speakers, sudden changes in direction, introduction of a new assessment element, etc.

C Teaching methods should take account of individual differences in learning style

Differences in learning style are a well-established feature of psychological research into learning. While the exact implication of learning style for teaching methods can be difficult to gauge or control, the simple message here is to be alert to the need to *vary teaching methods and technologies* between, say, direct presentation of material and discovery or problem-solving methods; between the different levels of skills appreciation – informational, etc; between oral, written and visual reinforcement of material to be learned; between group and individual projects. Each of these choices may depend on an assessment on how best to teach skills material but they will also invariably suit some students' (and tutors') styles more than others so that a varied and balanced approach should be aimed for.

At the level of how students differ in their ' management' of their learning on a course, a useful research-based classification of different student orientations to a course[14] (not necessarily translated into skilled performance!) is:

O deep approach (seeking to *understand* and relate principles of the course to earlier learning and wider principles);
O surface approach (seeking to *reproduce* what is thought to be required by the tutor by way of separate task assignments and information);
O strategic approach (seeking to *maximise grades* by systematic management of time and study efforts, and by being alert to assessment cues, past papers, etc).

It is to some extent within the control of tutors which approach most closely matches course objectives, and how much these approaches and their respect-

---

* A view apparent in several of the materials – see the comments in the communication skills materials and the interviewing tutor instructions.

ive skills are made explicit in the course programme in early course discussions. The orientations and their advantages and disadvantages can
usefully be explored within an introductory 'study skills' session.

D Practice is an essential element in skills training

Unless one is seeking merely to provide an 'awareness-raising' tour of various
skills, it is essential to incorporate opportunities to practise (ie repetition of
skills performance) into the course design, linked to course objectives and
priorities. Only by this means is it possible for students to learn and be guided
on the essential elements within the skill, to know which 'cues' are most
important in the sequence of choices and actions a skilled performance
requires. Practice under different conditions also assists with the *transfer* of
skills from the immediate learning situation into other contexts. The need for
practice is a justification for suspicion of single 'task' exercises and case studies
which demand large chunks of time on a course. Lengthy practical exercises
(eg participating in a mock conveyancing case from client approach to property transfer) are best used to achieve one or more of three purposes:

(a) as a means of bringing together the various threads of learning on a course
     (where the major skills areas have already been or are concurrently the
     subject of some practice);
(b) as a means of imparting confidence that one can learn about and cope with
     the complexities of practice;
(c) as a means of providing 'face validity', ie to show that what one is doing is
     obviously related to the 'real world'.

E Feedback is an essential facet of learning

The saying that 'practice makes perfect' is of course inaccurate. The saying is a
shorthand way of stating that 'Practice, the results of which are known and
acted upon, makes perfect'. Students can be guided on the results of their
performance by tutors or fellow students, or by themselves where the learning
situation is appropriately structured to reveal the successful and unsuccessful
elements of their performance and how to repeat, improve, or remedy them.
The success of feedback on a course will rest, first, on how well one can make
explicit the nature of the skills that one is assessing and the elements of
successful performance, and second, on one's ability to help the student
re-form his or her initial performance by adequate teaching methods and
support for behaviour which moves toward this performance. Feedback is
most effective when it closely follows performance of the relevant element in
the technique (either in time or through a video replay).

The belief by many practitioners that 'experience is a great teacher' does
justice to the role of practice and feedback in learning but of course ignores the
gross inefficiencies, distorted learning outcomes and frequent failures of this
particular school of learning!

F The structure and sequence of learning materials are important

In all learning programmes, the way in which particular units of a course are
structured can have an obvious impact on student learning. Structures and
tasks which are 'meaningful', which are readily remembered, which relate to
existing student knowledge, and which create interest and motivation are,

other things being equal, more likely to be learned. This requires of the tutor a search for methods of skills learning which lead to effective understanding of the nature of the skill and of the features in skilled performance which most readily typify effectiveness. In skills learning as in other areas of learning, confusion amongst the learned is likely to be reflected back in confused students. ('Confusion' in this sense is of course not the same thing as controversy – there may be controversy over whether, say, co-operative or competitive negotiating is more effective, but the differences between their 'cues' for skills learning can be readily identified.)

It is also important to assess whether or not aspects of the programme are dependent on, or assisted by, prior learning of other units of the course. There should ideally be a 'linked progression' of tasks, skills, information and methods. There are various approaches to creating linked progression in the structure of skills learning. For example:

(a) *building blocks* – students are taught the constituent techniques which form part of the task or operation (eg summarising, reflecting feeling) before being required to practise the task or operation itself (interviewing);

(b) *spiral* – students are given simple versions of an operation such as an interview and then gradually introduced to more complex exercises, learning to cope with micro-skills in the process through discovery or analysis and explanation by tutors, before they finally face a full client interview;*

(c) *problem-centred/clinics* – students are given various problems that might face a lawyer in practice, and required to work their way through them as might a practitioner handling a case, eg seeing the client, corresponding with the other party, issuing a writ, etc;

(d) *backward chaining* – the student is brought into a skilled performance near the final stage of that performance, and asked to complete the final stage, eg given a set of pleadings with only one element missing; asked to do a plea in mitigation.** The point of this approach is to give an early sense of achievement where otherwise learning a skilled performance may be arduous. They are then gradually taken back through the stages until all have been mastered in reverse order.

The demands on skills tutors to make explicit the significant elements† and situational cues in skilled performance (often only implicit amongst skilled performers), leads readily to an emphasis on *'research-led'* teaching programmes.

G Learning to learn is an essential feature of good skills training

Many of the skills in legal education veer towards the complex rather than the simple, ie they are often more accurately described as a *collection or repertoire* of skills, they involve complex reasoning and judgment processes, they are interactive (involve social skills), reactive (cues from the environment have to be used to guide choice of action), and socially responsive (change with societal variations and developments). For these reasons, effective skills teach-

* An approach perhaps most closely represented by the Kingston Polytechnic materials.
** Compare the approach of the Hong Kong materials on drafting ('amending' a first draft) with the Inns of Court 'bottom-up' approach.
† Note, for example, the helpful cues to effective speaking provided in the counselling materials.

ing can rarely be equated with 'instruction in techniques'. Flexibility in the performance of a skill and readiness to learn from others and from experience are necessary ingredients of effective skills training. The skills tutor must therefore be able to balance the fact that there are some readily identifiable techniques that are part of skilled performance and essential to learn with the fact of complexity in practice and human conduct. While this can be part of students' *intellectual* awareness of the subject, thought should be given to methods of reinforcing it in terms of the other dimensions we identified of attitudes and performance. This will depend in part on the 'role model' students identify with in the profession and the educational institution. It can also be encouraged by sessions with practitioners who use different approaches; by skills exercises in different settings and on varied topics (to encourage transfer of learning); by observation of similar skills in different professional or occupational settings; by some exercises on unusual situations (eg dealing with 'difficult' clients).

Teaching methods and technologies

We have already identified the use of the terminology of 'skills' as having the advantage of emphasising the need for more student-active teaching methods. Allied to this, the discussion on learning principles – the different types of skills and levels of skilled activity; different learning styles amongst students; the need to retain motivation; the need to encourage a learning to learn orientation – all of these should also indicate that one should initially approach a course with the assumption that a variety of teaching methods are essential to optimise learning on the course. The various methods are well documented, but not as widely used as would be merited by an emphasis on activity methods.

A Presentation methods

These methods are primarily intended to provide new information or a process of familiarisation with concepts, principles and rules or to identify for learners the significant features of a topic. The methods used include lectures/lecture-discussions/tutorials/seminars/slide or film presentations/reading/demonstrations. The advantage of these methods is their simplicity in presenting material in a structured fashion based on previous learning. Some of them, however, leave the learner relatively inactive. It is a common notion amongst younger teachers that they only really understood a topic when they had to teach it. This folklore reinforces the criticism of such methods, that the lecturer is in fact practising the behaviour expected of the students.

B Activity methods

Under this heading come the various techniques which focus on practice and on increased effectiveness in the *behaviour* of students. They are therefore generally an essential complement to skills-building programmes. The range of possible activities is effectively as wide as an imaginative tutor seeks to make it, but would commonly include: role-playing, case-study analysis, problem-solving exercises, project work, clinics, games, group discussion, interactive video, programmed or computer-assisted learning.*

* Some of the presentation methods do of course contain activity elements related to skills-building. Seminars and tutorials, for example, may be said to have activities related to presentation/discussion/reasoning skills, although these functions often may take second place to substantive, information acquisition purposes (reflecting an overlap, or confusion, of objectives which tends to reflect the muddied waters of other debates on objectives and methods in the legal curriculum, eg whether to teach reasoning skills directly or indirectly).

It would be foolish to advocate any particular method as more 'effective' since each of these methods must itself be used 'skilfully' to operate well. Also, there is apparently little research to evaluate practical methods despite their widespread use.[15]

Skills development – an eight-point plan

In choosing a technique to match the learning objectives of the course, guidance can be drawn from using a well-practised sequence for skills-training:

(1) Establish what can be regarded as a model of effective performance (teaching and learning *objectives*).
(2) Present an overview of the nature of skilled performance (provide a cognitive framework or '*map*' of the nature of the skill as a guide in future activities).*
(3) Provide a model of effective performance (*demonstration*, leading to imitation learning).**
(4) Provide opportunities to practise behaviours which approximate to the model (student *practice*).
(5) Provide students with knowledge of their results in relation to the model (*feedback*).
(6) Support and highlight elements of the performance which show progress towards the model ('*shaping*' behaviour through reinforcement or reward; demonstration; cognitive 'restructuring').
(7) Repeat (3)–(6) (*consolidation* through practice).
(8) Repeat (1)–(7) under different/more difficult conditions (consolidation/ *transfer* of learning).

There are three common reasons for courses *not* following such a model in skills-building:

(a) learning objectives have not been well-defined;
(b) effective performance is not demonstrable (query – is your objective a skills-based one? or do you need to approach the performance question by talking about the behaviour as a collection of skills, *some* of which are demonstrable but which in total cannot easily be demonstrated?);
(c) a *discovery* method of learning is being used, that is, students are not initially given a model of performance but the model is expected to emerge from practice on the behaviour (eg negotiating) and the conclusions/ behaviour adjustments† which they discover in the process.† This is a respectable alternative approach to the 'demonstrate-practice-review' model, which appeals to many educators and to the autonomy and self-respect (and hence motivation to learn) of students. The cautions against it – does it suit all your students' learning styles? is the discovery method being used to conceal an inadequate sense of objectives or under-

---

* For a useful example of a prior cognitive map, see the criteria-referenced drafting checklists used by the University of Hong Kong.
** Provided in a number of the materials by a video, or a 'model' draft, though often such models are used less for their imitation value than for their ability to stimulate critical observation.
† For a simple version of a discovery exercise, see the non-verbal communication game played in the interviewing materials, pp 37 ff. Discovery is emphasised strongly in the Kingston Polytechnic and Inns of Court materials.

standing of the skills? is it an inefficient learning technique when an appropriately structured demonstration would speed learning through imitation?*

An abbreviated form of the eight-point approach can be found in the practice of 'micro-teaching', now widely used in teacher training. The system involves a 'teach-evaluate feedback-reteach' sequence to improve basic teaching skills.[16]

Individual v Group?

Most educators face the dilemma of how much to orient a course or skills-building in terms of group or individual activities. A response to this could depend on:

(a) what resource limitations might there be?
(b) to what extent does the skill in real-life demand group contributions? and of what kind?
(c) to what extent would group work provide opportunities for effective demonstration? feedback and reinforcement? cognitive restructuring? support for experiment?
(d) what are the course certification or assessment requirements?

4 Assessing learning

The essential questions in assessment relate to *validity* – how far are we measuring what we claim to be measuring? and *reliability* – how consistent are such measurements across students and tutors? The problems in assessment can be related to many of the problems already discussed in terms of teaching and learning objectives. Some questions to ponder:

○ How specific are our learning objectives and criteria for accomplishment of them?
○ Are we assessing the skill in terms of performance (eg in a client interview) or cognitive skill (eg a negotiation journal setting out their thinking on strategies, tactics, outcomes of a negotiation they participated in?) or attitudes (eg extent to which they display enthusiasm in their practicals) or a mix?
○ Are we assessing learning in relation to others in the group ('norm-referenced' tests) or past groups or in relation to standards of performance ('criterion-referenced' or competence tests)?
○ Are we assessing individual *progress* or individual *competence* at the end of a course? (individuals may have differed in initial levels of competence they brought with them to the course) or in terms of predictions of achievement?
○ Are we assessing the effectiveness of teaching methods?

---

* In higher education in particular there has been a strong resistance to 'model' answers on grounds of preserving individuality and creativity, an unconvincing stance in this author's view. See, however, the argument for this position in the introduction to the Inns of Court materials on writing a legal opinion, and note the subsequent (perhaps contradictory?) statement that students may learn from good and bad examples in practice *after* they know the principles underlying effective practice.

○ Are we using assessment to monitor student progress and/or motivate students?

○ Does the skill or course merit a group assessment element?

○ To what extent do we use subjective judgments by observers? self-assessment? peer assessment?

○ When and how often do we assess?

None of these prove easy in practice to answer or to deal with skilfully. However, skills tutors sometimes feel bound to find a more exact science of assessment because they are dealing with observable behaviour or because of reasons of politics in introducing skills programmes into institutions suspicious of them. The consolation for the tutor should perhaps be a comparison with their colleagues' existing assessment systems – 'Many contemporary methods of student assessment predate the Renaissance, and academic inertia has proved to be stronger than the scientific revolution.'[17] Traditional academic methods of assessment are themselves not a precise instrument but rely on a great deal of intuition and cross-checking of subjective judgments. Nor do such systems always measure clearly what course designers might claim. Assessment of complex skilled performance will inevitably lean more towards impressionistic systems, but there is some evidence that the use of agreed checklists or rating scales to list what is being assessed will improve validity and reliability. 'In many respects examining students should be regarded like a piece of research. Many of the same precautions should be taken, and many of the same questions should be asked.'[18]

5 How do we evaluate course effectiveness?

Yes, back to objectives and how to assess them! This time, however, one might refer to 'meta-objectives' – what are the objectives of evaluation, in addition to known course objectives? While there are various interesting 'paradigms' of course evaluation,[19] the essential questions centre around decisions on which aspects of the course should be evaluated and on what criteria to use for evaluation. As a starting point, it can be helpful to list the various 'stakeholders' in the course – students, tutors, profession, institution, society – and their likely interests in the evaluation and its outcomes. Use should be made of outsiders to provide a fresh viewpoint. Course evaluation can be a sensitive period for staff involved if not handled well and should be treated from the beginning as part of an opportunity for, and part of, staff development as much as a critique of outcomes.

Staff development and motivation are neglected aspects of most writing on educational skills. This is regrettable given that some of the research on teaching effectiveness tends to suggest that tutor enthusiasm and interest in a topic can be a better guide to whether students will learn (and certainly to their satisfaction and interest in a topic) than the nature of the methods used. The vital missing ingredient in much of the literature is how to develop and maintain amongst educators a sense of freshness and enthusiasm for course design and practice. In educational terms, the need to maintain enthusiasm suggests a need for courses to include access to research opportunities, study leave and sabbaticals, contact with other disciplines and developments, periods of placement in the profession, use of outside lecturers, and so on. The exercise of skill in education, like skill in other areas of professional life, also depends on maintenance of the springs of creativity, motivation and enlightenment. The skilled tutor, in other words, does not live by skills alone.

NOTES

1 I am not aware of a compelling description of this approach in legal skills education, but a good example of an 'alternative' paradigm in skills teaching can be gleaned from W T Gallwey *The Inner Game of Tennis* (1975, London, Cape).

2 A J Pirie 'Objectives in Legal Education' in The Journal of Legal Education (1987) vol 37, 4, 576–597.

3 Quoted by G Tamsitt 'Teaching Interviewing and Negotiating: The Impossible Dream' in The Journal of Professional Legal Education (1983) 59–71. For lawyer views on learning skills from experience, see F K Zemans and V G Rosenblum *The Making of a Public Profession* (1981, Chicago, American Bar Foundation).

4 See, for example, O Hargie 'Communication as Skilled Behaviour' in O Hargie *A Handbook of Communication Skills* (1986, London, Croom Helm).

5 R Nelson-Jones *Human Relationship Skills: Training and Self-Help* (1986, Norwich, Cassell).

6 See W Twining 'Legal Skills and Legal Education', paper given to CNAA Law Teachers' Conference, 6 October 1987, London; now (1988) 22 The Law Teacher 4–13.

7 See D A Schon *The Reflective Practitioner* (1983, New York, Basic Books). Also, *Educating the Reflective Practitioner* (1987, New York, Jossey Bass).

8 P Bergman, A Sherr and R Burridge 'Learning from Experience: Non-legally Specific Role Plays' in J of Legal Education (1987) vol 37, 4, 535–553, 536.

9 See, for example, M Knowles *The Adult Learner: A Neglected Species* (1978, Chicago, Gulf); A G V Tobin 'Criteria for the Design of Legal Training Programmes' in The Journal of Professional Legal Education (1987) vol 5, 1, 55–63.

10 See, for example, I K Davies *Objectives in Curriculum Design* (1976, London, McGraw-Hill); A J Romiszowski *Designing Instructional Systems* (1981, London, Kogan Page). For a discussion of the lack of objectives in higher education, see G Squires *The Curriculum Beyond School* (1987, London, Hodder and Stoughton). For an attempt at a taxonomy of objectives in professional education, see R Carter 'A Taxonomy of Objectives for Professional Education' in Studies in Higher Education (1985) vol 10, 2, 135–149.

11 For examples in legal education, see A J Pirie 'Objectives in Legal Education' in The Journal of Legal Education (1987) vol 37, 4, 576–597; G Tamsitt 'Methods of Instruction in Interviewing and Counselling and Negotiation' in The Journal of Professional Legal Education (1986) vol 4, 1, 33–39.

12 This approach is based on Robert Mager's work, outlined in Romiszowski, op cit.

13 See Romiszowski, op cit and L B Curzon *Teaching in Further Education: An Outline of Principles and Practice* (1985, 3rd edn, London, Holt Rhinehart).

14 N Entwistle 'A Model of the Teaching-Learning Process' in *Student Learning: Research in Education and Cognitive Psychology* (1987, Milton Keynes, SRHE) pp 13–28.

15 See D Bligh, D Jaques and D W Piper *Seven Decisions When Teaching Students* (1981, 2nd edn, Devon, Exeter University Teaching Services) ch 5.

16 Op cit, pp 197–198, 278–280.

17 Op cit, p 56.

18 Op cit, p 56.

19 Op cit, ch 6.

Part 2

Practical skills

3 Communication skills

Mary Holmes, Judith Maxwell,
David Cruickshank and Andrew Pirie

I COMMUNICATION SKILLS FOR LAWYERS: A TEACHING PROGRAMME

Mary Holmes and Judith Maxwell

Introduction

This course in communication skills has been developed over the last six years and it will continue to develop as our experience increases. The reason for introducing communication skills to undergraduate law students was a recognition that the only skills training offered to students was mooting which, though very important in developing forensic skills, was a skill that the majority of students were unlikely to use much in their professional life. It was felt that there was a need to enable students to develop skills that, in addition to their forensic skills, they would find of continuing use. A precipitating factor in the genesis of our communication skills training course was our participation in the UK Client Interviewing Competition.

During our time of research into the teaching of communication skills we have been encouraged by the interest in our work shown by the legal profession. This has taken the form of support and help in developing the course from individual members of the profession and also financial support from the Mid Surrey Law Society who provide the prize for an annual Kingston Law School Interviewing Competition. Additionally we have provided information to the Law Society and the Council of Legal Education both on our work at Kingston and the importance generally of encouraging lawyers and undergraduate law students to participate in communication skills training. The Law Society has now adopted our course for articled clerks and newly qualified solicitors as part of their continuing education programme. The Inns of Court School of Law has also expressed an interest in organising courses in this field and we are helping them to establish a pilot scheme for such a course in the next academic year (1988/9).

We are currently offering at Kingston three courses in communication skills, two for undergraduates and one as part of the continuing education scheme. In addition we offer practice interviewing to those students interested in entering the UK Client Interviewing Competition. The following communication skills programme relates to the foundation course that we offer to undergraduates. Students are required to take this course before they can participate in the internal or external competitions or the subsequent casework course. This latter course, unlike the foundation course, requires the student lawyer to deal with one role play client through a series of meetings, correspondence and telephone calls as the case is developed. This course also allows for the development of negotiation skills as different student lawyers will be dealing with all the parties.

The following programme is, we hope, for the most part self-explanatory and is designed to be used by the instructors or facilitators organising the course. Although the course is set out with tasks for two facilitators, A and B, as a programme of team teaching, it could be adapted for use by only one facilitator and there is also no reason why the 'team' should not consist of more than two people. The materials given to the students should be kept to a minimum. The reason for this is a feeling that this is a course that must be taught in a different way from the normal undergraduate teaching and in its presentation should be as unlike as possible. We try to establish the different nature of the course from the beginning by using our working space in a different way, sitting as a single group in a non-hierarchical manner. We also make it clear that, although we may be directing the activities, what is learnt from them is learnt by all of us as a group and that our experiences with the course in any year may lead to subsequent modifications and improvements.

The ability to communicate is seen as so much an integral part of the human condition that to suggest to a person that they cannot communicate skilfully, or that there is much more to learn about it, is potentially threatening. We are aware that this type of skills training, if mishandled, can have a destructive effect upon the participants rather than the constructive and confidence-building effect that we hope to achieve. For this reason we work very hard to provide a supportive environment; we encourage constructive criticism and actively discourage destructive criticism. It is very important that students should be made aware of the need for and the implications of confidentiality in their relations with other members of the group. This needs to be stressed both because of the nature of the course itself and with particular regard to what is required of the students in certain of the exercises. We feel that it is important that we are not seen as all powerful, all knowledgeable lecturers with our comments being given undue importance or weight, rather we hope to be accepted as two members of the group which is engaged on a joint enterprise. It is the students' course as much as it is ours. Clearly in trying to establish a relationship of this nature we have to tackle our own feelings and prejudices concerning the teacher role, as well as dealing with the students' perceptions of this role.

Communication skills are not, for the majority, things that can be learnt in a hurry. We feel it is important that training should begin at undergraduate level and should continue to be developed through professional training, articles or pupillage and beyond. Clearly, this type of training can be very labour-intensive and it will be seen from a perusal of the programme that many areas are only dealt with in brief. Apart from individual interviews it is estimated that each workshop will last up to an hour and a half. For our students this course is voluntary and is in addition to their normal academic workload; because of this and the personal nature of the course, we do not require students to make a permanent commitment to see the course through to the end. The course has been very popular and we have found that the optimum number of students for one group is 24; in years where numbers are greater than this we have run two concurrent courses.

Example exercises are incorporated into the programme – these will change from year to year. We find through experience that some things work well but that others need modifying. With some groups the exercises do not always work in the way that we anticipate that they should but, even where an exercise has not worked out as hoped, it is still always possible to make some useful points, even if they are not necessarily the ones originally intended. By the same token we see a certain amount of flexibility in the order of the workshops and, for instance, with some groups it may be desirable to do the workshops and exercises dealing with body language and mannerisms before those requiring students to talk about things that are personal to them. A number of example roles are incorporated in the programme, these are also changed or modified from year to year or to suit a particular role player. Although the roles come complete with personal details we encourage role players to change them: their performance may be more natural, for instance, if they use their own name, address or other personal details rather than those given. Our views with relation to members of the group role playing for each other have been modified[1] and we now feel that this can be very useful at all stages in the programme. We also feel that keeping the programme under review, modifying the exercises and changing the roles makes us constantly aware of the purpose of the enterprise.

Finally, we would like to emphasise the vital importance of feedback and debriefing after exercises and interviews. Feedback and debriefing are both very important parts of the learning process and it is important that participants have an opportunity to relieve their feelings once they have done an exercise or interview. With regard to interviews both the interviewing lawyer and the role play client may be in an emotionally charged state and both should be given an opportunity to relieve their feelings about the interview and be gently encouraged back to reality. It is of particular importance that role players who have been asked to portray a difficult or victimised client should be able to express their feelings about the interview as the client and that they should also be given an opportunity to work themselves out of the role so that they do not leave still thinking themselves victims.

All members of the group are encouraged, with the exception of the interviews done in Workshops 11 and 12, to observe as well as participate in interviews. Their comments are also solicited in the feedback session, after the interview, but it should be made clear that this should be constructive and that little is to be gained from negative or destructive criticism.

This programme presents only an outline course of workshops which raise a number of important issues both for the learning and teaching of communication skills. There is a variety of answers to the questions posed. We would not wish to impose our responses to these questions, although we have a clear idea of the objectives sought. We would suggest, however, that facilitators should anticipate and consider possible responses and the way in which they may be tied in with the perceived objectives of each exercise. We hope that our programme might be of help to others trying to design a similar teaching programme and we will be happy to offer any further assistance and information that we can. We would also be very grateful for any comments about the programme and would be interested to hear from others working in the same area.

NOTES

1 Mary Holmes and Judith Maxwell 'The Use of Role Play and Video in Teaching Communication Skills to Law Students', *Journal of Professional Legal Education*, vol 5, 151. A version of that article was given as a paper at the Workshop on Professional Legal Skills at the University of Nottingham in December 1986.

COMMUNICATION SKILLS PROGRAMME

Workshop 1

A asks the students why they have elected to do the course and what their expectations are. (**B** makes a note so that these may be referred back to at the end of the course.)

B then goes on to set out what is, for the designers of the course, their manifesto:

(1) the course is designed to assist the students to develop their communication skills generally and although the latter part of the course is structured in the form of law office interviews the course has, potentially, a much wider application to their lives;

(2) this course is only the foundation for a learning process that will continue throughout their professional lives;

(3) the course is a chance to try out skills in a non-threatening and supportive environment, something that is less likely to happen in the professional environment;

(4) we hope to look at problems and issues in a way that allows students to develop their own skills in a personal way – there is no intention to impose rigid approaches to communication skills or interviewing techniques;

(5) we would like all members of the group to share their experiences and to articulate why they feel a particular approach works for them;

(6) that all members of the group should be constructive and positive in their comments on the efforts of other members of the group;

(7) that the ultimate choice as to what is accepted and rejected from the course must rest with the students and that all we can offer is a structured opportunity for self development.

B will continue by discussing the issue of CONFIDENTIALITY and its importance for the successful running of the course.

Students are asked to discuss personal matters in some of the exercises and it is necessary for the cohesion of the group that they may feel that they can trust each other. This is also a useful point at which to discuss the issue of confidentiality in their professional lives.

B describes briefly the structure of the course and stresses the following points:

○ Because of the nature of the course we do not expect students to make a firm commitment. If at any time a student wishes to leave the course we assume that they have their reasons for doing so and that they are under no obligation to divulge those reasons to us. Although we need to know, once interviews have been set up, that students will attend, if they are unable to attend at any particular time we only need to be informed of that fact; reasons or excuses are not necessary.

A leads the group in a discussion of their experiences of being interviewed by, eg doctor, dentist, prospective employer, admissions tutor at college etc (**B** notes comments).

A finally poses the question as to whether we can learn to improve our own interviewing skills from our experiences of being interviewed.

Workshop 2

B reminds everyone of the comments made in the previous workshop concerning experiences of being interviewed – thus providing a foundation for this workshop.

A shows VIDEO. (This is a video made by the Communication Skills group of a previous year and shows, in an exaggerated way, extracts from interviews with lawyers who are less than satisfactory in their approach, eg the joker, the moralist, the money-grabber, the smoker, the drunkard etc).

B asks the students to get into groups of four and gives them the following instructions:

(1) discuss the elements of a good interview;
(2) decide which are the three *most important* elements of a good interview;
(3) the time limit for this exercise is FIVE MINUTES.

At the end of five minutes **A** gets the small groups back into one large group. **A** then asks each group for the three most important elements of an interview and lists these on the blackboard. (**B** makes a note.)

A gives the students an opportunity to comment on the final list.

Workshop 3

Listening exercise

The students are not told beforehand the aim of this exercise as it will defeat the purpose.

A asks the students to find partners and then gives them the following instructions:

(1) Both partners have FIVE MINUTES each in which to tell their partner about one of the following:

    (a) their family and relations;
    (b) their likes and dislikes;
    (c) their experiences with examinations;
    (d) person(s) who have had an influence on their lives.

(All groups will be talking about the same things. **A** and **B** will have selected one of the categories from (a) to (d) beforehand)

(2) While one partner is telling his or her story the other is only to listen and is not to ask any questions or comment.

A will announce when the first five minutes are up so that the story-telling role can change. **A** calls time after the second five minutes.

B then asks each partnership to team up with another partnership, to make groups of four, and gives the following instructions:

(a) each person in the group has three minutes in which to relate to the other members of the group the 'story' that she/he has just heard;
(b) other members of the group are not to ask questions or comment on their 'story' when it is being told.

B announces each three-minute interval so they know when to change speakers. At the end of the twelve minutes **B** asks the small groups to reform as one large group.

A then leads a discussion about the exercise, first stressing that it is not necessary to reveal or comment directly on the stories told. The discussion will be based around the following, and similar, questions:

(1)   How easy did you find it to listen to the story that you were being told?
(2)   How did you think your partner felt about telling his/her story?
(3)   Did your partner retell your story accurately?
(4)   Did she/he get the details correct?
(5)   How did you feel hearing your original partner telling your story to others?
(6)   Were you selective about what you revealed? Why?
(7)   Did you change or alter any of your story before you told it? Why?
(8)   How difficult is it to listen and understand a story told to you for the first time?
(9)   What could you have done to help you better understand and remember the story told to you?
(10)   What have we learnt about listening to and understanding other peoples' stories?

Workshop 4

Fact-finding exercises

A distributes information cards to all members of the group and gives them the following instructions:

(1)   members of the group should get into pairs;
(2)   each partner takes it in turn to read off the description on his/her card and after each description the partner should state what they think that the object might be;
(3)   once both have gone through their cards they swop them for new ones with **A** and **B**;
(4)   partners try to get through as many cards as possible in five minutes.

Each card names an object and then lists five 'pieces of information' about that object. As each one is read off to the partner, the partner must try to guess what the object is.

EXAMPLE CARD

Object: telephone box

(1)   it is red;
(2)   it is made of concrete, metal and glass;
(3)   it has been known to hold up to 22 people;
(4)   you have to pay to use it;
(5)   it is used for the purpose of communication.

The purpose of the cards is to build up a picture of an everyday object through describing certain of its features which are 'true' but may not necessarily be the obvious ways of describing it.

B leads discussion on the difficulty of identifying objects if you have only partial information. Leading on to discuss the importance of questioning to elicit information and warning of the pitfalls of deciding too early on that you know what is being described.

A then leads a game of twenty questions. A volunteer thinks of an object and members of the group take it in turns to ask questions to gain information about the object. The volunteer may only answer yes or no to the questions put. Questioners should try to build on questions that have gone before. Any member of the group may ask 'is it ...' as her/his question.

A leads discussion after three or four rounds of twenty questions have been played covering the following points:

(1) Did any of you work out what the object was before a solution was suggested by a particular questioner?
(2) Were you convinced, from the information that you received that you knew the solution, only to find that you were wrong?
(3) How can we develop questioning to obtain the information that we need?

B will then lead a discussion on asking questions, talking about open and closed questions etc.

Workshop 5

In this workshop members of the group are given their first opportunity to interview a 'client'. The aim of this interview is for the interviewer to establish the pertinent facts to the problem presented; the interviewer is not required to give any advice to the client. These interviews should take between ten and fifteen minutes and each one will be observed by **A** or **B**. Once interviewers have done their own interview they will be encouraged to stay and observe subsequent interviews and join in feedback.

The role players will be briefed with one of the following roles:

Role 1: The accident

You are a student at ... College studying a subject other than law. You receive a grant but your father has to make a parental contribution. At the beginning of this term you were at a careers evening arranged by your college. You left at about 8.30 pm intending to return to your flat on your bicycle. As you rode out of the main gates you were knocked down by a car. You lost consciousness for a few minutes and when you came to the police and an ambulance had been called by your fellow students. You were turning right when the accident occurred and you were hit by a car that was also going down the hill. When the car hit you you were thrown towards the pavement but your bicycle was run over by the car that hit you and the car that was following it; in fact you do not remember this detail yourself but you have been told that this is what happened. Do not tell the solicitor that you don't actually remember being hit unless you are asked about it directly. The driver of the car that hit you stopped, although the one following did not.

The police took a statement from the driver of the car that hit you at the scene of the accident; he was then allowed to go. The police did not take a statement from you until you had had some initial treatment in the casualty department of the hospital. You were given a painkiller which you think made you rather dozy. When the policeman tried to question you you remember telling him that it was all your fault and bursting into tears. A nurse then asked the policeman to leave. You had some x-rays and it was found that you had broken your arm, this was set in plaster and you were kept in overnight for observation. The next morning the policeman came to see you again and you told him that you had cycled out of the college and at the time the car had not been in sight. The policeman gave you the name and address of the driver of the car and told you that he claimed that you had no lights on your bicycle. The policeman also told you that the bicycle was so badly damaged it had been impossible to establish whether the lights had been turned on or not.

The broken arm is not your writing arm but the doctor at the hospital seems to think that there might be some permanent damage. You can no longer lift your arm any higher than your shoulder. Your bicycle is a complete write off and you would be afraid to ride a bicycle now anyway. You also suffered minor injuries to your face and legs. The plaster was taken off your arm last week. Your parents are now paying for you to have physiotherapy because the doctor said you needed it but there was a six week waiting list for treatment on the NHS. (Your father's firm pays a BUPA subscription for him and his family.)

You have come to the solicitor, at the insistence of your parents, because you have been in touch with the driver who hit you and he says that the accident was your fault and his insurance company will not pay up. He says that you will have to sue him but he has a good defence.

Give the following information only if you are asked directly about it:

(1) You were drinking wine at the careers evening and probably had three or four glasses.
(2) You cannot truthfully remember whether you turned your lights on or not. You are sure you must have because it's an automatic reaction when you get on your bike.
(3) The names and addresses of three fellow students who saw the accident.
(4) You can't really remember whether you looked to see if any cars were coming down the hill. What you really remember is thinking that the road was nice and clear.
(5) You were wearing navy blue trousers and a navy blue jacket, nothing that was light or bright.
(6) You have broken this arm before, two years ago, and have had some stiffness in it ever since.

Role 2: *The car*

You can be yourself (name, age etc) as far as it is consistent with the following facts concerning your purchase of a car:

You are a travelling salesperson and naturally as you cover a large area need a car. Three months ago you bought a secondhand car from George's Garage,

Kingston. You know nothing about cars and you took a friend along although she/he doesn't know much more about them than you do. You were told that the car had only had one previous owner and that it had only done 20,000 miles. You now suspect that it must have done a great deal more as it is continually breaking down and you don't seem to have had a single trouble-free week of driving. When you bought the car you asked if there was a guarantee and the salesman said, 'Our cars are so good we don't need any guarantee' – you were impressed by that. Later he had said, 'If you have any problems bring it back and we will fix it', and you had thought he meant they would do it for nothing because of what he had said earlier. You now know better. You have complained to the manager but over the weeks he has become increasingly abusive and you find it really difficult to talk to him.

You are getting increasingly worried about the situation. You need your car to do your job and your boss has not been very happy that because of car trouble you have had to have time off work. Also you have had to spend a great deal of money getting the car fixed every time. As a result you have a substantial overdraft and the bank manager has said that you cannot have any more credit. You don't think that you can sell the car and you cannot afford to buy another. You think that there must be some way that you can sue the garage.

Give the following information only if you are asked directly about it:

(1) Shortly after you bought the car a friend's boyfriend who is interested in cars offered to tune the engine for you; he spent a whole weekend taking the engine apart and putting it together again.
(2) The first time that you complained to the manager of George's Garage he offered to change the car for another similar one, but you refused because you didn't like the colour of the other one.

BRIEFING ROLE PLAYERS

Role players need to be carefully briefed before their interviews in order that they can play their part in a realistic manner. Thus they need to be advised of the following matters:

(1) they may be asked for the names, addresses and telephone numbers of any of the people that they mention in their story and so need to have a 'stock' of such details to hand;
(2) they must be careful of giving information too readily and in the form in which it has been presented to them. They need to think about how people tell their stories; they should decide on the issues in a particular story that *they* think most important to talk about first. There are details that they are unlikely to think very important and will not mention unless asked specifi-cally about them;
(3) they should not deliberately conceal information unless they have been asked to as part of a particular role;
(4) as long as they keep to the essence of the problem that they have been given they are free to make changes to minor details if it is easier for them to remember the details that they provide etc;
(5) if they are playing a person with whom they have little in common then they should try to think themselves into that person so that they know that person very well and could, if asked, give any details of that person's life;
(6) it is important that they should participate actively in feedback sessions.

FEEDBACK

After each interview it is important that the interviewer should receive *positive* feedback from observers. As critical self-awareness develops interviewers will be able to feel and articulate what was wrong with a particular interview for themselves; it is counter-productive for observers to be destructive in their criticism.

_____

Workshop 6

A opens the workshop with a discussion concerning the interviews done in the previous workshop. This will involve not only getting the members of the group to talk about their feelings while interviewing and what they learnt from the experience but also how they felt about the feedback that they received immediately after the interview. It is very important to check how members of the group feel about feedback and to deal with any hostility or negative feelings that may have arisen.

B discusses the importance of note-taking for the interviewer and the problems this creates. Issues discussed may include:

(1) the need to explain to clients why notes are being taken;
(2) how you can take notes while at the same time attending to the client;
(3) whether a tape recorder might be used as an alternative means of recording the interview;
(4) the type of information that would need to be noted if you were dealing with (a) a road accident case, (b) a criminal case, (c) a divorce etc.

A asks the members of the group to pair off and in pairs to spend five minutes discussing the information that would need to be noted when dealing with a particular type of case (one that has not already been discussed).

A leads final discussion/pooling of information from the previous exercises (**B** takes a note).

_____

Workshop 7

This workshop will consist of a note-taking interview that will not be observed. The notes taken will be looked at by **A** and **B** when the interviews have been completed.

Each member of the group will have a role play client to interview for ten to fifteen minutes as a fact-finding, note-taking exercise. They will have been briefed beforehand as to the area of law which will be involved (it will not be an area covered in Workshop 6).

The role play clients will be briefed with details to play one of the following clients:

(1) a victim of a road accident;
(2) a spouse seeking a divorce;
(3) a student who has been caught dealing in drugs;
(4) a wealthy testator.

Workshop 8

In this workshop it is intended to move from fact-finding to emotions and how to deal with a client in an emotional state.

A hands back notes taken during Workshop 7 with comments. Members of the group divide into pairs and take each other's notes. They are then asked the extent to which they could understand the case using the information in his/her colleague's notes.

B asks members of the group to form new pairs. Each member is then given five minutes to tell his/her partner of a happy incident and a sad incident in his/her lives which has affected him/her in a personal way. When this has been done **B** will lead a discussion as to how people felt talking about happy and sad occasions in their lives. The discussion may cover some of the following points:

(1) Did anyone feel uncomfortable talking about these things? Why?
(2) Did anyone react inappropriately when listening or talking, eg laughing when the subject was sad?
(3) Would it be easier or more difficult to talk about these things to a complete stranger?

A then develops this discussion into a more general discussion about emotions, covering some of the following points:

(1) How do we recognise the emotional states of another person, particularly if we do not know them? eg by body language;
(2) How do we respond to another person who is in an emotional state?
(3) How can we deal with someone who is angry, violent, in tears, etc?

B gives a short introductory talk on the importance of the counselling dimension of interviews in professional practice.

Workshop 9

Body language and mannerisms

A divides the group into pairs and gives them the following instructions:

(1) one partner is to spend three minutes talking about their day so far, what classes they had, what they learnt etc.
(2) the other partner is not to make a sound but to convey to the story teller that this is the most boring story that they have ever heard (this information should only be conveyed to the listening partners).

B re-forms the group and leads a discussion about the exercise including the following points:

(1) How did you feel your story was received? How did you know?
(2) How were people using their faces and bodies to convey those feelings or emotions?
(3) How might we expect someone to express concentrated interest in something that we were telling them?
(4) Could we tell from the way someone sat how they were feeling?

B then asks every one in the group to express some or all of the following emotions simply by using their body and facial expression: anger, amusement, hatred, sorrow, boredom, exhaustion, fear etc.

B asks the group to get into threes and gives them the following instructions:

(1) one member of each group of three is to tell the other two why s/he is studying for a law degree and what s/he intends to do with the degree;
(2) the two other members of the group must act, individually, to try and distract the person talking from their story. In performing this task they must not touch the storyteller or speak themselves (this information should only be conveyed to the listening partners);
(3) the storyteller to speak for three minutes.

A leads a feedback discussion on the previous exercise including the following points:

(1) Was the storyteller distracted by the other two in his/her group?
(2) Did the two 'distractors' know the kind of things to do to put people off telling their story?
(3) Generally what kind of mannerisms or behaviour do we find distracting?
(4) Are we aware of our own mannerisms and how they might affect those that we come into contact with in a professional/personal relationship?
(5) Can members of the group identify mannerisms of other members of the group, including **A** and **B**? If any are identified to what extent are the perpetrators aware of them?

Workshop 10

A opens the workshop by discussing with the group the fact that we frequently have to tell people, in both professional and private life, things that they don't want to hear. In professional life this may involve telling a client that you cannot do anything for them or that they are in an even worse position than they think that they are. Discussing finance is also something that does not come easily, although it is crucial to the smooth running of the relationship that the client should understand and accept his/her financial obligation to the professional helper. It is also important that the client should understand the financial implications of any course of action that s/he chooses to take and what is being done for the fee that s/he is paying.

B asks for two volunteers to role play before the whole group and gives them the following instructions: they are in a bank manager's office, one is the rather stern bank manager, the other a student trying to increase his/her overdraft to last until the end of term.

Alternative scenarios:

(1) son/daughter trying to borrow money from parent for girlfriend's/own abortion;
(2) someone trying to borrow money from a friend to buy drugs, something of which the friend is slightly disapproving.

B allows role playing to run up to five minutes and then leads the group in a general discussion about the difficulty of asking people for money, including some of the following points:

(1) Why do we feel embarrassed asking people for money?
(2) Are there ways of overcoming this embarrassment?
(3) Do we find it difficult to ask people for money that they owe us?
(4) Why is it important to discuss finances with clients?

A then asks for two volunteers to role play in front of the whole group. Volunteers are given the following instructions:

○ one is a doctor and s/he is telling the other, the patient, that her/his illness is terminal.

Alternative scenarios:

(1) social worker telling parent that his/her child is to be taken into care because of suspected child abuse;
(2) tutor telling student that the student has failed examinations and must withdraw from the course.

A allows role play to run for up to five minutes and then leads a discussion resulting from the exercise.

B winds up the workshop by leading discussion on the importance of the client's choice when it comes to deciding on a course of action and further developing the theme of the counselling dimensions of the professional interview.

Workshops 11 and 12

Each member of the group will be given a role play client to interview for an initial interview of half an hour. These interviews will be recorded separately in the video studio and each individual will look at their own interview, alone.

Sample roles for clients follow.

Role play 1

○ You are Susan Morgan.
○ You are about 23 years old.
○ You teach in Kingston Comprehensive School.
○ You are unmarried and live alone.

YOUR PROBLEM

You were going to be married on 20 July 1987 but a week before the wedding your fiancé suddenly told you that he needed more excitement in his life than you could give him and broke off the engagement. Since then you have seen him occasionally with his rather glamorous secretary. You are now very isolated. You met your fiancé whilst you were still at school and in consequence you did not maintain a relationship with your schoolfriends; the only friends that you had were his friends. His friends seem to have dropped you as well. Naturally you have been desperately unhappy and you found last term very difficult.

During this difficult period one of the boys that you taught, and still teach in the fifth form, seemed to understand how you felt; he stopped the other kids ragging you. You came to depend on him, he was always willing to run errands for you and often stayed behind after school to talk to you. You found him both intelligent and sensitive and almost without realising it, over the term, you had told him all about your problems and your unhappiness.

After the school's Christmas party he went home with you and you embarked upon a sexual relationship with him that is continuing. The problem is that he is only fifteen and will not be sixteen until August 1988. The affair is very intense, he wants to marry you as soon as he is sixteen. You are rather ambivalent about marrying him; you can see many problems, not least that his parents are very ambitious for him and would be unlikely to consent. (His parents do not, of course, know about the affair.) Despite the fact that you do not think you want to marry him you feel at the moment that you could not break off the relationship. Clearly you need someone to care for you deeply, though you may not be honest enough to admit that it is not this particular boy that matters but anyone who was madly in love with you would do.

Unfortunately an older colleague has found out what is going on and is blackmailing you. First he borrowed things that he didn't return, including small sums of money. Last weekend he came to your flat, drunk. He was very abusive and made you have sex with him by threatening to expose you to the headmistress and the police. Not unnaturally this was a disastrous and unpleasurable episode and since then he has been very unpleasant towards you. He is now threatening to go to the police unless you agree to give him the money to buy the new stereo that he says he needs. Although you could afford to give him some money from your savings, you can see that this is unlikely to be the end of it. He really seems rather unbalanced and you are not confident that paying him will prevent him from going to the police. You have decided that the best thing to do is to consult a solicitor to see what will happen to you. You are distraught both as a result of your own emotional problems and the realisation that you have ruined your career and may go to prison. You are desperately in need of help and advice.

Role play 2

o You are ... (give yourself a name).
o You are about your own age.
o You are a second year student at Kingston Polytechnic studying drama.
o The local authority only pay your college fees: you do not receive a subsistence grant. Your parents make you an allowance for living expenses.

YOUR PROBLEM

Three nights ago you were at a disco in Kingston. It was raided by police looking for drugs. You were quite drunk by the time the raid took place and were carted off to the police station and put in a cell, where you remained, you think, for a couple of hours, by which time you had sobered up a bit. When you were interviewed by the police they showed you a packet of pills which they said were amphetamines and which they claimed to have found in your jacket pocket. You do not remember being searched but you were *very* drunk. The police said that if you told them the name of your pusher they would not press charges against you. They interrogated you for what seemed a very long time – and finally let you out on police bail. You are to appear in court next week.

You had no drugs on you that evening and you think they must have been planted on you either by the police or someone else at the club. This often happens; when people realise there is a raid they put their stuff in the nearest available pocket.

You do, however, use drugs from time to time but you could not tell the police where you get them from because you get them from a very close friend. The police know that you use drugs because you were successfully prosecuted, in similar circumstances, only three months ago and one of the policemen recognised you.

Your parents were very angry about your prosecution and have threatened that if anything similar happens again they will no longer pay your allowance, which would mean leaving Kingston Polytechnic.

Your greatest concern is to prevent them finding out. You don't know whether to plead guilty and try and get it all over and done with and hope that it is not reported in the papers or whether you should plead not guilty as you are innocent.

Role play 3

○ You are Sarah Gray, a student studying sociology at Kingston Polytechnic.
○ You share a house, 3 Kilvert Road, Kingston, with four other students.
○ The house is a three-bedroomed house and one of the rooms downstairs is used as a bedroom. You all share a sitting room, kitchen and bathroom.
○ Two of the students share a bedroom, the rest of you have a room of your own.

YOUR PROBLEM

You moved into the house in September 1986 and the others have moved in at various times since. As far as you know the house has always been let to students; those leaving usually finding someone else to take their place which is how you ended up there in the first place.

You each pay £25.00 a week to Mrs Tucker, the landlady, which she comes to collect on a Saturday morning. You think she is nosey and interfering; she loves to come to collect the rent really early, about 10 am, to catch you all still in bed so she can make some rude comments about the youth of today.

You are now having serious problems with Mrs Tucker and you have all clubbed together to pay for you to come and see a solicitor to get a stiff letter sent to her. The problem has arisen from the following facts.

About three weeks ago when Mrs Tucker came to collect the rent she said that she was putting the rent up for each of you by £10. You were all very indignant both at the amount of the increase and the way she did it and have decided as a matter of principle that you won't pay and you informed her in writing of that decision. You also said in your letter that it was about time she redecorated the house as it was in a pretty poor state of decoration and also that she should replace some of the shabby furniture and the broken window in the kitchen. Admittedly the window was broken during one of your parties,but why should you pay to repair *her* house.

She replied by solicitor's letter giving you all one month's notice to quit effective from 14 January 1988. You don't want to leave because it will be difficult to get other accommodation and you think that you are protected by the Rent Acts, though you are unsure of their scope. You think as she has sent you a solicitor's letter that you should reply in like mode pointing out that she can't evict you.

You also have some idea that when you moved in the rent had been fixed by the rent office – you are sure that one of the others living there at the time said they had had the rent fixed. You want to tell her in the letter that she can't raise the rent and doesn't she have some obligation to redecorate and repair?

You are all on full-time local authority grants and have no other income.

Role play 4

○ You are Mary Stubbs; you have two children aged three and four.
○ You were divorced from your husband two years ago.
○ You are a teacher; your salary is £8,000 per annum; your ex-husband pays you £100 per month for the maintenance of the children.

YOUR PROBLEM

With two growing children finances are always rather difficult and so you were exceptionally disappointed that after having saved up for two years to take the children on holiday, the whole thing was such a disaster.

You had booked a holiday, with Aurora Holidays, for two weeks in Greece in September. The hotel that you booked was specifically geared to single parent families and provided child-minding facilities in the evenings and organised evening events for the parents. All the rooms in the hotel were large family rooms with their bathrooms ensuite, and balconies. You were all very excited as it looked as though the hotel was nice (and served English food) and there would be other children and adults in the same position as yourselves to socialise with.

When you got there you were told that there had been an over-booking and that you could not stay at the hotel but had to stay in a taverna instead. This was most unsatisfactory – the room was small, cramped and stuffy. It had a balcony, but this was at street level which meant choking exhaust fumes all day and that the windows had to be locked at night. There were no child-minding facilities, no entertainments (except for a small bar) and there were no other English people staying there, and all the other guests were German. Additionally only Greek food was served which the children hated and it meant a lot of expensive eating out.

You have written to Aurora Holidays and they wrote back drawing your attention to the small print in the brochure which says, 'The company accepts no liability for changes to a similar type of accommodation.' They said that the accommodation was similar and anyway it was nothing to do with them and that you would 'have to sue the Greeks'. Finally they argued that you were offered, by their courier, the opportunity to use the entertainment facilities at the hotel and were offered the opportunity to transfer to the original hotel for the last five days of the holiday. (This is all true, but in fact you were having a holiday romance with Klaus, one of the guests at the taverna and so you didn't want to move out.)

You want the price of the holiday and the additional expense of eating out back from the company. Also you want compensation for the lack of entertainment and enjoyment and for the disappointment. You want this sum in order to take the children on a proper holiday this year because you feel rather guilty that you neglected them for Klaus last year. You are prompted by a similar case that you read about in the newspaper recently.

Workshop 13

Feedback session on the interviews done in Workshops 11 and 12. Members of the group will be asked to evaluate and discuss their performance and to identify their strengths and weaknesses.

A will then distribute the handout (following) and take the group through it. The handout provides guidelines *only* and members of the group will be encouraged to reflect on their own style of interviewing in the context of the suggestions contained in the handout.

HANDOUT FOR DISTRIBUTION IN WORKSHOP 13

Interviewing and counselling skills

Professionals are increasingly realising that expertise in their own field of competence is not sufficient. Professionals need to be able to communicate with their clients which is done most effectively through the interview. The client who comes for an interview with a problem may also need counselling. For the lawyer, interviewing and counselling skills are not the same as forensic skills, but like these latter skills they need to be learned.

Interviewing is a skill. The purpose of a solicitor's interview with a client is presumably to extract the required information from the client accurately and quickly. The interview is of great importance to the lawyer and is as necessary a tool as law books. During the course of the interview the lawyer should discover the extent of the client's problem; assess the problem from the legal point of view and the client's personal view; explore with the client the options available to the client and, finally, prepare a plan to assist the client to pursue the chosen option.

The interview needs a structure but beware of allowing structure to dominate, it must be a flexible structure. A suggested structure is:

(1) *Welcoming the client*: allow the client to orientate to the unfamiliar surroundings by making general comments; put the client at ease, as a client

who is not at ease will not be very forthcoming. Establish what is the nature of the problem and whether it is one that you are competent to deal with before you proceed to discussing anything else.

(2) *Finance*: this should be dealt with sensitively – most clients will realise that they have to pay and until the lawyer has dealt with this the client may be rather anxious at the prospect of finding themselves landed with a rather large bill.

(3) *The problem*: in order to obtain the maximum information concerning the client's problem it is necessary to **listen** and **reflect**.

Listening:
(a) give the client your whole attention keeping interruptions to a minimum;
(b) remember what your client has said – you will need to take some notes;
(c) listen for what is not openly said and watch for non-verbal clues to help understand the client's feelings;
(d) do not be stampeded into asking lots of questions by silences – some of the things that your client will discuss with you will be painful – allow them time and silence to collect their thoughts – let them explain in their own way and time. Silence can also be a useful tool to get a client talking;
(e) empathise – try to understand the client's problem as the client sees it and avoid making judgments and criticisms.

Reflecting:
(a) keep questions to a minimum except when:
(i) you need precise information;
(ii) you want to open up the interview and then ask open-ended questions;

(b) use minimal prompts: mm ... yes ... or repeat the last few words that the client has spoken;
(c) paraphrase or reflect accurately what the client has told you as a way of prompting reassurance that you have heard or checking that you have heard accurately;
(d) avoid speaking too soon ('yes, I'm sure I can help' before you know the full extent of the problem), too often (destroying the client's concentration on his story), and too long.

When you have heard the problem in detail:

(4) *Summarise*: the main points to make sure that you have recorded the essential details accurately – this also gives you time to synthesise what you have heard.

(5) *The solution*: this may not be obvious. There will usually be more than one way of dealing with a problem; a non-legal solution may be better for the individual client. When discussing the options with the client the lawyer needs to point out the advantages and disadvantages of each option and discuss all the implications, including financial ones, with the client.

(6) *Preference for a particular course of action*: once the client has indicated a preference discuss what both of you will do to implement that particular

course of action. Don't confuse the client by harking back to discarded options. Make sure that the client knows what you are going to do and when and what he needs to do.

(7) *Reassurance*: before winding up the interview make sure that the client's immediate fears (eg eviction etc) have been dealt with as well as long-term permanent strategy.

Some Do's and Dont's

 (1) Keep to a *logical* sequence of questions.
 (2) Avoid *multiple* questions.
 (3) Avoid *ambiguous* questions.
 (4) Avoid *legal jargon* and *technical words*.
 (5) Ask *open* questions.
 (6) Ask *probing* questions.
 (7) Avoid *yes/no* questions.
 (8) Avoid *leading questions*.
 (9) Avoid *interrupting*.
(10) Avoid *overt or implied criticism*.
(11) Avoid *extreme mannerisms*.
(12) Look *interested*.

Workshops 14, 15 and 16

During these workshops all members of the group will be provided with a role play client to interview for half an hour as a first interview. These interviews will be observed by **A** and **B** and other members of the group will be encouraged to watch and contribute to the feedback session which will take place immediately after each interview.

Sample roles for clients follow.

Role play 5

○ Your name is Susan Wade.
○ You are your own age.
○ You are unemployed and live on income support.
○ You live in a squat where you have your own room but the kitchen, bathroom and living room are shared by the other six people in the squat.
○ One of the people in the squat has suggested that you come and see a lawyer because you can get free legal advice.

YOUR PROBLEM

You left home and school when you were fifteen and have drifted about ever since. Your parents live in Leicester but you haven't been in touch with them since you moved to London. You haven't ever really had a proper job, although you have done occasional work in bars and boutiques. You have mostly lived in various squats, have dabbled with drugs and generally lived rather on the fringes of society. A year ago you had a baby but unfortunately suffered from post-natal depression and the baby was taken into care.

After the baby was born you were so depressed that you could see no future for yourself or your baby and you think that you agreed to the baby being in care. You have also been told that you agreed that the baby could be adopted but you don't remember doing that. You feel much better now and, although you are probably not entirely over your depression, you are still taking anti-depressant pills and see your doctor regularly. You have an appointment to see the psychiatrist, who treated you when you were in hospital, next month.

Your baby is in a foster home, quite a distance away from where you live, and you weren't allowed to see it until it was nearly four months old. Since then you have been to see it regularly every week at least once and sometimes twice. You don't get on at all well with the foster mother; you think she resents you and wants to keep your baby. She never even offers you a cup of tea when you are there and often won't let you give your baby a bottle or change its nappy. You think that she tells lies about you to your social worker.

Last week the social worker told you that you were not to be allowed to visit your child for a while because the foster mother said that the child was very upset by your visits. You think it's the foster mother who is upset by your visits because you think that she wants to adopt your child. You told the social worker that you would go anyway but she said that if you did the child would be moved to another home and you wouldn't be allowed to know where. She also said that it would be much better for your child if it was adopted because you have no future to offer it. She said you would never be allowed to keep a child in the squat because she says it is filthy. This isn't true, it's just that all the furniture is old and you are all a bit untidy. You don't want to leave the squat; you get support from the people that you live with.

You want to be able to visit your child but most of all you want your child to come and live with you. You are sure that you could look after the child properly and you could afford it because you would get more money from social security. You agreed to your child being taken into care and you think you should be able to have the child back now that you want to and you don't see why a stuck up snobbish social worker should prevent you.

Role play 6

○ You are Gordon Browne.
○ You are aged twenty-five years.
○ You are a computer programmer earning £20,000 pa.
○ You are divorced and your wife got the house but you have just purchased a very small one bedroomed flat.

YOUR PROBLEM

You have come for advice on the best way to get your children away from your ex-wife who you think is a very bad mother. You need something to be done immediately because she is endangering their health and their morals.

You met your wife when you were both students; she is now a teacher and works full time. You married when you were twenty and have two children, aged two and three. You were divorced a year ago.

You realise now that you and your wife were always incompatible. She objected to you belonging to a rugby club and a cricket club and playing these games most weekends in their season. You argued about politics as well; you are pretty middle of the road while she has become more and more left wing and involved with women's groups and vegetarianism. You don't think, for a start, that it can be healthy for children to be brought up on a vegetarian diet.

As your wife works you only pay maintenance for the children and you must admit you have been a bit erratic in your payments but your wife uses this to prevent you having access to the children. She says if you won't pay for them you can't see them. But she doesn't seem to realise that you've just had to buy and equip a new home for yourself, having got no share in the previous home.

The main reason that you wish to get the children away from your wife is that, you now realise, she is a lesbian and has her woman friend living with her in the house with your children. You are really horrified by this development and can't cope with the idea that your wife prefers a woman to you. What will the lads at the rugby club say? Also you are concerned about your children's morals and that they might catch AIDS. You spoke to your wife about this situation once and she made it quite clear that she was going to keep the children and that she and her woman friend would adopt them as a couple and keep you away from them.

Be suitably outraged and determined to leave no stone unturned to get your children back from this sick woman.

Role play 7

- ○ You are Peter Lee.
- ○ You are your own age.
- ○ You are a charge nurse in a psychiatric hospital.
- ○ You earn £9,230 plus £728 London weighting per annum.
- ○ You are married but separated from your wife and three months ago Mary moved in with you. She is also a charge nurse at the same hospital as you and she has two children aged seven and ten.

YOUR PROBLEM

You did your general training at Kingston Hospital. You trained with a good group and you worked hard and played hard. The young doctors used to hold some pretty wild and drunken parties to which all the nurses were invited. For all of you it was your first time away from home and things sometimes got a bit out of hand. Towards the end of your first year Anne told you that she was pregnant as the result of a brief affair that the two of you had had. Although neither of you were in love you thought that you should do the right thing and you got married. The marriage did not long survive the birth of your baby. Your wife went back to live with her parents taking your baby with her. Despite the distance that her parents live you have seen your child at least once a week and now that your child is older the child has stayed with you for the occasional weekend. You usually visit when your wife is at work because you get on better with your mother-in-law than you do with your wife. In fact you haven't spoken to your wife for about six months; all arrangements are made with her parents.

You have been very lucky financially. A legacy from an uncle enabled you to buy your own house a year ago, psychiatric nursing is better paid than general nursing and there is plenty of overtime. Your wife on the other hand is finding life something of a struggle although she is supported financially by her parents. In order to have some time with her child she only works part time and you know that she resents being so dependent on her parents. As things stand your wife could never afford to buy her own house. To give herself the chance to do so she has taken a very well paid job, in Saudi Arabia, for three years. During that time she is going to leave your child with her parents. You are most unhappy about this arrangement. Your parents-in-law are elderly and you doubt that they are up to bringing up a child on their own which will be the case despite the fact that your wife gets a three week holiday in England for every six months that she works. You think that a child should be with its natural parents. Now that you are living with Mary you can offer your child a proper home life and you would like your child back. You and your wife have never bothered to get divorced but you think that you should now do so as you are sure that any court must give you custody of the child. What worries you a little bit is that your wife's parents have spoken about adopting your child themselves and you think that this is a ploy to take away your rights over your child.

You have come to the solicitor today because you want to divorce your wife and seek custody of your child and to prevent her parents adopting the child.

Only volunteer the following information if you are asked directly:

(1) Your present relationship is not very stable; Mary is older than you and you don't get on very well with her kids.
(2) Mary is not very happy about having a young child added to the household.
(3) You have never paid any maintenance to your wife or your child – you are a bit mean and don't see why you should.
(4) You would have been quite happy to let the situation remain as it is at present but resent your wife just dumping your child. You don't think she should be allowed to do so.

Role play 8

○ You are Jessica Higgins.
○ You are aged thirty-five.
○ You are happily married and you have three children.
○ You and your husband are both dentists so you have a high joint income.

YOUR PROBLEM

Your problem is really your problem child. Your oldest child, Simon, aged sixteen, is well behaved, good at his school work and helpful at home; he has never given you a moment's trouble. Your youngest child Alice is three and utterly adorable but the middle child, Helen, aged 15, has been nothing but trouble since she was born and a great deal worse since Alice was born.

Because Helen was so badly behaved at school her headmistress insisted that she saw an educational psychologist. You were worried about Helen and so you agreed. She has been seeing John Edmundson, the educational psychologist, for about eighteen months. You have become increasingly concerned about Helen's relationship with John. You are fairly sure that Helen has slept with a number of boyfriends since she was thirteen, although she has never admitted it to you. These were boys of about her own age – you didn't know what to do about it and so did nothing. John is, you estimate, much nearer your own age and you think that Helen has been having a sexual relationship with him for about the last six months. Again she would not admit it and you did not know what to do.

You have decided that it is time to take action because you are convinced that Helen is pregnant; all the signs are there as any mother knows. You challenged Helen last week and she became quite hysterical, accusing you of all sorts of things, threatening to kill herself etc, but she denied that she was having an affair or that she was pregnant.

Although your feelings about this troublesome child are, and have always been, somewhat ambivalent, you are still very concerned for her welfare. You are particularly concerned that Edmundson will persuade Helen to have an abortion which you think will be disastrous for Helen; besides you object to abortion as a method of birth control. Also you do not think that Edmundson should be allowed to get away with this. It's not just Helen, what about all the other young girls that he is supposed to be helping?

Role play 9

○ You are Sabah Quazi.
○ You are twenty years old.
○ You are divorced.
○ You married when you were sixteen and you have never worked. Since you separated from your husband you have been living on income support.
○ You have a son who is two years old.
○ Decide where you live – this is a council flat, the rent is paid through housing benefit. You do not have a telephone.
○ Your husband is not English (decide on his name and nationality).
○ You know that your legal fees will be paid by legal aid because that is what happened when you got divorced.

YOUR PROBLEM

You were married when you were sixteen and at first you were very happy. After you had your baby things started to go wrong – your husband was very moody and you argued a lot. You also discovered that he was seeing another woman. Eventually he left you and moved in with her. Six months ago you were divorced and you were allowed to keep you son although your husband was allowed to visit him every Sunday and take him to stay for the weekend once a month. You were quite happy with these arrangements. You actually thought that your husband would soon tire of taking his son out because he hadn't to that point shown much interest in him. Contrary to your expectation, your ex-husband seems to be getting very fond of the child.

About six weeks ago two unsettling things happened. First, your ex-husband's girlfriend left him and he has taken to coming round to your flat more often, two or three times a week, saying that he wants to see his son. Sometimes you have found it quite difficult to get rid of him. He hurt you very much and you still feel bitter and resentful towards him and you certainly don't want to encourage him to hang around. What is even more worrying is that a few weeks ago his brother came from (his home country) and you know he is trying to persuade your husband to go 'home' – despite the fact that your husband has lived here for some time. Your husband's brother also seems very taken with your son and keeps bringing him round presents.

You are getting very suspicious that your ex-husband is going to snatch your son and take him to his home country. You are very concerned about this and feel that there is some way that he can be stopped and that is why you have come to seek advice from a solicitor today. You would like to stop your husband seeing your son at all.

Role play 10

○ You are Pete Andrews.
○ You are about your own age.
○ You live with your parents.
○ You work as a clerk in the local tax office and you have done so since you left school.
○ You earn £6,000 pa and you have £3,200 in a building society account.
○ You are a rather shy and solitary person and you do not have many friends nor do you go out much.
○ You have one previous conviction, some four years ago, for indecent assault and you were put on probation for one year.

YOUR PROBLEM

On Thursday and Friday of last week you had two days official holiday. You didn't do much in your two days off, so mostly you sat at home. Your parents, who are now retired, were away visiting your aunt. On Friday afternoon you went shopping in Kingston where you were stopped by the police and asked to take part in an identification parade. You took part in the parade and to your horror you were picked out by the two young girls who were brought in to see if they recognised anyone. The girls were in school uniform and you think that they were about eleven years old.

After the parade you were taken to a room and informed that the two girls claimed that someone had exposed himself to them in Richmond Park that morning. You were cautioned (but not told of your right to a solicitor or to contact a friend) and then the police interrogated you until quite late in the evening. You had not committed the offence but the police kept on and on at you telling you that the court would be much harsher in sentencing you if you pleaded not guilty. They also said that the case would be splashed all over the local papers and the whole thing would drag on for much longer if you didn't plead guilty and you would probably not get bail while on remand. In the end you 'confessed' and signed a written confession.

You appeared before the magistrates on Monday morning. They said it was a very serious case and that they would remand the case for two weeks in order that you should get yourself legal representation. You were devastated by this because you think that it means they will send you to prison and also you hoped that the case would be over before your parents came home at the end of the week. You still think that in view of what the police said to you and your previous conviction you should plead guilty.

Workshop 17

This workshop will be a general feedback session and a planning session.

Members of the group will be encouraged to discuss their experiences on the course and what, if anything, they feel they have got out of it. Suggestions for changes or improvements will also be sought.

II INTERVIEWING

David Cruickshank and Andrew Pirie*

INTERVIEWING SEMINAR 1

Interviewing exercise 1

TIME: 1 hour 15 minutes

1 Skill

Interviewing 1.

2 Topic

Definition, goals, problems.

3 Objectives

By the end of the activity, you will:
(a) be able to define the term 'interviewing';
(b) be able to state two major goals of the interviewing process for a lawyer; and
(c) be able to describe at least ten major problems in achieving the goals of the interviewing process for a lawyer.

4 Preparation

(a) Read Binder and Price *Legal Interviewing and Counselling* pp 1–5.

5 Description of activity

Through the use of short lawyer–client interview role plays and through feedback on these experiences, we will provide an introduction to the interviewing process for lawyers. The focus will be on the major goals of the legal interview and the major problems typically encountered by the new lawyer in the interviewing process.

6 Notes

None.

* The authors acknowledge the permission of the Professional Legal Training Course, CLE Society of British Columbia, Canada and the Institute of Professional Legal Studies of New Zealand who made possible the creation and republication of these materials.

Instructor material

7 Instructor preparation

(a) Same as for students.
(b) Review *Problems in the interviewing process* handout (see p 57 below).

8 Resources

(a) Handout – interviewing exercise 1, Lawyer instructions, Client facts and Confidential client instructions.
(b) Handout – *Problems in the interviewing process* (p 57 below).

9 Instruction

Timetable

9.30–9.45	Welcome students to the first seminar of the Programme. Objectives for the entire interviewing seminar are pointed out. Objectives for this activity are explained.
9.45–10.00	The definition and goals of interviewing.
10.00–10.30	Problems for the lawyer in the interviewing process.
10.30–10.45	Coffee break.

9.30–9.45

(1) This is the start of the first seminar. Welcome the students and assure them that they should find the three day interviewing seminar an exciting and rewarding learning experience.
(2) Point out briefly to the students that at the end of the three day seminar, they can expect to be able to perform all the Interviewing Seminar 1 objectives.
(3) Explain briefly the specific objectives for this activity. Explain that understanding the definition, goals and problems of legal interviewing is essential before going on to learn interviewing skills.
(4) Ask if any matters need clarification.

9.45–10.00

(1) Refer students to the definition of legal interviewing on p 5 of *Binder and Price*.
(2) From this definition, point out to the students that the major goals of legal interviewing are:
  (a) identifying the client's problems;
  (b) gathering relevant information on which to base a solution to the problems.
(3) Briefly distinguish the interviewing process from the counselling process, the latter being the lawyer helping the client reach a decision. You may want to point out the definition of counselling at p 5 of *Binder and Price*. While these processes are obviously closely connected, they will be treated separately.

(4) Stress the importance to lawyers of legal interviewing. Without all the skills necessary to identify client problems effectively and gather relevant information, lawyers could never be effective problem solvers. Point out to the students that all lawyers, whether doing barristers' or solicitors' work, interview clients.

10.00–10.30

(1) Explain to the students that despite the apparently simple definition and straightforward goals, legal interviewing is a difficult process to master.
(2) In order to understand interviewing problems, tell the students that you would like them to participate in a short role play between a lawyer and a client.
(3) Emphasise the guidelines for effective role playing.
(4) Divide the students into pairs. Let the students choose who will play lawyer and client. Hand out lawyer instructions, client facts and client instructions. Tell the lawyers that they will be given 10 minutes to interview the client. During the interviews, the lawyers and the clients should be trying to identify the problems that arose that made it difficult for the lawyer to interview effectively.
(5) Conduct the 10 minute interview. Please end the interviews after 10 minutes even though the interviews are not completed.
(6) From their experiences in the role plays, experience with lawyer interviews or their general knowledge, ask the students to identify the major problems new lawyers might encounter when interviewing a client.
(7) Record these problems on the blackboard. Do not take time to evaluate the problems or provide solutions. Try to ensure that everyone understands the nature of the problem being described.
(8) After completing the list, describe briefly for students other problems on the handout or other problems you are familiar with through your experience. Advise the students that during the seminar they will be developing skills and acquiring knowledge to assist them in overcoming these major interviewing problems.
(9) Hand out the sheet entitled *Problems in the interviewing process* (pp 57 ff). Tell the students that they should add to this list any additional problems they encounter throughout the first and the second interviewing seminars.

10.30–10.45

Coffee break.

10 Notes

None.

INTERVIEWING SEMINAR 1

Interviewing exercise 1

Lawyer instructions

Your secretary has advised you that a person involved in a motor vehicle accident would like to see you.

Please commence the interview (10 minutes).

INTERVIEWING SEMINAR 1

Interviewing exercise 1

Client instructions

You are a taxi driver. Your taxi was involved in a collision with a truck owned by the City two weeks ago. You spent a week in hospital with cuts and bruises.

You have come to see a lawyer because you rely on your taxi for a living and it was a 'write-off' in the accident. You just don't know what to do.

Please invent the necessary facts about the accident, your job, injuries etc as required in the interview (10 minutes).

INTERVIEWING SEMINAR 1

Interviewing exercise 1

Confidential client instructions

Shortly into the interview, question the competence of the lawyer because of gender. You would rather have a lawyer of the opposite sex. How will the lawyer respond?

INTERVIEWING SEMINAR 1

Interviewing exercise 1

Confidential client instructions

Be hesitant to talk about the accident. It was very traumatic and you have difficulty going back to talk about the accident.

Interviewing exercise 1

Confidential client instructions

You are very angry and upset at the accident. Express these feelings strongly in the interview. How will the lawyer respond?

———————————

Interviewing exercise 1

Confidential client instructions

The accident was clearly your fault. You were speeding and didn't have time to stop. Don't admit this fact but give the lawyer clues you are lying about the speed.

———————————

Interviewing exercise 1

Confidential client instructions

Play the 'rambling' client. Be very talkative about everything. How will the lawyer respond?

———————————

Interviewing exercise 1

Confidential client instructions

Demand to know very early into the interview what your chances are. Be persistent. Try to get the lawyer to tell you that your case is good.

———————————

INTERVIEWING SEMINAR 1

Interviewing exercise 1

Confidential client instructions

Be very hesitant to talk. This is your first visit to a lawyer. You are quite unsure of yourself. Will the lawyer set you at ease?

INTERVIEWING SEMINAR 1

Interviewing exercise 1

Confidential client instructions

Demand to know what the legal fees will be early on in the interview. Be persistent until you have a clear understanding of the cost.

INTERVIEWING SEMINAR 1

Interviewing exercise 1

Confidential client instructions

The police found some marijuana in your taxi when they investigated the accident. It isn't yours but you have been charged. You would like the lawyer's help with this also. However, only tell the lawyer about the criminal charge if the lawyer asks if you have other concerns.

INTERVIEWING SEMINAR 1

Interviewing exercise 1

Confidential client instructions

As you tell your story leave lots of gaps in the information. Jump around with the facts. Move from topic to topic. Don't be complete unless the lawyer is able to get you on track.

————————————

Problems in the interviewing process

The following is a list of some of the problems commonly encountered by lawyers when interviewing clients:

○ difficulty in responding to 'emotional' clients;
○ inability to control the rambling client;
○ misses information or gets inaccurate information as a result of poor quest-ioning;
○ confusion with client whose problem is outside area of expertise/experience;
○ doesn't know where or how to start the interview;
○ interview lasts too long;
○ difficulty in interviewing client when serious time constraints;
○ gives client 'premature' advice;
○ fails to be clear about legal fees;
○ not able to set client at ease;
○ problem in dealing with client who is not truthful;
○ fails to identify all of client's problems;
○ client has difficulty talking about sensitive topic;
○ distractions or noise in the office become disruptive to the interview;
○ fails to get clear instructions at end of interview.

————————————

INTERVIEWING SEMINAR 1

Interviewing exercise 2

TIME: 1 hour 45 minutes

1 Skill

Interviewing 1.

2 Topic

Listening and observing.

3 Objectives

At the end of the activity, you will:
(a) be able to list the major internal and external impediments to effective listening;
(b) be able to list the major sources of distortion for effective observing;
(c) be able to list the techniques that can improve listening and observing skills;
(d) be able to exhibit attending behaviour when communicating with a client;
(e) be able to summarise communicated verbal information without omitting any facts, given an oral communication of 10 minutes; and
(f) be able to describe the minimal elements of a person's physical behaviour, given an oral communication of 10 minutes.

4 Preparation

(a) Read *Listening and observing notes* below.

5 Description of activity

Lawyers constantly perform tasks that require them to listen and observe effectively. However, lawyers do not often recognise all the factors which adversely affect their listening and observing skills. By referring to techniques and skills to overcome barriers to listening and observing and through a role play of a lawyer–client interview, we will get a chance to improve our listening and observing skills.

6 Notes

None.

Listening and observing notes

(1) A lawyer is required to listen and observe carefully in the course of many legal functions, particularly in the contexts of interviewing, counselling, negotiation and advocacy.

Examples of such professional situations include:

(a) obtaining complete client instructions;

(b) using specific statements in negotiation, preparing pleadings, cross-examining a witness or summarising evidence at trial;

(c) assessing the response of an audience, judge, jurors, witness, client, negotiator or other lawyer.

(2) The skills of listening and observing are the foundation for the more complex skills of effective speaking and questioning, interpreting behaviour, responding and reacting, and creating conditions for communication. The questioning of a witness illustrates the interaction of these skills: the lawyer must be able simultaneously to think ahead to the next question, listen to the response to her or his previous question, and observe and interpret the non-verbal behaviour which accompanies the response. Otherwise, the lawyer would miss important data upon which to formulate and adjust her or his line of questioning.

(3) Physical distractions such as noise, lighting and interruptions constitute the major *external impediments* to effective listening. Common *internal impediments* to listening include:

(a) boredom;

(b) preoccupation or mental distraction;

(c) impatience;

(d) over-saturation;

(e) bias (eg hearing only those parts which seem to support our point of view);

(f) focusing on the speaker's delivery or appearance;

(g) listening intellectually to the verbal statement alone, ignoring non-verbal cues which may reinforce, amplify or contradict the verbal statement.

Some of the internal impediments to listening are attributable to the time differential between speaking and listening: one thinks at 4 or 5 times the normal speed of speech. Thus, particularly if the subject matter does not seem very interesting, it is easy to use this time lag to go off on private mental tangents (eg tomorrow's deadline on another file).

(4) The following *techniques* can improve your ability to listen to and accurately recall oral communications:

(a) exclude, where possible, distracting noises and interruptions (eg hold calls; shut office door);

(b) prepare yourself mentally to listen. Discipline yourself to stop thinking about the other things that would be competing with the speaker for your attention;

(c) prepare yourself physically to listen. Physical alertness affects mental alertness and communicates your interest in what the speaker is saying. Therefore, sit up and adopt a posture that is conducive to listening;

(d) trace the development of ideas being communicated;

(e) concentrate your attention and interest continuously on the speaker and what that person is saying;

(f) mentally repeat or summarise key ideas or statements, or associate related ideas, as they are being communicated. Use the fact that you can think faster than anyone can speak to your advantage;

(g) withhold evaluation of what the person is saying, controlling any judgmental emotional responses to the content. Be alert to words or subjects that reduce your desire to listen further or interfere with your objectivity;

(h) note the non-verbal cues which accompany what the speaker is saying (eg changing tones and volume of voice, facial expressions, gestures, body movement). The speaker does not always put everything that is important into the words;

(i) if possible, take notes of the key ideas or facts. Do not, however, allow extensive note-taking to divert your attention from listening;

(j) do not interrupt the speaker (unless it is necessary to clarify), finish sentences or change the subject;

(k) avoid playing with pencils or pens, paper clips, etc;

(l) listen responsively. Offer some non-verbal and verbal signs of understanding (eg nod your head or encourage speaker by saying 'uh-huh' occasionally).

(5) Perception during observation can be *distorted* by many of the same factors which interfere with accurate listening (eg physical distractions, preoccupation). Other potential sources of distortion in observation include the following:

(a) the cultural conditioning, education and personal experience of the observer. These may result in preconceived notions about a particular client, witness, lawyer, judge, etc.

(b) projecting one's own needs, desires or expectations onto those being observed, causing the observer to see only what he or she wants to see (ie selective perception);

(c) focusing on one particular aspect of appearance or behaviour and observing it very closely, but missing other simultaneously occurring behaviours. This may happen because the behaviour receiving the scrutiny may be bigger, more active or just more interesting. Also, one may notice unusual behaviour more closely than expected behaviour;

(d) attending to several people, conversations or events at the same time;

(e) variability in the language used to express perceptions (eg 'she slapped her child' or 'she gave her child a love tap');

(f) the influence of order effects (ie some feature of another's behaviour may influence one's perceptions of what follows, just as a person's last act may cause one to re-analyse and re-interpret the behaviour that preceded it);

(g) confusing factual descriptions of behaviour with inferences or interpretations about that behaviour;

(h) making simple explanations for complex behaviour;

(i) factors within the observer (eg mental or physical illness; intoxication, fatigue, poor vision);

(j) factors within the environment (eg general noise level, degree of illumination, proximity to what is being observed);

(k) the manner in which the observer's perceptions are elicited (eg questions which suggest the answer).

(6) A lawyer must be aware of the variability and fallibility of observation in relation to her or his own observation (of a client, other lawyer, witness, judge) as well as in relation to the observations of clients, witnesses and others. Pages 48–51 of Binder and Price *Legal Interviewing and Counselling: A Client-Centered Approach* (St Paul, 1977).

Knowledge of these factors may be useful to a lawyer in several ways. A lawyer frequently encounters situations where what her or his client says conflicts with another person's or witness's report of the same event. Knowledge of factors which tend to influence perception and recollection may help the lawyer to:

(a) determine which person's account is more accurate or reliable;
(b) assess whether or not the client is fabricating or merely mistaken;
(c) test a witness's observation on cross-examination;
(d) determine the best way to question a client in order to stimulate accurate recall and reporting.

(7) The lawyer's ability to observe and accurately report her or his observations can be improved by using the following *techniques*:

(a) exclude, where possible, distracting noises and interruptions;
(b) concentrate your attention and interest continuously on the person you are observing and his/her verbal and non-verbal behaviour;
(c) check your observations against the independent reports of others (eg ask your secretary if the client appeared apprehensive while waiting in the reception area);
(d) check the consistency of your observations at several different points over an extended period of time;
(e) observe and describe what you are observing to yourself, trying to keep an open frame of mind. Avoid premature judgment by verifying important perceptions with repeated observation or, in the case of a client, by explicit discussion with the client;
(f) adopt an alert posture;
(g) if possible, take notes.

Effective observation requires close attention to physical appearance and behaviour, including the degree to which a particular behaviour was performed (eg client stared out the window briefly or for an extended period of time).

ADDITIONAL READING

Capp, Glenn R *How to Communicate Orally* (New Jersey: 1966) pp 40–57, ch 3, 'Acquire Listening Facility'.
Knapp, Mark L *Essentials of Non-Verbal Communication* (New York: Holt, Reinhart and Wilson) pp 243–257.
Montgomery, Robert L *Listening Made Easy* (New York: AMACOM, 1981).
Nichols, Ralph G 'Listening is a 10 Part Skill' (July 1957) 45 Nation's Business 56–60.
Strong, Lydia 'Do You Know How to Listen' *Effective Communication on the Job* (New York: American Management Assoc Inc, 1956).

INTERVIEWING SEMINAR 1

Interviewing exercise 2

Instructor material

7 Instructor preparation

(a) Same as for students.

8 Resources

(a) Handout – Interviewing exercise 2; lawyer instructions; Client instructions.

9 Instruction

Timetable

10.45–11.00	Introduction to the importance of listening and observing skills for lawyers.
	Objectives for this activity are explained.
11.00–11.15	Impediments to effective listening and observing.
	Techniques and skills to improve listening and observing skills.
11.15–11.30	Exercise on attending behaviour.
11.30–12.30	Lawyer–client interview exercise to practise listening and observing skills.

10.45–11.00

(1) Explain to students that in performing many tasks, lawyers must carefully listen and observe to obtain information. These skills are particularly important to the goals of interviewing. Refer to the brief list of such tasks in the *Listening and observing notes* (pp 59–61 above) and ask students to identify *other important tasks*. You might also add to this list from your own experience.

(2) Ask students to identify the type of problems lawyers might experience if they are ineffective listeners and observers. Some of these problems might be:

(a) embarrassment, extra costs, at having to contact clients for information missed in the interview;

(b) inaccurately assessing a client's credibility or ability to give evidence because of missed information;

(c) failed negotiations or an inappropriate settlement because of missed information from another lawyer;

(d) creating a negative impression with a judge or jury by failing to hear or see certain communications from them;

(e) ineffective cross-examination of a witness in a trial because information communicated by the witness, both orally and by behaviour, has been missed.

11.00–11.15

(1) Emphasise to students that effective listening and observing is a two step process. First, lawyers must be able to identify the impediments to effective listening and observing. Second, lawyers must be able to perform in such a way that these impediments are reduced or eliminated.

(2) Refer students to the *impediments* to effective listening and observing in the *Listening and observing notes* (above). Ask the students if there are any points that require clarification. Then ask the students if other problems can be identified from their own professional or personal experience. Record any additional problems on the blackboard.

(3) Repeat the task in paragraph 2 for the *techniques to improve* listening and observing in the *Listening and observing notes*).

11.15–11.30

(1) Ask for one student volunteer for a 2–3 minute demonstration. The student will role play the client using the fact situation from the previous activity plan (the taxi driver accident). The instructor will role play the lawyer.

(2) During the interview you may ask questions but you must exhibit non-attending behaviour.

(3) Stop the interview after 2–3 minutes and ask the class for feedback on what the lawyer did that helped or hindered effective listening and observing.

(4) From these comments you should be able to make the point that the lawyer wasn't attending to the client. The key elements of this listening skill are:

S – squarely facing client
O – open stance
L – slight forward lean
E – appropriate eye contact
R – relaxed

(5) Emphasise to the students that attending skills will improve listening and observing. In a legal interview, this skill will assist the lawyer in identifying problems and relevant information and help ensure important information or behaviour is not missed.

11.30–12.30

(1) Advise the class that they will now have an opportunity to practise their listening and observing skills. Before the exercise, ask the class if any points need to be clarified.

(2) Divide the class into groups of four. Each group should have a lawyer, a client and two observers. The lawyer is to interview the client for approximately 10 minutes. The client should be instructed to create facts using the general client instructions that are handed out to the client and the observers. Handout Interviewing Exercise 2: Lawyer Instructions, Client Instructions.

(3) Before starting the interview, tell the students that at the end of 10 minutes the lawyer and observers must summarise in writing the verbal information communicated by the client and also describe the client's physical behaviour. The client should also summarise this information. Emphasise

to the class that lawyers normally make memos to file at the completion of interviews.
(4) Supervise the 10 minute interviews.
(5) Ask the lawyers, observers and clients to summarise in writing the verbal information communicated (10 minutes).
(6) When this task is completed, in the groups of four, ask the students to compare their results. Ask them to identify what techniques or skills made their listening and observing more effective and what behaviour hindered listening and observing (10 minutes).
(7) Ask each group to share with the entire class important points that arose from the exercise. Focus discussion on what lawyers can do to improve listening and observing particularly in the interviewing process, if a student describes behaviour that hindered listening and observing, try to have the class identify what can be done to solve the problem.

12.30–2.00

Lunch break.

10 Notes

None.

INTERVIEWING SEMINAR 1

Interviewing exercise 2

Lawyer instructions

Your secretary has advised you that a person who has just lost his/her job would like to see you.

Please commence the interview (10 minutes).

INTERVIEWING SEMINAR 1

Interviewing exercise 2

Client instructions

Your name is Ann/Andrew Tamati. You are in your early twenties, a Maori and 'boiling mad about what happened to you'. You feel you lost your job as a parking attendant in a busy downtown parking lot because of racial discrimination by the owner.

This just happened over the weekend. You are very worried about how you are going to continue to make rental, car and other payments.

Please create the details about one or two events that suggest racial discrimination (ie owner used derogatory names, told racial jokes in your presence etc). You should also tell the lawyer, reluctantly, that there have been a series of petty thefts from cars while you have been on duty. You did not take anything but you know the owner was very suspicious. Your job, in fact, is just to issue parking tickets and collect money. No one patrols the three storey parking lot.

The interview will be only for 10 minutes.

INTERVIEWING SEMINAR 1

Interviewing exercise 3

TIME: 2 hours

1 Skill

Interviewing 1.

2 Topic

The Three-Staged Interview Model.

3 Objectives

By the end of the activity, you will:

(a) be able to describe the major component parts of a three-staged interview; and
(b) be able to identify the advantages and disadvantages of a systematic interviewing process.

4 Preparation

(a) Read Binder and Price *Legal Interviewing and Counselling* pp 53–103.
(b) Read *The principal stages of interviewing* (below).

5 Description of activity

Through class discussion and a videotape of a lawyer–client interview, the three-staged interview model and its effective use will be illustrated.

6 Notes

None.

The principal stages of interviewing

(1) Preparation for the interview
(2) The interview

    (a) Beginning the interview
    (b) Preliminary problem identification
    (c) Chronological overview
    (d) Theory development and verification
    (e) Ending the interview

(3) Documenting the interview

1 Preparation for the interview

(1) Schedule appointment for interview and initiate relevant office procedure (eg open new file; check client index for conflict).
(2) Where possible, at time appointment is made:

    (a) ascertain the general nature of the problem or information which will be the subject of the interview;
    (b) request the person to bring any relevant documents or information to the interview.

(3) If appropriate, refer the client to another person or agency for assistance.
(4) Gather or prepare appropriate legal checklist(s) or precedents.
(5) Carry out preliminary legal or factual research to familiarise yourself with the general area to be canvassed in the interview.

2 The interview

A Beginning the interview

(1) Meet, seat and greet the client.
(2) Ensure you will have privacy (no distractions).

B Preliminary problem identification

(1) Allow the client to explain *general problem* in his or her own way.
(2) Build rapport by appropriate use of:

    (a) active listening responses which reflect understanding of the facts and feelings communicated by the client;
    (b) communication facilitators (ie recognition, confidentiality);
    (c) attending behaviour (squaring, sitting openly, inclining to client, eye contact, relaxed).

(3) Identify preliminarily:

    (a) the underlying transaction or situation which caused the client to seek legal assistance;
    (b) the client's principal concerns, both legal and non-legal;
    (c) the relief or solution the client desires.

(4) Avoid too much detail at this point. You simply want a 'snap shot' of the underlying matter, concerns and desired solution.
(5) Communicate to the client your understanding of client's concerns and desired solutions.
(6) Where appropriate, in light of the client's problems, refer the client to another person or agency for assistance. This may be invaluable assistance for non-legal problems.
(7) If the client raises legal fees at this stage, provide clear details of fee arrangements in a professional manner to the extent possible at this point.
(8) Explain what will take place for the rest of the interview, clarifying lawyer and client roles (the preparatory explanation).

C Chronological overview

(1) Obtain a chronological overview of the facts through appropriate use of:

   (a) open-ended questions;
   (b) narrow questions for clarification or to fill chronological gaps;
   (c) active listening responses;
   (d) communication facilitators;
   (e) attending behaviour.

(2) Avoid chronological gaps.
(3) Avoid side-tracking client with questions for details. At this stage you want an 'overview'.
(4) Organise the facts obtained, taking notes in a manner that does not inhibit communication.
(5) Obtain relevant documentary information in the client's possession.
(6) Avoid premature legal advice.

D Theory development and verification

(1) At the conclusion of the overview, you will have identified applicable legal and non-legal issues, substantive, procedural, and ethical, that arise out of client's problems and desired solutions.
(2) Where you lack sufficient legal or factual information to be able to identify or evaluate the legal issues, either:

   (a) adjourn the interview until you have had the opportunity to engage in the necessary research, or
   (b) refer the client to another lawyer who is familiar with that area of law, or another appropriate person or resource.

(3) Explore and evaluate the legal and non-legal issues you have identified. This requires you to obtain more detailed information. You must seek out the facts that are necessary or relevant with respect to the particular issue being evaluated.
(4) Use appropriate questioning (ie T-funnel, narrow) to motivate and exhaust client's recall of relevant facts.
(5) Identify deficiencies in available facts, what further facts are required and the methods of obtaining those facts.
(6) Avoid premature legal advice.

E Ending the interview

(1) Where you lack sufficient knowledge or experience to manage the client's problems competently, refer the client to another lawyer who is familiar with that area of law.
(2) In circumstances where further fact investigation or legal research is required to ascertain fully the client's legal position, adjourn the interview without a definitive analysis of the case. However, provide the client with a very basic legal analysis including a description of further work or research that must be done. *Avoid premature legal advice.*
(3) If not dealt with at an earlier point, provide clear details of fee arrangements to the client in a professional manner.
(4) Clarify your retainer with the client.
(5) Clarify follow up tasks for you *and* the client.

2 *Documenting the interview*

(1) Complete your notes of the interview.
(2) Carry out or initiate any relevant office procedures (eg diarising the file and next interview).
(3) Prepare a memo to file which organises and records the substance and details of the interview including:

    (a) the salient facts, noting any relevant factual or behavioural inconsistencies;
    (b) the client's concerns and desired solutions;
    (c) the legal and non-legal issues, procedural, substantive and ethical;
    (d) the fee arrangement agreed upon;
    (e) follow-up tasks to be performed by lawyer and client;
    (f) the next scheduled meeting with the client;
    (g) other relevant information.

(4) Organise the documents and file.
(5) Draft any documents, correspondence or memoranda which are required, sending a copy of each to the client.

Interviewing assessment guide ©

Student: Instructor:
Final Assessment:
Date:

This Guide is designed to assist you in providing feedback on the strengths and weaknesses of the lawyer's performance. *Be constructive.* Focus on what you hear and observe in the interview. Comments will make your feedback more helpful. For each performance objective, please note whether it was successfully completed (s) or not successfully completed (NS). Specific comments should be provided for all performances that are not successfully completed.

At the end of the Guide, please make your final assessment on whether the whole interview was successfully completed or not successfully completed.

A Beginning the interview   COMMENTS

[ ] (1) Meets, seats and greets client.
[ ] (2) Ensures privacy (no distractions).

B Preliminary problem identification

[ ] (1) Allows client to explain problem in own way.
    (2) Establishes rapport by use of:

[ ]   (a) active listening;
[ ]   (b) communication facilitators;
[ ]   (c) attending behaviour.

    (3) Obtains *general description* of:

[ ]   (a) underlying matter;
[ ]   (b) client's principal concerns;
[ ]   (c) client's desired solution.

[ ] (4) Summarises lawyer's understanding of the underlying matter, client's principal concerns and desired solutions.
[ ] (5) Explains what will take place for rest of interview, clarifying lawyer and client roles (the preparatory explanation).

C Chronological overview

    (1) Gets client to relate story chronologically using:

[ ]   (a) open-ended questions;
[ ]   (b) occasional narrow questions for clarification/elaboration;

[ ]   (c) active listening;
[ ]   (d) communication facilitators;
[ ]   (e) attending behaviour.
[ ] (2) Avoids chronological gaps.
[ ] (3) Avoids side-tracking client with question for details.
[ ] (4) Obtains relevant documentary information.
[ ] (5) Avoids premature legal advice.

D Theory development and verification

(1) Systematically explores potential relevant legal, and non-legal, issues obtaining information necessary to assess:

[ ]   (a) procedural steps;
[ ]   (b) substantive law;
[ ]   (c) professional responsibility concerns.
[ ] (2) Uses appropriate questioning techniques to motivate and exhaust client's recall of relevant facts.
[ ] (3) Identifies deficiencies in available facts, what further facts are required and methods of obtaining those facts.
[ ] (4) Explains legal terms and procedures where necessary in order to continue fact gathering.
[ ] (5) Avoids premature legal advice.

E Ending the interview

[ ] (1) Refers client to another lawyer where insufficient knowledge or experience.
[ ] (2) Clear details about fees given.
[ ] (3) Provides preliminary analysis of case unless further investigation unnecessary.
[ ] (4) Clarifies retainer.
[ ] (5) Clarifies follow-up tasks for lawyer and client.

F Documenting the interview

(1) Prepares a memo to file which includes:

[ ]   (a) client concerns and desired solutions;
[ ]   (b) relevant facts, factual or behavioural inconsistencies;
[ ]   (c) legal and non-legal issues;
[ ]   (d) fact deficiencies;
[ ]   (e) follow-up tasks of lawyer and client;
[ ]   (f) fee arrangement;
[ ]   (g) next scheduled meeting with client;
[ ]   (h) other relevant information.

G Communication skills

(1) Throughout the interview

[ ]   (a) exhibited attending behaviour;
[ ]   (b) used appropriate communication
             facilitators;
[ ]   (c) used active listening techniques.

H Questioning skills

[ ] (1) Throughout the interview, chose questions
          effectively.

Assessment   (Tick one)

[ ] The interview was successfully completed.
[ ] The interview was not successfully completed.

Additional comments

_____

INTERVIEWING SEMINAR 1

Interviewing exercise 3

Instructor material

7 Instructor preparation

(a) Same as for students.
(b) Review videotape (Interviewing 1 – Three-Staged Model).

8 Resources

(a) VCR, monitor, videotape (Interviewing 1 – Three-Staged Model).
(b) Handout – Interviewing exercise 3; Lawyer instruction A, B, C, D; Client
     instruction A, B, C, D.

9 Instruction

Timetable

2.00–2.20	Introduction to the Three-Staged Model. Objectives for this activity are explained.
3.30–3.50	Advantages and disadvantages of the Three-Staged Model.
3.50–4.00	Hand out Interviewing Assignment.

2.00–2.30

(1) Advise the students that all of the skills they have been learning will assist them in reaching the goals of the interview – to identify the client's problems and to gather relevant information on which to base a solution to those problems.

(2) However, none of the skills learned to date go specifically to the *process* or *method* lawyers use to reach these goals. This question of a suitable approach has probably already been apparent to students in their role plays.

(3) Tell the students that what you would like to do is briefly describe a systematic approach to interviewing that can be taken by lawyers, provide a videotaped demonstration of that approach and then get the students to evaluate the approach by identifying its advantages and disadvantages.

(4) Briefly describe the component parts of the three-stage interviewing model. Advise the students this summary is from *Binder and Price* pp 53–103.

(5) Your description can follow the *Principal stages of interviewing*.

(6) Ask the students if there are any questions although you can point out that they will have an opportunity to observe a demonstration of the model and then evaluate its usefulness.

2.30–3.30

(1) Prior to screening the videotape, tell the students that the primary goals are to demonstrate the three-staged interviewing model and to get their feedback on how well the lawyer applied the model. However, tell them that there will also be an opportunity to provide feedback on the lawyer's communication and questioning skills.

(2) Screen the videotape (approximately 30 minutes).

(3) Ask the students to provide feedback on the application by the lawyer of the interviewing model. It can be useful to focus on one part of the model at a time so that the students clearly understand what occurred in each part. Try to focus the feedback at this point on whether the model was clearly followed and what the lawyer did that helped meet the goals of each part of the model. Try to postpone an evaluation of its effectiveness.

(4) After discussing each part of the model, ask the students whether there is other feedback about the lawyer's communication or questioning skills.

3.30–3.50

(1) Tell the students that while it is this interviewing model that they will be asked to demonstrate tomorrow and in the interviewing assessment, it is important to understand both its advantages and its limitations.

(2) While this evaluation will be an ongoing process, particularly in practice, ask the students to divide into groups of four and brainstorm for 10 minutes. Compile a list of as many advantages and disadvantages as they can identify, at this point, for the three-staged interviewing model.

(3) After 10 minutes get the groups to report on the advantages and the disadvantages of the three-stage model. Record their findings on the blackboard.

(4) You may want to add to the list from your own experience or from the following list:

Advantages

○ helps establish rapport and trust with client (lawyer explains interview process, client tells own story etc);
○ gives the new lawyer a clear direction;
○ focuses on the goals of interviewing;
○ helps avoid premature 'hardening of the categories' (jumping to conclusions);
○ helps to ensure no gaps or omissions in information;
○ puts an important focus on the role of the client;
○ promotes efficient use of time in the interview;
○ is flexible to different clients and situations.

Disadvantages

○ may appear inappropriate if urgency or time constraints;
○ may appear like a lengthy process and therefore inefficient;
○ may appear inappropriate to some types of legal problems (eg client who wants to make a will);
○ may not be acceptable to lawyer who wants to dominate the interview;
○ may seem too inflexible.

(5) It is important that you stress that many perceived disadvantages disappear once the model is learned and its flexibility is understood. For example, the client who wants to make a will will probably not provide information in a chronological order. The ordering device might be a focus on general topics such as assets, family members, nature of bequests, beneficiaries, etc so that full information is gathered. Similarly, with clients you have seen before, the preparatory explanation can be amended and abbreviated if the client understands what is to follow.

(6) Finish by stressing to students that this model is widely accepted, has many benefits for lawyers and will serve as a solid foundation to build on. The flexibility in the model must not be ignored. Tell the students they will have further opportunities for evaluation after the interviewing exercise tomorrow.

3.50–4.00

(1) Tell the students they will have an opportunity tomorrow to practise all of the skills they have learned, including applying the interviewing model.
(2) Divide the students into groups of 4. Students will be either client A, B, C or D.
(3) Hand out the client instructions and corresponding lawyer instructions. Stress that the client instructions are confidential so that the interviewing exercise will be more enjoyable and realistic.
(4) Tell the students that in addition to the preparation they do overnight, all the lawyers for clients A, B, C and D will meet for one hour in the morning to finalise their preparation. The clients should have their stories and instructions fully considered.
(5) Refer the students to the *Interviewing assessment guide*. Tell the students they will receive feedback on their performance based on the criteria in the *Guide*. This is not a final assessment.

10 Notes

None.

INTERVIEWING SEMINAR 1

Interviewing exercise 3

Lawyer instructions

Your secretary has advised you that a person involved in a motor vehicle accident would like to see you. This person is a taxi-driver and has lost the use of their taxi.

Please prepare for and conduct the interview (30 minutes).

INTERVIEWING SEMINAR 1

Interviewing exercise 3

A: Client instructions: John/Joan Smythe

I INTRODUCTION

The purpose of this exercise is to provide students assuming the lawyer's role with experience in interviewing a client. We ask you to assume the role of John or Joan Smythe and consult the lawyer with respect to the problem described below. Your appointment with the lawyer has been arranged by telephone. You obtained the name of this particular lawyer from the radio controller of the co-operative taxi society with which you are affiliated. The controller has never consulted the lawyer concerned personally, but has heard of the lawyer from other drivers belonging to the same society. The lawyer does not act for the taxi society, only for some of the drivers.

II STATEMENTS OF FACTS

You earn your living by driving a taxicab. You own the taxi that you drive. You are a member of the Erewhon Co-operative Taxi Society. You have held a driver's licence for approximately 20 years. You have been driving taxis for about 15 years, and have owned your own taxi for the past 8 years. You are married, and have three children whose ages are 14, 12 and 9 years. Your financial contribution to the running of the matrimonial home is considerably greater than that of your spouse. Your driver's licence, and the taxi, are vital to the family's ability to pay for its living expenses. You are very concerned that nothing should be allowed to happen that would jeopardise that position.

About three weeks ago you were working in the cab on a Wednesday afternoon. You accepted an instruction over the radiotelephone at about 1.30 pm to pick up a fare in Belgravia who wanted to go to New Eden. Your route to Belgravia took you north east along the Great Northern Highway to Felstone, and then west along the East Coast Road to Belgravia. There is a major intersection at Felstone. It is controlled by traffic lights. The road is divided into four lanes, and widened for the intersection by the addition of a left turn lane. This lane provides for a free turn into the East Coast Road, it is marked with an arrow and the words 'Left Turn Only' painted on the tarseal and has a signpost at the corner saying 'Turning Traffic Give Way to Pedestrians'. The middle two lanes are dedicated to traffic moving straight on along the Great Northern Highway to Sampsonville, and they, too, have arrows painted on the road surface. The lane in the centre of the road provides for traffic turning into Shelley Bay Road. In addition to the arrow painted on the roadway, it has a separate green light to allow traffic to turn right.

At the start of the specially widened, left turn lane there is a bus shelter. There was only one person waiting at the bus stop, but quite a large number of teenage children wearing school uniforms were milling around on the pavement and the car park behind it. The car park is a large one. It is associated with a Foodville Supermarket and an Alabama Homestyle Chicken Restaurant. About twelve metres nearer to the corner than the bus shelter is a driveway. It goes into the car park, which occupies nearly a hectare. There is a sign on this entry way. It is placed just inside the car park, points to the road, and says 'No Entry'. It looks just like the signs used by the Ministry of Transport, but you have subsequently learned that it belongs to the supermarket. People meaning to use the car park are meant to get into it by way of two further drive ways, which are around the corner in the East Coast Road.

It was a fine day. The road surface was dry. The sun was shining from an unclouded sky. Traffic was very heavy, but it always is at that intersection.

As you came towards the intersection, you turned on your left indicator. The traffic lights were red, and traffic was building up in the middle lanes. The second to last vehicle in the left of the middle two lanes was a large truck. It was towing a freight pan which was emblazoned with the insignia of the Foodville Supermarket. *It was not, to your very clear memory, indicating an intention to make a turn.* You kept to the left of the carriageway, and started passing the vehicles in the middle lanes. When you were nearly past the entry way, there was a tremendous thumping noise and the rear of your car was swung to the left.

You immediately stopped to find that the truck had swung over towards the entry way, hit your car, and severely damaged it. The damage to the truck was, of course, not nearly as severe. You were very upset by the evident bad driving of the truckie, and immediately used your radiotelephone to contact the Ministry of Transport. It was a short time (maybe 15 minutes) before the officer arrived. He looked briefly at the damage and asked that the vehicles be moved around the corner in order to clear the road, which was becoming heavily congested.

When you came back around the corner after supervising the movement of your car, the traffic officer was talking to two people near the site of the accident. He next spoke with the truck driver. Finally he spoke to you, and you told him your version of the events. When you finished, he said that the truck driver had said that he had been indicating a left turn, that the person waiting at the bus stop confirmed this, and that the driver of the car behind the truck had said that you had zapped up the left lane at high speed thus causing the accident. The officer thereupon issued a traffic offence notice against you, alleging careless use of a motor vehicle.

You then radioed for a towing truck which took your taxi to Sue's Auto Repairs Ltd. Your vehicle has been off the road for 15 days because of the extensive damage. Sue's has advised you that the repairs will cost $2750.00. You have not yet arranged to have the repairs done. The reason for this is that the day after the accident you reported the accident in person to your insurer, Auto Insurance of New Zealand, and obtained a claim form. When you eventually lodged your claim, about one week after the accident, you were advised by your insurers that your insurance premium had not been paid. This payment should have been made one month before the accident. You cannot account for your failure to do so and your insurer notified you about one week ago that they are refusing to accept liability for the damage to your vehicle. They are also refusing to accept liability for your claim for loss of profits. On average, you take in approximately $80.00 per day net. You generally work 5 days per week.

In addition, just last week you received a letter from the Foodville Super-market chain telling you that they intend to sue you for damages.

You remain absolutely adamant that the accident was no fault of yours.

III ROLE PLAY INSTRUCTIONS

(1) You can create facts about your address and other details as you see fit. However, any facts that you create should be consistent with the above information.
(2) You have three documents with you. They are:
   (a) a sketch plan of the intersection that you made some time after the accident;
   (b) the traffic offence notice (ticket) issued to you by the officer;
   (c) the letter from the insurer, threatening to sue.

   You have left all your insurance documents at home. Do not disclose the existence of the documents you have unless specifically asked about them or whether you have any relevant documents.
(3) You have a number of worries that you want to talk to the lawyer about. They are:
   (a) Whether you have a chance of recovering the heavy repair bill you have had to pay to fix the cab (this came to $2750.00) and the lost profits. Can you recover from the supermarket or from your insurer.
   (b) Whether being convicted will cause you to lose your licence.
   (c) How to manage with day-to-day expenses for your family. You have not worked as a taxi driver since the accident. You have made a little bit of money working as a bartender.
   (d) Legal fees.

   Unless the lawyer asks you about other concerns, only tell the lawyer that you are worried about (a).
(4) During the interview, make the lawyer work hard to get out all the facts. The lawyer will probably try to get you to tell the story in chronological order. Allow yourself to ramble a little, and do not fill in all the gaps, unless the lawyer forces you to do so.

(5) You will be very reluctant to reveal one fact. It is that you were in a hurry on the afternoon in question, and are not at all sure what speed you were doing. You might well have been speeding. Only reveal this information if the lawyer satisfies you it is important.

(6) Please display a range of at least two emotions that fit the character you are playing during the interview. Unless the lawyer acknowledges these feelings in a helpful way, continue to display them until you are satisfied that the interviewer is adequately dealing with both your legal needs and your feelings.

(7) If the fee is going to be more than $350, you are going to have to borrow money from a family member whom you do not get on with very well. Please display some feelings such as dismay, or irritation at the amount the lawyer has said the matter will cost.

IV AFTER THE INTERVIEW

After the interview please discuss with the lawyer your evaluation of how well the interview went.

Prudential Insurance Company
44 Riskless Drive
AUCKLAND

Dear Sir or Madam,

We have been advised that you have been involved in a collision with a Foodville Supermarket delivery truck. We are the insurers of that vehicle.

We are holding you fully responsible for the damages caused. Please contact the undersigned, or arrange for your insurer to do so, in order that this claim can be settled.

Yours sincerely,

Robyn Elliot

Robyn Elliot
CLAIMS MANAGER

EAST COAST ROAD

GREAT NORTHERN HIGHWAY

SHELLEY BAY ROAD

LEFT TURN ONLY

Z

A

Y

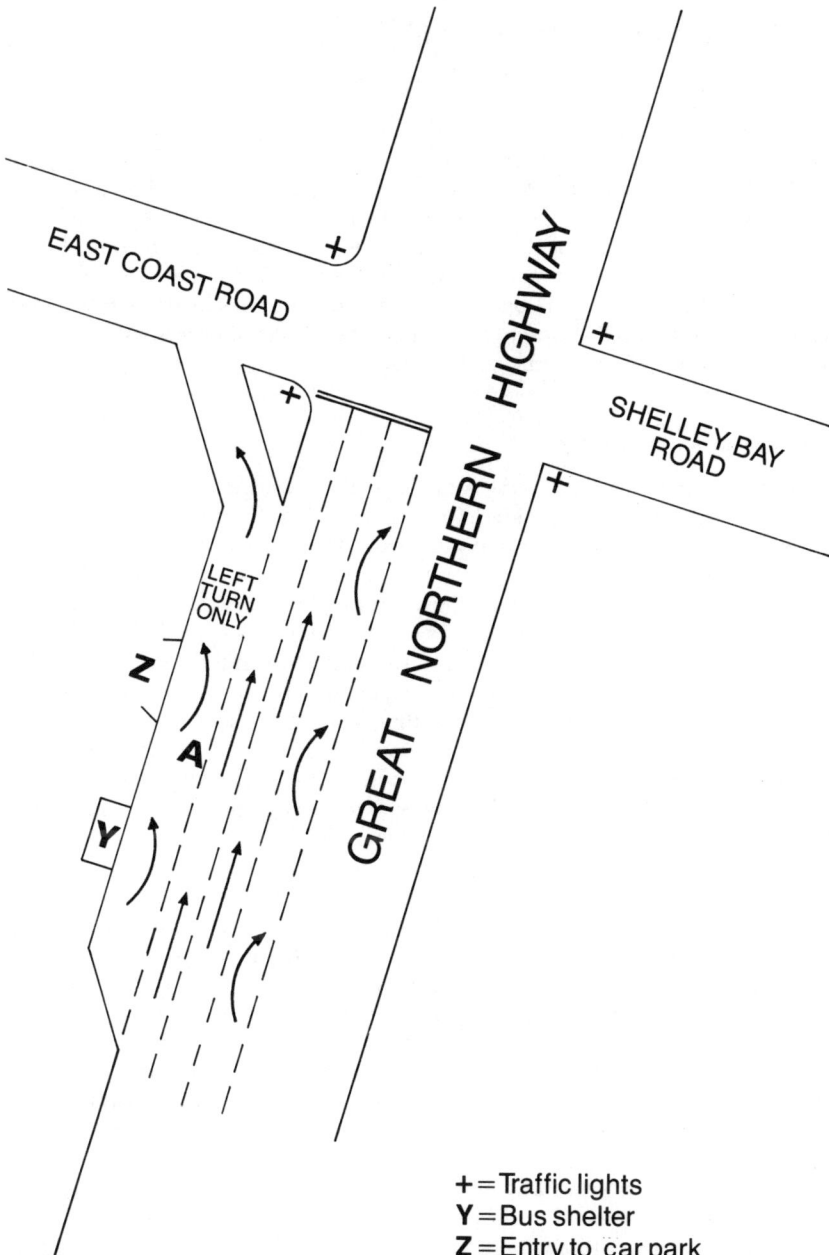

+ = Traffic lights
Y = Bus shelter
Z = Entry to car park
A = Approximate place
     of collision

INTERVIEWING SEMINAR 1

Interviewing exercise 3

B: Client instructions: John/Joan Simpkins

I INTRODUCTION

The purpose of this exercise is to provide students assuming the lawyer's role with experience in interviewing a client. We ask you to assume the role of John or Joan Simpkins and consult the lawyer with respect to the problem described below. Your appointment with the lawyer has been arranged by telephone. You obtained the name of this particular lawyer from the radio controller of the co-operative taxi society with which you are affiliated. The controller has never consulted the lawyer concerned personally, but has heard of the lawyer from other drivers belonging to the same society. The lawyer does not act for the taxi society, only for some of the drivers.

II STATEMENT OF FACTS

You earn your living by driving a taxicab. You own the taxi that you drive. You are a member of the Erewhon Co-operative Taxi Society. You have held a driver's licence for approximately ten years. You have been driving taxis for about five years, and have owned your own taxi for the past four years. You are married, and have three children whose ages are four, two and one years. Your financial contribution to the running of the matrimonial home is considerably greater than that of your spouse. Your driver's licence, and the taxi, are vital to the family's ability to pay for its living expenses. You are very concerned that nothing should be allowed to happen that would jeopardise that position.

About three weeks ago you were working in the cab on a Wednesday afternoon. You accepted an instruction over the radiotelephone at about 1.30 pm to pick up a fare in Belgravia who wanted to go to New Eden. Your route to Belgravia took you north east along the Great Northern Highway to Felstone, and then west along the East Coast Road to Belgravia. There is a major intersection at Felston. It is controlled by traffic lights. The road is divided into four lanes, and widened for the intersection by the addition of a left turn lane. This lane provides for a free turn into the East Coast Road, it is marked with an arrow and the words 'Left Turn Only' painted on the tarseal and has a signpost at the corner saying 'Turning Traffic Give Way to Pedestrians'. The middle two lanes are dedicated to traffic moving straight on along the Great Northern Highway to Sampsonville, and they, too, have arrows painted on the road surface. The lane in the centre of the road provides for traffic turning into Shelley Bay Road. In addition to the arrow painted on the roadway, it has a separate green light to allow traffic to turn right.

At the start of the specially widened, left turn lane there is a bus shelter. There was only one person waiting at the bus stop, but quite a large number of teenage children wearing school uniforms were milling around on the pavement and the car park behind it. The car park is a large one. It is associated with a Foodville Supermarket and an Alabama Homestyle Chicken Restaurant. About twelve metres nearer to the corner than the bus shelter is a driveway. It goes into the car park, which occupies nearly a hectare. There is a sign on this entry way. It is placed just inside the car park, points to the road, and says 'No Entry'. It looks just like the signs used by the Ministry of Transport, but you have subsequently learned that it belongs to the supermarket. People meaning to use the car park are meant to get into it by way of two further drive ways, which are around the corner in the East Coast Road.

It was a cloudy day. The road surface was wet from a recent rain. Traffic was very heavy, but it always is at that intersection.

As you came towards the intersection, you turned on your left indicator. The traffic lights were red, and traffic was building up in the middle lanes. The second to last vehicle in the left of the middle two lanes was a large truck. It was towing a freight pan which was emblazoned with the insignia of the Foodville Supermarket. You kept to the left of the carriageway, and started passing the vehicles in the middle lanes. When you were nearly past the entry way, there was a tremendous thumping noise and the rear of your car was swung to the left.

You immediately stopped to find that the truck had swung over towards the entry way, hit your car, and severely damaged it. The damage to the truck was, of course, not nearly as severe. You were very upset by the evident bad driving of the truckie, and immediately used your radiotelephone to contact the Ministry of Transport. It was a short time (maybe 15 minutes) before the officer arrived. He looked briefly at the damage and asked that the vehicles be moved around the corner in order to clear the road, which was becoming heavily congested.

When you came back around the corner after supervising the movement of your car, the traffic officer was talking to two people near the site of the accident. He next spoke with the truck driver. Finally he spoke to you, and you told him your version of the events. When you finished, he said that the truck driver had said that he had been indicating a left turn, that the person waiting at the bus stop confirmed this, and that the driver of the car behind the truck had said that you had zapped up the left lane at high speed thus causing the accident. The officer thereupon issued a traffic offence notice against you, alleging careless use of a motor vehicle.

You then radioed for a towing truck which took your taxi to Sue's Auto Repairs Ltd. Your vehicle has been off the road for 15 days because of the extensive damage. Sue's has advised you that the repairs will cost $4,000.00. You have not yet arranged to have the repairs done. The reason for this is that the day after the accident you reported the accident in person to your insurer, Auto Insurance of New Zealand, and obtained a claim form. When you eventually lodged your claim, about one week after the accident, you were advised by your insurers that your insurance premium had not been paid. This payment should have been made one month before the accident. You cannot account for your failure to do so and your insurer notified you about one week ago that they are refusing to accept liability for the damage to your vehicle. They are also refusing to accept liability for your claim for loss of profits. On average, you take in approximately $80.00 per day net. You generally work 5 days per week.

In addition, just last week you received a letter from the Foodville Supermarket chain telling you that they intend to sue you for damages.

You remain absolutely adamant that the accident was no fault of yours.

III ROLE PLAY INSTRUCTIONS

(1) You can create facts about your address and other details as you see fit. However, any facts that you create should be consistent with the above information.

(2) You have three documents with you. They are:

    (a) a sketch plan of the intersection that you made some time after the accident;

    (b) the traffic offence notice (ticket) issued to you by the officer;

    (c) the letter from the Foodville Supermarket insurer, threatening to sue.

You have left all your insurance documents at home. Do not disclose the existence of the documents you have unless specifically asked about them or whether you have any relevant documents.

(3) You have a number of worries that you want to talk to the lawyer about. They are:

    (a) Whether you have a chance of recovering the heavy repair bill you have had to pay to fix the cab (this came to $4,000.00) and the lost profits. Can you recover from the supermarket or from your insurer.

    (b) Whether being convicted will cause you to lose your licence.

    (c) How to manage with day-to-day expenses for your family. You have not worked as a taxi driver since the accident. You have made a little bit of money working as a bartender.

    (d) Legal fees.

Unless the lawyer asks you about other concerns, only tell the lawyer that you are worried about (a).

(4) During the interview, make the lawyer work hard to get out all the facts. The lawyer will probably try to get you to tell the story in chronological order. Allow yourself to ramble a little, and do not fill in all the gaps, unless the lawyer forces you to do so.

(5) You will be very reluctant to reveal one fact. It is that you may recall seeing the indicator light on the truck was showing a left turn but that you thought it would wait until you were past. You are worried this will hurt your case. Only reveal this information if the lawyer satisfies you it is important.

(6) Please display a range of at least two emotions that fit the character you are playing during the interview. Unless the lawyer acknowledges these feelings in a helpful way, continue to display them until you are satisfied that the interviewer is adequately dealing with both your legal needs and your feelings.

(7) If the fee is going to be more than $350, you are going to have to borrow money from a family member whom you do not get on with very well. Please display some feelings such as dismay, or irritation, at the amount the lawyer has said the matter will cost.

IV AFTER THE INTERVIEW

After the interview please discuss with the lawyer your evaluation of how well the interview went.

Prudential Insurance Company
44 Riskless Drive
AUCKLAND

Dear Sir or Madam,

We have been advised that you have been involved in a collision with a
Foodville Supermarket delivery truck. We are the insurers of that vehicle.

We are holding you fully responsible for the damages caused. Please
contact the undersigned, or arrange for your insurer to do so, in order that
this claim can be settled.

Yours sincerely,

Robyn Elliot

Robyn Elliot
CLAIMS MANAGER

INTERVIEWING SEMINAR 1

Interviewing exercise 3

C: Client instructions: John/Joan Simpkins

I INTRODUCTION

The purpose of this exercise is to provide students assuming the lawyer's role
with experience in interviewing a client. We ask you to assume the role of John
or Joan Simpkins and consult the lawyer with respect to the problem described
below. Your appointment with the lawyer has been arranged by telephone.
You obtained the name of this particular lawyer from the radio controller of
the co-operative taxi society with which you are affiliated. The controller has
never consulted the lawyer concerned personally, but has heard of the lawyer
from other drivers belonging to the same society. The lawyer does not act for
the taxi society, only for some of the drivers.

II STATEMENT OF FACTS

You earn your living by driving a taxicab. You own the taxi that you drive.
You are a member of the Erewhon Co-operative Taxi Society. You have held a
driver's licence for approximately 25 years. You have been driving taxis for
about 10 years, and have owned your own taxi for the past eight years. You are

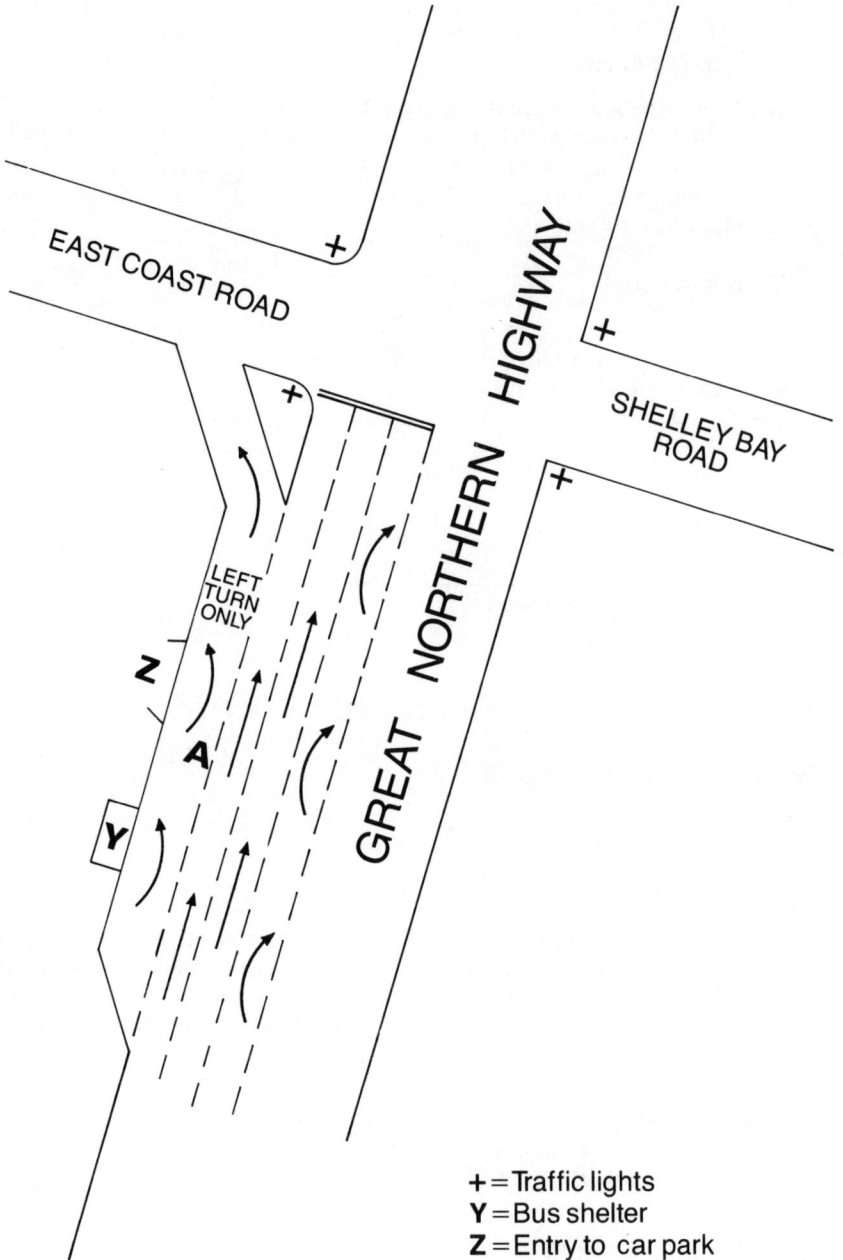

EAST COAST ROAD

GREAT NORTHERN HIGHWAY

SHELLEY BAY
ROAD

LEFT
TURN
ONLY

Z

A

Y

+ = Traffic lights
Y = Bus shelter
Z = Entry to car park
A = Approximate place
     of collision

married, and have two children whose ages are 12 and 9 years. Your financial contribution to the running of the matrimonial home is considerably greater than that of your spouse. Your driver's licence, and the taxi, are vital to the family's ability to pay for its living expenses. You are very concerned that nothing should be allowed to happen that would jeopardise that position.

About three weeks ago you were working in the cab on a Wednesday afternoon. You accepted an instruction over the radiotelephone at about 4.00 pm to pick up a fare in Belgravia who wanted to go to New Eden. Your route to Belgravia took you north east along the Great Northern Highway to Felstone, and then west along the East Coast Road to Belgravia. There is a major intersection at Felston. It is controlled by traffic lights. The road is divided into four lanes, and widened for the intersection by the addition of a left turn lane. This lane provides for a free turn into the East Coast Road, it is marked with an arrow and the words 'Left Turn Only' painted on the tarseal and has a signpost at the corner saying 'Turning Traffic Give Way to Pedestrians'. The middle two lanes are dedicated to traffic moving straight on along the Great Northern Highway to Sampsonville, and they, too, have arrows painted on the road surface. The lane in the centre of the road provides for traffic turning into Shelley Bay Road. In addition to the arrow painted on the roadway, it has a separate green light to allow traffic to turn right.

At the start of the specially widened, left turn lane there is a bus shelter. There was only one person waiting at the bus stop, but quite a large number of teenage children wearing school uniforms were milling around on the pavement and the car park behind it. The car park is a large one. It is associated with a Foodville Supermarket and an Alabama Homestyle Chicken Restaurant. About twelve metres nearer to the corner than the bus shelter is a driveway. It goes into the car park, which occupies nearly a hectare. There is a sign on this entry way. It is placed just inside the car park, points to the road, and says 'No Entry'. It looks just like the signs used by the Ministry of Transport, but you have subsequently learned that it belongs to the supermarket. People meaning to use the car park are meant to get into it by way of two further drive ways, which are around the corner in the East Coast Road.

It was a fine day. The road surface was dry. The sun was shining from an unclouded sky. Traffic was very heavy, but it always is at that intersection.

As you came towards the intersection, you turned on your left indicator. The traffic lights were red, and traffic was building up in the middle lanes. The second to last vehicle in the left of the middle two lanes was a large truck. It was towing a freight pan which was emblazoned with the insignia of the Foodville Supermarket. *It was not indicating an intention to make a turn.* You kept to the left of the carriageway, and started passing the vehicles in the middle lanes. When you were nearly past the entry way, there was a tremendous thumping noise and the rear of your car was swung to the left.

You immediately stopped to find that the truck had swung over towards the entry way, hit your car, and severely damaged it. The damage to the truck was, of course, not nearly as severe. You were very upset by the evident bad driving of the truckie, and immediately used your radiotelephone to contact the Ministry of Transport. It was a short time (maybe 15 minutes) before the officer arrived. He looked briefly at the damage and asked that the vehicles be moved around the corner in order to clear the road, which was becoming heavily congested.

When you came back around the corner after supervising the movement of your car, the traffic officer was talking to two people near the site of the accident. He next spoke with the truck driver. Finally he spoke to you, and you told him your version of the events. When you finished, he said that the truck driver had said that he had been indicating a left turn, that the person waiting at the bus stop confirmed this, and that the driver of the car behind the truck had said that you had zapped up the left lane at high speed thus causing the accident. The officer thereupon issued a traffic offence notice against you, alleging careless use of a motor vehicle.

You then radioed for a towing truck which took your taxi to Sue's Auto Repairs Ltd. Your vehicle has been off the road for 15 days because of the extensive damage. Sue's has advised you that the repairs will cost $5,000.00. You have not yet arranged to have the repairs done. The reason for this is that the day after the accident you reported the accident in person to your insurer, Auto Insurance of New Zealand, and obtained a claim form. When you eventually lodged your claim, about one week after the accident, you were advised by your insurers that your insurance premium had not been paid. This payment should have been made one month before the accident. You cannot account for your failure to do so and your insurer notified you about one week ago that they are refusing to accept liability for the damage to your vehicle. They are also refusing to accept liability for your claim for loss of profits. On average, you take in approximately $80.00 per day net. You generally work 5 days per week.

In addition, just last week you received a letter from the Foodville Supermarket chain telling you that they intend to sue you for damages.

III ROLE PLAY INSTRUCTIONS

(1) You can create facts about your address and other details as you see fit. However, any facts that you create should be consistent with the above information.

(2) You have three documents with you. They are:

    (a) a sketch plan of the intersection that you made some time after the accident;

    (b) the traffic offence notice (ticket) issued to you by the officer;

    (c) the letter from the Foodville Supermarket insurer, threatening to sue.

You have left all your insurance documents at home. Do not disclose the existence of the documents you have unless specifically asked about them or whether you have any relevant documents.

(3) You have a number of worries that you want to talk to the lawyer about. They are:

    (a) Whether you have a chance of recovering the heavy repair bill you have had to pay to fix the cab (this came to $5,000.00) and the lost profits. Can you recover from the supermarket or from your insurer.

    (b) Whether being convicted will cause you to lose your licence.

    (c) How to manage with day-to-day expenses for your family. You have not worked as a taxi driver since the accident. You have made a little bit of money working as a bartender.

    (d) Legal fees.

Unless the lawyer asks you about other concerns, only tell the lawyer that you are worried about (a).

(4) During the interview, make the lawyer work hard to get out all the facts. The lawyer will probably try to get you to tell the story in chronological order. Allow yourself to ramble a little, and do not fill in all the gaps unless the lawyer forces you to do so.

(5) You will be very reluctant to reveal two facts. It is that you were in a hurry on the afternoon in question, and are not at all sure what speed you were

doing. You might well have been speeding. In addition, you talked with the truck driver before the traffic officer arrived. You said to her 'I guess I wasn't paying as much attention as I should have'. Only reveal this information if the lawyer satisfies you it is important.

(6) Please display a range of at least two emotions that fit the character you are playing during the interview. Unless the lawyer acknowledges these feelings in a helpful way, continue to display them until you are satisfied that the interviewer is adequately dealing with both your legal needs and your feelings.

(7) If the fee is going to be more than $350, you are going to have to borrow money from a family member whom you do not get on with very well. Please display some feelings such as dismay, or irritation at the amount the lawyer has said the matter will cost.

IV AFTER THE INTERVIEW

After the interview please discuss with the lawyer your evaluation of how well the interview went.

Prudential Insurance Company
44 Riskless Drive
AUCKLAND

Dear Sir or Madam,

We have been advised that you have been involved in a collision with a Foodville Supermarket delivery truck. We are the insurers of that vehicle.

We are holding you fully responsible for the damages caused. Please contact the undersigned, or arrange for your insurer to do so, in order that this claim can be settled.

Yours sincerely,

Robyn Elliot

Robyn Elliot
CLAIMS MANAGER

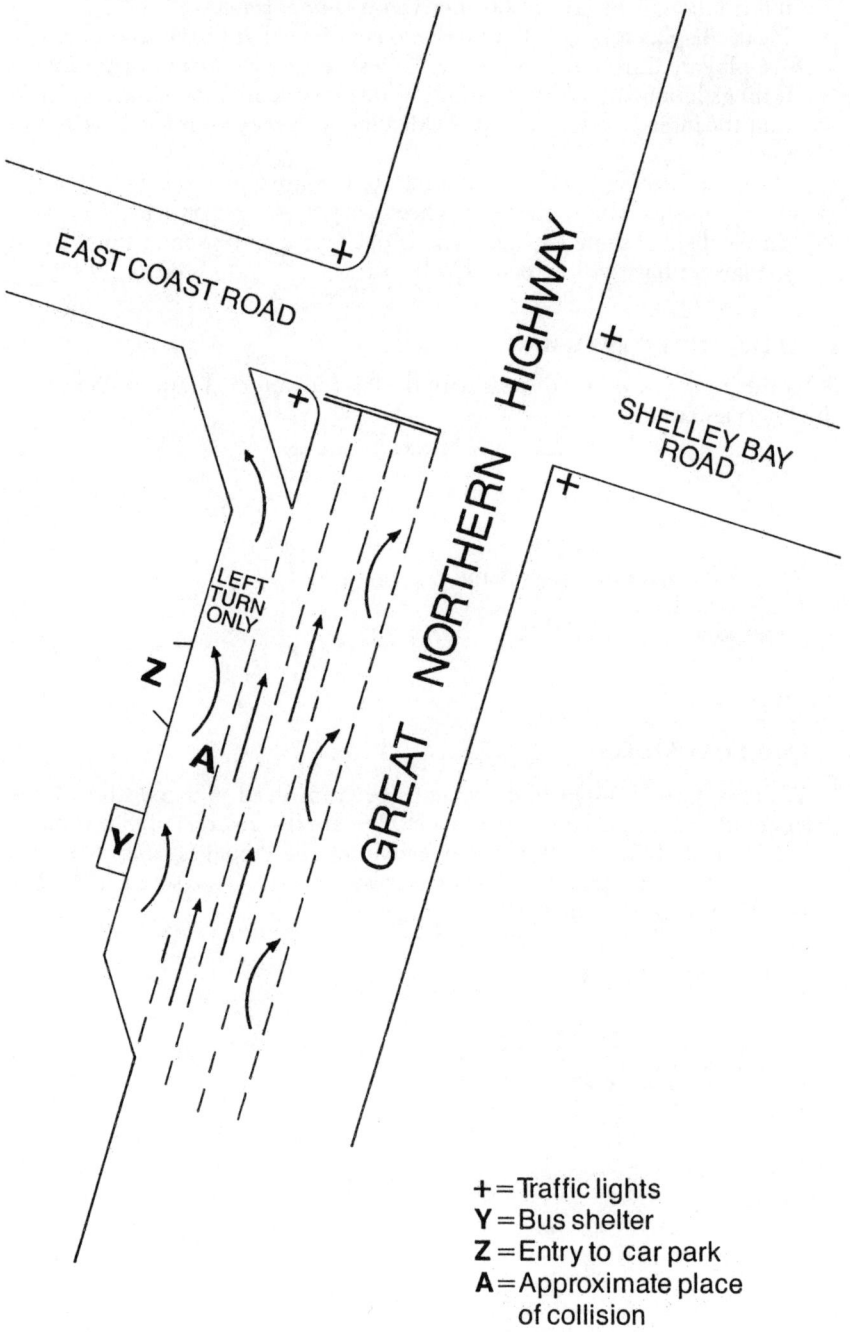

EAST COAST ROAD

SHELLEY BAY ROAD

GREAT NORTHERN HIGHWAY

LEFT TURN ONLY

Z

A

Y

+ = Traffic lights
Y = Bus shelter
Z = Entry to car park
A = Approximate place
    of collision

Interviewing exercise 3

D: Client instructions: John/Joan Simth

I INTRODUCTION

The purpose of this exercise is to provide students assuming the lawyer's role with experience in interviewing a client. We ask you to assume the role of John or Joan Simth and consult the lawyer with respect to the problem described below. Your appointment with the lawyer has been arranged by telephone. You obtained the name of this particular lawyer from the radio controller of the co-operative taxi society with which you are affiliated. The controller has never consulted the lawyer concerned personally, but has heard of the lawyer from other drivers belonging to the same society. The lawyer does not act for the taxi society, only for some of the drivers.

II STATEMENT OF FACTS

You earn your living by driving a taxicab. You own the taxi that you drive. You are a member of the Erewhon Co-operative Taxi Society. You have held a driver's licence for approximately five years. You have been driving taxis for about three years, and have owned your own taxi for the past year. You are married, and have four children whose ages are 5, 3, 2 and 1 years. Your financial contribution to the running of the matrimonial home is considerably greater than that of your spouse. Your driver's licence, and the taxi, are vital to the family's ability to pay for its living expenses. You are very concerned that nothing should be allowed to happen that would jeopardise that position.

About three weeks ago you were working in the cab on a Wednesday afternoon. You accepted an instruction over the radiotelephone at about 8.30 am to pick up a fare in Belgravia who wanted to go to New Eden. Your route to Belgravia took you north east along the Great Northern Highway to Felstone, and then west along the East Coast Road to Belgravia. There is a major intersection at Felston. It is controlled by traffic lights. The road is divided into four lanes, and widened for the intersection by the addition of a left turn lane. This lane provides for a free turn into the East Coast Road, it is marked with an arrow and the words 'Left Turn Only' painted on the tarseal and has a signpost at the corner saying 'Turning Traffic Give Way to Pedestrians'. The middle two lanes are dedicated to traffic moving straight on along the Great Northern Highway to Sampsonville, and they, too, have arrows painted on the road surface. The lane in the centre of the road provides for traffic turning into Shelley Bay Road. In addition to the arrow painted on the roadway, it has a separate green light to allow traffic to turn right.

At the start of the specially widened, left turn lane there is a bus shelter. There was only one person waiting at the bus stop, but quite a large number of teenage children wearing school uniforms were milling around on the pavement and the car park behind it. The car park is a large one. It is associated with a Foodville Supermarket and an Alabama Homestyle Chicken Restaurant. About twelve metres nearer to the corner than the bus shelter is a driveway. It goes into the car park, which occupies nearly a hectare. There is a sign on this entry way. It is placed just inside the car park, points to the road, and says 'No Entry'. It looks just like the signs used by the Ministry of Transport, but you have subsequently learned that it belongs to the supermarket. People meaning to use the car park are meant to get into it by way of two further drive ways, which are around the corner in the East Coast Road.

It was a cloudy day. The road surface was wet and it was rainy. Traffic was very heavy, but it always is at that intersection.

As you came towards the intersection, you turned on your left indicator. The traffic lights were red, and traffic was building up in the middle lanes. The second to last vehicle in the left of the middle two lanes was a large truck. It was towing a freight pan which was emblazoned with the insignia of the Foodville Supermarket. You cannot recall if it was indicating an intention to turn. You kept to the left of the carriageway, and started passing the vehicles in the middle lanes. When you were nearly past the entry way, there was a tremendous thumping noise and the rear of your car was swung to the left.

You immediately stopped to find that the truck had swung over towards the entry way, hit your car, and severely damaged it. The damage to the truck was, of course, not nearly as severe. You were very upset by the evident bad driving of the truckie, and immediately used your radiotelephone to contact the Ministry of Transport. It was a short time (maybe 15 minutes) before the officer arrived. He looked briefly at the damage and asked that the vehicles be moved around the corner in order to clear the road, which was becoming heavily congested.

When you came back around the corner after supervising the movement of your car, the traffic officer was talking to two people near the site of the accident. He next spoke with the truck driver. Finally he spoke to you, and you told him your version of the events. When you finished, he said that the truck driver had said that he had been indicating a left turn, that the person waiting at the bus stop confirmed this, and that the driver of the car behind the truck had said that you had zapped up the left lane at high speed thus causing the accident. The officer thereupon issued a traffic offence notice against you, alleging careless use of a motor vehicle.

You then radioed for a towing truck which took your taxi to Sue's Auto Repairs Ltd. Your vehicle has been off the road for 15 days because of the extensive damage. Sue's has advised you that the repairs will cost $3,000.00. You have not yet arranged to have the repairs done. The reason for this is that the day after the accident you reported the accident in person to your insurer, Auto Insurance of New Zealand, and obtained a claim form. When you eventually lodged your claim, about one week after the accident, you were advised by your insurers that your insurance premium had not been paid. This payment should have been made one month before the accident. You cannot account for your failure to do so and your insurer notified you about one week ago that they are refusing to accept liability for the damage to your vehicle. They are also refusing to accept liability for your claim for loss of profits. On average, you take in approximately $80.00 per day net. You generally work 5 days per week.

In addition, just last week you received a letter from the Foodville Supermarket chain telling you that they intend to sue you for damages.

You remain absolutely adamant that the accident was no fault of yours.

III ROLE PLAY INSTRUCTIONS

(1) You can create facts about your address and other details as you see fit. However, any facts that you create should be consistent with the above information.

(2) You have three documents with you. They are:

    (a) a sketch plan of the intersection that you made some time after the accident;

    (b) the traffic offence notice (ticket) issued to you by the officer;

    (c) the letter from the Foodville Supermarket insurer, threatening to sue.

You have left all your insurance documents at home. Do not disclose the existence of the documents you have unless specifically asked about them or whether you have any relevant documents.

(3) You have a number of worries that you want to talk to the lawyer about. They are:

    (a) Whether you have a chance of recovering the heavy repair bill you have had to pay to fix the cab (this came to $3,000.00) and the lost profits. Can you recover from the supermarket or from your insurer.

    (b) Whether being convicted will cause you to lose your licence.

    (c) How to manage with day-to-day expenses for your family. You have not worked as a taxi driver since the accident. You have made a little bit of money working as a bartender.

    (d) Legal fees.

Unless the lawyer asks you about other concerns, only tell the lawyer that you are worried about (a).

(4) During the interview, make the lawyer work hard to get out all the facts. The lawyer will probably try to get you to tell the story in chronological order. Allow yourself to ramble a little, and do not fill in all the gaps, unless the lawyer forces you to do so.

(5) You will be very reluctant to reveal one fact. It is that you were in a hurry on the afternoon in question, and are sure you were speeding – about 20 km/hr over the limit. Only reveal this information if the lawyer satisfies you it is important.

(6) Please display a range of at least two emotions that fit the character you are playing during the interview. Unless the lawyer acknowledges these feelings in a helpful way, continue to display them until you are satisfied that the interviewer is adequately dealing with both your legal needs and your feelings.

(7) If the fee is going to be more than $350, you are going to have to borrow money from a family member whom you do not get on with very well. Please display some feelings such as dismay, or irritation at the amount the lawyer has said the matter will cost.

IV AFTER THE INTERVIEW

After the interview please discuss with the lawyer your evaluation of how well the interview went.

EAST COAST ROAD

SHELLEY BAY
ROAD

GREAT NORTHERN HIGHWAY

LEFT
TURN
ONLY

Z

A

Y

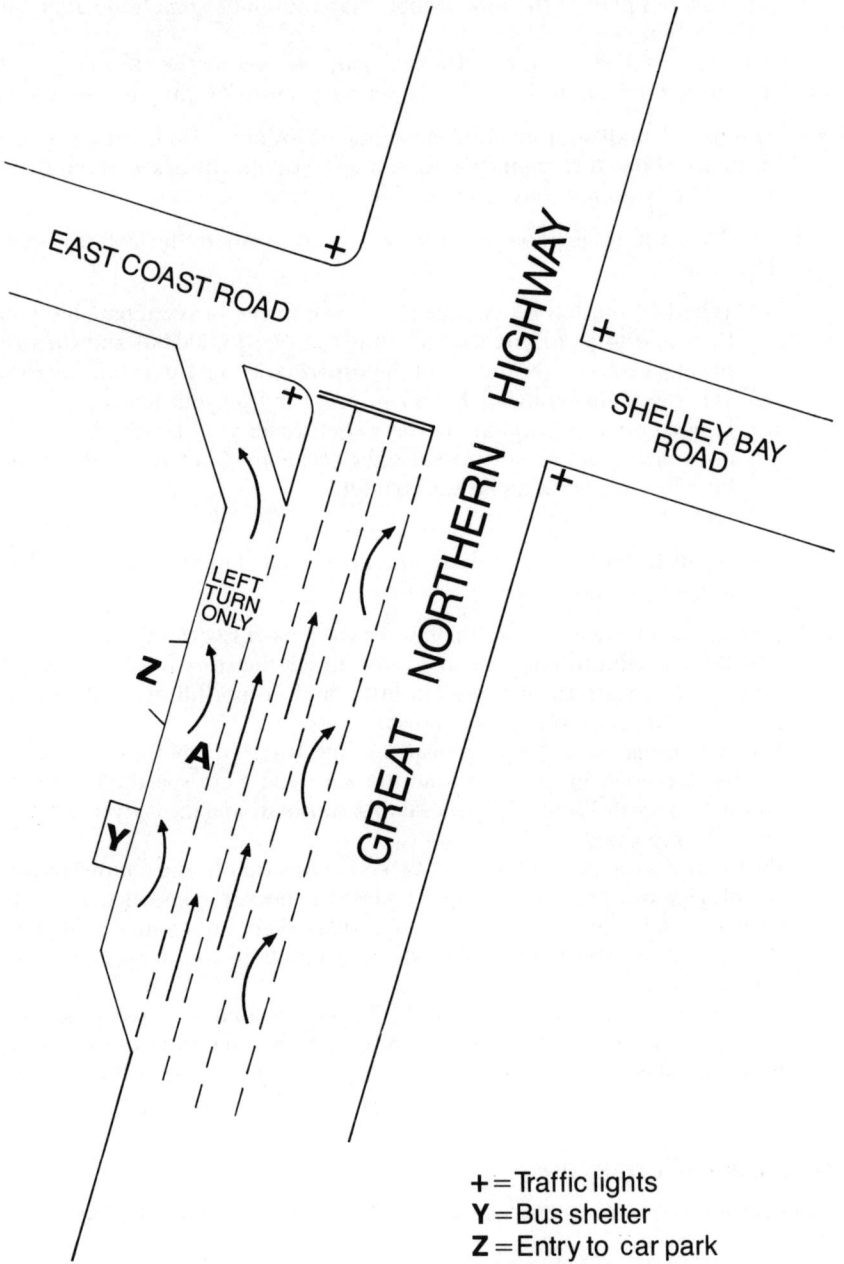

+ = Traffic lights
Y = Bus shelter
Z = Entry to car park
A = Approximate place
     of collision

Prudential Insurance Company
44 Riskless Drive
AUCKLAND

Dear Sir or Madam,

We have been advised that you have been involved in a collision with a
Foodville Supermarket delivery truck. We are the insurers of that vehicle.

   We are holding you fully responsible for the damages caused. Please
contact the undersigned, or arrange for your insurer to do so, in order that
this claim can be settled.

Yours sincerely,

Robyn Elliot

Robyn Elliot
CLAIMS MANAGER

_____

III COUNSELLING

David Cruickshank and Andrew Pirie*

COUNSELLING SEMINAR 1

Counselling exercise 1

TIME: 1 hour 15 minutes

1 Skill

Counselling 1.

2 Topic

Definition, goals, problems.

3 Objectives

By the end of the activity, you will:
(a) be able to define the term counselling;
(b) be able to state four major goals of the counselling process for a lawyer; and
(c) be able to describe at least ten major problems in achieving the goals of the counselling process for a lawyer.

4 Preparation

(a) Read Binder and Price *Legal Interviewing and Counselling* pp 135–155.

5 Description of activity

Through the use of short lawyer–client counselling role plays and through feedback on these experiences, we will provide an introduction to the counselling or advising process for lawyers. The focus will be on the major goals of counselling and the major problems typically encountered by the new lawyer in the counselling process.

6 Notes

None.

* The authors acknowledge the permission of the Professional Legal Training Course, CLE Society of British Columbia, Canada and the Institute of Professional Legal Studies of New Zealand who made possible the creation and republication of these materials.

Instructor material

7 Instructor preparation

(a) Same as for students.
(b) Review handout – *Problems in the counselling process* (p 98 below).

8 Resources

(a) Handout – Counselling exercise 1: Facts; Confidential client instructions.
(b) Handout – *Problems in the counselling process* (below).

9 Instruction

Timetable

9.30–9.45	Welcome students to the Counselling Seminar 1.
	Objectives for the entire counselling seminar are pointed out.
	Objectives for this activity are explained.
9.45–10.00	The definition and goals of counselling.
10.00–10.30	Problems for the lawyer in the counselling process.
10.30–10.45	Coffee break.

9.30–9.45

(1) This is the start of the counselling seminar. Tell the students that the next three days will be devoted to counselling skills for the lawyer. The students will do more advanced work in counselling skills in Week 8 in Counselling Seminar 2.
(2) Point out briefly to the students that at the end of the three day seminar, they can expect to be able to perform all the Counselling Seminar 1 objectives.
(3) Explain briefly the specific objectives for this activity. Explain that understanding the definition, goals and problems of legal counselling is essential before going on to learn counselling skills.
(4) Ask if any matters need clarification.

9.45–10.00

(1) Refer students to the definition of counselling on p 135 of *Binder and Price*. The term is often used interchangeably with 'advising'.
(2) From this definition, point out to the students that the major goal is to '*help* clients reach decisions'. This goal is broken down into

 (a) identifying potential solutions for each problem,
 (b) identifying probable positive and negative consequences for each solution,
 (c) weighing the consequences, and
 (d) deciding which alternative is most appropriate.

(3) Stress the importance of the two previous skills seminars to the counselling process. Counselling is a decision-making process. The lawyer must have competently completed the interview process in order to identify the

client's problems and to gather all the relevant information in order to determine which solutions are available. Legal and analysis skills are essential in order to identify and assess potential solutions.

(4) Counselling, therefore, naturally follows the interviewing process and incorporates legal and analysis skills.

(5) Finally, stress the importance of counselling skills to lawyers. Clients come to lawyers with problems for which they want solutions. Effective counselling skills will enable lawyers to help clients reach decisions about solutions to their problems. Point out to students that all lawyers, whether doing barrister or solicitor's work, counsel clients.

10.00–10.30

(1) Explain to students, just as with interviewing, that despite the apparently simple definition and straightforward goals, counselling is a difficult process to master.

(2) In order to understand counselling problems, tell the students that you would like them to participate in a short role play between a lawyer and a client.

(3) Divide the students into pairs. Let the students choose who will play lawyer and client. Hand out Counselling exercise 1: Facts to each person. Hand out the Confidential client instructions to clients. Tell the lawyers that they will have 5 minutes to review the facts and then be given 10 minutes to counsel the client. During the counselling process, the lawyers and clients should try to identify the problems that arose that made it difficult for the lawyer to counsel effectively.

(4) Give the lawyers 5 minutes to prepare. Conduct the 10 minute counselling sessions. Please end the counselling after 10 minutes even though the interviews are not completed.

(5) From their experiences in the role plays, practical experience in law firms or their general knowledge, ask the students to identify the major problems that new lawyers might encounter when counselling a client.

(6) Record these problems on the blackboard. Do not take time to evaluate the problems or provide solutions. Try to ensure that everyone understands the nature of the problem being described.

(7) After completing the list, describe briefly for students other problems on the handout or other problems you are familiar with through your experience. Advise the students that during the seminar they will be developing skills and acquiring knowledge to assist them in overcoming these major counselling problems.

(8) Hand out the sheet entitled *Problems in the counselling process*. Tell the students that they should add to this list any additional problems they encountered throughout both the first and the second counselling seminars.

10.30–10.45

Coffee break.

10 Notes

None.

COUNSELLING SEMINAR 1

Counselling exercise 1

FACTS

Your client is Brad/Janet Freeman.

About three months ago your client loaned a car to a friend to use. The car is owned by your client and is a 1971 Volkswagen Beetle. It's value is approximately $3,000. Your client's friend lives in the next province. Apparently your client agreed to loan the car to the friend, who didn't have a car, just as a 'favour'.

Your client would now like to have the car back. Despite numerous promises over the last few weeks, the friend has not returned the car. Your client wrote a letter to the friend two weeks ago but there has been no response.

Your client would like to resolve the problem.

COUNSELLING SEMINAR 1

Counselling exercise 1

Confidential client instructions

The purpose of this meeting is for the lawyer to help you decide what to do about the car. Try and get as much information from the lawyer as possible with respect to any solutions that are suggested. You are a lay person. Make sure the information the lawyer gives you is clear.

Also, in the first few minutes, raise one or more of the following points:

○ tell the lawyer you want to immediately sue your friend, no ifs, ands or buts;
○ get the lawyer to give you a figure immediately as to legal fees;
○ tell the lawyer, almost immediately, you just want to do what the lawyer thinks is best;
○ tell the lawyer you are really embarrassed about getting in this mess and you can't do anything if there is any publicity at all;
○ you are so angry with your friend. You would like to arrange for the car to have an 'accident' at night and then sue your friend. Can you do this to get 'even' with your friend.

Problems in the counselling process

The following is a list of some of the problems encountered by lawyers when counselling clients:

○ confuses the client with legal jargon or technical terms;
○ has difficulty in explaining substantive or procedural law to client;
○ fails to give the client complete information;
○ fails to give the client clear or accurate information about legal fees;
○ provides no organisation to the counselling session and this confuses the client;
○ fails to recognise or deal with 'non-legal' issues that affect the client's decision;
○ counsels clients in areas outside lawyer's experience or expertise;
○ pushes the client into a decision the lawyer thinks is best;
○ difficulty in counselling the client who can't make up his/her mind;
○ difficulty in responding to the client who is making a 'bad' decision;
○ lets the client pressure the lawyer to take steps or actions that are unethical;
○ doesn't get clear agreement from the client on steps that are to be taken;
○ similar communication problems as in interviewing.

Counselling exercise 2

TIME: 1 hour 45 minutes

1 Skill

Counselling 1.

2 Topic

The Counselling Model.

3 Objectives

By the end of the activity, you will:
(a) be able to describe the principal stages of the counselling process; and,
(b) be able to identify the advantages and disadvantages of a systematic counselling process.

4 Preparation

(a) Read Binder and Price *Legal Interviewing and Counselling* pp 156–191.
(b) Read *The principal stages of counselling* (pp 115–117 below).

5 Description of activity

Through class discussion and a video tape of a lawyer–client counselling session, a systematic approach to counselling will be illustrated and evaluated.

6 Notes

None.

Instructor material

7 Instructor preparation

(a) Same as for students.
(b) Review videotape (Counselling 1 – The Counselling Model).

8 Resources

(a) VCR, monitor, videotape (Counselling 1 – The Counselling Model).
(b) Handout – Counselling exercise 2: Facts.
(c) Handout – *Counselling preparation outline.*

9 Instruction

Timetable

10.45–11.15	Introduction to the Counselling Model. Objectives for this activity are explained.
11.15–12.00	View videotape of lawyer–client counselling session. Class discussion of videotape.
12.00–12.20	Advantages and disadvantages of the Counselling Model.
12.20–12.30	Hand out Counselling exercise 2.

10.45–11.15

(1) Since counselling is, in effect, a decision-making process involving the lawyer and the client, the lawyer will not be an effective counsellor if the client is not fully informed or does not understand information communicated.
(2) Tell the students that taking a planned and systematic approach to counselling is a major step to avoid omitting information or creating confusion.
(3) Accordingly tell the students that you would like to describe briefly a systematic approach to counselling that can be taken by lawyers, provide a videotape demonstration of that approach and then get the students to evaluate the approach by identifying its advantages and disadvantages.
(4) Briefly describe the component parts of the counselling model. Your description should follow the *Principal stages of the counselling model* (pp 115–117 below).
(5) Ask the students if there are any questions. However, you should point out that they will have an opportunity to observe a demonstration of the model and then evaluate its usefulness.

11.15–12.00

(1) Prior to screening the videotape, tell the students that the primary goals are to demonstrate the counselling model and to get their feedback on how well the lawyer applied the model.
(2) Screen the videotape (approximately 30 minutes).
(3) Ask the students to provide feedback on the application by the lawyer of the counselling model. It can be useful to focus on one part of the model at a time so that the students clearly understand what occurred in each part. Try to focus the feedback at this point on whether the model was clearly followed and what the lawyer did that helped reach the goals of counselling. Try to postpone an evaluation of the effectiveness of the model.
(4) After the feedback, draw to the students' attention that effective counselling will not only require a planned and systematic approach but also the use of communication skills. The communication skills important to interviewing are equally important in counselling. Tell the students that in their counselling role plays they will have further opportunities to practise and develop expertise in these skills:

   (a) attending;
   (b) behaviours that facilitate communication;
   (c) active listening;
   (d) questioning.

12.00–12.20

(1) Tell the students that while it is this counselling model that they will be asked to demonstrate in this seminar and in the counselling assessment, it is important to understand both its advantages and its limitations.

(2) While this evaluation will be an ongoing process, particularly in practice, ask the students to divide into groups of four and brainstorm for 10 minutes. Compile a list of as many advantages and disadvantages as they can identify, at this point, for the counselling model.

(3) After 10 minutes get the group to report to the class on their findings. Record their findings on the blackboard.

(4) You may want to add to the list from your own experience or from the following list:

Advantages

- ○ focuses specifically on goals of counselling;
- ○ gives the new lawyer a clear direction;
- ○ promotes full and informed decision-making;
- ○ less likely to be gaps or omissions in information communicated;
- ○ puts an important focus on the role of the client;
- ○ recognises decision making by client involves both legal and non-legal considerations;
- ○ promotes efficient use of time in the interview;
- ○ is flexible to different clients and situations.

Disadvantages

- ○ may appear like a lengthy process and therefore inefficient;
- ○ may appear inappropriate if urgency or time constraints;
- ○ may conflict with a client's expectation of who makes decision or how decisions made;
- ○ may not be acceptable to a lawyer who wants to tell the client what to do;
- ○ may seem too inflexible;
- ○ may seem inappropriate for some areas of practice.

(5) It is important that you encourage students not to make premature judgements about the value of the counselling model until they have had more experience using it. Many of the perceived disadvantages disappear once the model is learned and its flexibility is understood.

(6) Stress to students that this model is widely accepted, has many benefits for lawyers and will serve as a solid foundation to build on. Tell the students they will have further opportunities for evaluation after counselling sessions tomorrow.

12.20–12.30

(1) Tell the students that one of the most important stages of the counselling process is the preparation stage. Tell the students that they will have an opportunity after lunch to complete this stage.

(2) Divide the students into groups of 4.

(3) Hand out to each student Counselling exercise 2 and *Counselling preparation outline*.

(4) Tell the students that after lunch each group will have until 3.00 pm to prepare for a counselling session based on the information they have been given. Each group should follow the steps in the preparation stage. Each group will be asked to report to the class at 3.00 pm on the results of their work.

(5) Ensure that each group lets you know where the group will be working so that you can move from group to group to offer assistance.

10 Notes

None.

COUNSELLING SEMINAR 1

Counselling exercise 2

FACTS

Your client is Brad/Janet Freeman.

Your client purchased a used 1971 BMW three weeks ago from a local dealer. The purchase price was $10,000 cash which your client borrowed from the bank as a personal loan.

Since purchasing the car, there has been trouble. On five mornings in the last three weeks the car has refused to start. Each of these times your client had the car towed to the dealership. On each of these occasions the dealer said he 'fixed' the car and returned it (usually at the end of the day) to your client. The dealer said on each occasion that there had been a problem with the fuel pump and your client had to remember that foreign cars, especially used ones, 'are always acting up'.

Your client is 'fed up' with the problems. Your client uses the car to drive to and from work and needs reliability.

Apart from the fuel pump problem the car seems fine at the present time. However, your client is worried about the dealer's statement that these cars are 'always acting up'. Your client is worried that other problems might start appearing soon. While your client had an opportunity to fully inspect and drive the car before buying it, your client does remember the salesperson saying that 'because of the car's age, we can't offer any official guarantee or warranty but you won't have any problems. The car's in great shape.'

To date your client has paid out $500 for these troubles ($50 towing charge plus $50 labour, on each occasion the car wouldn't start).

Your client has told you that he/she would ideally like to return the car, get the $10,000 purchase price plus the $500 expenses back and invest the money in a new car with a good solid warranty.

If the car cannot be returned your client would like to get the $500 back and get some security against future repair bills.

Counselling preparation outline

This outline should be completed by the lawyer prior to meeting with the client to counsel him or her on solutions to the client's concerns.

In completing this outline, it will be necessary for you to use research and analysis skills.

The information in this outline must be thorough and accurate. The client will be relying on this information.

A Client concerns, relief desired	**B** Alternative courses of action	**C** Legal and non-legal consequences

(continue as necessary)

COUNSELLING SEMINAR 1

Counselling exercise 2

Instructor material

1 Instructor preparation

(a) Same as for students.

2 Resources

None.

3 Instruction

Timetable

| 3.30–3.35 | Introduction to the activity. Objectives for this activity are explained. |
| 3.35–4.00 | Short role plays and class feedback on performances. |

3.30–3.35

(1) Advise the students that even if a lawyer understands and applies a systematic approach to counselling, ultimately the lawyer must *communicate* information to the client. Accordingly, in addition to the communication skills already learned, effective speaking skills are critical to the counselling process (as well as to a wide variety of other functions where lawyers must speak effectively).

(2) Refer the students to the *Effective speaking notes* (below) and the *Elements of effective speaking* (below). Tell the students that most often ineffective speaking occurs because lawyers are either careless about or not aware of these basic skills.

(3) Tell the students that no specific instruction is planned with respect to speaking skills but you would like them to practise these skills. Effective speaking will be an integral part of the counselling process that they will be doing tomorrow.

(4) Ask the students if there are any questions about the *Elements of effective speaking* or if the students see any omissions.

3.35–4.00

(1) Tell the students that you would like to have volunteer lawyers who would take 3–5 minutes to begin explaining and describing to a client *one* of the solutions that was identified in the previous activity (the defective BMW case). (These solutions should still be on the blackboard.) The client will simply be the person sitting on either side of the volunteer lawyer. At the end of 3–5 minutes, you would like the class to provide constructive feedback to the lawyer on her/his speaking referring specifically to the Speaking Guide, *Elements of effective speaking*.

(2) Encourage volunteer lawyers.

(3) Ask the first volunteer lawyer to take 3–5 minutes to speak to the client. The rest of the class will observe.

(4) Supervise the feedback for 2–3 minutes. If there are speaking problems with content, language or presentation, ask the students to identify what the lawyer could have done or said to overcome the problem.

(5) Repeat the role plays as many times as possible until 4.00 pm.

(6) Finish the activity by advising the students that they can practise their speaking skills in any setting.

4 Notes

Before the students leave, remind them that they will be counselling a client based on the facts in Counselling exercise 2 (the defective BMW case). Students should ensure they are fully prepared to counsel a client in the morning although they will have forty minutes to complete their preparation.

Effective speaking notes

(1)   A lawyer is required to be an effective speaker in the course of many legal functions, particularly in the contexts of counselling, negotiation and advocacy.

Examples of such professional situations include:

(a)   informing a client about a particular course of action;
(b)   communicating information in a negotiation;
(c)   making opening or closing statements in a trial.

(2)   Effective speaking involves organisational skills respecting appropriate content, mastery of grammar and language, and effective delivery. As well, the speaker must be able to listen to and observe her or his audience in order to gauge its comprehension and receptiveness, and tailor the presentation accordingly. The following points outline some techniques and skills for effective speaking.

(3)   Restrict your subject to fit the time at your disposal. Do not try to cover too much ground. In a brief talk, of less than 5 minutes, you can only expect to get one or two main points across. In a longer talk, up to 30 minutes, do not try to cover more than four or five main ideas. Avoid irrelevant or superfluous information.

(4)   Develop your subject logically by using the sequence most appropriate to your material. This may be chronological or topical. In counselling, the client will also have important input into the order in which the subject matter is presented.

(5)   Enumerate your points as you make them, directing your listeners, point by point, to your conclusion or summation.

(6)   Avoid legal or technical terms and jargon wherever possible, particularly when speaking to clients. Explain what is unfamiliar to your audience by comparing it to something which your listeners understand.

> The greatest weapon in the arsenal of persuasion is the analogy, the story, the simple comparison to a familiar subject. Nothing can move the jurors more convincingly than an apt comparison to something they know from their own experience is true.
>
> It is worth some real effort to develop analogies to use in final argument . . . Here is . . . one on the point that what is ordinary care depends on the circumstances: 'If you were loading potatoes into a wagon in the field, you'd pick them up on the fork and heave them toward the wagon. You wouldn't be much concerned if one potato fell off, would you? One potato isn't worth much, and if it fell off, it wouldn't hurt anyone. But suppose you were loading nitroglycerin. Then how carefully, how gingerly, you would carry it and place it in someone else's hands, wrapped in foam or cotton and protected against vibration. Both acts would be done with ordinary care; ordinary care in handling great danger, nitroglycerin and ordinary care in handling non-dangerous potatoes.
>
> In this case the defendant was handling that silent assassin, electricity. With what care should he handle it? Ordinary care, her honor will tell you, but care dependent upon the circumstances. Where the danger is great, care that is ordinary in degree must be great in amount.'
>
> (C Spangenberg 'Basic Values and the Techniques of Persuasion' (1977) 3 (4) Litigation 13 at 16–17.)

(7)   Use language appropriate to your audience. If you must use legal or technical terms, do not introduce them until you have first explained what they mean. Much legal jargon is confusing to the lay person. Substitute clear and ordinary words whenever possible.

(8)   Use concrete, vigorous words which evoke mental pictures. Compare the following:

> 'It's just trading one set of problems for another, not solving them.'
> 'It's just rearranging the deck chairs on the Titanic.'

Don't say 'The defendant slandered and defamed the plaintiff'. Say instead: 'This corporation called John Smith a thief'. Take your listeners to the lowest level of abstraction.

(9)   Use visual aids such as pictures, diagrams or demonstrations, making sure they can be seen clearly by the entire audience.

(10)   Illustrate your points by using concrete examples and comparisons. For example, your explanation of a legal procedure or agreement may be more enlightening for your client if you explain how it worked in another case. Audiences have difficulty relating to an abstract concept or generalisation.

(11)   Emphasise your most important points at the outset and conclusion, because of the effects of primacy and recency, ie people tend to remember best what they hear first and what they hear last. Cue the audience that you are reaching the end of your presentation ('In conclusion . . .').

(12)   Avoid fillers (eg 'like', 'um', 'you know'). Read your discovery and trial transcripts with a critical eye and ear, looking for awkward words and phrases that impede clear speech. Once aware of your own common verbal obstructions, you will cure many of them automatically. James W McElhaney in 'The Language of Examination' (1977) 3(3) Litigation 45 (at 46) suggests another technique for eliminating poor speech patterns:

> Even though you make an effort to be simple and direct, you will find that some bad habits persist; usually crutch words and phrases you use without being aware of them. Part of the cure for this is better preparation so you will not need verbal crutches. The other device is a simple and effective one which will work on your 'ums' and 'ers' as well as 'let me ask you this' and 'I see' . . . It is based on the realisation that most speech patterns are subconscious. We simply do not think fast enough to consciously choose each word . . . [W]rite the word or phrase on several small cards, drawing a large red X through it. Put these around your home (and office, if you do not mind telling people why you have crossed out 'prior to that occasion') where you are bound to see them every day. Your mind will automatically do the rest.

(13)   In a longer presentation, end with a brief summary of the important points. This is part of the adage: 'First, tell them what you are going to tell them; then tell them; then tell them what you have told them.' Restate your ideas in different words to avoid irritating repetition.

(14)   The speaker's body language is also an essential component of communication and persuasion, as more than half of all communication is conveyed non-verbally – that is, by voice, manner and movement. John Stefano, in 'Body Language and Persuasion' ((1977) 3(4) Litigation 31 at 55), underscores the importance for lawyers of avoiding contradictions between verbal and non-verbal behaviour:

> What it comes down to for the lawyer is this: If you have correctly understood the situation, if you know what you are doing, and if you believe in it, your

body, voice, emotions and intellect will work together in the act of communicating with other human beings ... If, on the other hand, you do not know what you are doing or you do not believe in it, or you are afraid of revealing what you feel, your body and voice will betray you, no matter how much you attempt to manipulate them. You will either be acutely, painfully aware of both of them, as will your audience; or, if you choose to avoid the pain by not feeling, your audience will remain unmoved and unpersuaded.

I have argued that congruence of feelings and words is necessary for a communication to be accepted as potentially true. Direct attempts to produce this congruence – that is attempts to manipulate the body and the emotions – will fail, as will most attempts to mask them. Congruence is achieved through integrity, not technique. But emotionless speech is ambiguous and unpersuasive. For those of us not addicted to machiavellianism, that leaves only one alternative: know what you believe, and say it with feeling.

(15) Use your body language to emphasise, not distract from, what you are saying. Some common distracting movements are foot tapping, finger drumming, head scratching, etc. Mentally pick out a person in the audience and talk to this person. If you are communicating conversationally, you will naturally use a variety of gestures, inflections and rates of speaking, as the occasion and material dictate.

(16) Use the active voice in preference to the passive voice. The passive voice is weak. (Eg 'I shall always remember my first trial' instead of 'My first trial will always be remembered by me'.)

(17) Speak with a pleasant pitch; a high pitch often sounds shrill. Relaxing the throat muscles helps to keep the pitch down.

(18) Speak at an appropriate volume. Your audience should not have to strain to hear you. Low volume suggests low enthusiasm about the subject. A strong voice comes, in part, from breathing, supported by the diaphragm. If your abdomen sags, you will not have sufficient volume because your diaphragm will be slack. Therefore, when speaking, adopt a good posture with your head up and shoulders relaxed.

(19) Speak at an appropriate pace, neither too slow nor too fast. If you speak too quickly, it is sometimes helpful to concentrate on pausing between phrases and ideas, rather than to try to slow down the actual rhythm of what you are saying. This will give your listener a chance to catch up and process what you have said.

(20) Do not memorise or read what you are going to say, as it will lack spontaneity. If you write out your speech, questions or arguments in full, it is likely that you will read it, losing important eye contact with your audience. Instead, after preparing what you want to say, make an outline of the points you want to cover. Use this outline to cue your memory during your questioning or presentation.

(21) Carefully 'read' your audience before and during your presentation. If your audience is fidgeting or the faces of the listeners have a quizzical expression, they may be telling you to speak louder, faster, give more examples, or modify your language. You must be able to adjust what you are saying in response to feedback from the audience. That is why it is important never to read a speech or questions as you will miss important messages from your audience.

(22) Nervousness about speaking in public is not uncommon. A certain amount of stage fright is useful, as it keys you up to think faster, and speak with more fluency and intensity than usual. A lot of nervous symptoms which may seem painfully obvious to you, cannot be detected

by your listeners. It is important to divert your attention off yourself just before you turn to speak. Concentrate on what the other speaker is saying (eg opposing counsel's opening statement) or on the audience. Look for two or three responsive, sympathetic faces among your listeners, and look to them for reinforcement when you first start to speak. Communicate directly to them until your nervousness has diminished. Their positive feedback will buoy you up.

(23) When you make a mistake, such as mispronouncing a word, do not bother to apologise. Simply stop and start over, with your eyes up, using strong emphasis and inflection to make the correction. Retaining the appearance of calm is half the secret of recovering calm. Project confidence, even if you don't feel it, and you will ultimately feel more confident.

To calm yourself before speaking, take several deep breaths. The physical movement of pouring and drinking water at the podium may help relax you. Find an inconspicuous way of letting your body release its tension in a minimally disruptive way (eg press your thumb hard against the side of your index finger, allowing the rest of your hand to hang naturally).

ADDITIONAL READING

Capp, Glenn R *How to Communicate Orally* (2nd edn, Englewood Cliffs, Prentice Hall Inc, 1966).
Carnegie, Dale *The Quick and Easy Way to Effective Speaking* (New York, Pocket Books, 1977).
Gondin, William R and Mammen, Edward W *The Art of Speaking Made Simple* (New York, Doubleday & Company Inc, 1954).
Stone, Janet and Bachner, Jane *Speaking Up: A Book for Every Woman Who Wants to Speak Effectively* (New York, McGraw-Hill Book Company, 1977).

Speaking guide

Elements of effective speaking ©

The elements of effective speaking detailed below are grouped under three headings: Content, Language and Presentation.

A Content   COMMENTS

[ ] (1) Information accurate;
[ ] (2) Information complete;
[ ] (3) No irrelevant or superfluous information;
[ ] (4) Information well organised and logically developed;
[ ] (5) Smooth transition between topics;
[ ] (6) Concrete examples given;
[ ] (7) Uses visual aids where appropriate;
[ ] (8) Appropriate to the time limit;
[ ] (9) Emphasises most important points at outset and conclusion.

B Language   COMMENTS

[ ] (1) Language appropriate to the audience and
          purpose of speech;
[ ] (2) Legal or technical terms avoided;
[ ] (3) Explains legal or technical terms, if used;
[ ] (4) Modifies language if client appears to have
          difficulty understanding it;
[ ] (5) Avoids fillers (eg 'like', 'um' 'uh');
[ ] (6) Uses concrete, visual language (where
          appropriate).

C Presentation

  (1) Voice:

[ ]   (a) appropriate volume;
[ ]   (b) pleasant pitch;
[ ]   (c) clear enunciation;
[ ]   (d) correct pronunciation;
[ ]   (e) appropriate pace (varied, not too fast
                or slow).

  (2) Body movement

[ ]   (a) maintains and varies eye contact;
[ ]   (b) not too dependent on notes;
[ ]   (c) good posture;
[ ]   (d) relaxed manner;
[ ]   (e) gestures and body language convey
                speaker's interest in topic.

Counselling assessment guide ©

Student:

Date:

Instructor:

This Guide is designed to assist you in providing feedback on the strengths and
weaknesses of the lawyer's performance. *Be constructive*. Focus on what you hear
and observe in the interview. Comments will make your feedback more
helpful. For each performance objective, please note whether it was successfully completed (S) or not successfully completed (NS). Specific comments
should be provided for all performances that are not successfully completed.

   At the end of the Guide, please make your final assessment on whether the
whole counselling session was successfully completed or not successfully
completed.

A Beginning the counselling session   COMMENTS

[ ] (1) Meets, seats and greets client.
[ ] (2) Ensures privacy (no distractions).

B Preparatory explanation

[ ] (1) Asks client whether any new matters (information, documents) have arisen.
[ ] (2) Summarises new information acquired by the lawyer.
[ ] (3) Explains what will take place for rest of counselling session, clarifying lawyer and client roles (the preparatory explanation).
   (4) Establishes rapport by use of:

[ ]   (a) active listening;
[ ]   (b) communication facilitators;
[ ]   (c) attending behaviour.

C Identifying alternatives

[ ] (1) Priorises order in which client concerns are to be discussed.
[ ] (2) Describes briefly each alternative solution to the client's problem, including alternatives identified by the client.
   (3) Exhibits elements of effective speaking in describing the alternatives in relation to:

[ ]   (a) content;
[ ]   (b) language;
[ ]   (c) presentation.

[ ] (4) Checks client understanding of information.

D Analysing the consequences

[ ] (1) Priorises order in which alternatives are to be discussed.
[ ] (2) Systematically explores and describes the consequences, both legal and non-legal, for each alternative.
[ ] (3) Gets client to classify consequences as negative or positive where possible.
   (4) Exhibits elements of effective speaking in describing the consequences, in relation to:

[ ]   (a) content;
[ ]   (b) language;
[ ]   (c) presentation.

E Obtaining the client's decision

[ ] (1) Clarifies alternatives or consequences as necessary.

[ ] (2) Assists client in selecting course of action and obtains clear client instructions.

[ ] (3) Provides client with time to make decision where necessary.

[ ] (4) Avoids making decision for client.

[ ] (5) Clarifies follow up tasks for lawyer and client.

F Documenting the decision

(1) During the counselling session, completes the Counselling Guide setting out:

[ ]   (a) client concerns on relief desired;

[ ]   (b) alternative courses of action;

[ ]   (c) positive and negative consequences for each alternative;

[ ]   (d) the client's decision, if made.

G Communication skills

(1) Throughout the counselling session:

[ ]   (a) exhibited attending behaviour;

[ ]   (b) used appropriate communication facilitators;

[ ]   (c) used active listening techniques.

(2) Exhibited effective speaking (Speaking Guide) in relation to:

[ ]   (a) content;

[ ]   (b) language;

[ ]   (c) presentation.

H Questioning skills

[ ] (1) Throughout the counselling session, chose questions effectively when necessary.

ASSESSMENT (Tick one)

[ ] The counselling session was successfully completed.

[ ] The counselling session was not successfully completed.

ADDITIONAL COMMENTS

COUNSELLING SEMINAR 1

Counselling exercise 3

TIME: 3 hours

1 Skill

Counselling 1.

2 Topic

Integration of counselling skills.

3 Objectives

By the end of the activity, given a 20 minute counselling session between a lawyer and a client, you will:

(a) be able to counsel a client following the principal stages of the counselling process;
(b) be able to exhibit the elements of effective speaking relating to content, language and presentation;
(c) be able to exhibit attending behaviour;
(d) be able to exhibit all behaviours that facilitate communication from the client;
(e) be able to use active listening techniques;
(f) be able to choose questions effectively when necessary.

4 Preparation

(a) review Binder and Price *Legal Interviewing and Counselling* pp 135–191 as necessary;
(b) review *Effective speaking notes* (p 105) and *Speaking guide, Elements of effective speaking* (p 108);
(c) review materials from previous seminars where applicable to counselling skills;
(d) complete preparation for Counselling exercise 3 (based on Counselling exercise 2 – Facts);
(e) Read *Counselling assessment guide.*

5 Description of activity

Through the use of a hypothetical client fact situation, we will have an opportunity to integrate counselling skills learned to date in a 20 minute counselling session with a client.

6 Notes

None.

Instructor material

7 Instructor preparation

(a) Same as for students.
(b) Write schedule (9.40–12.30 pm) on the blackboard (see 9.30–9.40, para (3) below).

8 Resources

(a) Hand out – *Counselling assessment guide.*
(b) Hand out – Counselling exercise 3: Client instructions.

9 Instruction

Timetable

9.30–9.40	Introduction to activity. Objectives for this activity are explained.
9.40–10.00	Preparation for counselling role plays.
10.00–12.15	Counselling role plays and feedback.
12.15–12.30	Class discussion of counselling role plays.

9.30–9.40

(1) Tell the students that they will now have an opportunity to integrate in a counselling role play all the skills they have learned to date. Refer the students to the learning objectives for this activity.
(2) The counselling role plays will take place in groups of four. This will enable feedback to be given from both peers and instructor.
(3) Divide the class into groups of four. Have the following schedule on the blackboard:

9.40–10.00	Complete preparation stage
10.00–10.20	Counselling session 1
10.20–10.30	Feedback in small groups
10.30–10.45	Coffee break
10.45–11.05	Counselling session 2
11.05–11.15	Feedback in small groups
11.15–11.35	Counselling session 3
11.35–11.45	Feedback in small groups
11.45–12.05	Counselling session 4
12.05–12.15	Feedback in small groups
12.15–12.30	Debriefing whole class

(4) Tell the students they can decide amongst themselves the order in which they will role play lawyers and client. Each student must participate once

as a lawyer and once as a client. When not role-playing lawyer or client, students should act as observers and complete for each lawyer the *Counselling assessment guide*. Hand out to each student Counselling exercise 3 – Client instructions for their roles as clients.

(5) Hand out two *Counselling assessment guides* to each student.
(6) Ask if there are any questions for clarification.

9.40–10.00

(1) Tell the students they can work individually or in groups to complete their preparation for the counselling sessions.
(2) Ensure that each group of four for the counselling session advises you of the location where they will be conducting the sessions in order for you to observe as well.
(3) During the final preparation, provide assistance as necessary.

10.00–12.15

(1) During the counselling sessions, you should sit in as an observer. Try to remain for one complete session (counselling 20 minutes, feedback 10 minutes) with each group.
(2) Try to facilitate the feedback sessions but do not dominate them. Encourage students to provide their constructive feedback. All observers should complete a *Counselling assessment guide* and give it to the lawyer for her or his information.
(3) As you observe the counselling, collect information for the class on what is being done well and areas where improvement is necessary.

12.15–12.30

(1) Start by providing the students with encouragement on their performances. You will undoubtedly have observed many positive performances.
(2) Refer the students to the goal of counselling. Ask for comments or specific examples of what knowledge, skills or techniques helped lawyers reach these goals in the role plays. Also identify problems that arose that created problems for lawyers. Try and identify what the lawyer could have done to resolve these problems.

10 Notes

None.

The principal stages of counselling

1 Preparation for counselling

2 The counselling session

   A Beginning the counselling session
   B Preparatory explanation
   C Identifying the alternatives
   D Analysing the consequences
   E Obtaining the client's decision

3 Documenting the decision

1 Preparation for counselling

(1) Schedule appointment for counselling.
(2) Review client file and identify all client concerns or problems and the relief desired by the client.
(3) Carry out appropriate legal research and fact analysis to identify alternative courses of action that are available *at this point* with respect to each client problem.
(4) Analyse and predict the likely *legal* consequences of each alternative. You can also complete this step, using your experience, for the likely *non-legal* consequences (economic, social, psychological) of each alternative.
(5) Complete the *Counselling preparation outline* (p 103).
(6) From the *Counselling preparation outline*, fill in as much information as possible on the Client counselling guide.

2 The counselling session

A Beginning the counselling session

(1) Meet, seat and greet the client.
(2) Ensure you will have privacy (no distractions).

B Preparatory explanation

(1) Ask the client whether any new matters (information, documents) have arisen since the last meeting, that you may not be aware of.
(2) Summarise any new matters that have arisen since the last meeting, that the client may not be aware of.
(3) Explain what will take place for the rest of the counselling session, clarifying lawyer and client roles.
(4) Continue to build rapport by appropriate use of:

   (a) active listening responses which reflect understanding of the facts and feelings communicated by the client;
   (b) communication facilitators (ie recognition, confidentiality);
   (c) attending behaviour (squaring, sitting openly, inclining to client, eye contact, relaxed).

C Identifying the alternatives

(1) Determine, in consultation with the client, which of the client's concerns or problems should be discussed first. Priority may have to be given to a problem which requires immediate attention.
(2) Provide a brief description of each alternative solution that you have identified using the Client counselling guide. This description will enable the client to identify the non-legal consequences.
(3) Ask the client whether he or she can identify other alternatives. If other alternatives are raised, describe them also and write them on the Client counselling guide.
(4) Your description of alternatives should exhibit the elements of effective speaking in relation to:

    (a) content;
    (b) language;
    (c) presentation.

(5) Ensure the client fully understands the information communicated.

D Analysing the consequences

(1) Determine, in consultation with the client, which alternative course of action should be discussed first.
(2) For each alternative, analyse and predict the legal and non-legal consequences. You will be in the best position to predict the legal consequences. The client will be best able to predict economic, social or psychological consequences.
(3) In classifying consequences of a particular action as positive or negative, encourage the client to make this determination. What you regard as negative may not be for the client.
(4) Ensure the client is fully involved in this process.
(5) Your description of consequences should exhibit the elements of effective speaking in relation to:

    (a) content;
    (b) language;
    (c) presentation.

E Obtaining the client's decision

(1) Assist the client to select which course(s) of action, if any, he or she wishes to pursue.
(2) Clarify any alternatives or consequences as necessary.
(3) Avoid making decisions for client.
(4) Where the client requires time to make a decision and time is available, adjourn the counselling session. Provide the client with a summary of the information communicated in the counselling session if needed by the client.
(5) Clarify follow up tasks for you *and* the client.

3 Documenting the decision

(1) Complete your notes of the counselling session.
(2) Carry out or initiate any relevant office procedure.
(3) Prepare a memorandum to file which organises and records the substance and details of the session including:

 (a) new information communicated by the client;
 (b) the alternative courses of action;
 (c) the positive and negative consequences for each alternative;
 (d) the client's instructions, where obtained;
 (e) the fee arrangement, if different than previously agreed upon;
 (f) the next scheduled meeting with the client.

(4) Draft a letter to the client, confirming:

 (a) the client's instructions and the agreement for services;
 (b) the fee arrangement;
 (c) the steps to be taken, if agreed upon, by you and the client,
 (d) the next scheduled meeting with the client.

(5) Draft any documents, correspondence or memoranda which are required, sending a copy of each to the client.

4 Writing a legal opinion

Susan Blake

The skills involved in giving a legal opinion, whether written or oral, have tended to be ignored even in these days when the teaching of other skills such as interviewing is being developed. Because there are no formal legal rules about giving advice to a client, there is the tendency to think there is nothing to learn and anyone can do it, as used to be the case with interviewing. This is very unfair to the client, who may be left confused by the advice he gets, may become convinced that his lawyer does not really understand his case, or may feel that the best is not being done for him. This leads to a bad public image for the lawyer and it really is vital to develop skills in this area to do a proper professional job for the client.

There are two main areas needing work, to be dealt with in slightly different ways. The first is one commonly complained of – that many young people do not now have skills in using words, be it in grammar, the correct use of words or in logical and precise structure of written work. The second is knowing how to approach the task of giving advice in an organised way. Many young lawyers currently advise their first client without having thought much, if at all, about how to set about it, let alone receiving training and practice . . . the real client is the guinea-pig!

As to the first problem, the inability of current students to use English well is widely commented on in many professions – grammar is often not coherently taught, vocabulary tends to be limited and used inaccurately, and the importance of structure in written work is rarely emphasised. Although this is widely observed, solutions are not easy to find. Some years ago teaching moved to emphasising the importance of freedom of expression in writing rather than adhering to strict rules, but the time may have come to swing the pendulum back slightly towards the appreciation of formal rules.

There is a tendency to pass the buck back down the line – the professional training institute blames the university, the university blames the school, and the school blames the nursery school. The problem is now such that all levels need to try to find ways of teaching, and of identifying, those who do have problems right up to the level of professional training. There can be a problem in 'selling' this to students – who may feel offended if they are told that they cannot write well as if it were a personal criticism. However, exercises in using words, summarising points and constructing pieces must somehow be introduced, made interesting and taken seriously. Students shown good examples will usually appreciate their merits.

The second problem, of teaching students how to give structured and useful advice, is what I am primarily concerned with here. Experience has tended to show that how to give a legal opinion is not initially best taught by giving examples. Presented with examples the student will seek to copy them, rather than building an independent strength and style, which is crucial for a good lawyer. The best approach is rather to alert the student to how to prepare and develop style with comprehensive checklists that can easily be learned and used. These checklists, as evolved while teaching, are given to the students, with relatively few examples of actual opinions.

Once the checklists have been understood and absorbed, the student or young lawyer can more usefully learn from example, seeing what established lawyers in practice do, but being able to apply discrimination as to what is good practice that he or she could usefully follow, rather than copying bad practices and mistakes without thought.

Building a successful case in court begins from the earliest stages, so the following lists are central to being a good lawyer rather than peripheral. The lawyer who is really in control of the case from the start is most likely to win, and most likely to get the client returning, because the client has real confidence in the advice that was given and the way his or her case was conducted!

The checklists which follow were developed in teaching students studying for the Bar Examinations at the Inns of Court School of Law in London. Various teaching methods were used by different members of staff, the emphasis always being on building individual skills and style rather than following models, but this sort of checklist approach was quite common. The students worked in tutorial groups of 10–12, dealing with small legal problems in the basic legal areas of contract, tort, trusts and crime, being given a basic factual situation and asked to write a legal opinion as to the merits of the case, as if they were a barrister acting in the case. Students would work on each problem alone and then discuss their work in the tutorial groups. Further examples of the checklist approach suggested here, with further supporting material, are provided in *A Practical Approach to Legal Advice and Drafting* (3rd edition, 1989) published by The Blackstone Press, which is recommended for the Bar Finals Course.

In fact the course at the Inns of Court School of Law is currently being redesigned, with a New Vocational Course commencing in September 1989. This new course will put the writing of legal opinions into an even more practical context, linking it with the other skills of a lawyer, such as advising in conference and conducting a negotiation. The clear objective of this new course is that the skills of the lawyer will be more integrated to put the writing of a legal opinion into the context of managing facts and carrying out legal research. However, the basic approach of providing checklists and encouraging students to build up individual style and confidence rather than following set examples will remain central.

These checklists are designed to be of use to the barrister practising in the legal system of England and Wales, where the provision of a written opinion is a central element of practice. However, similar principles could be used in training lawyers to provide an opinion in any legal jurisdiction. While the checklists relate primarily to giving written advice they could be adapted fairly easily to the provision of oral advice.

PREPARING*

Writing a good legal opinion begins with good preparation!

○ Getting full and clear information from the client in an interview.
○ Getting all supporting evidence that is available, be it from documents or witnesses.
○ Getting all other relevant information, be it factual or technical.
○ Carrying out appropriate legal research.

This must all be done in the right frame of mind:

○ The decision as to what type of case the client has should not be taken too early (or there is the temptation to make the case fit the preconceived idea).
○ All material relating to a case should be read for the first time when the lawyer is in a receptive state of mind rather than tired, or concerned with some other matter.
○ All material relating to a case should be read carefully to avoid any misunderstanding.
○ The lawyer must approach the case from the point of view of his client, not as the judge of the case!

These points will now be broken down into more detailed work plans.

BEFORE WRITING THE OPINION

The opinion should be the polished final product rather than a rambling set of notes. First stages are separate from, and as important as, the final product. It is as necessary to develop good habits in preparatory skills as in wording the final result.
    The main stages in this are as follows:

1 The client's specific instructions and objectives must be obtained and kept clear in the mind at all times.
2 All material that may be relevant to the case must be collected.
3 The material in the case must be ordered.
4 The material in the case must be attentively read.
5 Clear and thorough notes must be made from the materials.
6 Any gaps must be identified and dealt with.
7 A specific decision must be taken about the future of the case.

To explain each point in more detail:

---

1 The client's instructions and objectives must be kept clear The client is the reason for the whole action, and must come first:

- o He or she must be interviewed in a way that will get all relevant details.
- o Everything said should be written down and checked with the client for accuracy and omissions.
- o The client must be asked specifically what he or she hopes to achieve in the case.
- o If there are alternatives in how to pursue the case, these must be explained to the client, who must decide.

---

2 It is important to collect all relevant information The following should be available while the opinion is being prepared:

- o The written statement of the client, including all the facts and the client's objectives in the case.
- o All other relevant written documents, such as contracts.
- o Statements from any witnesses.
- o Statements from experts if appropriate.
- o Pictures, plans, photos, diagrams etc to understand fully the situation (where this is vital as in a road accident, a plan should always be where it can be seen).
- o Any existing correspondence should be read for relevant matter.

---

3 The material must be ordered It should preferably be ordered even before it is read so it can be properly understood and does not give a false impression, but this is not always possible if some information is not yet available.

- o All material should be collected together in one place at one time.
- o Each item of material should be identified.
- o A suitable basis for ordering should be decided on (most important documents first, chronological etc).
- o Every document should be put in order with the chosen system.

4 The material must be read

o The material should be read when the lawyer is attentive.
o The material should be read without preconceptions as to fact or the likely cause of action.
o Each item should normally be read personally by the lawyer.
o The lawyer should keep his or her mind open right to the end of reading as to the type of case and the strength of it.
o Each item should be read twice, after some interval, to avoid misunderstanding or missing anything.

5 Thorough notes should be made, then checked and ordered   A good clean copy of these notes should be retained for easy reference while writing the opinion or giving oral advice. It may also be useful if the case comes back for further advice, or for easy reference when presenting the case in court.

o Notes of all times and places should be made from all relevant material. These should then be sorted and ordered.
o Basic notes of all material facts should be made, with any relevant detail.
o Any discrepancies in the information given should be noted and checked.
o Anything that is unclear or ambiguous should be noted and checked.
o Notes should be kept of references to relevant points so they may be found again easily.
o Possible causes of action should be noted.

6 Any gaps in information should be identified and dealt with   If anything major is missing it must be got or checked before proceeding.

o Think through the factual situation – is it realistic? are there any gaps in it?

o Notes should be made of any further document or information that needs to be sought.
o Notes should be made of points where further evidence is needed.
o Notes should be made of points that need further legal research.

7 A decision must be taken about the future of the case   This needs a clear and specific decision with a structured time scale.

○ Immediate action may be necessary, such as seeking an injunction. If so, get on with it!
○ If further information is needed, can you proceed without it or should you wait for it? If you need to wait, decide exactly what is needed and who will get it, and when by.
○ If you do not need to wait, take the next step, eg issue proceedings.
○ If there are further decisions to be taken, they should be clearly put to and taken by the client.

WRITING THE OPINION

The main stages in writing the opinion are:

1 Notes for the opinion should be made.
2 The opinion is written or given.
3 Professional polish.
4 Practical polish.
5 The opinion should be read and/or checked.

1 Notes for the opinion should be made
○ Each possible cause of action should be noted, with the elements it will be necessary to show to succeed.
○ The facts and evidence in support of each should be noted.
○ The potential weaknesses of each should be noted.
○ Every possible remedy should be noted, with relevant facts (especially relating to quantum of damages).
○ The potential contents should be ordered before beginning to write. The opinion should not ramble (especially to the extent of possibly contradicting itself!).

2 The opinion is written, based on the notes made

o Choose a suitable order for the material and overall structure for the advice. This may differ with different types of case.

o Choose a suitable line of approach, building up arguments to assist the client rather than writing a judgment.

o Choose a suitable layout – subheadings and numbered paragraphs are easier to read.

o Choose a suitable style of writing to communicate properly, and in which you feel comfortable. Should you write at length or briefly? Do you tell jokes or not? In any event, the opinion is NOT an academic thesis.

o Choose a suitable vocabulary – you do not communicate with a confused old lady in the same way as with the managing director of a new company. Who are you writing or speaking to? There is no magic in long words, or unnecessarily obscure terminology!

o Choose a suitable level of legal content – some have to have detailed argument, many need relatively little. Also choose carefully the necessary level for quotation of statutes and cases. Anything that is particularly authoritative, close on the facts or recent should be there. Long quotes may be boring unless they are really helpful!

o Choose a suitable length – you are not paid by length and there is no merit in repetition.

o Summarise conclusions at the beginning or the end for clear and easy reference.

3 The importance of the professional approach

o Be careful to take the tone of the legal adviser, not of the judge.

o Keep legal argument clearly separate from personal views.

o The opinion should not be too strongly phrased in the first person – the case is the client's, not the lawyer's.

o Don't be unjustifiably optimistic or pessimistic as to the likely success of the client's case.

o Never force your own decisions on the client – it is his case!

4 The practical approach makes the good lawyer
- Think of your case practically to work out what exactly might have happened and what evidence might be available.
- Pretend you are the lawyer for the other side to imagine the weaknesses in your own case and the possible arguments for the other side.
- Read your own advice critically as if you were the client – does it really help and cover everything, or is it vague and leave you with unanswered questions?
- Beware of making any assumptions, of fact or attitude.
- Don't develop clever legal arguments that do not have a realistic chance of success, which the client ends up paying for.
- Deal with potential remedies thoroughly.

5 Read and check the opinion If you are talking, check your notes to see you have covered everything. If you are writing, set the opinion aside and come back to it later to check:

- Does it cover all the facts?
- Does it make clear what the possible causes of action are, and the strengths and weaknesses of each?
- Does it make as clear as possible what the client may hope to gain from any action?
- Does it put the choices to be made clearly to the client, and make it clear that the choices are for the client, although it may also make clear what the lawyer recommends.
- Is it clear and concise in the way it is set out, the words it uses, what is covered and what is referred to? (Go through it with a pencil crossing out what is unnecessary!)

NEVER LOSE SIGHT OF THE FACT THAT THE OPINION'S MAIN AIMS ARE:

(1) TO COMMUNICATE
(2) TO HELP THE CLIENT.

SUGGESTED BASIC OUTLINE FOR AN OPINION IN A CIVIL CASE

OPINION

1 Introduction

The facts of the case are summarised briefly to give context, and the main issues to be dealt with identified.

2 Summary of advice

The main elements of the advice the lawyer is giving can usefully be summarised, so they can be easily and quickly grasped, and followed through the opinion.

3 Cause of action

Each possible cause of action in the case should be set out and analysed. Identify all the legal elements of each, and assess if each is present in the case. Identify any legal, factual or evidential difficulties for each element. If there is more than one possible cause of action, analyse strengths and weaknesses of each and possibly suggest which is best. All possible arguments in the client's favour should be examined.

4 Defences

Examine every possible defence to the client's claim. This should include anything specifically raised in the papers in the case, and any other possible defence the lawyer feels could arise. Include full and partial defences. Examine the factual, legal and evidential difficulties of each, whether it is considered likely to succeed, and what the effect on the case might be.

5 Remedies

All possible remedies that might be available to the client if he or she succeeds should be explained. If there is a choice of remedies, that choice should be put to the client.

   If damages are sought, the lawyer should try to give as close an estimate as possible of the sum likely to be recovered, with some estimate as to the likely chances of success. Investigate fully all possible loss the client has suffered, and all possible deductions.

6 Other points

These are things that may be dealt with in the course of the opinion, or at the end.

(a) Any point which the client has specifically asked the lawyer to deal with because it is important to him.
(b) *Evidence* The best argument can fail if you cannot prove your case, so deal with what evidence there already is with any appropriate comment, and what further evidence is needed, with clear directions where it should be sought.
(c) *Procedural points* The lawyer should explain appropriate legal procedure to the client, and should deal with any particular procedural step that may be of use to the client in the case.

7 Conclusions

Any conclusions, and any future steps to be taken in the case, and any decisions that the client has to take should be set out clearly. Some indication of chances of success may be appropriate. Don't leave any questions unanswered.

Dated   Signed by the lawyer

5 Drafting

Stephen Nathanson and Susan Blake

I INTRODUCTION TO TEACHING MATERIALS ON DRAFTING

Stephen Nathanson

These materials are from a course called 'Commercial Law and Practice' which is part of the curriculum leading to a Postgraduate Certificate in Laws (PCLL) at the University of Hong Kong. Recipients of the PCLL may be permitted to serve under articles or pupillage and thereafter be admitted to practice as solicitors or barristers.

The 'Commercial Law and Practice' course aims to develop skills such as drafting, writing, problem-solving and negotiation in a commercial law context. Classroom instruction takes place one day each week and consists of a lecture in the morning and a small group activity in the afternoon. These materials constitute the first activity plan in drafting. They describe the activity which takes place in small groups after the first lecture on commercial drafting, which includes a discussion of drafting models as well as criteria for effective drafting. As the activity plan shows, instruction in drafting is criteria-referenced and remains so throughout the drafting component of the course. In the first lecture and this first activity, the objectives of the instruction are to develop three abilities:

(1) to be able to explain the criteria or principles of effective drafting;
(2) to be able to identify and explain drafting errors by reference to those principles;
(3) to be able to apply some of those principles in drafting.

Principles of drafting are labelled in generic terms so that they can be rehearsed in subsequent activities in different legal contexts, although this and subsequent activities devote some time to an analysis of legal issues peculiar to the legal context under discussion in the activity. A brief discussion of the reasons for using this instructional method is set out at p 133 of the activity plan. It should be noted that the activity plan format and the *Drafting guide* included in these materials are based on material first developed when this writer was an instructor at the Professional Legal Training Course (PLTC) in Vancouver, British Columbia. Pages 129–132 of the activity plan are for students and lecturers. Pages 132–136 are for lecturers only.

TEACHING MATERIALS

1 Objectives

(1) You will be able to explain a set of criteria for effective legal drafting.
(2) Given a simple commercial contract you will be able to identify and explain drafting weakness or errors by reference to these criteria.
(3) You will be able to redraft one clause of this contract to correct weaknesses or errors.

2 Preparation

(1) Read Exercise A and the sales contract below.
(2) Review the Sale of Goods Ordinance (SOGO) and identify what SOGO provisions are relevant for the purpose of drafting the sales contract.
(3) Read Goode *Commercial Law* chapters 3 and 13, pp 365–372.
(4) Read 'Drafting – law, fact, and language' (from Robinson *Drafting*).

3 Description of the activity

(1) Lecturer gives talk on drafting. Class discusses criteria for effective drafting as set out in the *Drafting guide* (pp 131–132).
(2) Students divide into pairs to do Exercise A below.
(3) When doing the exercise, identify and characterise drafting weaknesses or errors in the sales contract by reference to criteria in the *Drafting guide*. When you see a drafting error, circle it or make a notation with the applicable *Drafting guide* item number beside it. For example:

> Buyer? ⑨　㉗　　Seller? ⑧
> If the party of the first part shall default, the party of the second part shall be entitled
> ⑧　　　　　　　　　　⑦a
> to receive the sum certain of $100,000.
> ⑦a　　receive from whom? ⑩

After identification of errors or weaknesses students redraft clause 3 of the sales contract.
(4) Class discusses solutions to Exercise A.
(5) Lecturer hands out sample redraft of sales contract. Class critiques the sample.

4 Notes

(1) **Exercise A**
Assume you act for Wah Luen Machinery Ltd, a textile machine manufacturer. Wah Luen has agreed to sell three knitting machines to Che

Lak Knitting Ltd. The price is $270,000–$30,000 on execution of the agreement, the balance in three equal instalments: 15 January, YR+1, 1 March, YR+1 and 1 April, YR+1. The machines are to be delivered on 15 January, YR+1. The sales contract which follows needs redrafting. Your task, however, is limited to the following:

(a) Identify and characterise drafting errors and weaknesses by the method described in heading 3, para (3) above.
(b) After identification of errors and weaknesses, redraft clause 3 of the sales contract.
(c) Assume any other facts consistent with those given.

(2) There is an exercise which must be completed and handed in. See AP4 for details.
(3) Always read ahead to find out what the weekly course requirements are.

Sales Contract

AGREEMENT   Made the 14th day of November, YR0

BETWEEN   Wah Luen Machinery Ltd whose place of business is at 79 Hung To Road, Kwun Tong, Kowloon (hereinafter referred to as 'the Seller')

AND   Che Lak Knitting Ltd whose place of business is at 14–16 Fui Yiu Kok Street, Tsuen Wan, New Territories (hereinafter referred to as 'the Buyer')

THE VENDOR AND THE PURCHASER have agreed as follows:

1   The Seller agrees to sell to the Buyer three knitting machines namely: two Atlas Heavy Duty Knitters Model AK43B manufactured by Atlas Engineering Ltd, serial numbers AK43B7942H702 and AK43B8742H703 and one Atlas Special Adjustable Knitter, Model 3X100 manufactured by Atlas Engineering Ltd, serial number 3100X4791H927 ('the Machines').
2   The Seller agrees to deliver the Machines to the Buyer at 14–16 Fui Yiu Kok St, Tsuen Wan, New Territories.
3   The Buyer agrees to pay $270,000 payable as follows: $30,000 on the signing of this agreement, the balance of $240,000 by four consecutive monthly instalments on the fifteenth day of January YR+1, the first day of March YR+1, and the first day of April YR+1.
4   Title in the Machines shall remain vested in the Seller until payment of the final instalment specified in clause 3 has been received by the Seller.
5   Risk shall pass when the machines are delivered to the Buyer as specified in clause 2.
6   The Buyer shall arrange full insurance of the machines from the date hereof.
7   The Seller warrants that the Goods are of merchantable quality and are fit for the particular purpose required by the Buyer and have been modified to enable the production of high quality knitted jumpers as specified in Schedule A.

8   In the event of any dispute arising between the Buyer and the Seller efforts will be made to reach settlement through direct negotiation but should this fail the dispute shall be referred to arbitration under the provisions of the Arbitration Ordinance and its amendments.

9   This agreement and all obligations created shall be construed and enforced according to Hong Kong law.

In witness whereof this agreement has been made the day and year first above mentioned.

Wah Luen Machinery Ltd

per: .... C/S

Che Lak Knitting Ltd

per: .... C/S

Completed by: ....
Completed for: ....
Date: ....

Drafting guide

Instructions

This guide is designed to assist you in providing detailed, descriptive feedback on the strengths and weaknesses of drafting.

COMMENTS

[ ]   (1) Meets client's goals and carries out client's instructions.

[ ]   (2) Accurately addresses all relevant legal issues.

[ ]   (3) Uses precedents critically, demonstrates understanding of what they mean.

(4) Is organised logically:

[ ]   (a) uses appropriate and logical categories to organise material;

[ ]   (b) includes appropriate material in each category;

[ ]   (c) sequences all material logically;

[ ]   (d) uses appropriate paragraphing, subparagraphing, tabulation.

(5) Forms a consistent and coherent whole:

[ ]   (a) avoids internal contradictions;
[ ]   (b) uses same words to mean same thing;
[ ]   (c) uses definitions where appropriate;
[ ]   (d) uses defined terms in their defined sense throughout.

[ ] (6) Uses correct grammar.
(7) Uses appropriate language:

[ ]   (a) uses active rather than passive voice;
[ ]   (b) uses modern rather than archaic expressions or legal jargon (except where these have special juridical meaning);
[ ]   (c) uses present rather than future tense;
[ ]   (d) uses deliberate vagueness, where appropriate.

[ ] (8) Is succinct (no superfluous language).
[ ] (9) Is precise (no ambiguity).
[ ] (10) Where appropriate, ensures content is expressed in legislative sentences (ie meets the 'who? what? when? where?' test).
(11) In contracts:

[ ]   (a) provides internal remedies for breach;
[ ]   (b) provides conditions precedent or 'subject to' clauses, where appropriate;
[ ]   (c) provides other special clauses, where appropriate (see (2) above).

[ ] (12) Meets any formal requirements.
[ ] (13) Maintains a standard of care which does not prejudice the interests of client.

FROM HERE TO END OF PLAN FOR LECTURERS ONLY:

5 Resources

(1) Sample Redraft of Sales Contract (pp 137–138) – copies for students.
(2) Sale of Goods Ordinance.
(3) Transparency of Sales Contract.
(4) R M Goode *Commercial Law*.

6 Suggestions to lecturers for instruction

A Discuss objectives

B Talk on drafting and *Drafting guide*

1 You might start the talk by posing questions about the teaching methods and suggest answers:

Q Why learn drafting by this criteria-based method?
A If criteria for effective drafting are specifically labelled, as they are in the *Drafting guide*, once learned it is easier to *transfer* them from exercise to exercise. Labelling thus facilitates transfer and learning.

Q But drafting considerations in, say, a joint venture agreement are entirely different from those in a sales contract. How can they both be 'learned' with the same set of criteria?
A Some criteria transfer readily and some (such as (2) 'legal issues'), do not. For example, although the criterion 'uses same words to mean the same thing', is applicable to all drafting, the legal issues coverable in a sales contract are necessarily different from those in a joint venture agreement. Still, covering or 'addressing' legal issues *generally*, is a criterion that must be met in all effective drafting.

2 Discuss items on the *Drafting guide*. It is suggested that you discuss some items this activity and some the next. The ones chosen for discussion for this activity are emphasised in Exercise A. They are items: (1), (2), (4)(d), (5)(a), (5)(b), (5)(c), (5)(d), (8), (10), (11)(a).

3 Most, if not all, of these criteria, are dealt with in the readings on drafting, but a few may require some explanation:

(7)(d) Uses deliberate vagueness, where appropriate.

eg in a contract drawn for a banker, a clause stipulates: 'ABC bank shall act as a reasonable lender'.

This is 'deliberately vague' and so favours the bank in the day-to-day operation of the contract. On the other hand, 'deliberate vagueness' can backfire if there is litigation because such clauses are usually construed against the drafting party.

(10) Where appropriate, ensures content is expressed in legislative sentences (ie meets the 'who? what? when? where?' test).

This criterion rests on the proposition that contractual terms are a form of legislation, ie private legislation governing legal relations between private parties. As such, contractual terms should contain all the elements necessary to create binding legal obligations. Those elements are usually (but not always) statements about

(1) *who* is to perform the obligation;
(2) *what* obligation is to be performed;
(3) *when* the obligation is to be performed;
(4) *where* the obligation is to be performed.

When one or more of these elements is missing from a contractual term it *may* have the effect of either releasing one of the parties from an intended obligation or creating sufficient ambiguity to provide one of the parties with an issue to litigate, eg:

> Notwithstanding the foregoing, the Vendor shall receive payment of $10,000.

This contractual term is deficient because it omits:

○ *who* is to pay;
○ *when* the payment is to be made;
○ (*where* the payment is to be made; this may or may not create a problem, depending on the other terms of the contract).

(4)(a) Provides internal remedies for breach

These are remedies for breach written into contracts which can save the client the expense of litigation. Examples of such clauses are liquidated damages and acceleration clauses.

Arbitration is *not* an internal remedy in the sense that the remedy is provided by the arbitrator, not the terms of the contract.

C Perform Exercise A

1   Divide students into pairs. Each pair should do the exercise as described above.

D Discuss solutions to Exercise A

1   Discuss errors and weaknesses by reference to the criteria. Here, you might suggest to students that their drafting exercises will be marked according to the *same* set of criteria and in the *same* way that the students are 'marking' this sales contract. The criteria – though not invariably applicable to all drafting – are thus better remembered and put into practice. The recommended technique for conducting this discussion is to make a transparency of the Sales Contract and refer to its specific parts on the overhead as the discussion proceeds.

It is not recommended that you use a transparency of the Criteria-Assessed Sales Contract (CASC), because if this is displayed on the overhead, students tend to lose interest in what they have done and, instead, focus interest on what 'you' have done.

2   Use the CASC, however, to guide the discussion. Most of the *Drafting guide* items marked on the CASC are self-explanatory, but what follows are some notes particularly directed to legal issues (*Guide* item (2)).

(a) Clause 4, CASC – Title remains vested in the seller until payment of the final instalment. See ss 40–43 SOGO – unpaid seller has a lien on goods even after 'property passes'. The evident purpose of the draftsperson is to give the seller *more* than a lien – to permit him to retain title even after delivery. This can be accomplished by effective drafting (see *Goode* p 372). This retention of title provision, therefore, can be further improved by adding disposition and repossession clauses (see clauses 5 and 6 of the Redraft which you can discuss later). (*Guide* item 11.)

(b) The contract, as a whole, should provide the seller with another internal remedy, in addition to disposition and repossession: interest on overdue amounts. (See clause 4 of redraft.)

(c) Clauses 5 and 6 of the CASC, of course, are inconsistent (*Guide* item (5)(a)) because the buyer should not have to arrange insurance from the date of the contract, only when risk passes, ie at delivery. Also, prior to delivery, buyer has no insurable interest in the machines. (See *Goode* p 216.)

3 Review the students' performance in redrafting clause 3 of the CASC. Have one student reproduce his/her solution on the overhead. Class can then critique it. (See clause 3 of Sample Redraft.)

E Hand out Sample Redraft – discuss and critique

Emphasise that this is not *the* solution to the exercise. Drafting can never be perfect. The purpose of critiquing, practising, and critiquing is simply to improve.

8 Notes

(1) The talk on drafting (in 6B) can be lengthened or abbreviated depending on how much has already been covered in the lecture.
(2) What follows is the Criteria-Assessed Sales Contract. Please do not hand this out to students. Use it for your own reference to guide the discussion.
(3) Remind students to complete next week's exercise on time.

Criteria-Assessed Sales Contract

AGREEMENT   Made the 14th day of November, YRO

BETWEEN   Wah Luen Machinery Ltd whose place of business is at 79 Hung To Road Kwun Tong, Kowloon (hereinafter referred to as 'the Seller')

AND   Che Lak Knitting Ltd whose place of business is at 14–16 Fui Yiu Kok Street, Tsuen Wan, New Territories (hereinafter referred to as 'the Buyer') THE VENDOR AND THE PURCHASER have agreed as follows:

1 The Seller agrees to sell to the Buyer three knitting machines namely: two Atlas Heavy Duty Knitters Model AK43B manufactured by Atlas Engineering Ltd, serial numbers AK43B7942H702 and AK43B8742H703 and one Atlas Special Adjustable Knitter, Model 3X100 manufactured by Atlas Engineering Ltd, serial number 3100X4791H927 ('the Machines').

2 The Seller agrees to deliver the Machines to the Buyer at

(14–16 Fui Yiu Kok St, Tsuen Wan, New Territories.) ⑧

⑩ to whom?

3   The Buyer agrees to pay $270,000 payable as follows: $30,000

∧

① three equal

on the signing of this agreement, the balance of $240,000 by ̶f̶o̶u̶r̶

consecutive monthly instalments on the ̶f̶i̶f̶t̶e̶e̶n̶t̶h̶ day of January

YR+1, the ̶f̶i̶r̶s̶t̶ ̶d̶a̶y̶ ̶o̶f̶ ̶M̶a̶r̶c̶h̶ YR+1, and the first day of April *⑤a*

YR+1.

③ *Seller's rights on default?*

4   Title in the Machines shall remain vested in the Seller until

⑪ *internal remedies?*

payment of the final instalment specified in clause 3 has been

received by the Seller.

– interest on overdue amounts
– repossesion
– disposition

⑤a

5   Risk shall pass when the Machines are delivered to the Buyer

To be consistent, date machines insured s/b

as specified in clause 2. *Same as date risk passes.*

⑤b upper case "M" or lower case?

6   The Buyer shall arrange full insurance of the machines from

the date hereof.

⑤d

7   The Seller warrants that the Goods are of merchantable qual-

ity and are fit for the particular purpose required by the Buyer

② No declaration of purpose by the buyer

and have been modified to enable the production of high quality

knitted jumpers as specified in Schedule A.

8   In the event of any dispute arising between the Buyer and the

Seller efforts will be made to reach settlement through direct ne-

gotiation but should this fail the dispute shall be referred to arbi-

tration under the provisions of the Arbitration Ordinance and its

amendments.

9   This agreement and all obligations created shall be construed

and enforced according to Hong Kong law.

In witness whereof this agreement has been made the day

and year first above mentioned.

Wah Luen Machinery Ltd

per: . . . . C/S

Che Lak Knitting Ltd

per: . . . . C/S

SAMPLE REDRAFT

Sales Contract

AGREEMENT   made the 14th day of November YR0
BETWEEN   Wah Luen Machinery Ltd whose place of business is at 79
             Hung To Road, Kowloon Tong, Kowloon ('the Seller')
AND   Che Lak Knitting Ltd whose place of business is at 14–16 Fui
             Yiu Kok St, Tsuen Wan, New Territories ('the Buyer').

The Buyer and Seller have agreed as follows:

1 The Buyer agrees to buy from the Seller and the Seller agrees to sell to the
Buyer three knitting machines ('the Machines') namely:

(a) Two Atlas Heavy Duty Knitters Model AK43B manufactured
    by Atlas Engineering Ltd, serial numbers AK43B7942H702 and
    AK43B8742H703 respectively,
(b) One Atlas Special Adjustable Knitter, Model 3X100 manufactured by
    Atlas Engineering Ltd, serial number 3X100X4791H927.

2 The Seller agrees to deliver the Machines to the Buyer at its place of
business on the 15th day of January YR+1.
3 The Buyer agrees to pay $270,000 due and payable as follows:

(a) $30,000 on the execution of this agreement
(b) $80,000 on the date of delivery
(c) $80,000 on the first day of March YR+1
(d) $80,000 on the first day of April YR+1.

4 The Buyer shall pay all sums to the Seller on or before the due dates. Delay
of payment is subject to the consent of the Seller but interest at the rate of
twelve per cent per annum is charged against all overdue amounts.
5 Until all sums specified in the previous clause have been paid to the Seller,
title in the Machines shall remain vested in the Seller.
6 In default of payment of any sum by the due date the Seller has the right to:

(a) dispose of the Machines and charge the Buyer for any loss incurred,
(b) enter into premises where the Machines are installed and to remove and
    repossess the Machines.

7 Risk shall pass to the Buyer when the Machines are delivered to the Buyer
as specified in clause 2.
8 The Buyer shall arrange full insurance of the Machines from the date of
delivery, and shall, prior to delivery, furnish written proof thereof satisfactory
to the Seller.
9 The Seller warrants that the Machines are of merchantable quality and are
fit for the particular purpose required by the Buyer, which purpose has been
communicated in a letter from the Buyer to the Seller dated November 8 YR0
and attached hereto as Schedule A. The Seller warrants that the Machines
have been modified, in accordance with Schedule B, for that particular purpose.

10   In the event of any dispute arising between the Buyer and the Seller, other than a default of payment, efforts will be made to reach settlement through direct negotiation but should this fail the dispute shall be referred to arbitration under the provisions of the Arbitration Ordinance and its amendments.

11   This agreement and all obligations created shall be construed and enforced according to Hong Kong law.

In witness whereof this agreement has been made the day and year first above mentioned.

Wah Luen Machinery Ltd

per: .... C/S

Che Lak Knitting Ltd

per: .... C/S

———————————————

II DRAFTING A LEGAL DOCUMENT

Susan Blake

Drafting a legal document is all too often regarded as boring, or at the very least mechanical. It can be difficult to convince students and young lawyers that they have to do anything other than look up a precedent and copy it, and training courses and literature have tended to follow this approach. Vast volumes of precedents are published, but there are few works on general techniques of drafting; though there are on other skills such as advocacy. While advocacy is more obviously important to a case, drafting can be as important, given that few of the cases begun actually go to court for advocacy to have any relevance, and that the strength of a case begins with a good draft.

The intention here is to give some guidance on general techniques of drafting, designed to encourage students to think what they are doing and build up a good approach that may be applied to all drafting. The comments and examples here relate to drafting pleadings for a court case, but similar principles could also be used for drafting other documents, such as contracts or leases.

The good draft needs to have a clear purpose, clarity and conciseness – a legal draft does not have to be long, boring and incomprehensible, though to see many examples one would not guess it! It is clear and concise wording and structure that matter, not the number of four-syllabled words and sub-clauses. It is frightening how many students are so buried in Victorian examples that they start producing drafts with sentences that don't even have verbs rather than thinking what they are doing! The right word is always better than the impressive one.

Part of the reason for putting relatively little emphasis on teaching the skills of drafting is clearly that some of the old crucial importance of drafting has gone. Historically, many centuries of legal practice went into developing very complex rules for pleading, and well into this century, a small error in drafting could lose a case. Drafting formulae had to be copied slavishly, and many rules had to be followed, but this is no longer the case.

Now that procedural rules have been modified so that errors in drafting can be remedied by amendment there appears to be a feeling that skills of drafting are not especially important – you can just copy something roughly right and sort out any problems later – but this can lead to sloppiness not just in drafting but in the overall approach to a case.

It is still important to learn basic and general skills in drafting, and this can best be done by training the mind in the necessary approach and objectives for a good draft rather than just giving examples. It is important to emphasise what one is trying to achieve with the draft, and then encourage the students to build up their own style and confidence.

It is of course still important to look at examples of drafts, but this should be done once the basic principles are appreciated, and done critically. You do not copy a draft from a book or a draft produced by an older lawyer without question just because it comes from a book or an older lawyer – the questions should always be there whether the draft really does it's job within the objectives of good drafting.

If the lawyer has a thorough knowledge of the facts and issues in his or her case, a good draft should follow virtually automatically.

There are several reasons why such good drafting remains an important skill:

○ A weak draft is a sign of a badly prepared case. The clear and confident draft indicates a well-prepared case, and is more likely to win.
○ The draft is the first thing the judge will see in many cases, possibly even before he or she comes into court, and a good, strong, clear pleading is the best way to attract the judge's attention to the strengths of your case.
○ Good drafting remains crucial in some cases – if a vital fact is not pleaded it may defeat the case, or if the right remedy is not sought, the court may not have the power to grant it.

It is important to stress to students how important good drafting is. While bad drafting will rarely lose a whole case, a good case can look weak if it is badly drafted, and a mediocre case can look much better if it is clearly and concisely drafted, impressing the other side, as well as the judge.

The materials given here are checklists of objectives and working patterns for students to learn to work with rather than finished examples. The materials were developed in teaching at the Inns of Court School of Law in London, for training students on the one year vocational course for those who had already obtained a law degree and had chosen to qualify as barristers.

The basis of the teaching was a set of lectures on the principles of drafting at the start of the course, followed by small group tutorial work in groups of 10–12 students, in which the development of drafting skills was elaborated, with approaches like the checklists here being used. Sample drafts were provided to students in the basic areas of contract, tort, trust law and crime, and in some other areas depending on options chosen. Students were given short problems in a legal context for which each was asked to prepare a draft personally, which was then discussed in the tutorial group.

The Bar course at the Inns of Court School of Law is in fact being redesigned at the time of writing, with a New Vocational Course to start in September 1989. The teaching of drafting has already evolved, and in the new course it will be extended, with lectures being abandoned in favour of large group work in which the students will practise preparing elements of drafts either in class or between classes, covering comprehensively all basic types of draft. The tutorial work will be more strongly based on giving the students small 'briefs' rather than simple legal problems, with drafting skills increasingly being integrated with other skills, so that students will for example be asked to draft an order after a negotiation, conduct an advocacy exercise on the basis of their own draft etc. However, the basic checklist approach for building up skills and encouraging individual style rather than providing models will very much underlie the new course.

The checklists provided here relate to drafting basic pleadings for taking a case to court, as these are central to the work of a barrister, but they can easily be adapted as required to relate to drafting other legal documents.

PRINCIPLES OF PLEADING AND DRAFTING

It is very important to have the basic principles and objectives of pleading in the mind all the time one is drafting.

Any draft should be intended to make issues clear so as to save time and money, and to prepare genuinely for the trial. It should be as brief a summary as possible of the material facts in the case.

○ The draft should summarise the case of the party.
○ The draft should sufficiently clarify the case of the party.
○ The draft should limit and define the issues in the case.
○ The draft should inform the other side of the case against them.
○ The draft should establish those issues on which evidence will be required.

It needs a logical structure. Be clear. Be brief.

CHOOSING THE TYPE OF DRAFT

Choose the right kind of draft – often this will be obvious, but if there is any choice to make, make it.

Choose the right type of draft within the general classification. A precedent may well be useful, but only in a very general sense to give overall contents and layout. Rather than leaving the precedent in front of you, note its contents for order and specific content to get a skeleton outline, then put the precedent away and draft your own pleading.

Look up all precedents that are possibly relevant, making intelligent choices what headings to look at. Usually factors from several different specimen drafts will need to be put together for use in a particular case.

Beware of the following:

○ Copying a precedent without considering whether it really applies. Do not just look up a general category in a collection of precedents, find one that looks vaguely right or deals with a similar subject and copy that.
○ Being too used to a particular type of draft and therefore failing to take sufficient care each time to make it suit the current case in every detail.
○ Copying something another lawyer has done without questioning whether it really does its job.

Precedents are increasingly kept on word processing machines in legal offices. This is generally a very good thing, but care must be taken to ensure that the sample is fully and correctly adapted for each case. No sample should be used just because it is there – if there is no really appropriate sample, start from scratch.

---

* Checklists on pp 141–147 copyright © 1987 Susan Blake.

TECHNICAL RULES

The lawyer should of course be fully aware of the technical rules for drafting in his or her own jurisdiction. In England and Wales, as apparently in a number of other jurisdictions, these rules are not available in a coherent form. Some are found dotted around the rules of Court, some are in Acts of Parliament and some are tradition. It would be a good step forward to have a single work containing all the technical rules of drafting to keep to hand while working. It is vital for the young lawyer to know what is regulation that he must adhere to, everything else is personal style, that should be adapted to best suit the case.

CONTENTS OF A DRAFT

A draft should contain:

○ A summary of material facts in numbered paragraphs.
○ All the material facts.
○ All the factors needed for the intended cause of action.
○ Detailed particulars of any fact necessary, eg of a general allegation of negligence or misrepresentation.
○ All the material facts and figures for the remedy sought.

This contrasts strongly to what an advice to a client should contain. That should cover every possible option – the draft is limited to basic issues of the cause of action decided on. The opinion may make presumptions or deal with possibilities – such things have no place in a draft, which should be thoroughly founded on facts and law.

Matters which may be omitted

○ Immaterial facts.
○ Evidence (except eg relevant parts of documents). Evidence is to prove the case in court, it should only be briefly in the pleading if it is part of telling the story. But don't forget that every point pleaded will need to be proved.
○ Law (unless it has crucial relevance, eg a statutory defence). Law is only needed if, eg a statute, gives the court power to act.
○ Matters presumed by law.
○ Legal argument. Legal argument is for advocacy in court.

PREPARATION FOR PLEADING

It is important to prepare properly before beginning to draft.

- All available material relating to the case should be read. Any fact that is not clear must be checked before it is pleaded.
- If any important material is not yet available, it may be necessary to wait for it.
- Concise notes of all dates, places, and people should be made and kept available to refer to while drafting.
- The client should be consulted and agree before the case is launched.
- The cause/causes of action should be decided and notes made of all the legal elements in each. The cause of action must be chosen carefully.
- Do any basic legal research before starting to draft – it is no use finding out later that a cause of action is not available!
- List all the remedies to be sought. Not only obvious remedies such as damages or orders, but keep a comprehensive list of every remedy that may be sought in a type of action and see if it is relevant.

Be thoroughly prepared before starting. It is wrong to take the view you can always amend the draft later – this wastes time, is the sign of someone who does not get round to preparing the case properly, and easily gives a poor opinion of the case.

Note that material facts may include facts before the main cause of action where one thing is conditional on another.

CHOOSING A CAUSE OF ACTION

- List all possibilities.
- List all the legal elements of each, with the evidence you have or should be able to get on each, and any legal uncertainty.
- Decide which is strongest, which weakest.
- Consider tactical factors.
- Don't make serious allegations like fraud unless convinced they are justified on the evidence.
- Decide which to use. It is usually possible to have more than one claim in a case, so long as the claims have some link of fact.
- Beware of pleading contradictory or conflicting causes of action, even if they are in the alternative.

Choose the parties correctly too – is there any choice, who is the strongest case against, who has the money.

PLANNING THE DRAFT

As a basic approach for beginners, though it can help in complex cases too, once you have read all the material in a case, write down the material facts in numbered sequence:

1 The plaintiff was walking across the High Street.
2 The defendant drove his car into the plaintiff.
3 The plaintiff's leg was broken.
4 The plaintiff's suit, costing £200, was ruined.

That is a basic outline of a statement of claim!
   Also, try writing down all the legal elements of the cause of action in numbered sequence:

1 Was a duty of care owed by the defendant to the plaintiff?
2 Was the duty of care operative at the time?
3 Was the plaintiff injured or did he suffer loss?
4 Did the injury or loss result from the defendant's negligence?

Check the first list against the second to ensure that everything has been covered.

WRITING THE DRAFT

○ Get the formal parts right – it makes a very bad impression if you do not!
○ All the allegations should be in a logical order.
○ Each allegation should be in a separate numbered paragraph.
○ Every allegation should be specific not vague, unless it is strictly necessary, wait for extra information if you have to. Only plead wide if you really don't know something.
○ Alternative allegations should be separate and clearly alternative.
○ Plead remedies sought as fully as the cause of action, including details such as interest.

STYLE OF WRITING

○ Use ordinary words! Long words and complicated structures should only be in if they are really justified, because the point is complex or there are many alternatives.
○ Always use the same word to refer to an item – consistency avoids confusion!
○ Some phraseology is a matter of law – where one is quoting a statutory cause of action. Where there are rules they must be adhered to.
○ If words from documents or conversations must be included they must be quoted accurately.

TACTICS

o Think positively, phrase every allegation as strongly as you reasonably can.
o If you don't put something in, you cannot normally give evidence on it
  at the trial.
o If you don't put something in, it cannot normally be raised on appeal.
o Don't anticipate what the other side may argue or you are doing their
  work for them.
o If you put too much in it may help the other side.
o What you put in the pleading will bind you at trial.
o Tactics are especially important in the amount of particulars pleaded.
o Details can make the case look strong – you are not afraid to give
  them!
o Pleading evidence or legal argument may be of assistance to the other
  side.

CHECKING THE DRAFT

Having drafted a pleading, always try to leave it for a little while and
then read it through. Check:

o It makes sense as a document on its own, without reference to any
  other material.
o It does not leave out any vital elements of fact or law.
o There are no inconsistencies to undermine the case.
o Cross out anything not directly relevant.
o Cross out anything that is not part of your case, even if it may be
  relevant for the other side. You should not do their pleading for them!
o Cross out any words that are superfluous.
o Check every word used accurately and unambiguously.

  Try reading it as if you were the lawyer for the other side to see what
the weaknesses are!
  The pleading should not leave you asking 'How?' or 'Why?' on any
issue because something vital has been left out.
  Always check the pleading later if necessary – especially before the
trial begins. It may need to be amended.
  Don't let familiarity with a type of draft weaken your accuracy.

DEALING WITH DRAFTS AT LATER STAGES

Drafting defences

There should be a similar approach to that outlined above for general approach, preparation and wording, but there is a need to centre attention on replying to the pleading before, any defects in it and how to put in one's own allegations.

o Read the preceding thoroughly and go through it with the client, discussing and clarifying every point.
o Decide your reaction to every allegation.

    (a) Admit it if it is true, or time and money will be wasted, but only if it is really true.
    (b) Deny the allegation if it is not true.
    (c) Confess and avoid, if you wish to add extra information to put a different light on things.
    (d) Just leave the other side to prove their case.

o Plead any positive allegations you wish to add.
o It is not necessary to plead to anything which was not in the statement of claim in the first place.

Dealing with defective drafts

There are various ways of dealing with defective drafts, depending on the needs of the case and the tactics you wish to adopt.

o If the pleading leaves out vital information, it should probably be sought (but beware of just prodding the other side into preparing their case better!).
o If the draft is very weak, it may be possible to get it struck out, to show one is taking the case seriously, but if it is not struck out there is the same possible drawback as above.
o Amend your own draft if necessary to put your case properly in time for the trial.
o Most systems allow other ways, such as interrogatories, to get more information from the other side.

There is rarely a great deal to be gained from taking petty points or being obstructive – the full and clear draft is the best!

BASIC STATEMENT OF CLAIM

IN THE HIGH COURT OF JUSTICE   1987:A:No
QUEENS BENCH DIVISION

BETWEEN   A   B   Plaintiff
                   and
           C   D   Defendant

STATEMENT OF CLAIM

1 [Establish as far as is relevant to the action who the parties are.]
2 [Plead any relevant facts prior to the cause of action arising.]
3 [Plead the basic relationship or situation from which the cause of action arises, eg contract, trust.]
4 [Plead any relevant details, eg terms of the contract.]
5 [Plead specifically the cause of action, eg breach.]

PARTICULARS OF

[Plead any appropriate details of breach etc]

6 By reason of the matters aforesaid the plaintiff has suffered loss and damage.

PARTICULARS OF DAMAGE

(Set out details of figures so far as known)
(Also plead particulars of injury where relevant)

7 [Plead the basic fact of any general or continuing loss which cannot yet be quantified.]
8 [Plead any further or alternative cause of action.]

AND the plaintiff claims:

1 [List in separate paragraphs all the remedies sought.]
2 [Include claims for interest, costs etc.]

Served etc   (Signed by lawyer)

BASIC DEFENCE AND COUNTERCLAIM

IN THE HIGH COURT OF JUSTICE   1987:A:No

QUEENS BENCH DIVISION

BETWEEN   A   B   Plaintiff
                                        and
                                   C   D   Defendant

DEFENCE

[Plead to all the allegations in the Statement of Claim in separate numbered paragraphs. The following are examples of possible paragraphs that may be adapted for use.]

1 The defendant admits paragraph   of the Statement of Claim.
2 The defendant denies paragraph   of the Statement of Claim.
3 The defendant denies paragraph   of the Statement of Claim, save in that ...
4 The defendant denies that the Plaintiff has suffered loss and damage as alleged in the Statement of Claim.
5 Further or in the alternative, the defendant denies that the alleged loss and damage were caused by the defendant.
6 Save as is herein specifically admitted or not admitted, the defendant denies each and every allegation contained in the Statement of Claim as though the same were set out herein and specifically traversed.

COUNTERCLAIM

7 [Plead the facts giving rise to the counterclaim in separate numbered paragraphs as though pleading a Statement of Claim.]
8
9

AND the Defendant counterclaims:

1 [Set out in separate numbered paragraphs the reliefs sought on the counterclaim.]
2

Served etc   (Signed by lawyer)

6 Trusts/contracts

Christopher Allen

The course at the Inns of Court School of Law prepares students for the Bar Final Examination. This examination currently contains two General Papers which are designed to reflect the sort of paperwork with which a newly qualified barrister might be expected to deal. General Paper I covers selected topics in tort and criminal law. General Paper II covers a substantial part of the law relating to trusts and contract.* Preparation for the examination includes a number of tutorials (each for about 10 students and lasting about an hour) in which problems similar to those appearing in the examination are discussed.

Re Prescott's Will Trusts is a tutorial problem which is currently dealt with at an early stage in the trusts tutorials. As the final paragraph indicates, students are asked to advise essentially on two matters: the devolution of Peachings Hall and the effect of clause 5 of Colin Prescott's will. In dealing with the first of these matters, most students appreciate that the effect of the provision in Albert's will has to be taken into account. Discussion generally focuses first on whether Albert used words sufficiently imperative to create a trust. The conclusion usually is that he did not and at that stage students often need to be reminded that for the purposes of drafting an originating summons all possibilities have to be considered. This leads on to the questions of certainty of subject matter and certainty of objects. The latter problem is of some significance in view of the claim made by Richard Prescott and invariably involves some discussion of the general problem of legal interpretation. Students are encouraged to work out an argument from the context of 'the words on the page' to defeat Richard's claim.

Clause 5 is seen by most students to raise the question of the meaning of 'my children'. At this stage it is usually realised that no interpretive guide is to be found in the 'words on the page' context and it is quite often assumed, without reference to authority, that extrinsic evidence can always be adduced to assist in interpretation of wills. (Perhaps surprisingly, this is not a topic dealt with in much detail in the standard student text books on trusts.) A smaller proportion of the students will see further that there is a problem about the manner of distribution. Some simply assume that the trustees will have a discretion and the inability of the courts to re-write inconveniently or badly drafted wills has to be emphasised. It is usually perceived that if 'my children'

---

* From September 1989 the General Papers will not form part of the New Vocational Course of the Inns of Court School of Law (p 119 above). They will, however, continue to form part of the old syllabus which will be available for candidates for Bar Finals who are not intending to practise at the English Bar.

includes non-adopted as well as adopted children there will be a difficulty in that some of the children cannot be traced. A few appreciate that the instructions are ambiguous here; does it mean that some cannot be identified as well as traced? An additional problem posed by clause 5 is when the distribution is to be made; it is not often that students perceive that clause 5 has to be read in the context of the preceding clauses and that the word 'thereafter' in clause 5 is ambiguous.

At various stages of the discussion students are encouraged to consider the effect of the failure of the various provisions and to deal with any necessary procedural matters such as the making of representation orders and the possible need for an order to allow advertising for claimants.

A less structured approach to the tutorial problem can sometimes be adopted in contract. In *Jackie Russell v Watchdogs Ltd* a group can be asked to operate as a team of lawyers discussing the problem among themselves and then presenting a conclusion in two stages.

The first stage is a consideration of liability: on what basis can Mrs Russell recover damages? It is quickly appreciated that the first step is to analyse the contractual situation. Were there two contractual obligations operating on the night in question, one to provide an all-night watchman and the other to provide the usual service? Was the original contract varied so as to provide for an all-night service instead of the usual one? Students are sometimes reluctant to rely on the oral agreement because they feel that there is insufficient evidence to support it. Opinions on this matter can be quite strongly expressed and it is necessary to remind students that quite often the lay client will see a copy of counsel's opinion and it is tactless to state too bluntly that the client is unlikely to be believed upon her oath. Those who initially have favoured reliance on the usual arrangement then have to struggle to see how breach led to the loss in question. Usually there are suggestions that some term should be implied, such as that the patrolman should have patrolled at regular intervals throughout the night, or should have patrolled at least once before 12.30. This leads obviously to thought about the circumstances in which courts will imply terms in contracts. Another question which those discussing the problem often perceive is this: suppose you could imply a term on the lines indicated, how could you show that its breach led to the loss?

The exclusion clause is often a difficulty: there is generally much anxiety about whether it can be implied in the agreement to provide an all-night watchman. Most groups come to the conclusion that the question is not a very important one because if there was such an agreement and Watchdogs failed to provide the watchman this was almost certainly because of negligence by one or more of their employees at some stage after the telephone call was received.

The second stage of debate concerns damages. How much is recoverable? This involves realisation that some calculations will involve double recovery. Initially some students wish to recover the 'value' of the dogs as well as sums in respect of lost prize money and stud fees. A causation problem may be seen to arise in relation to Poins as well as a problem of mitigation: did Mrs Russell do all that she could to inform her neighbours of the loss so that a greyhound found roaming would not be shot? (Would her neighbours have paid regard to this if the greyhound was worrying sheep?).

The problem of damages for distress does not always receive the attention that it deserves. Might this be a case falling within the sort of exceptions which have survived *Bliss v SE Thames Regional Health Authority* [1985] IRLR 308? Even if it is such a case, are any difficulties raised by the nature and extent of distress caused?

A final point concerns special damages; most students are ready to claim for the cost of repairs but many fail to appreciate that vet's fees were probably incurred as well.

The problems outlined above, and those in relation to *Re Prescott's Will Trusts*, are obviously not exhaustive but they tend to provide the main lines of discussion on the basis of which students may subsequently attempt to draft the appropriate pleadings.

Re Prescott's Will Trusts

Instructing solicitors act for Roberta Prescott and David Rafferty who are the executors and trustees of the will of Colin Prescott, who died on 10 January 1987. Probate was granted on 23 June 1987.

Colin Prescott was the only son of Albert Prescott, a successful industrialist who built up a business in textiles. Colin worked in the business all his adult life and inherited it on his father's death in 1960. He also inherited a large freehold house called Peachings Hall, Manor Street, Bradford. Albert bought Peachings Hall when he discovered that it had been built by his ancestors in the seventeenth century. He wanted to ensure that it remained within the family and the bequest to Colin in Albert's will (dated 30 September 1959) was in the following terms:

> I give my house and land known as Peachings Hall to my son Colin, in the confident hope that he will devise it to one or more of his children in his will and never allow it to pass outside the Prescott family; and in default of any such devise I desire that it shall pass to his eldest child then living and if there is no such child then to his closest living blood relative.

Colin ran the business profitably until he retired in 1982, when he sold it and devoted himself to his 'children'. He and Roberta married in 1942 but had no children of their own since tests revealed that Colin was incapable of fathering children. From 1960 they ran their home at Peachings Hall as a unique kind of children's home for orphaned refugee children from Third World countries. They looked after as many as 20 at any one time, bringing them up as their own children and treating them as such even after they had left. Some were legally adopted by Colin and Roberta, others were long-term or short-term foster children, some of whom took the Prescott name. Although Albert lived at Peachings Hall until his death, and did not disapprove of these children, he had very little contact with them.

By his will dated 19 July 1969 Colin appointed Roberta and David Rafferty (an old friend) to be his executors and trustees and after providing for the payment of all debts, tax and expenses he disposed of his estate as follows:

○ By clause 2 he gave assets to the value of £400,000 to Roberta.
○ By clause 3 he gave Peachings Hall to the trustees upon trust for sale, not to be sold until Roberta died or his youngest child attained the age of 21, whichever was later, and upon sale the proceeds to form part of the children's fund.
○ By clause 4 he gave the residue of his estate to the trustees upon trust to maintain Peachings Hall and provide for the children living there until the youngest child attained the age of 21, thereafter to form part of the children's fund.

○ Clause 5 reads: 'That part of my estate designated the children's fund shall be distributed by my trustees among my children.'

There are about 150 of Colin's 'children' living: nearly all can be identified and traced, but there are a few children who lived at Peachings Hall for such a short period that they never really became part of the family and their whereabouts are unknown. The oldest 'child' is Margaret Wong, but she was never legally adopted. The oldest adopted child is Czarina Prescott who was adopted by an order dated 15 October 1955. Another child, Simon Prescott, is willing to represent the class of children. The youngest child is Ranjit Prescott, aged 2, who is adopted.

Colin has only two known blood relatives: a niece, Angela Quincy, and a cousin, Richard Prescott, who claims to be entitled to Peachings Hall under Albert's will on the grounds that he lives only a mile away.

The residuary estate is worth approximately £1,250,000. Peachings Hall has been valued at £250,000.

Counsel is requested to advise as to the devolution of Peachings Hall and as to the effect of clause 5 of the will, and to draft an application to the court to determine such questions as may arise. (Instructing solicitors will draft affidavits.)

Jackie Russell v Watchdogs Ltd

Counsel is instructed on behalf of Mrs Jackie Russell, who is the owner of Falstaff Farm, Gadshill, Kent where she breeds and trains racing greyhounds.

At night the greyhounds are locked into the kennel compound, which consists of two kennels, each housing about 10 dogs, in a courtyard enclosed by a high wall with a single iron gate. Outside the courtyard is an exercise area entirely surrounded by a wire mesh fence. To keep watch, Mrs Russell hires a security firm, Watchdogs Limited ('Watchdogs'). By a contract made in January 1984 Watchdogs agreed, for a fixed charge (currently £32.60 per week), to provide a night patrol service whereby a patrolman would visit and check the kennel enclosure four times a night between the hours of 9 pm and 7 am. The contract contained the following clause:

> Under no circumstances shall the company be held responsible for any loss suffered by the customer through burglary, theft, fire, criminal damage or any other cause, except insofar as such loss is attributable to the negligence of the employees of the company acting within the course of their employment.

Throughout the period of the contract the regular patrolman has been Mr Harry Prince, whom Mrs Russell and her family have got to know quite well. However, on occasions (for example when prowlers have been seen, or the night before a major race meeting) Mrs Russell has felt that additional security is necessary and has telephoned Watchdogs who have provided an all-night watchman at a fixed fee of £45.40 per night. There is no mention of this service in the contract.

On 18 April 1988 Mr Prince reported to Mrs Russell that on two occasions the previous night he had seen prowlers near the perimeter fence who had run off when challenged. Mrs Russell asked him to be particularly vigilant the next night and immediately telephoned Watchdogs to ask for an all-night patrol that night, which they agreed. No payment in advance was requested and indeed nothing was said about money.

That night, Mrs Russell's daughter, Elizabeth, was in the Boar's Head Inn, which is 100 yards away from Falstaff Farm and saw Harry Prince drinking with a companion. He was there at 9.00 pm when she arrived and was still there at 11.30 pm when she left. Believing an all-night patrol had been arranged, she thought nothing of it. In fact no all-night patrolman turned up.

The next morning, 19 April, Mrs Russell found that raiders had broken into the kennels. Two greyhounds, Pistol and Poins, were missing and a third, Peto, was dead. A veterinary surgeon found that he had been strangled and put the time of death at around midnight. The police found evidence that two men had cut a hole in the wire fence, sawn through the padlock on the iron gate and picked the lock on the kennel door. All had been left open. The police estimate that it would have taken the raiders about one hour to get in.

Pistol has never been found and it appears that he was the raiders' target. Poins apparently escaped through the open fence and roamed the countryside for two days. He was shot dead by a local farmer when he attacked the farmer's sheep.

Pistol had just retired from racing and was now at stud. He was expected to earn around £10,000 a year over the next five years in stud fees. Poins and Peto were both successful dogs each of whom was expected to win races worth £5,000 in all in 1988 and again in 1989. They would then have retired. Poins would have gone to stud. The estimated value of the three dogs is: Pistol £20,000; Poins £17,500; Peto £8,000. Mrs Russell was deeply distressed at the loss of her three favourite dogs and suffered from depression for several months.

Instructing solicitors have received the following letter from Watchdogs:

Dear Sirs,

We must inform you that we have no record of any telephone conversation with your client on 18 April 1988 and we deny that any agreement to provide an all-night watchman service on that night was entered into. Mr Prince's log for that night shows that he made four visits, at 12.30, 2.30, 4.30 and 6.30 am. Your client's loss is plainly not attributable to any negligence on the part of our employees and we must accordingly deny any liability.

Yours etc

Mrs Russell on 2 July 1988 received a bill from Watchdogs containing the following items:

Night patrol service 1 April–30 June 1988	
12 weeks at £32.60	£391.20
All-night watchman service	
3 nights at £45.40	£136.20
	£527.40

Mrs Russell says she arranged for an all-night watchman on three occasions in the period covered by the bill: on 2 and 18 April and 31 May.

Counsel is requested to advise Mrs Russell as to liability and quantum and to draft a statement of claim.

7 Negotiation skills

David Cruickshank, Stephen Nathanson and Neville Carter

I NEGOTIATION SKILLS

David Cruickshank and Stephen Nathanson[1]

The half-day Negotiation Skills Activity Plan on pp 157 ff is an adaptation of a skills teaching exercise in a 10-week Professional Legal Training Course.* Negotiation is one of six major skills that are taught in the course and the teaching methodology here is representative of the methods used for other skills.** The curriculum design principles used for negotiation also reflect the principles used elsewhere in the course. Finally, the highly organised structure of the activities and the precise timing demonstrate the challenge faced by legal educators with a broad skills training and substantive law mandate.

Like all other skills in the course, negotiation is placed in a primary substantive context, which we call a 'file'.† We usually choose a personal injury in an auto accident as the context for negotiation.‡ In the materials which follow, a brief example of an office space negotiation has been selected to demonstrate. The choice of a file context depends upon whether: (1) it is a good vehicle for the skill; (2) it is a commonly occurring legal transaction in the early years of practice; and (3) there is a strong potential for the participants to integrate knowledge and skill as they learn. Furthermore, the file context must deliver up issues of professional responsibility in a realistic setting. These issues are not announced; they are buried in the discussions and exercises, awaiting discovery.

Negotiation takes $4\frac{1}{2}$ days of 39 instructional days available in the course. The organisational structure is as follows:

1 The authors acknowledge the permission of the Professional Legal Training Course, CLE Society of British Columbia, Canada, who made possible the creation and republication of these materials.

* The course is a post-graduate, pre-admission skills training course required by the Law Society of British Columbia for all articled students. The course is more fully described in David A Cruickshank 'Professional Legal Training in British Columbia' (1985) 3 Jo Prof Legal Ed 111.
** The other major skills taught are: advocacy, interviewing and counselling, writing, drafting and legal research.
† In Australian practical training courses, these are known as 'current matters'; others would see them as 'transactions'.
‡ In the outline that follows, not all negotiation exercises are in the personal injury field. In the early exercises, rather than opt for file 'purity', we attempt to run a short-preparation exercise that lays the skills foundation for the major exercise. That is why the example Activity Plan in this book deals with a more generic issue (rent for office space).

Day	*Activities*	*Resources*
1 *am*	○ substantive and procedural overview; ○ short answer test on readings; ○ introduce first negotiation exercise.	○ panel of three guest instructor experts on personal injury; ○ full-time instructors.
pm	○ negotiation exercise in pairs (no 1) on rent for office space* (objective: practice; negotiation strategies); ○ review and critique of videotape of lawyers demonstrating two different negotiation strategies.	○ full-time instructor (class of 16–20); ○ videotaped demonstration.
2 *am*	○ negotiation exercise in fours (two per side) (no 2) on a landlord-tenant dispute (objective: practice and observe specific tactics); ○ review outcomes of negotiations; feedback on strategy and tactics; ○ demonstrate stages of negotiations (videotape) and discuss.	○ full-time instructor; ○ videotape.
pm	major negotiation exercise in pairs (no 3) on auto accident case.	○ full-time instructor; ○ pre-assigned legal research on personal injury quantum cases.
3 *am &* *pm*	student pairs negotiate ($\frac{1}{2}$ hour of session must be on videotape).	○ videotaping cameras, recorders.
4 *am*	student pairs review videotape with skills guide and prepare negotiation journals.	○ video replay facilities.
pm	○ students review some peer tapes in class, compare results, discuss; ○ hand in negotiation journal (record of tactics, offers, settlement etc).	○ guest instructor expert; ○ full-time instructor; ○ video replay facilities.

Some of the curriculum design principles apparent here include:

○ depends on advance reading and research;
○ self-directed learning exercises to appeal to adults;
○ a building block approach from least complex to most complex;
○ integration of previously learned elements of skill (eg strategies) with new elements (eg stages) and substantive law;
○ regular feedback and analysis of progress at each stage of learning;
○ a detailed skill guide (checklist) used to track progress, assist in feedback.

* Plan in these materials

In most other skills this curriculum design pattern is followed by a skill test (eg videotaped interview performance, writing assignment). In negotiation, we have not yet developed a test that accommodates all negotiating styles while setting objective standards.

Finally, there are aspects of the teaching methods and the learning environment that are critical to the success of these Activity Plans. Those features are:

o skills teaching cycle of demonstration – practice – feedback;
o favourable instructor–student ratio (maximum, 1:20);
o minimum lecture content (3 hours in $4\frac{1}{2}$ days);
o peer critique and participation;
o effective use of videotaping;
o chronological, factual, and material realism in the design of the file;
o use of summary devices (student journal, results comparisons charts etc) to record and reflect on skills learned.

In conclusion, it must be said that negotiation is the most popular skill block in the Professional Legal Training Course. At the same time, it stirs up the most emotional responses and ethical concerns in the entire course. While we have learned a great deal about integrating negotiation skills and legal substance, our lesson plans have much to teach us. In our jurisdiction, there remains the challenge of learning how to 'unlearn' the adversary style of negotiation seen as the norm in the legal profession and develop a more principled, ethically sound model for beginning lawyers.*

---

* Our main skill reading to promote principled negotiation is Fisher and Ury *Getting to Yes* (New York, Penguin, 1983).

NEGOTIATION SKILLS ACTIVITY PLAN

TIME:

1 File

2 Objective(s)

(1) Given the background reading and a brief lecture, participants will be able to identify and describe negotiation strategies and the characteristics of certain negotiators.
(2) Participants will be able to identify the negotiating strategy of a partner in a role-played negotiation.
(3) Participants will be able to identify the characteristics and risks associated with each strategy in a negotiation.
(4) Participants will be able to respond to a partner's negotiation strategy in order to achieve a resolution of the dispute.

3 Preparation

(1) Read *Skills material*.
(2) Read *Negotiation outline* (p 166).
(3) Read summary of *Getting to Yes*.
(4) Optional reading: Fisher and Ury *Getting to Yes*.

4 Description of the activity

(1) There will be a brief introduction to negotiation.
(2) The participants will review their Confidential Instructions and prepare their negotiation.
(3) The participants will negotiate and at the end of the negotiation give each other feedback. A supervising instructor will assist.
(4) In giving feedback, consider the following:
   (a) Did your partner's strategy coincide with the strategy that you perceived?
   (b) Did your partner perceive his or her own strategy the same way that you did; or did it change during the course of the negotiation? If it did change, why did it change?
   (c) Identify what your partner lost or gained by use of a specific strategy. For example, did he/she risk breakdown by being too competitive or did he/she risk too expensive an outcome with a co-operative strategy?
   (d) Were any unilateral concessions made by your partner, and if so, what were the consequences?
   (e) Did your partner react emotionally to anything that you said and if he/she did was this 'real' emotion or merely a deliberate tactic?

(f) If your partner was competitive, did he/she create tension and mistrust between you?

(g) Did you use objective criteria in negotiating? (Did you put forward facts and figures in support of your argument and did you probe for facts and figures in your partner's position?)

(h) Did you invent any creative options for mutual gain?

(5) As you are doing the negotiation note down in writing specific language or behaviour that your partner used which you can point to as indicating a certain strategy or as being particularly effective or ineffective.

(6) The participants will discuss the outcome of the negotiation.

FROM HERE TO END OF PLAN FOR INSTRUCTORS ONLY

Instructor's preparation

As for students.

Resources

None.

Instruction

Timetable of instruction

1.30–2.00 pm	Overview of negotiation
2.00–2.15 pm	Preparation for negotiation
2.15–2.45 pm	Negotiation
2.45–3.00 pm	Feedback, recording of results, and summing up
3.00–3.15 pm	Coffee break

1.30–2.00 pm

I Overview of negotiation

(1) The instructor should introduce negotiation. (Paragraphs 2 to 4 of these notes are reproduced from the *Skills material.*

(2) The lawyer's duty to negotiate effectively   Why do so many lawyers not take more seriously their professional duty to negotiate effectively? All lawyers clearly have an ethical duty to serve the best interests of their clients, subject to rules of ethical conduct. Lawyers must identify the goals of their individual clients and set out to achieve them. For example, a typical plaintiff in a personal injury law suit wishes to recover as much money as possible, as quickly as possible, as cheaply as possible, and with the least emotional stress. Lawyers who fail to negotiate effectively for such clients have failed in their professional duty.

Effective negotiating, however, cannot always result in an agreement. Barristers who negotiate effectively but who do not settle an individual case can achieve much for their clients. They can learn a great deal about the other side's position, which will be potentially useful at trial. Lawyers who negotiate effectively can maximise the amount of information learned during the negotiation by effective questioning of other lawyers. Surely the professional duty to clients includes making effective efforts to learn as much about the position of others as is reasonably possible.

The professional duty of solicitors to negotiate effectively is an obvious one. For example, solicitors negotiating a contract must identify and set out to achieve the goals of their clients. A typical client wishes to achieve the most satisfactory result as quickly as possible, as cheaply as possible, and with as little emotional stress as possible. The most satisfactory result might not be limited to achieving the best result financially in the short term. Solicitors' clients will frequently want to establish a long-term effective relationship with other parties to the negotiation, as well as maintain a reputation for excellence and integrity in the community.

(3) Acquiring negotiation skills   Lawyers commonly accept that lawyering skills can be improved upon through education and practice. Though some lawyers will inevitably be superior to others in specific skill areas, lawyers commonly accept that they can improve their skills in such areas as legal writing, drafting, and advocacy. Some lawyers might not include the skill of effective negotiating in such a list, but increasingly lawyers and educators are becoming convinced that effective negotiating is a skill that can be learned and improved upon. Lawyers who make a serious effort to improve their negotiating skills are fulfilling their professional duty to serve effectively the needs of their clients.

(4) Negotiation strategies and tactics   Literature on negotiation commonly refers to two or three negotiation strategies. Those strategies are co-operative, competitive (also known as aggressive), and principled (also known as problem solving or rational). The readings in the skills material discuss all three. The most recently identified strategy is the strategy of principled negotiation discussed in Fisher and Ury's *Getting to Yes*. A section in the skill material discusses *Getting to Yes* in some detail.

Negotiators might deliberately or inadvertently adopt one of the three strategies, and might stick with that choice or shift from one to another over a particular negotiation. Fisher and Ury recommend using the principled negotiation strategy at all times.

The literature also discusses negotiation tactics (also known as 'techniques'). Regardless of the particular strategy which a lawyer adopts, tactics are also being employed. For example, the competitive negotiator might employ the tactics of anger, initial high demand, threats or delays.

Whether or not individual lawyers deliberately employ such tactics, learning about them is useful. In order to negotiate effectively, it is useful to identify the strategy and tactics being used by other lawyers. In that way, you are able more effectively to deal with other negotiators. Learning to identify what other negotiators are attempting to do is an important part of fulfilling one's ethical duty to negotiate effectively on behalf of clients.

(5)   Today we will take a brief look at three commonly identified negotiation strategies. We will discuss tactics (or techniques) in greater detail tomorrow.

(6) Characteristics of the Aggressive (Competitive) Negotiation Strategy:

(a) Aggressives move psychologically *against* their opponents; they use:

    (i) intimidation (demoralise, browbeat, perturb);
    (ii) threats (intent to hurt or injure);
    (iii) superiority (every kind, in every way);
    (iv) blame (problems are caused by client and opponent).

(b) Under the 'smokescreen' of the attack aggressives follow a four-fold strategy:

    (i) make extreme demands;
    (ii) make very few concessions;
    (iii) if concessions must be made, make very small ones;
    (iv) create 'false issues'.

(c) Dangers or risks of the aggressive approach:

    (i) creates misunderstanding between the two sides – agreement will take longer and consume more resources;
    (ii) increases the number of failures – trial rate is more than double, for example;
    (iii) raises strong likelihood of retaliation;
    (iv) when used as substitute for preparation, aggressive strategy yields low outcomes;
    (v) in repeated encounters, it is less profitable than a co-operative strategy – see Robert Axelrod *The Evolution of Co-operation* (Basic Books, 1984).

(d) Advantages:

    (i) it avoids the risk of exploitation.

(7) Characteristics of the Co-operation Negotiation Strategy:

(a) Co-operatives move psychologically *toward* their opponents:

    (i) establish common ground;
    (ii) emphasise shared values;
    (iii) are trustworthy (fair, objective, reasonable).

(b) Co-operatives establish credibility and good faith by:

    (i) making unilateral concessions;
    (ii) seeking highest joint outcome (both sides better off).

(c) Dangers or risks of the co-operative approach:

    (i) risk of manipulation and exploitation;

    Note: risk stems from an unexamined and unarticulated idea among co-operatives:

    The Co-operative Assumption

    (1) if I am fair and trustworthy, and
    (2) if I make unilateral concessions
    (3) then the other side will feel an irresistible moral obligation to reciprocate.

(ii) risk of righteous indignation when the opponent doesn't reciprocate (ie against most aggressives).

(d) Benefits of the co-operative approach:

(i) in repeat situations, a savvy co-operative strategy yields a higher individual profit than an aggressive strategy;

(ii) in virtually all situations, a savvy co-operative strategy yields higher *joint* benefits than an aggressive approach.

(8) Characteristics of the Principled (Problem Solving) Strategy This method is discussed in *Getting to Yes* (available at the reception desk).

o People find themselves in a dilemma. They see two ways to negotiate: co-operative or aggressive (soft or hard). Some negotiations fall between hard and soft, but each involves an attempted trade-off between getting what you want and getting along with people.

o There is a third way to negotiate. The method of *principled negotiation* is to decide issues on their merits rather than through a haggling process focused on what each side says it will and won't do. It suggests that you look for mutual gains wherever possible, and that where your interests conflict, you should insist that the result be based on some fair standards independent of the will of either side. The method of principled negotiation focuses on the merits. It employs no tricks and no posturing. Principled negotiation shows you how to obtain what you are entitled to and still be decent. It enables you to be fair while protecting you against those who would take advantage of your fairness.

o Every negotiation is different, but the basic elements do not change. Principled negotiation can be used whether there is one issue or several, two parties or many. The method applies whether the other side is more experienced or less, a hard bargainer or a friendly one. Principled negotiation is an all-purpose strategy. Unlike other strategies, if the other side learns this one, it does not become more difficult to use; it becomes easier.

Some concrete examples of the principled negotiation strategy are:

(a) Do not negotiate on positions; rather focus on the needs or interests of both parties.

Example
Generally, a position is likely to be concrete (eg my client wants $12,000.00); the interest underlying the position may well be unexpressed, intangible or maybe even inconsistent (eg I want $12,000.00 to pay for my doctor's bills or I want $12,000.00 because I have suffered enough and want some compensation for it, or I want $12,000.00 as vindication). Focusing on the needs or interests of both parties rather than the positions of the parties leads the negotiators to ask *why* the claims are being made and how the parties' needs can be satisfied.

(b) Invent creative options for mutual gain.

Example
If money is at issue in a dispute, there may be a creative option other than the payment of money to resolve the dispute. Inventing creative options is one of the natural results of focusing on the needs or interests of both parties. If we know that a claimant wants $12,000.00 for damaged prop-

erty and we know the reason why, we can then attempt to meet his/her needs and reduce our exposure (eg instead of paying money we might agree to repair the property which may be less expensive).

These three strategies are not mutually exclusive. A person may follow one strategy and move to another. A person may incorporate some of the aspects of one strategy in another. Certainly the style of negotiation suggested by *Getting to Yes* – principled negotiation – is consistent with both the co-operative and the competitive strategies.

(9)   Students are not being asked deliberately to choose a strategy. Most lawyers do not deliberately choose a strategy. Whatever your strategy, you must be effective with it, and therefore should study and refine it.

(10)   The instructor should encourage students to practise the principled negotiation strategy, and to decide individually whether it is more effective than traditional strategies.

(11)   Emphasise the following skills, which we have dealt with in other contexts and which are important in negotiation:

o   *Organising information* – preparation is absolutely essential to effective negotiation. Otherwise, there is little chance of success, and risk of being exploited.

o   *Speaking effectively* – your adversary in a negotiation is not the judge. However, he or she will often place him/herself in the shoes of a judge. Part of your job is to persuade him/her by speaking effectively. Though he/she may disagree with much of what you say, well articulated persuasion will usually sink in.

o   *Questioning* – questioning is a crucial skill in effective negotiation. There are many questions which are asked in the course of a negotiation which are 'blocked'. That is to say someone may ask you a question which you do not want to answer and you may answer it with a question or answer it with an answer to another question, or simply say that you are not answering it – thus blocking the question. It is important to phrase your questions very carefully and potentially to elicit valuable information and to overcome blocking techniques. Even if your question is blocked, it still makes your adversary realise you are on to something important. It will make you realise the same thing.

o   *Identifying and evaluating relevant facts and legal issues* – the book *Getting to Yes* stresses the need to develop *objective criteria* in negotiation. This involves both putting forward, and probing for, objective criteria in support of your and your opponent's side of the issue. (See pp 88–98 of *Getting to Yes*.) Ensure that you have factual and legal support for your claims and probe for factual and legal support in your adversary's claims. What cases does he/she have in support of his/her claim? Read the language of the cases carefully. Don't rely on his/her version of them. What facts are there in support of his/her claim? What evidence does he/she have in support of it? Can such evidence be produced – documents, witnesses, etc?

In *Getting to Yes* the use of objective criteria is called 'principled' negotiation as opposed to positional bargaining which seeks to stand on a fixed (usually quantified) position and work around it.

(12) Tell the students that over the next several days they will be discussing negotiation, conducting negotiations and viewing the negotiation process from basically three different angles:

(a) from the point of view of overall *strategy*;
(b) from the point of view of tactics which are the tools which implement or further an overall strategy;
(c) from the point of view of the stages of the negotiation process.

Starting this afternoon in these two activities we will define strategies, conduct a negotiation and see a video – all the while focusing on evaluating strategies for ourselves and identifying them in others.

Tomorrow morning there will be a discussion of negotiation tactics and students will conduct a team negotiation.

Tomorrow morning after the negotiation we will view a personal injury video, for the purposes of identifying the stages in the negotiation process, as well as effective strategies and tactics.

This is the major personal injury negotiation exercise which continues for two and a half days.

2.00–2.15 pm

II Preparation for negotiation

2.15–2.45 pm

III Negotiation

2.45–3.00 pm

IV Feedback – recording of results and summing up

Students should give feedback to each other as set out in the Description of Activity at paragraph E. The instructor should circulate and draw lessons from the negotiations that he/she can share with the class as a whole.

With this particular negotiation Shelly Filbert should have questioned Bobby Leonard carefully to obtain the information that Bobby Leonard was in fact quitting the practice of law and had to leave the province by 1 June YR0.

Bobby Leonard might have questioned Shelly Filbert effectively by finding out that Shelly Filbert's lease was expiring on 1 July YR0.

If Shelly Filbert was too competitive he/she might have jeopardised his/her chances of taking over part of Bobby Leonard's practice; on the other hand, Bobby Leonard might have rewarded hard bargaining.

Ask the students about the effectiveness of their particular strategy. (This problem was designed to encourage principled negotiation.) Emphasise the importance of effective questioning.

Notes

None.

Confidential instructions for Shelly Filbert

You are Shelly Filbert, a young sole practitioner in a small law office near Broadway and Oak. Your practice is just beginning to grow and prospects are very good. Your practice consists primarily of family, conveyancing, criminal and lately, because of contacts you've made with several physicians who lease offices in the same building as you, plaintiff's personal injury work. As a result of several exceptionally impressive trial successes, you are quickly developing a reputation as a skilful personal injury lawyer.

You own all your office equipment, which includes a word processor, two terminals, office furniture, filing cabinets, etc. Your lease is on a five year term with an option to renew but it is about to expire. Right now you are paying a flat rate of $700.00 per month – a phenomenally low rate – but because of the demand for office space in your area, your landlord, Joe Brown, has indicated that he is about to raise it substantially. You've been negotiating with him over the last several weeks and he has said that he must charge you what the market will bear, especially because he has had many inquiries about your space and besides, he has been quick to emphasise, he has greatly undercharged you for the last several years. His last offer, which you believe to be a firm one was $1,500.00 per month plus maintenance, utilities and taxes, which will work out to roughly $1,750.00 per month. You think this is far too much and are not prepared to pay it. He has told you that if you don't take up the option to renew he is going to have to ask you to leave. That option must be exercised, according to the terms of the lease, in five days.

It is now 10 May YR0 and your lease expires 1 July YR0. You have been frantically looking around for alternative office space but have found nothing to suit your budget. Given your present file load, your projected revenues, and the fact that you have a practice loan with the bank of $30,000.00 and a line of credit which, though it now sits at $15,000.00 runs out at $25,000.00, you can't really afford to pay more than $1,100.00 a month, all inclusive. Besides, you've estimated your moving expenses including phone and office equipment installation will be approximately $6,500.00.

You've just heard that a lawyer named Bobby Leonard, a downtown sole practitioner, has been advertising to sublet his/her premises. You have heard via the grapevine that he/she is a middle-aged practitioner with a varied litigation practice which includes, family, commercial and personal injury litigation. You have also heard from various sources that Bobby is moving out of his/her office to relocate and that under the terms of his/her lease he/she may sublet to any practising lawyer without the consent of the lessor. You like the idea of moving downtown.

Bobby's office is in a prestigious location right near the courthouse and you have just seen the interior which you are very impressed with. You have not yet met Bobby, but his/her secretary did show you around his/her office. The leasehold improvements are much more appealing than your own; also, the office's proximity to the courthouse and the land title office would greatly enhance your efficiency. If you could get his/her premises, you could justify a rent of $1,300.00 or perhaps even $1,400.00 a month. $1,400.00 would be stretching it, but given the downtown location you think that you could greatly improve your practice. You know that generally there is quite a large surplus of downtown office space so you are hopeful of clinching a good deal, preferably on a long-term basis. You are just about to meet Bobby Leonard to negotiate a sub-lease with him/her. You have heard that Bobby Leonard is a very busy lawyer and a fair-minded person. According to some people Bobby does a great deal of personal injury work and some major claims in that area. He/she has been known to refer his/her smaller claims to other lawyers because he/she has been overloaded. You would like to make a favourable impression on him/her so that he/she might consider you a candidate for referrals. In spite of this concern, however, your overriding goal is to negotiate the lowest possible rent for youself.

Make up any other facts, but these facts must be absolutely consistent with the facts in these instructions.

Before you start negotiating, select a negotiation strategy.

Confidential instructions for Bobby Leonard

You are a middle-aged sole practitioner named Bobby Leonard. Your practice consists entirely of litigation matters, namely commercial, family and major personal injury litigation. You are presently situated in a fine office with tasteful leasehold improvements in a very convenient location in the down-town area right near the courthouse and land titles office. Your rent, inclusive of parking, utilities, maintenance and taxes is $1,600.00 per month and you have three years left on a five year lease. Your rent will stay at about $1,600.00 per month until the expiry of that lease. It is now 10 May YR0 and there are 36 months remaining (June YR0 to May YR+3). You have just recently decided to leave the practice of law because you have been offered an excellent job in Calgary. You have just been hired as counsel for a large oil company and the salary and benefits are excellent. The job commences 1 June YR0 and you have to be there on that date. Your family, (your spouse and two teenage children) have already moved there. For the last three weeks you have been hastily winding up your practice. You've succeeded in selling all your office equipment and you've found jobs for your two secretaries. At first, when you found out you had the job in Calgary, you quietly spread the word that your practice was for sale but you gave up trying to sell it when you discovered you couldn't really find a suitable buyer. You're now more interested in ensuring that your clients are well served by whoever takes over your files. Accordingly, you have been winding up your practice by referring files to trusted colleagues and you have been very careful about your choices so that your clients will be left in the hands of competent counsel. Unfortunately, you have not been able to find a sub-lessee who is prepared to pay a reasonable rent for the premises. Your lease allows you to sublet to any practising lawyer without the consent of the lessor. The problem in finding a sub-lessee is that there is a surplus of office space downtown and your lease is not that attractive. Similar space in the area is renting for somewhat less than $1,600.00 a month, though leasehold improvements are generally not as luxurious as yours. The terms of your present lease allow you or the sub-lessee to extend the lease after expiry but the terms are open and fully negotiable. You expect that if business in three years is generally as poor as it is now, there is even a possibility that the rent may decline, as the landlord is anxious to fill up your building which is still not fully rented.

You've had one offer for the space from a lawyer named Albert Haywood, an immigration 'specialist' who, in your opinion, tried to take advantage of the situation by offering the paltry sum of $1,000.00 a month for the sub-lease. That offer is still open but you will only take it as a last resort, since it will cost you $600.00 a month for the next three years. You can afford this but it would make quite an uncomfortable dent in your salary.

You're about to meet Shelly Filbert, a young lawyer who your secretary has told you about. He/she came into your office the other day when you weren't there to look at the space and expressed interest. You have heard through the grapevine that Shelly is an up-and-coming competent trial lawyer who has recently made a reputation for himself/herself as a plaintiff's personal injury litigator. As it turns out, you still have about 20 files left and they are mainly plaintiff's personal injury work and some family cases. You would be prepared to refer Shelly the remainder of your practice if the conditions were right. Potential gross billings on those files are anywhere between $15,000.00 and $40,000.00 and you estimate your own work-in-progress on those files to be anywhere from $5,000.00 to $15,000.00 depending on the outcomes. You are not interested in 'selling' the remainder of your practice. However, with many but *not all* of the already 'referred' files you have agreed with new lawyers to credit you with work-in-progress when they get paid. Sometimes, depending on the size of the work-in-progress, and the likelihood of success on the file, you have waived your claim to payment.

Negotiation outline ©

When planning for negotiation you may wish to consider the following:

A Preparation

(1) Identify relevant facts.
(2) Identify relevant legal issues.
(3) Conduct legal research.
(4) Identify client's goals and interests, and prioritise.
(5) Identify other party's goals and interests and prioritise.
(6) Identify strengths and weaknesses of client's position.
(7) Identify strengths and weaknesses of other party's position.
(8) Identify possible concessions.
(9) Consider alternative settlement options.
(10) Consider alternatives available if negotiation fails.
(11) Develop agenda.
(12) Plan strategy (eg problem solving, aggressive, co-operative).
(13) Plan tactics (eg timing of offers, limited authority, silence, good guy –
     bad guy, split the difference, threats and promises, take it or leave it etc).

B The negotiation

(1) Obtain information through questioning.
(2) Separate the people from the problem:

   (a) listen to other party;
   (b) confirm understanding of other party's position;
   (c) allow other party to let off steam.

(3) Focus on interests not positions:

   (a) describe problem in terms of impact on client;
   (b) encourage other party to explain client's interests and goals;
   (c) explain own client's interests and goals;
   (d) identify shared interests and goals;
   (e) focus on present and future concerns not past grievances.

(4) Ascertain scope of other party's authority.
(5) Develop and discuss alternative settlement options.
(6) Make offers that are justified by objective criteria.
(7) Insist on and probe for objective criteria based on law, precedents, facts
     evidence.
(8) Be open to reason, closed to threats.
(9) Make a note of agreements and concessions as they occur.

NAME OF STUDENT FILLING THIS OUT.......................................
NAME OF OBSERVED STUDENT ....

Negotiation feedback sheet

A   Strategy: What was his/her strategy? Did it change?

....

....

B   Tactics and counter-tactics: (eg pattern of offers, large demand, false demand, threats, promises, silence, split the difference, effective questions, etc). List tactics and give particulars of how your opponent used them and whether they were effective or ineffective.

....

....

C   Characteristics: (eg trustworthy, argumentative, fair, dominating, obliging, bluffs, intolerant, hostile, willing to stretch the facts, etc). List the negotiator's characteristics and give particulars of what he/she did or how he/she behaved to evidence these characteristics.

....

....

D   What valuable information did your opponent reveal?

   (1) Through your questioning?

....

....

   (2) In the absence of questioning?

....

....

E   Did your opponent give you any non-verbal signals which assisted you? Give particulars.

....

....

F   Did your opponent effectively evaluate:
   (1) The facts?...
   (2) The legal issues? ....

G   Did your opponent allow your manner of presentation to interfere with the substance of the negotiation? Give particulars.

....

....

H   Comment on the negotiator's identification and handling of ethical or professional responsibility issues.

....

....

I Other comments (use additional pages if necessary).

....

....

———————

Negotiation journal

Table of contents

A Analysis

(1) Organise information received.
(2) Identify and evaluate relevant facts (including those which are confidential).
(3) Identify and evaluate legal issues as applied to this set of facts. (Do legal research, if necessary, and evaluate it.)
(4) Classify needs – yours and theirs (lawyer and client).

B Planning

(1) State your negotiation objectives (including range of acceptable settlements and non-negotiable issues).
(2) State anticipated negotiation objectives of other party.
(3) Select negotiation strategy to achieve your negotiation objectives.
(4) Anticipate your own strategy changes and reasons for changes.
(5) State characteristics you expect to demonstrate in pursuit of that strategy.
(6) State tactics to be used in furtherance of selected strategy.
(7) Set down agenda:

  (a) your position on each item;
  (b) estimate of your opponent's position.

C Discussion

(1) Preliminaries/orientation and positioning:

  (a) state summary of rapport and relationship seen by you in opening five minutes;
  (b) summarise each side's initial position on each issue.

(2) Discussion/argumentation:

  (a) outline 'most favourable case' you see on the other side;
  (b) list position changes by both sides on each issue;
  (c) summarise early concessions;

(3) Emergence and crisis:

  (a) list further position changes by both sides on each issue;
  (b) summarise concessions or refusals to consider on each issue;
  (c) describe changes in strategy used by each side (if any);

(d) list tactics actually used and tactics observed on the other side (also list counter-tactics);

(e) identify 'crisis points' in each issue.

(4) Agreement or final break-down:

(a) set out in point form the precise terms of the agreement or reasons for breakdown;

(b) write a self-evaluation of your strategy and tactics. Analyse your strengths and weaknesses in the negotiation, making specific reference to what you observed in your performance on your videotape and in what your opponent said in his/her Feedback Sheet. Be specific. For example, analyse why your strategy and/or tactics changed; why your anticipated agenda changed; whether you advanced your case or probed your opponent's case using objective criteria; etc.

Note:

Parts A and B of this journal must be completed before the negotiation and Part C, after the negotiation. Except for the last section (Part C4b) this journal may be completed in comprehensible note form.

The journal must be handed in to your instructor and the Feedback Sheet to your opponent.

The journal will be assessed for the logic and cogency of your preparation and demonstration of what you observed and learned about the negotiation process in this exercise.

Negotiation Grid

Group No.	A	B	C	D	E	F	G	H	I	J	K	L(p)	L(d)	M	N
1															
2															
3															
4															
5															
6															
7															
8															
9															
10															

KEY

A Settled at what amount?
B Did not settle – how far apart?
C Plaintiff's selected strategy.
D Defendant's perception of plaintiff's strategy.
E Plaintiff's selected tactics.
F Defendant's perception of plaintiff's tactics.
G Defendant's selected strategy.
H Plaintiff's perception of defendant's strategy.
I Defendant's selected tactics.
J Plaintiff's perception of defendant's tactics.
K Time spent negotiating.
L(p) Was valuable information revealed by plaintiff through questioning?
L(d) Was valuable information revealed by defendant through questioning?
M Did plaintiff do anything ethically questionable?
N Did defendant do anything ethically questionable?

II NEGOTIATION SKILLS

Neville Carter ©

The materials which follow are extracts from student and instructor Activity Plans from the thirteen week pre-admission skills course conducted in New Zealand for all law graduates seeking admission to practice as barristers and solicitors.

Negotiation skills are taught and practised during two seminars in the course, each of four days duration. Approximately 40 hours of instruction is devoted to this skill area, which represents about one eighth of all instruction in the 61-day programme.

The course itself comprises 16 skills seminars. Objectives and assessment criteria for each seminar are primarily referenced to the performance of skills as distinct from the acquisition of information in procedural or substantive law areas. At the same time all skills are taught and practised in the context of typical New Zealand law office transactions. In the later stages of instruction, the fact situations on which role plays and other activities are based derive from specimen law office files and involve students in comprehensive analysis of relevant legal principles and procedures.

There are eight primary skills taught in the course. Each skill is taught in the context of a variety of different legal transactions but becomes the major vehicle for instruction in one particular transaction:

Skill	*Primary transactional focus*
Interviewing	Debt recovery
Fact analysis	(a) District court civil and criminal practice
	(b) Conveyancing
Advising	Company, trusts, partnership
Negotiation	Sale and purchase of business
Writing and drafting	(a) High court pleading and procedure
	(b) Commercial leases, company incorporation
	(c) Will drafting
	(d) Probate, securities
	(e) *Preparation for assessment* based on fact patterns involving commercial clients setting up new business vehicles

These programmes demonstrate the binocular approach taken by course designers to skills training on the one hand and the teaching of relevant

© The author acknowledges the permission of the Institute of Professional Legal Studies of New Zealand who made possible the creation and republication of these materials.

practice and procedure on the other. The priority accorded to the skills aspect is reflected in Assessment Guides which prescribe a series of strategies, organisational methods, questioning skills, speaking skills and other behaviours which the student must demonstrate in order to pass assessments. At the same time there is a high degree of integration of elements of skills and substantive law, particularly at the final assessment stage.

All course materials have been systematically designed to ensure commonality of delivery of instruction in each of the four centres in which the course is conducted. Course activities maximise student participation and peer feedback and lecture content is kept to a minimum.

NEGOTIATING SEMINAR 1

Programme

Creative legal problem solving   Foreclosure

Mediation   Family law

Advocacy   District court civil and
                                                   general procedure

The Negotiation programme involves the following activities:

NEGOTIATION

DAY 1			*Activity*
am	(a)	**Discussion**	definitions and goals of negotiation
	(b)	**Short role plays**	identification of problems in the negotiation process
	(c)	**Negotiation game**	personal factors important in negotiation – competitive approaches, trust, mutual gain, ethics
	(d)	**Videotape exercise**	strategies and tactics 1
pm	(e)	**Role plays**	(one on one) based on commercial law fact patterns

DAY 2			
am	(a)	**Videotape demonstration**	strategies and tactics 2
	(b)	**Discussion**	the preparation stage, the Need Theory, negotiation journals
pm	(c)	**Role plays**	based on family law fact pattern

DAY 3			
am	(a)	**Negotiation game**	creating options for mutual gain
	(b)	**Preparation for team negotiations**	based on real estate specimen law office files
pm	(c)	**Discussion with guest instructor**	covering relevant real estate practice and procedure

DAY 4			
am	(a)	**Completion of negotiation journals**	for real estate negotiations

pm	(b)	**Real estate negotiation role plays and discussion**	

DAY 5

| *am* | (a) | **Panel discussion** | ethical issues in commercial conveyancing negotiations |
| *pm* | (b) | **Preparation for commercial negotiation** | based on Sales of Goods Act fact patterns |

DAY 6

am	(a)	**Commercial negotiation role plays and discussion**	
pm	(b)	**Guest instructor workshop**	based on sale and purchase of commercial business – practice and procedure
	(c)	**Preparation for assessment**	based on specimen files for sale and purchase of business

DAYS 7, 8

am, pm	**Assessments (as allocated)**	conducted in pairs and videotaped for student self evaluation and as a resource for instructors completing assessments

Interviewing skills are taught and practised in two three-day seminars involving about one sixth of total instruction time. The programme is structured as follows:

INTERVIEWING

DAY 1			*Activity*
am	(a)	**Discussion**	definitions and goals of interviewing
	(b)	**Short role plays**	identification of problems in the interviewing process
	(c)	**Discussion**	listening and observing skills
	(d)	**Group game exercise**	based on the principles of attending behaviour
	(e)	**Lawyer/client role plays**	providing practice in listening and observing skills
pm	(f)	**Discussion**	communication – inhibitors and facilitators
	(g)	**Communication game**	focused on non-verbal communication
	(h)	**Video exercise**	based on a demonstration of a lawyer/client interview

DAY 2

am	(a)	**Videotape exercise and discussion**	covering the technique of active listening
	(b)	**Role plays**	based on a contested will
	(c)	**Discussion and video**	questioning skills
pm	(d)	**Discussion**	introduction to Three Stage Model
	(e)	**Videotape demonstration**	Three Stage Model
	(f)	**Discussion**	advantages and disadvantages of structured interview models

DAY 3

am	(a)	**Role plays**	based on a town planning fact pattern
	(b)	**Discussion**	dealing with client reluctance
	(c)	**Discussion**	special problems of client reluctance and responses in criminal matters
am, pm	(d)	**Role plays**	based on criminal fact patterns
	(e)	**Discussion and evaluation of role plays**	

DAY 4

	(a)	**Guest instructor workshop**	focused on law and procedure to debt recovery work
	(b)	**Students prepare for assessments**	based on debt recovery fact patterns

DAYS 5, 6

	Assessments	(as allocated) half hour duration involving visitors in the role of clients and videotaping of performances for student self-assessment, and as a resource to instructors on assessment.

As with interviewing, counselling skills are taught and practised in two three-day seminars covering the following activities:

COUNSELLING

DAY 1			*Activity*
am	(a)	**Discussion**	definitions and goals of counselling
	(b)	**Short role plays**	identification of problems in the counselling process
	(c)	**Discussion**	introduction to the Counselling Model
	(d)	**Videotape exercise**	advantages and disadvantages of the Counselling Model
pm	(e)	**Discussion**	the preparation stage
	(f)	**Role plays**	based on a debt recovery fact pattern

DAY 2			
am	(a)	**Role plays**	based on an action under motor vehicle dealers legislation
pm	(b)	**Videotape exercise**	ethical considerations in counselling

DAY 3			
am	(a)	**Preparation for role plays**	based on a family law fact pattern and assisted by guest instructor
	(b)	**Role plays**	
pm	(c)	**Role plays (cont'd)**	
	(d)	**Discussion and evaluation of role plays**	

DAY 4			
am	(a)	**Discussion**	counselling difficult clients
	(b)	**Counselling game**	helping clients reach difficult decision
	(c)	**Role plays**	based on a criminal fact pattern
pm	(d)	**Guest instructor workshop**	law and practice – selection of business vehicles

DAYS 5, 6		
	Assessments	(as allocated) half hour duration involving visitors in the role of clients and videotaping of performances for student self assessment and as a resource to instructors on assessment.

NEGOTIATION SEMINAR 1*

Exercise 1

TIME: 1 hour 15 minutes

1 Skill

Negotiation 1.

2 Topic

Definition, goals, problems.

3 Objectives

By the end of the activity, you will:

(a) be able to define the term negotiation;
(b) be able to state the major goal of negotiation; and
(c) be able to describe at least ten major problems in achieving the goal of
      negotiation.

4 Preparation

(a) Read skills materials.

5 Description of activity

Though the use of short lawyer–lawyer negotiation role plays and through
feedback on these experiences, we will provide an introduction to the negotiation process for lawyers. The focus will be on the major goals of negotiation
and the major problems typically encountered by the new lawyer in the
negotiation process.

6 Notes

None.

Instructor material

7 Instructor preparation

(a) Same as for students.
(b) Handout – *Problems in the negotiation process* (p 182).

---

* The materials on pp 178–215 were devised and prepared by Professor Pirie, Institute of
  Professional Legal Studies of New Zealand.

8 Resources

(a) Handout – Negotiation exercise 1 – facts (p 181); Confidential instructions for Sally Swansong's lawyer (p 182); Confidential instructions for Lyric Opera's lawyer.
(b) Handout – *Problems in the negotiation process* (p 182).

9 Instruction

Timetable

9.30–9.45	Welcome students to the Negotiation 1 Seminar. Objectives for the entire negotiation seminar are pointed out. Objectives for this activity are explained.
9.45–10.00	The definition and goals of negotiation.
10.00–10.30	Problems for the lawyer in the negotiation process.
10.30–10.45	Coffee break.

9.30–9.45

(1) This is the beginning of the negotiation seminar. Tell the students that the next five days will be devoted to negotiation skills for the lawyer. The students will also do more advanced work in negotiation skills in Week 9 in Negotiation Seminar 2.
(2) Point out briefly to students that at the end of the five day seminar, they can expect to be able to perform *all* the Negotiation Seminar 1 objectives.
(3) Explain briefly the specific objectives for this activity. Explain that understanding the definition, goals and problems of legal negotiation is essential before going on to learn negotiation skills.

9.45–10.00

(1) Refer the students to the definitions of negotiation.
(2) From these definitions, point out to the students that the major goal of negotiation is to 'resolve, settle or manage matters in conflict'. More simply the goal is 'an agreement'.
(3) Stress to the students the extreme importance of negotiation skills to lawyers. Former Chief Justice Burger says that

> of all the skills needed for the practising lawyer, skill in negotiation must rank very high.

(4) Tell the students that because clients come to lawyers with problems or conflicts, negotiation skills that are focused on settling matters or getting an agreement are very important.
(5) Take a few minutes to get the students to identify particular areas of practice or examples where lawyers specifically use negotiation skills. Try to generate as wide a list as possible to emphasise the pervasiveness of negotiation in law practice. You may add to this list from your own experience.

10.00–10.30

(1) Tell the students that just as with other skills areas, negotiation is a complex process to master.
(2) In order to better appreciate problems lawyers are likely to encounter when negotiating, tell the students that you would like them to participate in a short negotiation role play involving two lawyers.
(3) Divide the students into pairs (or apples if you wish). Give each student a copy of Negotiation exercise 1 – Facts. For each pair, give one student – Confidential instructions for Sally Swansong's lawyer and the other student – Confidential instructions for Lyric Opera's lawyer.
(4) Tell the students that they will have *2 minutes* to prepare quickly for the negotiation and *8 minutes* to conduct the negotiation. The negotiation will end after *8 minutes* whether agreement is reached or not. After the negotiation, tell the students you would like to identify major problems they see existing for lawyers in the negotiation process.
(5) Give the students just *2 minutes to prepare*. Conduct the negotiations for eight minutes. Give students a one or two minute warning that the negotiation will end.
(6) Record agreements that were reached on the blackboard. Note the range of agreements.
(7) Tell the students that the purpose of the role play was not so much to assess how well each lawyer negotiated but rather to identify problems in the negotiation process.
(8) From the experience in the role play, practical experience in law firms or general knowledge, ask the students to identify the major problems that new lawyers might encounter when negotiating on behalf of a client.
(9) Record these problems on the blackboard. Do not take time to evaluate the problems or provide solutions. Try to ensure that everyone understands the nature of the problem being described.
(10) You may want to add to the list by describing other problems you are familiar with from your experience. Thank the students for their contribution and advise them that during the negotiation seminars they will be developing skills and acquiring knowledge to assist them in overcoming these major negotiation problems.
(11) Hand out the sheet entitled *Problems in the negotiation process* (p 182). Tell the students they should add to this list any additional problems they encounter throughout both the first and second negotiation seminars.

10.30–10.45

Coffee break.

10 Notes

None.

NEGOTIATION SEMINAR 1

Negotiation exercise 1

Facts

Sally Swansong, an aging soprano, has asked the Lyric Opera if she may sing the role of Manon Lescaut in the forthcoming production of that opera. Selection of the performer for that role has not as yet been announced, although the names of the performers for all the other roles were announced several weeks ago. The role is generally acknowledged to be a prize role for a young soprano, but Sally's voice is still very good, especially for her age, and she knows the part well, having sung it hundreds of times. Last year the soprano who sang the role for the Lyric was paid $25,000 for her performance.

NEGOTIATION SEMINAR 1

Negotiation exercise 1

Confidential instructions for the Lyric's lawyer

The Lyric hasn't announced the performer for the role of Manon because the soprano they had expected to sing the role has developed a benign throat tumour which will need surgery prior to the performance date. Every other good soprano contacted by the Lyric has been unavailable on the date of the performance. The Lyric is desperate. Even though Sally Swansong is old for the role, her voice sounds young and with proper make-up she could be outstanding in the part. Because of the time pressures, the management has authorised you to offer $15,000 more than the $30,000 which was to be paid to the sick soprano originally scheduled for the role. The show must go on and not to get Sally would result in its cancellation and a loss of $400,000 to the Lyric.

NEGOTIATION SEMINAR 1

Negotiation exercise 1

Confidential instructions for Sally's lawyer

Sally hasn't been able to get a good role in two years. If she can get this part it will give her a good chance at an important part in a forthcoming TV Special on the Opera. The TV Special would pay her $45,000 and lead to many other singing engagements. Accordingly she would gladly sing Manon for nothing, but because of professional pride, she would like you to get as much for her as possible.

Problems in the negotiation process

The following is a list of some of the problems commonly encountered by lawyers when involved in legal negotiations:

o is not fully prepared about facts, law, other negotiator;
o is confused about how to start, end a negotiation;
o doesn't know, what, if any, information to disclose;
o is too trusting of the other lawyer;
o makes too many concessions in the negotiation;
o makes agreements without clear client instructions;
o feels exploited;
o gets angry or reacts very emotionally in the negotiation and causes a breakdown;
o seems to just 'argue' and get nowhere;
o doesn't know how to break off or end negotiations;
o provides misleading information or 'lies' to the other lawyer;
o makes too high or too low an opening offer;
o knows that the client could have gotten a 'better' deal;
o finds own ego is preventing agreement from being reached;
o fails to accurately record any agreement;
o fails to listen or poor listening;
o underestimates the other side or overestimates own case.

Definitions of negotiation

The following are some common definitions of negotiation. They should help in understanding the negotiation process.

Negotiation

o To confer with another for the purpose of arranging some matters by mutual agreement; to discuss a matter with a view to settlement or compromise (*Shorter Oxford English Dictionary*, 1977).
o Any form of verbal communication, direct or indirect, whereby parties to a conflict of interest discuss, without resort to arbitration or other judicial processes, the form of any joint action which they might take to manage a dispute between them (Morley and Stephenson *The Social Psychology of Bargaining*, 1977).
o Communication for the purpose of persuasion (Goldberg, Green and Sander *Dispute Resolution*, 1985).
o Whenever people exchange ideas with the intention of changing relationships, whenever they confer for agreement, they are negotiating (Nierenberg *Fundamentals of Negotiating*, 1968).
o A problem-solving process in which two or more people voluntarily discuss their differences and attempt to reach a joint decision on their common concerns (Moore *Negotiation Materials*, 1983).

NEGOTIATION SEMINAR 1

'Win as much as you can' negotiation game

TIME: 2 hours

1 *Skill*

Negotiation 1.

2 *Topic*

Negotiation strategies, tactics

3 *Objectives*

By the end of the activity, you will:

(a) be able to describe the three major negotiating strategies;
(b) be able to list the major objectives and characteristics for effective and ineffective legal negotiators following each negotiating strategy;
(c) be able to define interests, positions, issues and options in negotiation;
(d) be able to describe at least [ten] negotiating tactics; and
(e) be able to describe the major risks or limitations for each negotiating strategy.

4 *Preparation*

(a) Read skills materials.
(b) Read Fisher and Ury *Getting to Yes* pp 3–14.

5 *Description of activity*

Different lawyers approach negotiation in different ways. Through the use of a negotiation game and a short videotaped lecture on negotiation, we will acquire a clearer understanding of the different approaches to negotiation and how lawyers can be more effective negotiators.

6 *Notes*

None.

Instructor material

7 *Instructor preparation*

(a) Same as for students.

(b) Review 'Win as much as you can' instructions, Scoresheet and Discussion comments.
(c) Review videotape – Negotiation 1: Negotiation strategies, Tactics lecture.

8 Resources

(a) Handouts – Instructions and Scoresheets – 'Win as much as you can'; XY cards.
(b) VCR, monitor, videotape – Negotiation 1: Negotiation strategies, Tactics lecture.

9 Instruction

Timetable

10.45–10.50	Objectives for this activity are explained.
10.50–12.00	'Win as much as you can' Game.
	Class discussion of game.
12.00–12.45	Videotape lecture on negotiation strategies and tactics.
	Class discussion.

10.45–10.50

(1) Tell the students that in this activity they will have an opportunity to understand more clearly the different approaches a lawyer might take to a negotiation. As a result of this knowledge, students should be in a position to be able to choose an approach that will help them be effective negotiators.

10.50–12.00

(1) To begin this process tell the students you would like them to play a negotiation game called 'Win as much as you can'.
(2) Set up the game by following these steps:
  (a) Divide the students into groups of four and get them to sit around a table facing each other. They will have to move chairs and tables to do this. The minimum size of each group is four. If there are extras, these students can play as teams of two in a group.
  (b) Distribute to each student one copy of the instructions, two scoresheets and the X and Y card.
  (c) Briefly go through the rules on the instruction sheet. Emphasise to students that there are no negotiations permitted until after round 4. Discussions are again permitted before round 8 and round 10. Point out also that scores are tripled, including losses, on rounds 5, 8 and 10.
  (d) Take a couple of minutes to ensure everyone understands how the game is played.
  (e) Play the game. Do your best to ensure there are no discussions until the end of round 4. Keep to the time limits. Make sure students record their results on the scoresheet as they play.
  (f) At the end of the game, record each group's results.
(3) Tell the students that before they discuss the results, you would like to give them an opportunity to play one more game. Arrange the groups so that the highest scores play together and the lowest scores play together.

(4) Play a second complete game. At the end of the game, again record each group's results.
(5) Begin the discussion of the game by telling students that everyone could have won $16 by always playing Y. The results will inevitably show most, if not all, scores well below $16. Ask students to explain the results.
(6) As the discussion proceeds focus students on:

  (a) what they learned about negotiation from this game;
  (b) what they learned about themselves as negotiators from this game.

(7) At least the following points should be made in the discussion:

  (a) lawyers tend to approach negotiation in a co-operative or competitive way;
  (b) competitive approaches will be taken even if the outcome is not optimal (winning is most important);
  (c) trust is critical in negotiation;
  (d) negotiators will not always approach a problem to get mutual gain;
  (e) a competitive approach to negotiation can create ethical problems.

12.00–12.45

(1) Tell the students that you would like them now to view a 30 minute videotape on negotiation. The videotape is a presentation by Professor Andrew Pirie, a Canadian law professor and lawyer, who has been teaching negotiation skills and working in this area for a number of years. Professor Pirie will speak on the materials. After the videotape is finished, there will be an opportunity for comment.
(2) Screen the videotape.
(3) Ask the class if any points need to be clarified or if they have any comments.
(4) Tell the class that after lunch they will have an opportunity to participate in team negotiations and to choose and implement a negotiating strategy and tactics.

10 Notes

None.

NEGOTIATION SEMINAR 1

'Win as much as you can' instruction

(A simulated negotiation for four players)

Directions: There are four players in each group. Each player receives a small card or piece of paper having an 'X' on one side and a 'Y' on the other. The objective of the game is given in its title; each player seeks to win as many hypothetical dollars as possible during the ten rounds of play. In this game, however, rather than flipping pennies, each player must display an X or a Y. The pay-off depends upon the mix of choices selected by the players in the group. Since there are four players in each group, five combinations of choices and five pay-offs are possible:

4 Xs: Lose $1.00 each
3 Xs: Win $1.00 each 1 Y: Loses $3.00
2 Xs: Win $2.00 each 2 Ys: Lose $2.00 each
1 X: Wins $3.00 3 Ys: Lose $1.00 each
4 Ys: Win $1.00 each

Order of play: Each player receives a card with an X on one side and a Y on the other. For each round of play, each player must 'shuffle' his or her card by holding it under the table and turning it over several times. Then the players cover their cards and place them, with the appropriate symbol face up (but their hands covering the symbol they have chosen), on the table. When all are ready, the players remove their hands, observe the combination of choices, and calculate their respective scores. Each player then records his or her score on the accompanying sheet and prepares for the next round of play.

Before the game and during the first four rounds of play, the players should not discuss strategy nor should any individual make any binding statement about how he or she will play. After the fourth round, the group may discuss strategy, although individual players remain free to play as they choose despite any dictates of the group. The group may again discuss strategy before the 8th and 10th rounds. The player with the highest number of hypothetical dollars at the end of the tenth round will be the winner.

NEGOTIATION SEMINAR

'Win as much as you can' scoresheet

Player's name ....

ROUND	PLAY		WHICH DID YOU CHOOSE AN X OR A Y? RECORD CHOICE	HOW MUCH DID YOU WIN THIS ROUND?	HOW MUCH DID YOU LOSE THIS ROUND?	ON ROUNDS 5, 8 & 10 YOU MULTIPLY YOUR SCORE BY THREE BONUS POINTS:	TOTAL SCORE FOR EACH ROUND
	TIME ALLOWED	CONFER WITH					
1	2 mins.	NO ONE					=
2	1 min.	NO ONE					=
3	1 min.	NO ONE					=
4	1 min.	NO ONE					=
5	3 mins. +1 min.	GROUP				BONUS ROUND: PAY-OFF×3	=
6	1 min.	NO ONE					=
7	1 min.	NO ONE					=
8	3 mins. +1 min.	GROUP				BONUS ROUND: PAY-OFF×3	=
9	1 min.	NO ONE					=
10	3 mins. +1 min.	GROUP				BONUS ROUND: PAY-OFF×3	=

TOTAL SCORE

TOTAL SCORES OF THE OTHER THREE PLAYERS IN YOUR GROUP: Player 2...............................

Player 3...............................

Player 4...............................

NEGOTIATION SEMINAR 1

'Win as much as you can': Discussion comments

(Reprinted from Williams 'Legal Negotiation and Settlement' *Teacher's Manual*, 1983)

If time permits, I suggest that the first negotiating experience be with the 'Win as much as you can' game, which can be played during a regular class session. A typical version of the game is included in this Manual. At first glance, the game appears somewhat complicated. In practice, it is not. As soon as the students have played one or two rounds the mystery disappears and the groups get intensely (and noisily) involved in the play.

As indicated in the description of the game, students are divided into groups of four persons each. Each person is given a small piece of paper with an 'X' written on one side and a 'Y' written on the other. For each turn of the game, each player must decide whether to show the 'X' or the 'Y'. If all four players show a 'Y', they each receive an imaginary pay-off of one dollar. If they all show an 'X', they all lose one dollar. If there is a mixture of 'X's' and 'Y's', then the imaginary dollars are distributed as indicated in the pay-off table. After each turn, the players fill in the appropriate line on their individual score sheets. If all four players show 'Y' every round, they each receive $16 (or 16 points).

The outcome is highly predictable. In several years of playing this game, I have rarely had a group in which all players receive the maximum pay off (16 – hypothetical – dollars). In every group there is at least one person (and generally more than one) who cannot resist the temptation to get the upper hand at everyone else's expense. Whoever does this receives an immediate, if temporary, financial gain. However, the higher their gain, the greater the tendency for someone else in the group to bring them down to size. Play quickly becomes less and less predictable, and all players end up with substantially less than they would have received if they had all played 'co-operatively'. I have never had a student win more than $16 (though it is theoretically possible), and many groups end up with three if not four players actually showing a loss at the end of 10 rounds. This, of course, is the catch of the title. A student can only win the maximum if everyone in the group foregoes competition in favour of co-operation, whereas the title implies that it is a competitive game. At least two or three full games should be played, so that students can see that there is no improvement in results over time; someone always tries to take advantage, and losses accumulate. The value of playing the game early in the course is *not*, in my opinion, to teach the virtues of co-operative behaviour. Issues of co-operation versus competition are confronted repeatedly throughout the course, and should not be resolved on so simple a test. The value of the game is almost the opposite. Highly co-operative students tend to believe that all the world is just as co-operative as they are, and that rational people do not seek for advantage at the expense of their peers. This game challenges that assumption, because a significant number of class members openly (and gleefully) seek their narrow self-interest through gamesmanship over the obvious mutual gains of co-operative behaviour. Co-operative students will not be fully convinced of this, but will at least be shaken in their faith, laying a foundation for more careful consideration of their assumptions about how other negotiators approach the bargaining task.

The game illustrates, then, that some law students (and presumably a proportionate number of lawyers) prefer competition so strongly that they will not forego it in exchange for an optimum outcome; they would rather out-manoeuvre their opponents than co-operate with them, *even if it means that they themselves (and their clients) receive substantially less in the transaction.* Their reward is in beating their opponents, not in optimising the economic value of the transaction. Assuming this is a correct description of reality (as I believe it is), there is hardly a more valuable lesson to be learned. To become an effective negotiator, a student must learn how other attorneys think and act in negotiating situations. This simple game, in which the economic pay-offs are so easily calculated, is an effective device for this purpose.

Negotiation exercise 2

TIME: 2 hours

1 Skill

Negotiation 1.

2 Topic

Demonstrating negotiation strategies, Tactics, Effective speaking in negotiation.

3 Objectives

By the end of the activity, given a thirty minute negotiation between lawyers, you will:

(a) be able to demonstrate the use of a negotiating strategy and at least two negotiating tactics. In demonstrating the negotiating strategy, you must
  (i) exhibit behaviours and attitudes of effective negotiators using that strategy;
  (ii) avoid exhibiting behaviours and attitudes of ineffective negotiators;
(b) be able to exhibit the elements of effective speaking relating to content, language and presentation.

4 Preparation

Review readings and notes from previous activity.

5 Description of activity

Through a role play of a negotiation between lawyers, we will have an opportunity to choose and implement a negotiating strategy and appropriate tactics and practise effective speaking in the negotiation.

6 Notes

None.

Instructor material

7 Instructor preparation

(a) Same as for students.

(b) Review handout – Negotiation exercise 2: Confidential facts for sellers; Confidential facts for buyers, factual summary.

8 Resources

Handout – Negotiation exercise 2: Confidential facts for sellers, Confidential facts for buyers, factual summary.

9 Instruction

Timetable

2.00–2.15	Introduction to this activity.
	Objectives for this activity are explained.
2.15–3.00	Preparation for negotiation exercise.
3.00–3.30	Team negotiations – tax law books.
3.30–4.00	Class discussion of negotiation exercise.

2.00–2.15

(1) Tell the students that they will now have an opportunity to negotiate using a particular strategy and appropriate tactics in a team negotiation exercise.
(2) The actual process of choosing a particular strategy involves a careful analysis of the problem and the parties. Tell the students that instruction will be provided on that analysis tomorrow. At this point, tell the students that in choosing an approach to take they should:

  (a) review the risks identified for each strategy – will they defeat the goal of negotiation;
  (b) consider whether client objectives and negotiating objectives match;
  (c) consider whether the behaviours and attitudes of the effective negotiator are compatible with your personality.

(3) Divide the students into teams of 2 and randomly pair teams. For the teams negotiating with each other, assign roles of buyers or sellers. Distribute confidential facts for sellers and for buyers.
(4) Tell the students that they will have until 3.00 pm to prepare. Refer the students to the performances that are to be exhibited in the negotiation. The preparation should be focused on being able to exhibit these behaviours, attitudes and skills. After the negotiation there will be an opportunity to provide feedback on the effectiveness of the negotiators.
(5) Advise the students that they must prepare as teams but that they may confer with lawyers on the same side. In this respect, you should ask all the buyers to prepare in one room and all the sellers in another room. At 3.00 pm ask all students to return to this classroom.
(6) Ask if there are any matters that require clarification.

2.15–3.00

Move from group to group and provide assistance as necessary. Ensure the students are focused on the objectives for this activity.

3.00–3.30

(1) Tell the students that the negotiations must be completed by 3.30 whether agreement is reached or not.
(2) Ask the students to move to locations to conduct the negotiations. Make sure the groups tell you where they will be located so that you can observe the negotiations in order to provide feedback.
(3) Move from group to group and observe the negotiations. Make notes of what you observe that illustrates effective negotiation and areas where problems are being encountered.
(4) As groups finish, give to each student a copy of the factual summary and encourage them to discuss the negotiation prior to the class meeting.

3.00–4.00

(1) Get each group to provide you with the results of the negotiation and record these on the blackboard. Make a note beside each result which negotiating strategies were used.
(2) Tell the students you would like their feedback on the exercise. Ask the students to share with the class what negotiating strategies (behaviours, attitudes) and tactics worked well and why. Also ask the students to identify problems they encountered that made reaching an agreement difficult or impossible.
(3) For problems that are identified, try and get the class to identify what the lawyer could have done or said to overcome the problem. For example, some students may have run out of time and rushed into a bad agreement. You can suggest that, where possible, a negotiation can be adjourned to get client instructions, collect more information or just to 'regroup'.
(4) Some of the problems may relate to areas to be dealt with later (ie how to prepare fully) and you can postpone discussion.
(5) Tell the students that tomorrow they will have an opportunity to observe and provide feedback to two senior lawyers negotiating on videotape.
(6) Finish by thanking the students for their hard work on the exercise and their comments.

10 Notes

None.

NEGOTIATION SEMINAR 1

Negotiation exercise 2

Confidential facts for sellers

You and your negotiating partner are junior solicitors in the medium-sized Auckland law firm of Peterson, Jones and Frazier. The firm has 8 partners, 9 solicitors, and a staff of about 20. The firm is engaged in general corporate practice, including commercial, securities, antitrust, and tax work.

Your law firm has recently entered into an agreement for the installation of a *Westlaw/System II* automated legal research system. The system will provide a new micro-video display terminal for the desk of each partner and senior solicitor, as well as two standard-size video-display terminals and printers for junior solicitors to use in the firm's library. Because of the excellent tax services available on *Westlaw*, the need for additional space in the library to accommodate the *Westlaw* terminals, and the heavy expense of maintaining its present collection of tax books, the firm has decided to dispose of about 800 basic volumes in its tax collection, replacing them with *Westlaw* online sources plus microfiche copies of tax materials not yet on *Westlaw*.

Three months ago, you and your negotiating partner were assigned by the firm to dispose of the tax collection as soon as possible. The firm needs the books out of the library within the next two weeks in order to install the *Westlaw* equipment and the microfiche storage shelves and equipment. It is possible, of course, for the firm to box the books and store them in a commercial warehouse, but this would involve an extra expense of about $1,500 and would make selling the books more difficult.

You have developed the following facts:

(1) The 800 volumes were purchased over a period of about 15 years. The total cost of purchasing them was approximately $16,500.

(2) The 800 volumes constitute a comprehensive basic library in tax law. All of the volumes are in good condition. About 25 per cent of the books have never been used at all.

(3) If purchased new today, the same collection would cost around $24,000 plus shipping. However, with the growing movement to automation, there does not appear to be much of a demand for such a collection, new or used.

(4) A national distributor of law books knows of the firm's desire to sell the books and he has written you a letter offering to purchase the entire collection for $4,000. You are relieved to have this offer and the firm has instructed you that you should sell to the distributor if no better offer materialises in the immediate future.

(5) Over the past several weeks, you and your partner have run ads in several legal newspapers and magazines. You have also personally contacted many tax-oriented law firms in the province, but you have found no one interested in the collection.

(6) Yesterday, your secretary told you and your partner that he knew of three young lawyers who were forming a new firm and who were planning to limit their practice to tax work. He said he had met two of them at a dinner party, and had mentioned the firm's tax collection to them. They had indicated that they were interested in possibly purchasing part or all of the collection if the price was within reach of their limited resources. This

morning, you received a telephone call from one of these young lawyers asking if they could talk with you about the possible purchase of the books. You informed the lawyer that you would only consider a sale of the entire collection, but that if they were interested you would like to meet with them.

The firm has given you and your partner full authority to conclude a sale at any price higher than the distributor's offer, on the condition the books be moved out of the library within the next two weeks.

NEGOTIATION SEMINAR 1

Negotiation exercise 2

Confidential facts for buyers

You and your negotiating partner have been practising law with a large Auckland law firm ever since you graduated from law school three years ago. You have both specialised in tax work, and you have recently decided to join with a third lawyer in forming your own three-person law firm specialising in tax work. You and your negotiating partner have a number of large corporate clients who have indicated they would bring their tax business to your new firm. In addition, the lawyer joining you is from a well-connected and wealthy family that has agreed to cover the initial costs of setting up a law office in a prime location and equipping it in appropriate fashion.

One of the most important matters of business you face is to assemble a collection of tax books that will provide the broad foundation in tax law information you will need to serve your clients successfully. You all agree that a good tax library is worth whatever expense may be involved.

Several nights ago you and your associate were at a dinner party and learned, from a legal secretary, that his law firm (the medium-sized firm of Peterson, Jones and Frazier) was switching to *Westlaw* and has an 800 volume collection of tax books for sale. You expressed interest, he sent you a list of the titles by messenger the next day, and you found that the collection covers most of the basic materials you had in mind to buy. You telephoned the responsible lawyers in that firm this morning and made an appointment to meet with them today to discuss the purchase of the books.

In your investigations so far, you have learned the following facts:

(1) You expect to have to pay $30,000 for a basic tax collection plus an additional $3,000 to $4,000 per year for subscriptions to the commercial tax up-date services. You have $30,000 on hand for those initial purchases.
(2) You estimate that the tax collection being offered by the law firm is about 80 per cent complete, in the sense that it will cover 80 per cent of your basic needs apart from subscription services.

(3) You estimate that the 800 books being offered by the law firm would cost very close to $30,000 if purchased brand new today (between $25,000 and $30,000). You are not sure how much the books originally cost.

(4) You have found that national distributors of law books deal in used books and that some of the titles you need could be obtained from them. However, it would be impossible to purchase anything resembling a complete set of used volumes, because they simply are not available. A dealer has estimated for you that if such a used set were available, it would cost in the neighbourhood of $18,000–$20,000.

(5) Because of the difficulty in even locating such a full collection of tax books, you have decided that you are willing to pay the law firm as much as $22,000 for the collection if all the books are in satisfactory condition.

(6) Although you have already signed a lease for your new office quarters, the leasing period does not begin for two more months, and in the meantime you would like to leave the books in their present location if possible. You have no objection to paying for them now and letting the selling law firm continue to use them in the intervening time.

NEGOTIATION SEMINAR 1

Negotiation exercise 2

Tax law books negotiation: factual summary

Sellers' facts	*Buyers' facts*
(1) The volumes cost (new) $16,500.	(1) Expect to pay about $30,000 for basic tax collection. That amount of money is on hand.
(2) All volumes in good condition; 25 per cent never used at all.	(2) Firm's collection comprises about 80 per cent of what you need.
(3) Collection would cost $24,000 new today, but demand is low due to automated systems.	(3) You estimate that collection would cost between $25,000 and $30,000 new today.
(4) Firm has offer from a national distributor to buy collection for $4,000. Firm will accept unless better deal immediately materialises.	(4) No used sets of tax law books are available in the used-book market. If they were, a used set would cost about $18,000 to $20,000.
(5) Extensive advertising by firm has brought forth no interested buyers.	(5) Due to above difficulties, you are willing to pay the firm up to $22,000 if books are in good condition.

(6) Firm's two negotiators have full authority to sell at any price above $4,000 on condition books can be moved out of library within two weeks.
(7) It would cost $1,500 to put books in storage.

(6) Lease for your new office does not begin for two more months; no place to put books in the meantime.

NEGOTIATION SEMINAR 1

Negotiation exercise 3

TIME: 4 hours 15 minutes

1 Skill

Negotiation 1.

2 Topic

The stages of negotiation: the preparation stage.

3 Objectives

By the end of the activity, you will:

(a) be able to describe the steps in the preparation stage for negotiation;
(b) be able to complete all the tasks identified in the preparation stage for negotiation; and
(c) be able to complete, in writing, a Negotiation Journal in the prescribed form.

4 Preparation

(a) Read skills materials: negotiation.
(b) Read Fisher and Ury *Getting to Yes* pp 41–57.
(c) Read *The principal stages of negotiation* (pp 199 ff).
(d) Read practice materials: family law, ss 7.01–7.23.

5 Description

Many mistakes are made when lawyers negotiate because they fail to understand fully the negotiation process. Particularly, many lawyers do not appreciate the exact nature and extent of the preparation necessary to be an effective negotiator. By better understanding the principal stages of negotiation, particularly the preparation stage, and by having an opportunity to prepare for a negotiation, we can move towards eliminating common mistakes in negotiation.

6 Notes

None.

The principal stages of negotiation

1 Preparation for negotiation

   A Analysis
   B Planning for negotiation

2 The negotiation

   A Preliminaries
   B Planning for negotiation
   C Agreement or final breakdown

3 Documenting the agreement

1 Preparation for negotiation

[* denotes steps or actions that would not always be taken by positional bargainers]

A Analysis

(1)   Complete *fact investigation*, subject to obtaining further facts during the negotiation.

(2)   Identify and prioritise the *issues* to be negotiated that are important to your client. These issues will be both legal and non-legal, and may be substantive, procedural or psychological.

(3)   Predict the legal and non-legal issues that you think will be important to the other party or parties to the negotiation.

(4)   Finalise the *legal research* on all legal issues. You should be fully familiar with the law (cases, statutes, regulations) relating to these issues.

(5)   Gather *information* about the parties (backgrounds, authority, experience, reputation etc) involved in the negotiation, including other lawyers. This information will help you in formulating your approach to the negotiation and in predicting actions taken by other parties.

(6)   For each issue, summarise the relevant facts.

(7)   Identify any *deficiencies in information*. Determine whether the negotiation can go ahead without this information or whether the information can be obtained in the negotiation or through some other course of action.

(8)*   Identify the *interests or needs* of your client which must be met if a negotiated solution is to be acceptable. Remember, interests are different than positions.

(9)*   Predict the interests that the other party or parties to the negotiation would like to have met.

(10)*   Identify alternative solutions that will satisfy your client's interests and resolve the issues.

(11)*   Identify alternative solutions that other parties might find acceptable.

(12)*   Determine whether common interests exist, whether any alternative solution might be acceptable to all parties and what differences exist among issues, interests and solutions.

(13)   Classify the negotiation as generally integrative (win-win) or distributive (win-lose).

(14)   Determine what other courses of action (legal proceedings, investigation etc) need to be taken in addition to the negotiation.

B Planning for negotiation

(1)   Institute other proceedings, including further information-gathering, to be carried on before and during the negotiation.
(2)   Predict the approach and tactics that will be used by other parties to the negotiation.
(3)   As a result of (2) and your analysis, choose an appropriate negotiating strategy and tactics. Remember that a focus on tactics can encourage positional bargaining.
(4)*   Develop objective criteria (such as custom, market values, social values, precedent) for resolving conflicting interests.
(5)   Develop, with your client, the *best alternative to a negotiated agreement* (BATNA) for your client and other parties.
(6)   Select an appropriate time and location for the negotiation session(s).
(7)   Draft an agenda to structure the negotiation. You will want to organise information and issues in the sequence where information is best presented and issues are best solved.
(8)   Clarify instructions from your client respecting the scope of your authority (disclosure of information, settlement).
(9)   Complete writing in your Negotiation Journal.

2 *The negotiation*

A Preliminaries

(1)   Initiate contact with the other negotiator.
(2)   Establish effective communication with the other negotiator, when appropriate, through the use of:

(a)   active listening responses which reflect understanding of the facts and feelings communicated by the negotiator;
(b)   communication facilitators;
(c)   attending behaviour.

(3)   Obtain further information (questioning, exchange of documents, listening and observing) respecting issues, interests, solutions, strategies or tactics.
(4)   Re-assess your analysis stage in light of any new information.
(5)   Obtain agreement on the time and location for the negotiation.
(6)   Advise your client.

B Discussion

Problem solving	*Positional*
(1) Agree on any necessary procedures to be followed.	(1) Agree on any necessary procedures to be followed.
(2) The parties define and clarify the issues to be discussed.	(2) Identify the issues and/or let other party identify them.

(3) Differences in information (data, perception) are discussed. Further information obtained (questioning, exchange of documents, listening and observing).

(4) Establish the sequence for discussing the issues.

(5) Identify and clarify the interests or needs of all parties. You should understand the needs of the other party as well as your own.

(6) Jointly generate alternative solutions that will satisfy the combined needs (develop options for mutual gain).

(7) Use appropriate negotiating tactics that are not inconsistent with problem-solving approach.

(8) Assess the alternative solutions based on the interests of each party.

(9) Eliminate unacceptable or unworkable alternatives and review most acceptable alternative.

(10) Generate proposals based on your assessment and review.

(11) Deal with deadlocks if they arise (summarise, move to different issue, make a disclosure etc).

(12) Adjourn the negotiation, if necessary, to obtain further information to discuss matters with client, to obtain instructions.

(13) If negotiating with a positional bargainer:

    (a) continue to focus on your client's interests; encourage the other negotiator to do the same;

(3) Obtain further information (questioning, exchange of documents, listening and observing).

(4) Put forward agenda.

(5) Parties present maximum position to meet needs.

(6) Discuss persuasively the reasons and arguments that support your position.

(7) Present counter-proposals.

(8) Use negotiating tactics (ie threats, bluffs, anger/aggression) to support or enhance your position, to discredit opposite position.

(9) Identify and narrow the bargaining range.

(10) Search for trade-offs, concessions and compromises.

(11) Adjourn the negotiation, if necessary, to obtain further information, to discuss matters with client or to obtain instructions.

    (b) don't argue; incorporate problem-solving techniques;
    (c) separate the people from the problem;
    (d) insist on objective criteria and not unprincipled pressure;
    (e) bring in a third party (mediator, expert, the parties themselves) where appropriate;
    (f) consider changing your approach or ending negotiations if risks high.

(14) Your discussions in the negotiation should exhibit the elements of effective speaking in relation to:

    (a) content;
    (b) language; and
    (c) presentation.

(12) Your discussions in the negotiation should exhibit the elements of effective speaking in relation to:

    (a) content;
    (b) language; and
    (c) presentation.

C Agreement or final breakdown

(1) If possible, reach agreement on an appropriate solution subject to client approval unless clear instructions to settle.
(2) Advise your client, obtain instructions and confirm in writing the agreement with all other negotiators.
(3) If no agreement is possible and the negotiation has reached an impasse, adjourn the negotiation, advise your client and obtain instructions as to alternative course(s) of action to be followed to a negotiated agreement.

3 Documenting the agreement

(1) Formalise the agreement where necessary and confirm in writing with all parties.
(2) Write your client a reporting letter confirming instructions and terms of the agreement.
(3) Carry out all relevant practice operations (registration, filing etc).

Negotiation Journal

A Negotiation Journal is required to be completed by you for certain negotiation sessions in the course. The purpose of the written journal is to provide information on which your preparation for a negotiation can be assessed by both your instructor and your peers and on which you can be given feedback.

The content of your journal will show whether you have successfully completed all of the steps competent lawyers would take in preparing for a negotiation. Those steps are referred to in *The principal stages of negotiation* at pp 199 ff.

In order to provide uniformity in student negotiation journals, we ask you to *prepare your journals accordingly to the following format.* Completed journals must be typed or written legibly. *The length will vary according to the nature of the negotiation problem.*

NAME(S):   **INSTRUCTOR:**

Negotiation exercise no:

Your client:

Name of other negotiator(s):

Their client:

[*may not be included by positional bargainers]

A Issues to be negotiated

○ a list and brief summary of questions the parties disagree about.

B Relevant facts

○ a brief summary of facts relevant to each issue;
○ deficiencies in facts and, if so, sources of further information should be identified.

C Relevant law

○ a brief summary of the law (cases, statutes, regulations) for each legal issue;
○ your summary should contain your opinion about how the issue would be resolved legally (the legal position).

D Personal information

○ a brief summary of information about the parties and other negotiators which might affect strategies, tactics, solutions.

*E Interests of parties

○ a brief summary of the interests or needs of each party to the negotiation which must be met if a negotiated solution is to be acceptable;
○ remember to differentiate between interests and positions;
○ interests are usually the reasons *why* a negotiator wants a particular solution;
○ identify objective criteria to resolve conflicting interests.

F Alternative solutions

○ a preliminary list of possible alternative solutions to resolve each issue;
○ positional bargainers will be establishing maximum or minimum positions.

G BATNA

○ a statement of the best alternative to a negotiated agreement for each issue or series of issues for your client and the other parties.

H Negotiating strategy and tactics

○ set out your choice of a negotiating strategy and tactics you intend to use to achieve the desired solution;
○ preliminarily predict strategy and tactics of other negotiators;
○ briefly summarise reasons for choice and identify risks you see associated with your choice.

I Draft agenda

○ prioritise order of issues to be negotiated.

J Client instructions

○ a brief summary of client instructions, particularly noting any limitations on the scope of your authority.

Instructor material

7 Instructor preparation

(a) Same as for students.

8 Resources

(a) Handout:

   ○ Negotiation exercise 3: Robert Bateman;
   ○ Confidential instructions lawyer A;
   ○ Confidential instructions lawyer B.

(b) Negotiation exercise 4:

   ○ General instructions;
   ○ Confidential information for Tom's lawyer;
   ○ Confidential information for Barbara's lawyer.

9 Instruction

Timetable

10.45–11.00	Introduction to activity.
	Objectives for this activity are explained.
	The principal stages of negotiation.
11.00–12.30	The preparation stage: the Need Theory of negotiation; the Negotiation Journal.
12.30–2.00	Lunch.
	Review negotiation problem.
2.00–3.30	Preparation for negotiation by class.
3.30–4.00	Class discussion of preparation stage.

10.45–11.00

(1) Tell the students that they will have already identified that many mistakes are made in negotiation because lawyers do not fully understand the steps that are normally followed in a negotiation. Because lawyers are not familiar with the stages of negotiation, they often omit steps, take them in the wrong order or inadequately complete them. One excellent example is poor preparation for negotiation.

(3) Refer the students to *The principal stages of negotiation.*

(4) Advise the students that this is a synthesis of various writings on the negotiation process. It breaks the negotiation process down into three major stages (Preparation, Negotiation, and Documenting the agreement) and describes the major tasks that effective negotiators would complete in each stage. *Briefly* describe the general steps in each stage. Each stage will be considered in more detail later.

(5) Tell the students that negotiation is a dynamic process. However, if these tasks are carefully completed and matched with effective negotiation behaviour, attitudes and skills, it is highly likely you will be a very effective negotiator.

11.00–12.15

(1) Tell the students that what you would like to do for the rest of the day is focus on competently completing the preparation stage. The first part of the activity will focus on the knowledge and skills necessary to complete the preparation stage. The second part of the activity, in the afternoon, will give the students the opportunity to actually prepare for a negotiation. Time will be spent tomorrow on the negotiation stage and documenting the agreement stage.

(2) Refer the students to the preparation stage in *The principal stages of negotiation.* Before answering questions or clarifying points, tell the students you would like to deal with *two difficulties* often encountered in preparing for negotiation.

(3) First, tell the students you would like them to watch a short demonstration of a negotiation between two lawyers. Hand out to all students the confidential instructions for lawyers (A and B) in Negotiation exercise 3.

(4) Ask the volunteers (lawyer A and lawyer B) to come to the front of the

room and begin the negotiation. (Negotiation exercise 3: Robert Bateman.)

(5) Allow the negotiation to continue for 4–6 minutes.

(6) Stop the negotiation. Ask the class to provide feedback on whether the negotiators were making progress towards an agreement and why. If they were not, why not.

(7) Conduct the discussion in accordance with the *Instructor's notes: Robert Bateman* (p 207).

(8) Finish by emphasising to students that it is important in preparing for a negotiation, whether you are taking a problem-solving approach or not, to identify the *interests or needs* of the parties. If the focus is only on positions (what the parties want) and not interests (why they want something), there is a risk of deadlock or breakdown or a risk options will be overlooked.

(9) Tell the students that steps 8 and 9 in Preparation stage: analysis (p 199) refer to the identification of the underlying interests or needs of parties to a negotiation.

(10) The second point respecting the preparation stage relates to the Negotiation Journal. Tell the students that in order for you and their peers to provide feedback on their preparation, you are going to ask them to complete a written Negotiation Journal. The Journal will be a written record of the preparation done.

(11) Refer each student to the Negotiation Journal form. Briefly highlight the headings and the nature of the content. Stress to the students the importance of learning to complete the Journal fully and accurately. A written journal will form an important part of the assessment in the Negotiation 2 Seminar.

(12) Ask the students whether they have any questions about the preparation stage or points to be clarified.

12.15–12.30

(1) Tell the students you would now like to hand out Negotiation exercise 4 to give them practice in completing the preparation stage.

(2) Divide the students into teams of two. Randomly pair teams. One team will represent client A. The other team will represent client B.

(3) Hand out the Confidential instructions for A's lawyers and for B's lawyers.

(4) Tell the students that they will have until 3.30 pm to work on the preparation for this negotiation problem. Tell them this preparation is important because tomorrow they will actually negotiate this problem.

(5) While each team of lawyers should prepare together, encourage all the lawyers representing A to prepare in the same room, to share ideas and help solve problems. Give the same directions for B's lawyers.

(6) Tell the students they do not need to complete fully the preparation. There will be time set aside tomorrow to finalise preparation before the actual negotiation (from 10.45 am–2.00 pm to prepare).

(7) Ensure you get the students to advise you where they will be preparing so that you can move from group to group to provide assistance.

2.00–3.30

(1) Move from group to group and provide the students with assistance in completing the preparation stage for negotiation. Don't give the answers

to the students directly. Provide direction if they are going off track. Focus them on specific steps in the preparation stage and the information required in the Negotiation Journal.
(2) Make sure you visit each team. In observing the preparation, try to identify what is being done that assists preparation and what problems are arising. This information will be used in the large group feedback session.

3.30–4.00

(1) With the whole class, tell them you would like to get reports on how the preparation is going. Get them to identify what they are doing that is helping preparation and what problems they are experiencing. Avoid disclosing information that would disrupt the actual negotiation tomorrow.
(2) For problems that arise, try to get the class to identify what can be done to overcome the problem.
(3) Finish the activity by reminding the students to retain their preparation work. There will be time tomorrow to finish preparation before the actual negotiation.

10 Notes

None.

Negotiation exercise 3

Instructor's notes: Robert Bateman

These notes are designed to assist you in the class discussion of this exercise.

The exercise is designed to illustrate the difference between *interests* and *positions* in a negotiation. Often a focus on positions can lead to deadlocks or a breakdown whereas a focus or interests can provide a wider scope for a solution.

In the years that I have been using this exercise, the negotiators rarely make much progress towards a solution. The class usually recognises this result but can have some difficulty understanding why this is happening. However, usually the negotiators focus on positions which in this case are diametrically opposed. (Lawyer A wants to buy the painting. Lawyer B does not want to buy the painting.) There is no bargaining range the way the problem is designed.

However, you can get the class to identify *why* each negotiator held the particular position. Why did lawyer A want to buy the painting? The facts disclose that she or he finds it aesthetically pleasing. The painting would fulfil an aesthetic need. Lawyer A is not really concerned about the appreciation value and the painting will not generate more business. On the other hand, lawyer B does not want to buy the painting because it threatens his or her family life. The extra monthly payment for each ($500) could break up the family. The interest of lawyer B is a very basic need for this type of security.

Once these interests are identified it is easy to see why no progress can be made towards an agreement unless lawyer B's needs are taken into account. Lawyer A's needs are easier to meet.

If the lawyers were making progress it will only be because they are trying to identify solutions that do not cost lawyer B any money.

Do not go on to discuss solutions that might solve the problem in light of these interests. The students will do an exercise tomorrow in which they will try to identify solutions to this problem. This exercise is designed to illustrate risks associated with positional bargaining and how interest of the parties to a negotiation can be identified.

NEGOTIATION SEMINAR 1

Negotiation exercise 3: Robert Bateman

Confidential instructions: lawyer A

You are a partner in a two person law firm. You have been practising with your partner for about five years and are building up a respectable practice. However, you and your partner have built up a large debt for office furnishings, law books and computers, and you both expect it will be another five years before this debt is retired.

You have asked your partner to meet you to discuss the possible purchase of a Robert Bateman painting entitled 'Eagle in Flight'. You would love to buy this painting. You find it extremely pleasing aesthetically. The cost of the painting is $25,000.00 and you have confirmed the bank would lend you this money. The loan would be paid back on 30 monthly instalments of $1,000 each. (This is the best, and only, loan arrangement that you can make.) You would gladly share these payments to have this beautiful painting in the office. *However it is clear the painting would not result in more business.* You know the painting will appreciate in value by 15 per cent per year. Although you find your monthly salary is 'tough to get by on', you are single and would be willing to pay an extra $500/month (your share) to enjoy such art.

Please meet with your partner.

NEGOTIATION SEMINAR 1

Negotiation exercise 3: Robert Bateman

Confidential instructions: lawyer B

You are a partner in a two person law firm. You have been practising with your partner for about five years and are building up a respectable practice. However, you and your partner have built up a large debt for office furnishings, law books and computers, and you both expect it will be another five years before this debt is retired.

Your partner has asked to meet you to discuss the possible purchase of a Robert Bateman painting entitled 'Eagle in Flight'. The cost of the painting is $25,000.00. You are absolutely opposed to purchasing the painting. While you like Bateman's paintings and know the painting would appreciate in value by 15 per cent per year, you simply *can't afford to reduce your monthly draws* to pay for this painting. You have a family and are already experiencing serious financial problems at home. Any further financial pressure would be more than you could handle. Even an extra $50 a month might break you. You hope you and your family can get by until the debt is retired.

However, you have agreed to discuss this matter with your partner.

NEGOTIATION SEMINAR 1

Negotiation exercise 4

General instructions

(adapted from Gerald R Williams 'Legal Negotiation and Settlement' *Teacher's Manual*, 1983)

The following facts are for use in a negotiation exercise involving Tom Winters and Barbara Winters.

Lawyers representing both parties are receiving the same general statement of the facts. In addition, lawyers for each party are receiving supplemental information that would normally develop in the course of handling the case. If in the course of negotiations, you are asked for information which has not been provided, simply indicate that the information is not available. You may create incidental facts which would be consistent with the character of your client so long as they are not unduly self-serving and do not distort the outcome.

FACTS

Tom and Barbara have been married for 15 years and have had five children, ages 3, 6, 10, 13 and 14. They met in fifth form and were wed two months after graduation. Tom works as a policeman and makes $25,000 a year salary. Two years ago he began working the undercover detail which has necessitated being 'on call' for almost 24 hours a day 6 days a week. During the last 3 months he has been assigned the graveyard shift so that he sleeps during the day and works from 11 pm to 7 am.

Tom has been able to save about $500, which is in a joint account with Barbara. Tom and Barbara bought a house in 1985 for $50,000 and its current value is about $75,000. Tom made the initial down payment ($8,000) and is making all mortgage payments by himself. The balance remaining due is $40,000. Barbara has spent considerable time and money remodelling the house. She claims that she has put at least $7,000 into remodelling and $3,000 into furnishings. The money she used was given to her by her parents as a graduation gift, to be used for university, but she realised that she would never return to school. The family has two cars, a 1982 Ford station wagon, for which 22 monthly payments of $285 each still remain and a 1980 Toyota pickup truck, which is paid for. Both cars are in good condition. The market value of the Ford is $7,500. The market value of the Toyota is $3,000. Ski equipment was purchased one year ago for both Tom and Barbara and the contract has a total of $1,880 outstanding which is due in monthly payments of $75 each. In addition, the family has doctor and dental bills totalling $385, which have accumulated in the past two months and the brand new stereo system requires $100 monthly instalment payments for the next 9 months in order to be paid for. Barbara's grandfather, who had been a resident of this city all his life, left her his entire art collection, which has recently been appraised at just over $160,000. He died two months ago and the estate is still in probate. It appears no one will contest the distribution of the estate mandated in the will. This process is expected to take another 10 months.

Tom appears to be easy going at work and in social situations, but he is a very strict father at home. He is fairly nice-looking and though his athletic build is sagging, he likes to reminisce about his fame in school. He would like very much to continue his education in university, but feels the pressure of a family will not allow him to do so.

Barbara looks quite young for her age and upon a first meeting, one would assume she was in her early twenties. While she was in high school, Barbara was very popular and dated whenever she pleased. She enjoys getting out and 'doing things' but Tom would rather spend a quiet evening at home. This is especially true since his job now necessitates his being out on the town all night. She doesn't like cooking and the two oldest daughters take turns cooking the evening meal and keeping house. Though Barbara never worked in an outside job, in the past 5 years she has run a day care centre for pre-schoolers in her home.

Approximately $2\frac{1}{2}$ months ago, Barbara started leaving the youngest children home and taking the two teenage girls with her to the neighbourhood park, where she watched the neighbourhood boys play tennis and softball. She and her two daughters would leave during the day and night, often while Tom was at work. Through her daughters, Barbara has become friendly with the boys who hang out at the park. She has become especially close to the tennis teacher who is in seventh form at the local school and has on several occasions invited him over at night when she is alone with the children. Barbara and her two girls have also been seen out dragging Main Street frequently.

Two weeks ago, a police unit saw the Toyota, apparently abandoned, at 3 am in the neighbourhood park. The officer had the dispatcher run a vehicle registration check and discovered the car belonged to Tom. After Tom was notified of the car's location, the officer walked through the park and met Barbara and Ren White, the tennis teacher, emerging from the baseball dugout. Tom arrived about 10 minutes later and had a quarrel with Barbara. He ordered Barbara to move out of the house. He took the car keys from her and she had her mother come for her that night. All the children stayed in the house with Tom, who arranged for a neighbour lady to stay with them at night. Barbara has not been back to the house or seen the children since the incident in the park two weeks ago. Tom called Barbara on the telephone each day for several days, but she refused to speak to him.

NEGOTIATION SEMINAR 1

Negotiation exercise 4

Confidential information – for Tom's lawyer

When Tom came in to ask you to negotiate a separation agreement, you let him talk and unload his pressures. With a little careful probing and questioning, he told you the following:

> I love Barbara very much, but I just don't know what's gotten into her. I married her because she was so much fun, but it's gotten to the point where she can't sit still for one minute. Since she's moved out, she spends all her time with that little tennis player. She's telling everyone we know that she's crazy for him and the whole town knows she dumped me. I don't know if

they actually sleep together, but you can bet your bottom dollar there's some hanky panky going on. I might even consider hiring some private detective to try and get something on them, even though I would kind of hate to use it in trial or make anything public. I'm a reasonable man. If she would just straighten up and come home, I could forgive her for this silly foolishness. I love her and more than anything would just like to see us get back together again.

She's also gone on some outrageous shopping sprees lately – just before she left, she ran up $500 on my mastercharge for new clothes she didn't need and we couldn't afford ... somehow she must have sneaked my card out of my wallet. Then she joined one of those health spas which racked up a $800 debt. As far as property, I don't really mind if she takes a car and I'd even let her have as much as half of the joint savings in order to get established.

I know that she probably wants the kids, but that's out of the question. Those kids are my life. She hasn't even come over one single time since she moved out, but she calls them sometimes at night when I'm at work. How's that for a fine mother! I come home during dinner break and stay with them as long as I can. I know that they miss their mother, but so do I. I think that her new friends have made her lose all common sense. If only she would come back, I'd try to change a little and let her do things she wants; I'd even try to take her out at night once in a while.

To tell you the truth, I'm also of the opinion that I should not pay Barbara any support so that I can use all my salary to raise the kids. Besides, her grandfather just died and left her a valuable art collection, so I think she can support herself in fine style. She should also give up any right to the house. After all, I paid for it, and I need a proper home to give to the children. But I could even give that up if I have to as long as I get the kids. If this goes through I don't care what I have to lose if I can just get custody. If you can't help me there, tell me now and I'll find another lawyer that can.

EXPERT MEDICAL REPORT

Dr James Simpson, the head of the community mental health centre, is an experienced child psychologist. In addition to extensive graduate research, he has over eight years practical interviewing, counselling, and treatment experience. He has served as an expert witness in numerous trials. At your request, he interviewed and tested Barbara. Her lawyer may know that Barbara recently saw a psychologist, but probably is not aware that the testing was done at your request and that you have the report in your file. Dr Simpson has summarised his notes and test results into the following informative report:

Patient is obviously reverting to later childhood adolescence. The constant domination by her husband Tom, who she sees as an authoritarian figure, is forcing her to rebel and she is acting as a teenager resisting rules. Now that her children are beginning to mature, she subconsciously wants to relive the years she missed while she was a young bride. Barbara wants fun and excitement for her two oldest girls, who she favours. This awakens old unfulfilled desires in her. She loves the children very much and wants custody of them because she fears that if they stay with Tom, his stern nature will cause them to rebel.

Barbara does not admit to any extra-marital infidelity, but she wants a divorce finalised quickly. It appears certain that she no longer loves Tom and will not return to him. Since she has had a taste of freedom, it is unlikely that she will give up the chance to be her own woman. She feels that she can be an individual in the current relationship with Ren White, the tennis player, although her interest in him is probably due to adolescent fantasies.

On the basis of this comprehensive interview and basic evaluative tests conducted, I feel it is safe to say that with a year or so of therapy, she would be an excellent mother. As it is now, I think that she might be competent, but probably below average as a mother figure. From what she tells me of Tom, I feel that he also has problems that could be helped with regular therapy. He sets unreasonably strict rules for the children and will not listen to logic or attempts at compromise. If he does not become more flexible in the next few years, serious parent/child conflicts are inevitable.

Please prepare for and conduct the negotiations with Barbara's lawyer. Do your best. Strive for an agreement that will serve the best interests of your client as you see them.

NEGOTIATION SEMINAR 1

Negotiation exercise 4

Confidential information – for Barbara's lawyer

When Barbara received a letter from Tom's lawyer saying Tom wanted a separation agreement, she was frantic. She came to you on a recommendation of her brother. During her first interview, she confided the following information:

> I know that I married Tom too early, but I wanted to get away from home. My father was so weak that I could do exactly what I wanted. I was so excited to find Tom because he seemed like such a man – so strong and handsome. How was I to know that he'd go overboard and never let me do anything but be his shadow and servant? He just wanted to stay home every night with a can of beer and watch football games. And its been even worse since he's been working those night shifts. Why, he wants me to sit home all day quiet while he sleeps and then sit home all night alone while he works. The only time we see each other is early afternoon and then I'm ready for a nap after handling kids all morning.
>
> Ren is just the opposite – alive, exciting and full of fun. He makes me feel like a woman again. He's quite good looking and I'm very attracted to him physically. I must have a divorce; the sooner the better. Ren is a very talented tennis player and is always winning awards and contests even though he's only in seventh form. He's very independent and has a place of his own as his father is dead and his mother remarried and moved to Australia. He teaches lessons for the city in the summer and in addition to that, lives on a small allowance from his mother. We've just got to get him into a university or his mother will stop the payments in 6 months when he turns 18. If we can convince some university, perhaps overseas, to ignore his bad grades and look at his great athletic potential, we can keep getting his allowance until he's 22.

I don't want you to think that money means all that much to me. I started the day care centre just so I could have a little money of my own. I hated crawling on my hands and knees to Tom for every penny that I needed. Though I usually spent it as I wanted, I did manage to save $3,000 over the years which I have in a separate account. Tom doesn't know about that.

I want the children. They want me and need me, and I know I can take care of them. It would be best for the kids if Tom and I could patch things up, but whatever excitement I thought I saw in him is gone. I couldn't live with him again. I also want to save the kids from growing up in the sterile environment that Tom and I were stuck in. I think I should get the house to raise the kids in and also decent support. Isn't that fair? I really deserve to keep the art collection too because it's for the kids. I haven't told Tom, but my grandfather's will says that any money from the collection is for them. I'm not sure that he trusted me.

Barbara also told you that before she came in for this interview, but after she received the lawyer's letter, Tom asked her to see a certain local psychiatrist, which she did.

OTHER INTERVIEWS

You send your capable summer clerk out to gather information for the case. She goes to neighbours and asks questions as to Barbara's reputation. They all answer that she is acting like a juvenile and give examples such as her involvement in water fights, flirting with her daughter's ex-boyfriends, and general 'hustling' at the park. When asked which parent they thought would be better for the children if the divorce were to be finalised, every person (of the 14 spoken to) selected Tom because he seemed to be more responsible and care about the welfare of all the children. Your clerk also spoke with the 4 teenaged boys involved who indicated that, at the most, Barbara was fun to be with, but that she was just their 'good friend' because she had something going with Ren White, the school tennis star. In addition, the children of Barbara and Tom were interviewed. The substance of their comments was as follows:

Chad: age 3 – 'I miss my mum and want her to come back.'

Jeff: age 6 – 'I love my mother, but she leaves me to play with Chad sometimes. She drives away with Laurie and Jill to play, but she only takes me to the grocery store. When I have a wet bed at night, she spanks me the next morning.'

Todd: age 10 – 'I love my mum and I love my dad. If I had to choose, I would rather live with my dad because he takes good care of me and reads me good night stories. When mum leaves Chad and Jeff here, I go play with my other friends on the block. She used to bring her friend home and make us kids stay in our rooms till he was gone.'

Laurie: age 13 – 'I love my mum, but I don't want to grow up like her. She's acting like one of my girlfriends, not like my mother. She doesn't care about the day care children either. When she takes Jill and I out for rides, she used to leave Jeff and Chad with the nursery children all morning while dad was asleep downstairs.'

Jill: age 14 – 'If my parents get divorced, I want to live with my dad. I love my mum – all of us kids do, but I think that there's something a little bit wrong with her the last little while. If the judge told me that I had to live with my mum, I'd run away.'

Please prepare for and conduct the negotiations with Tom's lawyer. Do your best. Strive for an agreement that will serve the best interests of your client as you see them.

8 Analysis of evidence

Terence Anderson and William Twining

Introduction

Nearly all study of evidence in law degrees and practical training courses concentrates on the law of evidence. Questions about what constitute valid, cogent and appropriate modes of reasoning about disputed questions of fact have recently attracted a great deal of theoretical attention, especially in relation to probability theory.[1] But the skills of analysis and reasoning associated with what John Henry Wigmore called 'the logic of proof' have rarely been developed by direct instruction in modern legal education. This is strange, because almost all lists of 'lawyering skills' include 'fact analysis' among the most important skills required in many kinds of legal practice.[2]

In 1913, Wigmore launched a bold presentation of a 'science of proof' which he claimed was both anterior to and of more practical importance than the law of evidence.[3] For nearly forty years he taught his science to law students at Northwestern University Law School, but he failed to persuade his contemporaries of its utility.[4] Today Wigmore is remembered mainly for his writings on the law of evidence rather than for his science of proof. One reason for his failure is that he was ahead of his time. A few years ago Professor David Schum, a psychologist who has done some interesting empirical research based on Wigmore's science, presented Wigmore's 'chart method' of analysing evidence without identifying its source to a group of computer analysts interested in 'expert systems'. None knew of a more advanced method for analysing and organising large amounts of data. When asked to guess when the method was devised, the earliest estimate was 1970.[5]

In recent years Schum and others have developed approaches based on Wigmorean analysis in training intelligence analysts, in research on inferential reasoning and in designing computer-based systems for assisting work on difficult evidential and inferential problems.[6] Such developments represent exciting future directions. Less ambitiously, during the past ten years we have used a modified version of Wigmore's method in courses on evidence in England and the United States. We have presented this as a simple form of applied logic, carefully distanced from the mathematics and the sophisticated technology that fascinates a few, but terrifies most, law students.

The materials in this section are intended as an introduction to this type of analysis. They include Wigmore's first, and most succinct, account of his method and some extracts from a set of course materials on analysis of evidence that have been prepared for use in American law schools.[7] The main objective is to demonstrate that it is possible to develop skills of analysis and

216

reasoning relating to evidence and inference in a direct, simple and practical way.

NOTES

1 See, for example, the extensive debate between Jonathan Cohen, Glanville Williams, Sir Richard Eggleston and others in the Criminal Law Review for 1979–80. See further the special symposium on Probability and Inference in the Law of Evidence, 66 Boston Law Rev Nos 3 and 4 (1986).
2 This is true even in England: Report of the Committee on Legal Education (the Ormrod Report), Cmnd 4595 (1971), paras 91, 101, 108, 185(5); cf *A Time for Change* (the Lady Marre Report) (London, 1988), ch 12; the formulation most directly relevant here is: 'An ability to analyse facts and to be able to construct and criticise an argument on a disputed question of fact' (p 114).
3 See p 223 below. See generally, J H Wigmore *The Science of Judicial Proof* (3rd edn, 1937).
4 On Wigmore's 'science' see William Twining *Theories of Evidence: Bentham and Wigmore* (1985) ch 3 and appendix.
5 Personal communication from Professor David Schum.
6 See especially D Schum *Evidence and Inference for the Intelligence Analyst*, 2 vols (University Press of America, 1987).
7 T Anderson and W Twining *Analysis of Evidence* (tentative edition, University of Miami Law School, 1987). Copies of this are obtainable on request from Professor Anderson at the University of Miami.

Contents
  I Inferential tasks
 II J H Wigmore 'The Problem of Proof'
III T Anderson and W Twining 'A Note on the Uses and Limitations of Wigmore's Method'
IV Sample inference charts

I INFERENTIAL TASKS

(From T Anderson and W Twining *Analysis of Evidence* (tentative edn, 1987, University of Miami Law School) 3–7)

Assessing the present and predicting the future: the intelligence analyst

(Schum *Evidence and Inference for the Intelligence Analyst* © (extracts))

The inference tasks performed by intelligence analysts share many character- istics in common with tasks in other areas [such as law, medical diagnosis and scientific research]. In common with legal fact-finding, analysts must fre- quently evaluate rich mixtures of nearly all the [standard] evidentiary forms. Juridical inference and intelligence analysis share a level of heightened aware- ness of and interest in source credibility not matched in other areas. The intelligence analyst shares the necessity for hypothesis and evidence gener- ation with the scientist and the medical diagnostician and, like the diagnostician, must consider multiple causes for observed data patterns. In addition, the structure of intelligence analytic problems is at least as difficult as those encountered in medical diagnosis. It is true of course that an analyst working in some discipline, inherits whatever inferential problems are peculiar to his/her scientific discipline. Thus, for example, the analyst asked to assess the intentions of Country A toward Country B must cope with the same indirect (or circumstantial) measurement problems that characterise academic research on intention and motivation in behavioral/social sciences. In common with law, medicine, and applied science, inference in intelligence analysis tends to be action-oriented. An interesting side constraint on our analysts is that their products are evaluated or 'graded' on their action or policy-relevance when, in fact, it is not always the case that analysts will be aware of what policies or actions are being considered.

An intelligence scenario 'from the top down'

As a weapon system analyst you have been following our own efforts to determine the feasibility of developing a certain tactical weapon system X. System X, though it provides decided improvements over an existing system Y, also promises to be very expensive. All of the relevant information you obtain suggests that development of X is quite feasible. Other information you have strongly suggests that system developers in Country A, a potential adversary, are also considering a weapon system whose characteristics are sufficiently similar to X that we can refer to theirs as X. They also have an existing system very similar to our existing system Y. As the acknowledged expert, you are tasked with determining how likely it is that decision-makers in Country A have decided to develop a prototype for the testing/evaluation of System X.

In this inference task you consider three possible major conclusions about the development of X in Country A:

○ H1: They have decided to build an X.
○ H2: They have decided not to build an X.
○ H3: They have not decided yet.

These hypotheses or major conclusions are immediately suggested by the nature of your assignment; a customer has stated a requirement that you can fulfill by an analysis showing the relative likelihood of these possible conclusions. Of course, it is true that any of these hypotheses, as stated above, could be redefined or reapportioned. For example, you might consider splitting H3 into:

○ H3: They have not decided yet but seem to be favouring development of X.
○ H4: They have not decided yet but seem to be against development of X.

This particular inference problem has some interesting features common to a variety of actual analytic inference tasks. One feature is that this problem requires an inference about the *intentions* of another country, group, or person; inferential work on this problem requires the analyst to place himself/herself in the position of other persons and to consider, among other things, what factors these persons would consider as well as the importance these persons would assign to these factors. Another feature is that the major hypotheses in this example allow one to deduce a rich variety of classes of hypotheses at several lower levels; lower level hypotheses are sometimes called indicators or *interim* hypotheses. Indicators or interim hypotheses simply prescribe possible evidence bearing upon hypotheses at the next *higher level* in a bottom-up chain of reasoning from the evidence.

It would certainly be nice if you had access to a credible person in Country A whose position made him/her privy to the decision we are concerned about and who would be willing to tell us which, if any, decision about X had been made. Absent such a 'nugget', we must proceed using more indirect means. So you ask yourself, what factors would decision-makers in Country A consider in such a decision. Here are three among the many factors you might suppose decision-makers in Country A would consider:

(1) Their assessment of the need for System X.
(2) Their assessment of the feasibility of developing X.
(3) Their assessment of the cost of X.

Each of these factors suggests certain reasoning chains in an inference about a decision made about System X in Country A. For our present purposes let us simply consider the first factor concerning need. The figure below illustrates one possible 'top-down' reasoning chain which suggests evidence we might obtain about their decision regarding X.

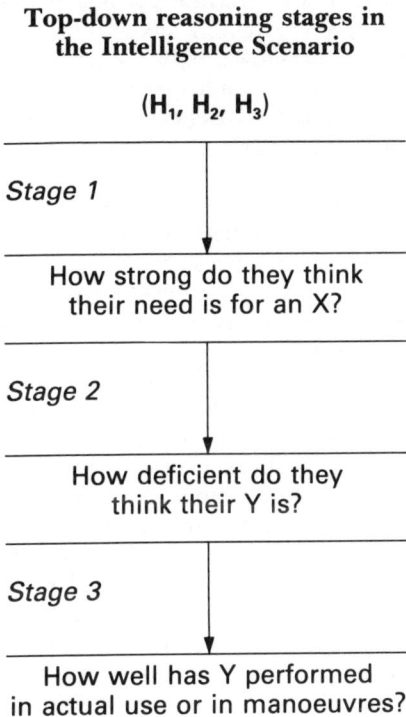

**Top-down reasoning stages in
the Intelligence Scenario**

(H₁, H₂, H₃)

Stage 1

How strong do they think
their need is for an X?

Stage 2

How deficient do they
think their Y is?

Stage 3

How well has Y performed
in actual use or in manoeuvres?

One deduction from our three possible major conclusions is that decision-makers in Country A have considered their need for System X; the question is: how strong do they think their need is for an X? Again, absent a credible source privy to decision-making in A, we are not likely to have direct evidence about their assessed need for an X. So we ask a further question and make a second deduction; the question is: what kinds of evidence might indicate how strongly they assess their need for an X to be? We may here be able to deduce many kinds of need-related indicators, for example, how deficient or obsolete do they consider is their current Y system, or, how important do they now consider X/Y systems generally in their tactical armamentarium. Let us just consider how deficient they believe is their existing Y system. Once again, we may or may not be able to obtain direct evidence of their beliefs on this issue and so we ask further questions about the kinds of evidence bearing upon their assessment of deficiencies in Y. One answer, of course, concerns how well their Y systems have performed in actual use or in evaluations during manoeuvres or other tests.

Here, finally, is a question whose answer does not involve an assessment by you of the state of mind of decision-makers in Country A; the answer involves observations of the actual performance of System Y. Presumably, we could make some of these observations or gather such evidence in other ways. For example, Countries A and B got into a scrap two months ago; the engagement was brief but intense. Several operators of Y systems from Country A were captured and interrogated by B personnel. In the process, the captured persons make assertions about their Y systems; these assertions (or, in truth, these alleged assertions) are passed along to us. With any luck at all, we may even be allowed to examine a captured Y system if any exist. We may discover that Country A's Y systems are inaccurate, jam, don't start in cold weather, overheat, or have parts that keep falling off.

This simple exercise in top-down deductive reasoning is an example of systematised expectation or anticipation of the kinds of evidence that may bear upon conclusions you have to reach. Depending upon the amount of time you have, your expertise in a problem area may allow you to construct an elaborate 'tree' whose 'branches' indicate the kinds of evidence you might expect to observe or consider. At the very outset of our discussions, we considered the importance of expectation and anticipation in any inference task. In many cases extensive top-down cascaded reasoning chains, in which your expectations are made explicit, can be formed before any evidence is considered.

Whether or not you could have observable evidence at any reasoning stage is an important issue. The above intelligence scenario was deliberately contrived to illustrate a situation in which several stages of deduction are necessary before we get to a stage at which there could be evidence observable to us. The more reasoning stages from hypotheses to an 'observable' stage, the weaker we expect evidence at this stage to be in inferences about top-level hypotheses. The assertions of the captured Y-system user from Country A provides an illustration of inferential remoteness. Suppose this person asserts: 'The Y system is inaccurate and jams all the time.' This assertion is just inconclusive evidence on how well Y systems perform; this source could be lying and, in any case, he is just a single user; others may have had different experiences with Y systems. In turn, the truth that Y systems perform badly is just inconclusive evidence that decision-makers in Country A believe Y to be deficient. They might believe, for example, that the system is excellent but the training of operators is poor. At the next stage, even a strong belief among decision-makers that Y is deficient is just inconclusive evidence of their belief in a need for X; they may have decided to do away with X/Y systems entirely. Finally, a strong belief in the need for an X system is inconclusive on whether or not they have decided to build one. They may need other systems as well and have decided to allocate resources elsewhere.

Questions

(1) What are the similarities and differences between

    (i) adjudication of a disputed question of fact;

    (ii) medical diagnosis of a patient with a complex combination of symptoms;

(iii) intelligence analysis directed to predicting the potential for survival of a military regime in a foreign country;

(iv) determination of an archeological puzzle?

(2) Do those different roles involve similar ethical choices and dilemmas in handling evidence?

Two murders

(1) *Charlie* C was murdered in his home at approximately 4.30 pm on 1 January. D states that she saw E enter C's house at 4.15 pm on that day. Show how D's statement tends to support the conclusion that it was E who murdered D.

(2) *Percy* Edith Thompson was charged with the murder of her husband Percy in that she either conspired with or incited her lover, Frederick Bywaters, to murder Percy.

(a) In the trial it was assumed that the fact that Edith was 28 and Freddie was 20 was relevant to the charge. Is this a reasonable assumption? If so why?

(b) Construct a chain of inferences from the fact that Edith was older than Freddie that supports the proposition that Edith incited him.

(c) Can the same fact be used as part of an argument in defence of Edith?

II THE PROBLEM OF PROOF

(From John H Wigmore 'The Problem of Proof' (1913) 8 Illinois Law Review 77.)

This article aspires to propose, though in tentative form only, a *novum organum* for the study of judicial evidence.

The study of the principles of evidence, for a lawyer, falls into two distinct parts. One is proof in the general sense – the part concerned with the ratiocinative process of contentious persuasion – mind to mind, counsel to juror, each partisan seeking to move the mind of the tribunal. The other part is admissibility – the procedural rules devised by law, and based on litigious experience and tradition, to guard the tribunal (particularly the jury) against erroneous persuasion. Hitherto, the latter has loomed largest in our formal studies – has, in fact, monopolised them; while the former, virtually ignored, has been left to the chances of later acquisition, casual and emphatic, in the course of practice. Here we have been wrong; and in two ways:

For one thing, there is, and there *must* be, a probative science – the principles of proof – independent of the artificial rules of procedure; hence, it can be and should be studied. This science, to be sure, may as yet be imperfectly formulated or even incapable of formulation. But all the more need is there to begin in earnest to investigate and develop it. Furthermore, this process of proof is the more important of the two – indeed, is the ultimate purpose in every judicial investigation. The procedural rules for admissibility are merely a preliminary aid to the main activity, viz. the persuasion of the tribunal's mind to a correct conclusion by safe materials. This main process is that for which the jury are there, and on which the counsel's duty is focused. Vital as it is, its principles surely demand study.

And, for another thing, the judicial rules of Admissibility are destined to lessen in relative importance during the next generation or later. Proof will assume the important place; and we must therefore prepare ourselves for this shifting of emphasis. We must seek to acquire a scientific understanding of the principles of what may be called 'natural' proof, – the hitherto neglected process. If we do not do this, history will repeat itself, and we shall find ourselves in the present plight of Continental Europe. There, in the early 1800s the ancient worn-out numerical system of 'legal proof' was abolished by fiat and the so-called 'free proof' – namely, no system at all – was substituted. For centuries, lawyers and judges had evidenced and proved by the artificial numerical system; they had no training in any other, – no understanding of the living process of belief; in consequence, when 'legal proof' was abolished, they were unready, and judicial trials have been carried on for a century past by uncomprehended, unguided, and therefore unsafe mental processes. Only in recent times, under the influences of modern science, are they beginning to develop a science of proof.

Such will be our own fate, when the time comes, if we do not lay foundations to prepare for the new stage of procedure. So far, there seems to be no attempt in English, since Bentham, to call attention to the principles of judicial Proof (distinguished from Admissibility) as a whole and as a system.

The problem of collating a mass of evidence, so as to determine the net effect which it should have on one's belief, is an everyday problem in courts of justice. Nevertheless, no one hitherto seems to have published any logical scheme on a scale large enough to aid this purpose. What is here offered is therefore only an attempt at a working method, which may suffice for lack of any other yet accessible.

Three questions naturally arise. What is the *object* of such a scheme? What are the necessary *conditions* to be satisfied? What is the *apparatus* therefore?

1 The object

The object, of course, is to determine rationally the net persuasive effect of a mixed mass of evidence. Many data, perhaps multifarious, are thrust upon us as tending to produce belief or disbelief. Each of them (by hypothesis) has some probative bearing. Consequently, we should not permit ourselves to reach a conclusion without considering all of them and the relative value of each. Negatively, therefore, our object is (in part) to avoid being misled (it may be) through attending only to some fragments of the mass of data. We must assume that a conclusion reached upon such a fragment only will be more or less untrustworthy. And our moral duty (in court) is to reach a belief corresponding to the actual facts; hence it is repugnant to us to contemplate that our belief is not as trustworthy as it could be.

Why is there such a danger of untrustworthiness? Because *belief* is *purely mental*. It is distinct from the external reality, or actual fact. Hence the approximation of our belief of a correct representation of the actual fact will depend upon how fully the data for the fact have entered into the mental formation of our belief. But those data have entered into the formation of our belief *at successive times*; hence a danger of omission or of inferior attention. 'Knowledge in the highest perfection would consist in the *simultaneous* possession of facts. To comprehend a science perfectly, we should have every fact present with every other fact. We are logically weak and imperfect in respect of the fact that we are obliged to think of one thing after another.' And in the

court room or the office the multitude of evidential facts are originally apprehended one after another. Hence the final problem is to co-ordinate them.
Logic ignores time; but the mind is more or less conditioned by it. The problem
is to remove the handicap as far as possible.

It may be answered that psychologically each evidential detail, when originally apprehended, did have [its] due effect, and that sub-consciously the
total impression is meanwhile being gradually produced. For example, when a
thousand bales of cotton are piled one by one in a warehouse, the whole
original thousand will finally be found there, available for sale, even though
they went in there piece-meal at different times. To rebut this argument, it is
enough to say that we do not yet know by psychological science that this
analogy is true of the mind in its successive apprehension of sundry facts;
hence we cannot afford to assume it. But furthermore, even if it were true
under certain abstract conditions, it is not the fact in the ordinary conduct of
justice. So many interruptions and distractions occur, both to the lawyer
in preparation [and] to the jurors in the trial, that facts cannot be properly
coordinated on their first apprehension. Hence our plain duty remains, to lift
once more and finally into consciousness *all* the data, to attempt to co-ordinate
them consciously, and to determine their net effect on belief.

Our object then, specifically, is in essence: *To perform the logical (or psychological) process of a conscious juxtaposition of detailed ideas for the purpose of producing
rationally a single final idea. Hence, to the extent that the mind is unable to juxtapose
consciously a larger number of ideas, each coherent group of detailed constituent ideas must
be reduced in consciousness to a single idea; until the mind can consciously juxtapose them
with due attention to each, so as to produce its single final idea.*

2 The necessary conditions

Any scheme which will aid in the foregoing purpose must fulfill certain
conditions, at least to a substantial degree.

(a) It must employ *types* of evidence, suitable for representing all kinds of cases
     presented. And these types must be based on some logical *system*, ie a
     system which includes all the fundamental logical processes.
(b) It must be able with these types to include *all the evidential data* in a *given
     case*. This requirement is mechanically the most exacting. The types of
     evidence and the processes of logic are few; but the number of instances of
     each one of them in a given case varies infinitely. Eg there may be in one
     case fifteen witnesses to a specific circumstance and two each to two
     others; while in the next case there may be neither circumstances nor
     witness of that sort, but thirty separate groups of other sorts; and this
     would be a simple example. Hence, the desired scheme must be capable
     mechanically of taking care of all possible varieties and the repeated
     instances of each.
(c) It must be able to show the *relation* of each evidential fact to each and all
     others. The process leading to belief is one of successive subsumings of
     single instances into groups of data and of the reduction of these groups
     into new single instances, and so on; hence the relations of the data to each
     other must be made apprehensible, and not merely the data per se. By
     'relations' of data is here meant that each believed fact does or does not
     tend to produce in the mind a belief or disbelief in some other specific
     alleged fact.
(d) It must be able to show the distinction between a *'fact' as alleged* and a *fact*

as believed or disbelieved; ie between the evidential data as *first proffered* for a purpose, and the effect of those data for the purpose *after* the mind has passed on them. Eg the party offers a witness as proving that the defendant was on a near-by street corner at a certain hour; yet when the tribunal proceeds to reckon that alleged fact as an item towards the main issue, it must have had some way of noting for later use whether it does or does not believe the witness and accept that alleged fact as an actual fact. Any scheme which fails to provide this would be like a bridge with the bolts left out of the truss angles; there would be nothing to show that it does not rest merely on an aggregation of hypotheses.

(e) It must be able to represent all the data as potentially *present in time to the consciousness*. The very aim of the scheme is to enable all the data to be lifted into consciousness at once. To be sure, the mind itself is not completely capable of this task, in other than the simplest cases. Numerous groups of subordinate data have to be first subsumed into other data by separate acts, until the number of those is small enough to be considered in a single continuous consciousness. Hence, the scheme in question *may* be so constructed that the records of these preliminary mental acts are not at all exhibited at once. Nevertheless, the mind will have to be sent back over these preliminary acts, from time to time, to verify, amplify, and correct them. And so (as first stated above) all of them must be at least *potentially* presentable to the consciousness, if the scheme is to be efficient.

(f) It must, finally, be *compendious* in bulk, and *not too complicated* in variety of symbols. These limitations are set by the practical facts of legal work. Nevertheless, men's aptitudes for the use of such schemes vary greatly. Experience alone can tell us whether a particular scheme is usable by the generality of able students and practitioners who need or care to attack the problem.

(g) But, negatively, the scheme need *not* show us what our belief *ought* to be. It can hope to show only what our belief actually *is*, and *how* we have actually reached it.

For example, assuming that the mind has accepted certain subordinate facts A, B, C, D, and E; and that A, B, and C point to X, the defendant's doing of an act, while D and E point to Not-X, ie his not doing it; there is no law (yet known) of logical thought which tells us that $(A+B+C)+(D+E)$ *must* equal X, or *must* equal Not-X. We know only that our mind, reflecting upon the five evidential data, *does* come to the conclusion X, or Not-X, as the case may be. All that the scheme can do for us is to make plain the entirety and details of our actual mental process. It cannot reveal laws which should be consciously obeyed in that process.

This is because no system of logic has yet discovered and established such laws. There are no known rules available, to test the correctness of the infinite variety of inferences presentable in judicial trials. Much indeed has been done that is theoretically applicable to circumstantial evidence; eg the method of differences, in inductive logic, may enable us, with the help of a chemist, to say whether a stain was produced by a specific liquid. But these methods must be pursued by a comparison of observed or experimental instances, newly obtained for the very case in hand, and usually numerous; hence they are impracticable for the vast mass of judicial data. Moreover, even so far as practicable in theory (so to speak), the required consumption of time would forbid their use in trials for any large masses of varied evidence. Hence, they do not serve our purpose. For testimonial evidence, also, those methods would be to some extent applicable in modern psychological experimentation. Yet merely to imagine two or three witnesses elaborately tested to determine their degree of trustworthiness as to memory or observation of sundry subjects of testimony, is to realise that such methods, by reason of the consumption of time alone, are not yet feasible in judicial trials. Finally, even so far as logic and psychology have gone with methods for estimating the probative force of individual inferences, they have apparently done nothing practical towards a method for measuring the *net effect* of a series or *mass of mixed data* bearing on a single alleged fact.

For these and other reasons, then, it must be understood that the desired scheme is not expected to tell us what *ought* logically to be our belief, – either as to individual subordinate data or as to the final net fact in issue.

What it *does* purport to achieve is to *show us explicitly* in a single compass how we *do reason and believe* for those individual facts and from them to the final fact. To achieve this much would be a substantial gain, in the direction of correctness of belief. Each separate proffered fact is tested in our consciousness, and the result is recorded. Perhaps we cannot explain *why* we reach that result, but we know at least that we *do* reach it. And thus step by step we set down the separate units of actual belief, – connecting, subsuming, and generalising, until the subfinal grouping is reached; then dwelling in consciousness on that; until at last a belief (or disbelief) on the final fact evolves into our consciousness.

Hence, though we may not be able to demonstrate that we *ought* to reach that belief or disbelief, we have at least the satisfaction of having taken every precaution to reach it rationally. Our moral duty was to approximate, so far as capable, our belief to the fact. We have performed that duty, to the limits of our present rational capacity. And the scheme or method, if it has enlarged that capacity, will have achieved something worth while.

We now proceed to the third and final topic: an Apparatus suitable as a working method for attaining the foregoing purpose while fulfilling the necessary conditions just set forth.

3 Explanation of apparatus for charting and listing the details of a mass of evidence

The apparatus consists of a Chart for symbols and a List for their translation. The types of evidence and logical processes have already been set forth in former chapters.

1 Symbols for kinds of evidence

Each human assertion, offered to be credited, is conceived of as a testimonial fact; each fact of any other sort is a circumstantial fact.

☐	Testimonial evidence affirmatory (M testifies that defendant had the knife).
⊓	Testimonial evidence negatory (M testifies that defendant did *not* have the knife).
○	Circumstantial evidence affirmatory (knife was picked up near where defendant was; hence, defendant had it).
∩	Circumstantial evidence negatory (knife was found in deceased's hand; hence, defendant did *not* have it).

⊟
⊓
⊖
⋂
¶

∞

Same four kinds of evidence, when offered by the *defendant* in a case. (These are the same four kinds of evidence; it is merely convenient to note which party offers them.)

Any fact judicially admitted, or noticed as a matter of general knowledge or inference, without evidence introduced.

Any fact presented to the *tribunal's own senses*, ie a coat shown, or a witness' assertion made in court on the stand. Everything actually evidenced must end in this, except when judicially noticed or judicially admitted.

>

Explanatory evidence; ie for *circumstantial* evidence, explaining away its effect (knife might have been dropped by a third person); for *testimonial* evidence, discrediting its trustworthiness (witness was too excited to see who picked up the knife).

◁

Corroborative evidence; ie for *circumstantial* evidence, strengthening the inference, closing up other possible explanations (no third person was near the parties when the knife was found); for *testimonial* evidence, supporting it by closing up possibilities of testimonial error (witness stood close by, was not excited, was disinterested spectator).

>
◁

Same two kinds of evidence, when offered by the *defendant* in a case.

2 *Relation of individual pieces of evidence, shown by position of symbols*

○ A supposed fact tending to prove the existence of another fact is placed *below* it.

○ A supposed explanatory or corroborative fact, tending to lessen or to strengthen the force of fact thus proved, is placed to *left* or *right* of it, respectively.

○ A single *straight* line (continued at a right angle, if necessary) indicates the supposed relation of one fact to another.

○ The symbol for a fact observed by the tribunal or judicially admitted or noticed (¶, ∞) is placed directly *below* the fact so learned.

3 *Probative effect of an evidential fact*

When a fact is offered or conceived as evidencing, explaining, or corroborating, it is noted by the appropriate symbol with a connecting line. But thus far it is merely *offered*. We do not yet know whether we believe it to be a fact, nor what probative force we are willing to give it, if a fact. As soon as our mind has come to the necessary *conclusion* on the subject, we symbolise as follows:

↑

(1) *Provisional credit* given to *affirmatory* evidence, testimonial or circumstantial, is shown by adding an arrow-head.

Provisional credit given to *negatory* evidence, testimonial or circumstantial, is shown by adding an arrow-head above a small cipher.

Particularly *strong credit* given to those kinds of evidence respectively is shown by doubling the arrow-head; this is usually applicable where several testimonies or circumstances concur upon the same fact.

(2) A small interrogation mark, placed alongside the connecting line, signifies *doubt* as to the probative effect of the evidence.

Similarly, for each kind of symbol, a small interrogation mark within it signifies a mental balance, an uncertainty; the alleged fact may or may not be a fact.

(3) A dot within the symbol of any kind of *alleged fact* signifies that we now *believe* it to *be* a fact. Particularly strong belief may be signified by two dots; thus ⊙ .

A small cipher within the symbol of any kind of alleged fact signifies that we now *disbelieve* it to be a fact. Particularly strong disbelief may be signified by two such ciphers; thus ⊙ .

(4) If a single supposed *explanatory* fact does, in our estimation after weighing it, detract from the force of the desired inference (in case of a witness, if it discredits his assertion), we signify this by an arrow-head pointing to the left, placed half way across the horizontal connecting line.

If a single *corroborative* fact is given effect in our estimation, we signify this by a short Roman letter X, placed across the connecting line.

Doubling the mark indicates particular strength in the effect, ie ⤙ , or ⤚ .

Ultimately, when determining the total effect, in our estimation of *all* explanatory and corroborative facts upon the *net probative value* of the specific fact explained or corroborated, we place a short horizontal mark or small X, respectively, upon the upright connecting line of the latter fact.

Thus, for *net probative value*, several grades of probative effect may be symbolised: † signifies that the inference is a weak one; ┬ signifies that it has no force at all; ⚔ signifies that it is a strong one; ⚔ signifies that it is conclusive. When the supposed inference is a *negatory* one, the same symbols are used, with the addition of the negatory symbol, ie ⚔ (witness asserts that defendant had *not* a knife in his hand; witness's credit is supported by the fact that he is a friend of the deceased).

4 Numbering the symbols

Each symbol receives a number, placed at the upper left outside margin. These numbers are then placed in the Evidence List; they are written down consecutively, and opposite each one in the list is written a brief note of the evidential fact represented by it.

The List is thus the translation of the Chart.

The separate pieces of evidence are given *consecutive* numbers in the List as they are being analysed and noted in symbols, till all the evidence is charted. They need not run consecutively on the *Chart*; though naturally the numbers in any one chain of inferences will be consecutive. Should a further analysis of a particular piece of evidence develop new appurtenant evidence, the additional evidence can be given a decimal of the main number (so that on the Evidence List it will be found conveniently near to the main fact). Eg if $^{27}\bigcirc$ is found later to have two new explanatory facts, one of them, with its appurtenant witnesses, may be numbered 27.1, 27.2, 27.3; the other may be numbered 27.4, 27.5, 27.6. NB that on the Chart it is immaterial whether the numbers are consecutive; the numbers serve merely to guide the eye quickly to the description of the fact on the Evidence List.

5 Analysing and classifying the evidence

(a) Each supposed piece of evidence must be *analysed*, so far as practicable and reasonably necessary, into all *its subordinate inferences*. Only in this way can the possibilities of explanation and corroborative facts be discovered. Eg the defendant's threats in *Com. v Umilian*; the inference really is: threats show a plan to kill, and plan to kill shows actual killing. This enables us to chart separately the possible explanations weakening the inference from threats, and the testimony, if any, asserting those explanatory facts.

(b) Where a *Human Act* is the issue, the classification in Part I of this work will be found convenient, ie Moral Character, Motive, Design, etc. Under Motive (Emotion) it is sounder to separate at the outset the distinct alleged motives, if any; eg desire for money, desire for revenge, etc, because they are in effect distinct and perhaps inconsistent probative facts.

(c) In the same way, the *discrediting* (explanatory) *facts for a witness's assertion* should be separated into their component items. Thus, if bias is the general nature of the impeachment, let eg $>^{18}$ be the supposed general fact of actual bias and let $^{19}\bigcirc$ and $^{20}\bigcirc$ be the two circumstances tending to evidence it, 19 being the witness's relation to the defendant as a discharged employee, 21 being another witness who testifies to this, and 20 being the impeached witness's strong demeanor of bias while on the stand.

Thus the whole representation would be:

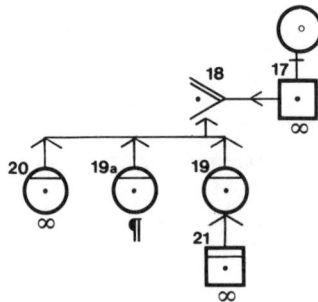

Here the added symbols of belief show that the probative effect has been that we refuse belief (if we do) to the fact asserted by this witness, because of his bias as shown by those facts.

Note that 19 is here supplemented by 19*a*, ie the supposed general truth that discharged employees are apt to have an emotion of hostility; the letter *a* added to the main number will indicate the appurtenant relation of this fact to 19.

In accordance with the analysis of impeaching evidence (as set forth in prior chapters) it is usually desirable to note separately on the Chart any supposed general truth implicitly or explicitly relied upon. This is more commonly the case where a *mediate* or second step of reference is involved, as in the above example. But even there a general truth may not always be involved; eg in the above example 20 ◯ is the specific language or demeanor from which an inference is made, without aid of a general truth, to the supposed emotion. Where an *immediate* inference is involved, the only cases where the supposed general truths need to be explicitly noted will usually be those involving external conditions, – light, sound, etc; in such a case the first symbol can be doubled, using the letter *a* with the main number to indicate the appurtenant general truth. For example, if the location of the witness is said to have obstructed his vision and thus discredited his statement, it would be thus indicated:

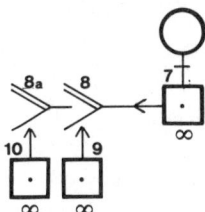

Here: 7 is the witness to be impeached; 8 is the facts of his location on the sidewalk, and 9 is a witness to those facts; 8*a* is the impossibility of correct vision from such location, and 10 is a witness to experiments showing such impossibility.

A special advantage in thus plotting separately the concrete facts and the general truths is that the witnesses thereto may then be plotted separately, and thus all the evidence thereon can be more clearly distinguished and weighed.

6 Plotting the chart

Use an oblong sheet of unruled paper.

Allot the right-hand half to the plaintiff or prosecution, the left-hand half to the defendant.

Allot the right-hand quarter to the plaintiff's testimonial evidence directly on the fact in issue; the next quarter (towards the left) to his circumstantial evidence; and so on for the defendant. If there are two or more distinct facts necessary in law to the issue, use a separate chart sheet for each; unless the mass of evidence is small enough for a single sheet (as in the annexed examples of charts).

Since the quantity of each kind of evidence varies in each case, the above allotments of one quarter each are of course provisional only. In practice, a smaller or larger fraction will usually be needed. But by beginning at the right-hand end and disposing of all of each kind of evidence before proceeding to the next, the spacing will adjust itself. If desired, a line can be drawn perpendicularly to mark off the mass of one kind of evidence when charted.

When beginning on the next kind, allow a little extra space for later discoveries in the kind of evidence just finished.

Use right-angled continued lines freely in connecting the symbols, so as to economise space and to keep together the same kind of evidence.

Use a sharpened lead pencil.

If new inferences are later discovered and no space is left, erase some former symbols and rechart them, prolonging the lines so as to leave the new space needed.

Wherever a disbelief or doubt symbol is found, there ought to be some explanatory fact (>) to account for it. Hence, if such has been inadvertently omitted, analyse it into consciousness, chart it, and describe it in the Evidence List.

Where two or more witnesses, as to whose credit no question is raised, testify to the same fact, one symbol in the Chart may serve for all; but as many numbers should be given it as there are witnesses, bracketing these numbers to one description in the Evidence List.

A fact is to be classed as negatory or affirmatory in itself and not according to the party offering it. Thus, as in Nos 51, 52, 48, 49, of *Hatchett v Com.* (see Chart), the defendant may offer an affirmatory fact to prove another fact which is negatory of his guilt.

7 Sundries

For clearness and quickness in studying the total effect of the mass of evidence when charted, coloured pencils may be used.

Use a *blue* pencil for important facts favouring the plaintiff's or prosecution's contention, and a *green* one for those favouring the defendant's. Mark the arrow point of the belief symbol (↑), or the cross of the disbelief symbol (†), respectively blue or green. Thus the subfinal facts can be conveniently concentrated in the mind, for the purpose of the net total effect on the mind. Varieties of detail in the use of the coloured pencil can be invented as convenient; eg a simple arrow point (↑), blue or green, can be used for the subordinate facts as the basis of a long line of inference, and a triangular arrow point for the subfinal facts when reached.

When ready to reach a final verdict, refresh the memory from the List, so that the tenor of the Chart symbols is as clear as possible in the mind. Then go over the whole Chart in the mind, force the subfinal facts into juxtaposition, and determine the net impression as to the ultimate fact in issue.

8 Finally, remember that

The logical (or psychological) process is essentially one of mental juxtaposition of detailed ideas for the purpose of producing rationally a single final idea. Hence, to the extent that the mind is unable to juxtapose consciously a larger number of ideas, each coherent group of detailed constituent ideas must be reduced successively to a single idea, until the number and kind is such that the mind can consciously juxtapose them with due attention to each. And the use of symbols has no other purpose than to facilitate this process. Hence, each person may contrive his own special ways of using these or other symbols.

As examples of the use of the Chart and List, the cases of *Com. v Umilian* (post) and *Hatchett v Com.* (post) are charted and listed in the following pages. Note that these Examples might have been charted with more economy of space, but in their present shape they show how the Chart develops in the actual making. The charter cannot know beforehand how many data will be found under each inference; hence he must allow space, which may not afterwards be needed.

Commonwealth v Umilian (1901) Supreme Judicial Court of
Massachusetts, 177 Mass 582

Indictment for murder, returned 12 June 1900. At the trial in the Superior
Court, before Sherman and Stevens JJ, the defendant at the close of the
evidence asked the judges to rule and instruct the jury: first, that there was not
sufficient evidence to warrant the jury in finding a verdict of guilty; and,
second, that there was not sufficient evidence to warrant the jury in finding a
verdict of guilty in the first degree. The judges declined to give either of these
rulings. The jury found a verdict of guilty of murder in the first degree; and the
defendant alleged exceptions.

J B O'Donnell, for the defendant. *J C Hammond*, District Attorney, for the
Commonwealth.

KNOWLTON J: The defendant was found guilty of murder in the first degree,
and the only question before us is whether there was any evidence to warrant
the verdict. He and Casimir Jedrusik were working together as farm laborers
for one Keith in Granby. On Sunday, 31 December 1899, Jedrusik disap-
peared, and was never afterwards seen alive. On 10 April 1900, his headless,
mutilated body was found inclosed in a bran sack in an unused well between
four hundred and five hundred feet from Keith's horse barn. His clothing was
found inclosed in another sack in the same well. His skull was afterwards found
buried in the cellar of the horse barn. the sacks were similar to those which
Keith had in the horse barn. The stone, which was inclosed in the sack of
clothing, exactly fitted a vacant place in a stone wall about in line between the
old well and the north door of the horse barn. On the day of the disappearance
there was no snow on the ground, and the surface of the ground was entirely
frozen. In the cellar of the horse barn pigs were kept, and there was soft mud
there. The clothing which was exhibited to the jury had mud upon it which the
Commonwealth contended on the evidence was like that in the cellar.
Mr and Mrs Keith drove away to church on 31 December, leaving the
defendant and Jedrusik about the barn. The defendant's wife was in the house,
where she was employed as a housemaid, and there was evidence tending to
show that the only other person who came there during the day was a young
woman who came to visit her. The defendant was outside of the house, about
the premises, for some hours after Mr and Mrs Keith went to church, and
when he came in he said that Jedrusik had gone to Granby. There were
wounds on the head of Jedrusik, which the Commonwealth contended were
made by a corn cutter that was in the horse barn, and was exhibited to the jury.
The evidence tended to show that the defendant had ample opportunity to
commit the murder, and that no other person had an opportunity to do it
without discovery.

On 18 November the defendant went to Chicopee to the house of a Polish
priest, to have the ceremony of marriage performed between him and a young
woman who had been living as a maid at Keith's house, and he found that the
priest had received a letter in a name which proved to be fictitious, charging
him with having a wife and children in the old country, and with receiving
letters from his wife asking for money for the support of himself and her
children. The priest refused to marry him, and sent a trusted person with him
to investigate. It turned out that Jedrusik wrote the letter, and that its contents
did not appear to be true. The defendant was then married by the priest, and
the evidence tended to show that he was very angry with Jedrusik, and that he
made strong threats of vengeance against him. There was evidence from
several witnesses that at different times between the defendant's marriage and

Jedrusik's disappearance, the defendant manifested deeply hostile feeling towards him, and made threats against him. On the morning of 31 December, there was a new manifestation of this feeling in charges made to Mr Keith that Jedrusik had stolen a plane and had stolen butter. There was evidence that, between the time of the disappearance and the discovery of the body, the defendant was seen to take up one of the planks covering the unused well, and also that when he was told in the daytime that Keith and one Olds had gone out of the house with a lantern, he said he 'knew what they were going to do. Mr Olds wants to buy the pump in the old well'. There was evidence that nothing had ever been said by Olds about buying the pump. Immediately after being told this the defendant went into the horse barn, and was seen looking out of a window from which the well could be seen. When others went to the well after the body was found, he did not go. There was also evidence that about the middle of January he gave away Jedrusik's rubber boots, and said that he did not think Jedrusik would come back. There were many other things in his language and conduct after Jedrusik's disappearance which the Commonwealth relied on as tending to show guilty knowledge, and much of his testimony in explanation of facts was in direct contradiction of other witnesses.

Without going more at length into the evidence, which was voluminous, we are of opinion that it would have been error to take the case from the jury. So far as we can judge from the bill of exceptions the evidence well warranted the verdict. *Exceptions overruled.*

EXAMPLE A: COMMONWEALTH V UMILIAN

> Evidence Chart. [See below, p 254.]
> Evidence List (*Com. v Umilian*).

1   Design to kill J.
2   Threats of unstated tenor, made on discovery of J's interference in prevention of marriage.
3   Anon. witnesses thereto.
4   Threats might have meant merely some lesser harm.
5   Threats of revenge at later time.
6   Anon. witnesses thereto.
7   Threats might have meant merely some lesser harm.
8   Revengeful, murderous emotion towards J.
9   J had charged him with intended bigamy 18 Nov, and had tried thereby to prevent his marriage.
10 Letter received by priest, stating that U already had family in old country.
11 Anon. witnesses to this.
12 J was author of letter, though it was in fictitious name.
13 Anon. witnesses to this.
14 Letter communicated by priest to U, with refusal to perform marriage; refusal later withdrawn.
15 Anon. witnesses to this.
16 Letter's statements were untrue.
17 Anon. witnesses to this.
18 U being innocent, and marriage being finally performed, U would not have had a strong feeling of revenge.
19 J remaining in daily contact, wound must have rankled.
20 Wife remaining there, jealousy between U and J probably continued.
21 U uttered threats and other hostile expressions between 18 Nov and 31 Dec.

22 Anon. witnesses to this.
23 U, on 31 Dec charged J to K with stealing K's goods.
24 Anon. witnesses to this.
25 Does not appear that these charges were false, hence not malicious.
26 U's opportunity in time and place was almost exclusive.
27 On 31 Dec U was on premises.
27.1 Witnesses to this.
28 U was only man so seen.
29 U's wife and woman visitor, were there.
30 Anon. witnesses to this.
31 Passing tramp-villain might have been there.
32 In time between 31 Dec and April others had access to J, if alive still.
33 U had uneasy consciousness of guilt about J's disappearance.
34 U lied about J's going to Granby.
35 U said J had gone there, although J was dead.
36 Anon. witnesses to this.
37 J might really have gone there, not being killed till later.
38 U was conscious that the well was a place where damaging things would be discovered.
39 He watched those who searched there.
40 Anon. witnesses to this.
41 That might have been due to natural curiosity of a farm hand at strange doings.
42 U lied about the reason for Olds and K searching the well.
43 Anon. witnesses to this.
44 U did not go to the well to see the body when found.
45 Anon. witnesses to this.
46 Several other reasons would explain this.
47 U knew that J was dead, though others did not.
48 He gave away J's boots and said that J would not come back; this was about the middle of January.
49 Anon. witnesses thereto.
50 Like others, U may merely have believed that J had given up work at the farm.
51 Data of slayer on J's body were of a person having free and intimate access to horse barn of K.
52 Wound-marks were those of a horse-cutter from barn.

EXERCISE A

Read the account of *Commonwealth v Umilian*, then
(a) complete the key-list on *data of slayer*; and
(b) draw an evidence chart for the case, using Wigmore's symbols.

III A NOTE ON THE USES AND LIMITATIONS OF WIGMORE'S CHART METHOD

(From T Anderson and W Twining *Analysis of Evidence* (tentative edn, 1987, University of Miami Law School, 77–87))

Introduction

The purpose of this note is to give our personal appraisal of Wigmore's Chart Method in terms of its value within legal education, as a device for practising lawyers, and as a method which might be adopted (and adapted) by other types of investigators involved in different kinds of factual inquiries, such as archaeologists, historians, or detectives.

The first question to be asked is whether the method has a sound theoretical basis. Wigmore's general approach falls squarely within the central tradition of Anglo-American evidence scholarship, which in turn is closely connected to the practice of lawyers and of the courts. It claims to be a systematisation and refinement of the methods of analysing evidence used by experienced and effective practitioners both in preparing and presenting cases. It draws on a central tradition of inductive logic – notably the work of Mill, Sidgwick, and Jevons.[1] Wigmore's method is solidly grounded in an intellectually respect-able tradition which has been developed and refined by others; to date, no one has developed an alternative method of organising and analysing masses of evidence which is comparable in sophistication and clarity.

In evaluating the utility of the method, it is important to distinguish between its pedagogical value as a form of mental training and its practical value as a technique usable by trial lawyers or others. The justification for training in formal logic or in pure mathematics is not seriously undermined by pointing out that the ordinary conditions of living do not often permit direct applications of these methods to the practical problems in everyday life. The conditions of the academy often permit greater purity and greater rigour than can be expected in the hurly-burly of practical affairs. But, even if judged solely in terms of practical value, a rigorous training in a method of analysis, which may be too time-consuming, demanding, or 'pure' for regular practical use, may have a gymnastic value as mental training and may set standards of rigour or provide an orientation sufficient to justify its use in academic exercises. Artificiality may be a reasonable price to pay for these benefits. Indeed, as we understand the argument, these are the very grounds upon which the American case-method of training lawyers was and is justified.

Similar considerations apply to Wigmorean analysis: even if the Chart Method in its purest form may be too laborious for everyday use by prac-titioners – a question which we leave open for the present – it does not necessarily undermine its value as an educational device. Accordingly, in evaluating the utility of the method, we need to separate its utility as a method of intellectual training from its utility as a daily tool for the working prac-titioner.

The practical values for students

What can students expect to learn from doing exercises in Wigmorean analy-sis? In our view, such exercises serve several purposes, only two of which need to be noted here. First, they create certain kinds of awareness: awareness that the counters in any argument, and particularly in arguments about evidence, are propositions and relations between propositions; awareness that in ordi-nary discourse, whether written or oral, many steps in the argument are typically glossed over or left implicit. We believe that one of Wigmore's main claims for the method is fully justified: that it brings into the open and makes explicit important steps in an argument and thereby makes it easier to judge both their soundness and their probative force. A student who has been through the process of analysing even one case in a disciplined way is made aware of how easy it is to make logical jumps, to rely upon unidentified generalisations, to get away with fallacies, to introduce irrelevant material, or, by a shift in standpoint, to switch ultimate probanda, and so on. All students, particularly in the early stages, find doing these exercises extremely laborious. Indeed they have a natural tendency to move quickly from over-confidence to despair and to be tempted to give up without suitable 'encouragement'. This should drive home the lesson that analysing evidence is essentially hard intellectual work. A student who has spent a mere fifty or a hundred hours analysing a rather simple case more readily grasps how it is that so many thousands of hours could have been spent on projects such as congressional investigations into the Kennedy assassination or the hunt for the Yorkshire Ripper (to take two extreme cases) or even on quite routine police investigations into a murder. Thus application of the method compels a disciplined and patient approach to evidence. Adapting Marshall Macluhan, if Wigmorean analysis is the medium, the message is that analysis of evidence involves hard work.

Second, the Wigmore chart method forces the student to take facts seriously. It forces the student to prepare a list of evidential propositions: some of these propositions might actually be asserted by a witness or supported by real evidence presented to the senses of the trier of fact during trial. It forces the student to relate this mass of evidential propositions to the ultimately controlling propositions of law in a rigorous and logically coherent manner, identifying each intermediate inference necessary to establish the relationship between the data and the ultimate probandum. Apart from its other values, this is enough to justify its use.[2]

An approach to Wigmore's methods

Mastering Wigmore's method is similar to mastering any complex analytical skill. In learning it, you should try to cultivate the habit of going through a regular sequence of operations step-by-step. We have identified a sequence of seven steps that seem necessary and helpful:

(1) clarification of standpoint, purpose, and role;
(2) formulation of potential ultimate probandum or probanda;
(3) formulation of potential penultimate and strategic probanda;
(4) formulation of theory and themes of the case: choice of strategic ultimate and penultimate probanda;
(5) compiling a key-list;
(6) preparation of the chart(s); and
(7) completing the analysis.

It is worth considering each of these in turn.

Step 1 Clarify the standpoint of the analysis by giving clear and precise answers to the questions. Who am I? At what stage in what process am I? What am I trying to do?

Standpoint is always a function of three dependent variables – time and location, objective (or purpose), and role. For Wigmore the principal, but not the only, temporal point of reference is the trial and the courtroom; the secondary point is the occurrence of the events giving rise to the dispute. He commonly directs his analysis to the evidence presented to the trier of fact in terms of the conclusions to be drawn with respect to the past events that gave

rise to the dispute. However, he is neither consistent in adopting that standpoint nor in identifying the particular standpoint he is using or its consequences to the analysis.

In academic law instruction, the point in time is typically post-trial and
post-appeal. Based upon the evidence in the record and the law applied, did
the trier of fact have a logical basis for the result reached? For the practitioner
(and, with appropriate exercises, for the student) the exercise may focus upon
any stage: reviewing a trial record for appeal, developing a closing argument
based upon evidence given, preparing a matter for trial based upon a completed investigation, investigating a matter in preparation for litigation or
trial, evaluating a client's claims in order to aid the decision whether to
litigate, or even advising a client on how to structure proposed conduct with
respect to the prospect of future litigation.

The standpoint is also a function of the objectives of the analysis. These can
usefully be divided into three main classes: organisational, evaluative and
advocacy objectives. One of the main values of the chart method is as a tool for
organising or ordering or structuring the evidence and inferences derived from
it, as a preliminary to pursuing some other objective such as evaluation or
presentation of an argument. For Wigmore (and for most academic analysis) the objective is ordinarily to evaluate the evidence offered to determine
whether the case was rightly or justifiably decided with reference to some
articulated standard – eg given the substantive law and the burden of proof the
court found applicable, did the evidence support the factual conclusion necessary to be reached? This evaluative analysis may be done for different purposes
– to determine whether the lawyer could have done better on closing or on
appeal, whether the rules of admissibility operated to further or frustrate an
inquiry to determine truth, etc. But all such exercises start from the assumption that the evidence presented to the trier of fact is fixed.

An advocacy objective is typically dominant when the student or the
lawyer seeks to perform the analysis to assist in determining an appropriate
course of conduct. What additional investigation or discovery should I seek
to strengthen (or weaken) inferences necessary to the development of my
client's (or my adversary's) case? What evidence must I highlight and what
evidence must I seek to exclude or minimise to develop my theory of the
case?[3]

A third variable is role. Role is always implicit once the objective is chosen.
But it may be useful to consider the variable separately both to clarify
objectives and to reveal possible personal biases of the person doing the
analysis. For example, the lawyer preparing for trial has a fixed role, but must
assume three standpoints and three roles in order to do the job: first, the role of
advocate for his or her client; second, the standpoint and role of his opponent;
and, finally, the role and standpoint of the trier-of-fact. To what extent will the
triers of fact share the generalisations (or biases) upon which the probative
force of my analysis and ordering of the evidence depend?[4]

Step 2   Formulate carefully and precisely the potential ultimate probandum
or probanda. This does not come as naturally to students as an experienced
lawyer might expect. It is surprising how often students fail to see that this is a
crucial preliminary step which provides the focal point for the whole analysis.
Without an ultimate probandum there is no touchstone of relevance; if it is
incorrectly or loosely formulated, the ensuing analysis is correspondingly
vulnerable.

The first step then must be to formulate (or identify) the controlling propositions of law. Typically, these can be divided into two categories, the substantive proportions (the elements of the crime, the standard of care, the rule of damages) and the propositions defining the standard of proof (beyond a reasonable doubt, clear and convincing, a preponderance of the evidence). The substantive propositions constitute the major premises; the ultimate probandum or probanda are the minor premises – those propositions of fact which, if found proven to the required degree, compel or support the conclusion that the party with the burden must prevail. The propositions defining the burden of proof govern the analysis of the probative force of the evidence.

The process is reflexive and involves judgment. For every case we may be able to identify abstract propositions of law that control and convert them into abstract propositions of fact. For example:

Major premise:	All contracts made in violation of positive law are void.
Minor premise:	This contract was made in violation of positive law.
Conclusion:	This contract was void.

But for the particular case, the propositions must be made specific.

Major premise:	If a landlord had knowledge at the time he signed a lease that conditions existed which violated the housing regulations and which rendered the premises unsafe and unsanitary then the lease was void as an illegal contract.
Major premise:	The landlord here knew on the date the lease was signed that three conditions existed, each of which constituted a violation of the housing regulations and which collectively rendered the premises unsafe and unsanitary.
	or
	The landlord here knew when he signed the lease that the commode was inoperable, that the stair railing was broken, and that the ceiling was too low, and those conditions made the apartment unsafe and unsanitary.
Conclusion:	This lease was void.

[The major and minor premises are drawn from *Brown v Southall Realty Co*, 237 A 2d 834 (DC Ct App 1968).]

The process is complex and reflexive. If the ultimate probandum is too abstract, it does not provide the touchstone of relevance; to the extent it is framed with too much specificity at the outset, avenues of inquiry that might otherwise be explored may be foreclosed. The need for judgment in addition to technical skill is clearest when the problem is viewed from the standpoint of the advocate. From the available legal authority, he or she must determine the most 'favourable' proposition of law that the court can be persuaded to accept as controlling. From that the ultimate probandum must be derived. But that judgment can only be finally made after the lawyer has analysed the evidence and made a judgment with respect to the most favourable proposition that he or she can persuasively argue it does not (or does) prove. Although the steps should be approached sequentially, all judgments should be tentative until the entire process has been completed.

Step 3 Formulate the potential penultimate probanda, that is to say the main propositions which stand immediately adjacent to the ultimate probandum or probanda.

Ordinarily the ultimate probandum or probanda are compound propositions with more than one condition which must be satisfied. Determining the penultimate probanda initially and at a minimum, requires that we break the ordinarily complex ultimate probandum into component simple propositions. But more is required to make the necessary strategic judgments. The person doing the analysis must adopt a tentative theory of the case. Based upon impressions derived from the evidence as a whole, what are the central problems and how can the necessary propositions be framed to enhance the prospects that the evidence properly analysed will (or will not) logically and persuasively satisfy the conditions identified. Art and intuition are both required, but at this stage care must be taken to identify and set down as many potentially useful alternatives as possible. Once these penultimate probanda have been tentatively formulated, the lawyer should be in a position to visualise the overall structure of the case and the potential ways in which the factum probans suggested by the available evidential data can be related to these penultimate probanda. An illustration may be useful at this point.

In *Brown v Southall Realty Co*, the court had established the specific major premise set out above and had applied it to the facts of that case – a broken commode, a broken stair railing and a ceiling less than the required height. Assume we have a tenant-client whose apartment had a broken commode, a leaky gas stove and rat infestation. Assume that each of these conditions violated a specific housing regulation. We seek to start our pre-trial evidence chart.

From the major premise in *Brown*, we might formulate our ultimate probandum.

(1) The landlord knew at the time the lease was signed that the apartment had a commode which was inoperable and a stove which leaked gas and was infested by rats, and these three conditions collectively made the premises unsafe and unsanitary. This complex and compound ultimate probandum may be translated into simpler penultimate probanda as follows:

(2) At the time the lease was signed, the apartment had a commode which was inoperable, a stove which leaked gas, and was infested by rats.

(3) At the time the lease was signed, the apartment had a commode which was inoperable.

(4) At the time the lease was signed, the apartment had a stove which leaked gas.

(5) At the time the lease was signed, the apartment was infested by rats.

(6) At the time the lease was signed, the landlord knew that these conditions existed.

(7) These conditions rendered the apartment unsafe and unsanitary. Using Wigmore's symbols, these propositions and their relationships might be plotted as follows:

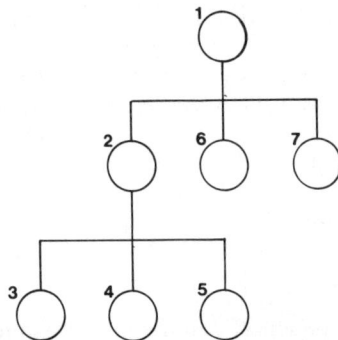

This formulation, however, also involved judgments and suggests a theory of the case. It is not, for example, entirely clear under *Brown* whether the landlord's knowledge need extend only to the specific conditions or whether he or she must also know that the conditions render the premises unsafe and unsanitary and/or that the conditions in fact violated the housing regulations. In formulating the ultimate probandum and the penultimate probanda, we make judgments that may limit our analysis of the evidence. These may be critical judgments. They should be consciously, carefully, and, at this stage, cautiously made.

Step 4   Formulate the provisional theories of the case and choose the strategic ultimate and penultimate probanda that best fit the theory or theories. The theory of the case is the logical statement formulated as an argument supporting one or more conclusions about the case as a whole. Up to this point we have operated with provisional theories. If the problem is a complex one involving a mixed mass of evidence, it is highly likely that there will be a range of possible theories each of which could lead the analysis in significantly different directions. In order to make the task manageable, it may be necessary to eliminate some possibilities and concentrate on one or more specific theories. Even historians and scientists do not have infinite time and resources to pursue endless lines of enquiry. Typically advocates have to settle for one theory (or at least a strictly limited number) at a fairly early stage. The precise timing of such choices naturally varies according to circumstances. Later we shall explore in some detail the nature of such theories, their relationship to 'story', 'situation' and 'theme' in the context of advocacy and their functions at different stages of litigation. At this stage, we wish merely to emphasise two related points: Choice of theory is one of the most important decisions that has to be made in trial practice.[1] Accordingly care must be taken both to consider the full range of possibilities, including variants, and to formulate the chosen theory or theories as precisely as possible.

Step 5   Formulate the key-list: identify those items of evidential data that are available to be offered and convert them into simple propositions: propositions involving only one condition and susceptible to the response 'true/false', 'proven/not proven', 'probable/not probable', etc. Then state each of the intermediate propositions necessary to relate them to one or more of the penultimate probanda.

From the universe of data available, the key-list may (and probably must) be limited to what is relevant (in some degree) to the ultimate probandum. But visualising what is relevant requires an intuitive application of the inductive process we are trying to make explicit. Beware of cutting out potentially relevant material too early; err on the side of over-inclusion in the first cut. It is simple to strike unnecessary evidentiary propositions from the key-list after the chart is complete; it may well be impossible to see significant relations if data have not been included.

The process of developing and organising the key-list is also reflexive. The ultimate and penultimate probanda suggest intermediate probanda we want to reach. But the evidential proposition may also suggest direct and intermediate inferences and combinations whose relevance will be apparent only when formulated. The propositions on the list should be ordered 'logically', but there is a danger that too early an effort at structure and coherence will cause us to overlook important hypotheses.

Several points deserve further comment. First, most of Wigmore's exercises involved ex post facto analysis of accounts of decided cases, typically of trial

1 See p 323 below.

records. His standpoint was, accordingly, that of some type of historian, even when the analysis was confined to reconstructing arguments about evidence actually presented by each side in an adversary proceeding. By definition, if that is the standpoint, all the evidence has been collected. The exercise then is to analyse a given mixed mass of evidence that constitutes the data on which the decision was based in light of a declared ultimate probandum. If this standpoint is adopted, the natural next step is to compile a key-list. This involves identifying, formulating, and ordering propositions which are direct-ly or indirectly relevant to the ultimate probandum or probanda as given.

But if the standpoint is that of an advocate, the concept of selection must be added. Selection implies a given collection of pre-existing propositions from which one chooses those which are relevant. But even where there is a finite body of material for analysis, such as a pre-trial collection of depositions and documents, the propositions are not already there, lined up like candidates on parade. A complex process of extracting, individuating and making explicit statements in propositional form is involved, allowing considerable scope for both choice and creativity. To be sure, there may be statements in the record which may be lifted verbatim into a key-list, but these are likely to be exceptional.

For example, in the foregoing landlord and tenant illustration, we have postulated that 'at the time the lease was signed the landlord knew these conditions existed'. this in turn requires proof showing (a) at what point in time the lease was signed; (b) that the conditions existed at that point in time; and (c) that the landlord knew at that time that these conditions existed. From the standpoint of tenant's counsel, the third element may pose the most difficulty. Absent an admission, what circumstantial propositions must be shown to establish the state of internal knowledge possessed by the landlord at a particular moment? If the fact is important, would it make a difference whether the landlord lived one or one hundred miles away from the apartment building? All the advocate is likely to have in the evidential data are the two addresses.

Selection also requires more than sorting out the relevant from the irrel-evant. A proposition is relevant if it has some probative connection with an ultimate probandum, that is, it tends to support, tends to negate, or tends to explain that probandum either directly or indirectly. Relevance is a necessary condition for inclusion of an evidential proposition on a key-list, but it is not a sufficient condition. There is an almost infinite possibility of regress and of more and more minute analysis of any body of evidentiary materials. Inclusion in a key-list inevitably involves making judgments of importance [non-trivi-ality] which go beyond mere theoretical relevance. Wigmore's science does not, and probably could not, provide a clear set of criteria of importance. The importance criterion is simple to state, but difficult to apply. The final product must include only those propositions that are relevant in fact and relevant in light of the theory of the case the advocate has adopted and the theory that he or she anticipates opposing counsel will adopt. Again, in the preliminary stages, caution must be exercised: weeding is easier than insertion.

Second, formulation of propositions on the key-list involves rather more than merely making explicit what was perhaps formerly implicit or only partially expressed. It also involves refinement of expression, analogous to what is involved in drafting a statute or formal document on the basis of a rough set of instructions. Indeed, the formulation of the ultimate probandum may well require the same level of drafting skill and precision. The formulation of evidential data into key-list propositions does not require, for most practical purposes, the same degree of precision and rigor as the drafting of legal instruments. The point at which precision becomes pedantry typically depends on context. But the analogy with drafting is nevertheless useful.

For example, every law student knows that formulating the holding (*ratio decidendi*) of a case requires judgment, art and skill. In the illustration above, the major premise was derived from *Brown v Southall Realty Co*. To students familiar with that decision, the statement of the rule may seem a rather conservative formulation of the holding for a tenant's lawyer to adopt. However, from the opinion it is not entirely clear whether the landlord had to know (a) only that the conditions in fact existed or, in addition (b) that these conditions constituted violations of the housing regulations, and/or perhaps (c) that collectively these conditions in fact rendered the apartment unsafe and unsanitary. The major premise as framed assumes away these ambiguities and represents the lawyer's judgment about the legal principle that will be applied to the case at hand or, more likely, the strongest ultimate probandum, the evidence in his or her case will support. From these judgments follow a series of dependent judgments about the ultimate and penultimate probanda. This requires high art indeed.[5]

There are no established rules for drafting propositions, but it is possible to give some guidance by way of advice. For example: Be precise. Be clear (avoid ambiguities). Normally, each proposition on the key-list should make one point only, and this should be signalled (eg, 'It was O who killed P' rather than 'O killed P'). Choose an appropriate level of generality for each proposition. So far as possible, use language which signals clearly the connections with immediately adjacent propositions. Be succinct, strive for economy, and so on. Again, skill in drafting a key-list involves art as well as science.

Finally, the propositions on the final key-list should be ordered so that the structure of the argument is, if possible, apparent on the face. Here too there is room for differences of taste and of judgment. For example, Twining is by temperament and training more at ease with words than with pictures or other symbols as means of communication. Accordingly, he finds it easier to grasp the structure and details of an argument about evidence from a key-list than from a chart. Indeed, for him a good key-list sometimes renders a chart almost superfluous. Others are different. Anderson, for instance, starts charting at an early stage and prepares his key-list and his chart simultaneously, moving backwards and forwards from one to the other. Wigmore himself, rather surprisingly to someone of Twining's temperament, saw the key-list as a mere adjunct to the chart: it is a key to the chart. Clearly, if the chart is the end product, there is no logical necessity for order within the key-list: the chart defines the order. But practically, reading the key-list and working through a chart are both enhanced if the propositions on the list are ordered logically. Here common sense, taking into account the purpose of the effort and the needs of the audience, is likely to be a safe guide.

Step 6 Preparing the chart(s). The end products are the chart and the key-list. The actual mechanics required to draw a chart are always laborious. They are specially laborious in one's first attempts. The struggle is not only with the logic but also with recalling the correct symbols and laying it all out on paper. Wigmore offers some suggestions (pp 231–232 above); we here add a few of our own.

(a) Always start with the ultimate probanda and work 'down' at least through the penultimate probanda. This will serve several purposes: it will help you to visualise the structure of the case; it will let you plan the 'space allocations' for the chart or charts; and it may show you ways of reorganising parts of your key-list. In the illustration above, for example, propositions 2 through 6 each require a showing of the 'time the lease was signed'. This suggests that repetition in the chart might be avoided if the lawyer organised all the evidential data with respect to the 'time the lease was signed' into one section of the chart and amended the penultimate probanda accordingly. Thus, assuming the evidential data, we might add as a proposition: '8. Both parties signed the lease on 27 December 19', and then amend proposition 2–6 to begin: 'On 27 December 19, . . .'.

(b) Break the chart into sectors and complete a part at a time. For example, in the *Brown* illustration, the existence of the three conditions (proposition 2) defines a possible separate sector. If the evidential propositions related to this penultimate probandum seem manageable in number, chart it first. (Unless you are or employ a professional draftsman, we suggest you do your 'sector charts' on separate sheets of paper and then identify these charts on a chart of your ultimate probanda. Thus, in the chart on the illustration above, we might simply print under circles 3, 4, and 5, 'See chart B'. It is annoying to see a new relationship or possibility after you have charted fifteen propositions in a sector; it is devastating to encounter the same problem after you have charted 150 propositions in a single sheet of paper.)

(c) Do not make the mistake of assuming that a proposition (evidential or intermediate) will appear only once in the chart. For example, the proof of one or more of propositions 3, 4, and 5 in the foregoing illustration is necessarily a part of the proof of propositions 6 and 7. So too, the fact the landlord had cancelled an extermination contract for the building in September might be relevant to support both the proposition that the apartment was infested with rats and the proposition that the landlord knew on 27 December that it was infested with rats. A logic chart is not a jigsaw puzzle.

(d) At every stage, check that each inferential relationship charted involves a genuine inference: Does the proposition added tend to support or negate the proposition to which it is tied. This step is critical. The function of the chart is to enable the preparer and the audience to spot flaws not before apparent in the analysis and to enable the advocate to correct or emphasise the error.

Step 7 Complete the analysis. The chart and key-list are means not ends. As a guide to work, the first five steps have proven useful in practice. But at each step the judgments made and the analysis were necessarily tentative. The end is to develop a logically sound analysis that, in light of the analyser's specific objectives, organises a mass of evidence and charts the inferences necessary to relate all significant relevant data to the ultimate proposition in issue. Typically, the process of revision and refinement is continuous, with judgments previously made being revised in each succeeding step of the analysis. But the chart and key-list completed through Step 6 provide the first real opportunity for analysing and evaluating the case as a whole and testing the judgments initially made. This is where the true value of the analysis as both intellectual exercise and practical work emerges most clearly. For that reason, the analysis of the whole should be done as a separate step.

Time permitting, this step should not be undertaken immediately and, in practice, should ordinarily be collegial activity. Lay the record, the key-list,and the chart aside for a few days or a week. Ask a fellow student or a partner to read the record, the key-list, and the chart to see if he or she can follow it, attack it, offer fresh insights. Then, using the first six steps as a guide, work through the materials and refine or adjust the key-list and chart as necessary.

For the trial lawyer, this is obviously and necessarily a continuous process. The early phases of an investigation have suggested a tentative theory: the available evidence, in light of established legal principles, suggests a plausible theory by which a desirable ultimate proposition might be proven. But new supporting and conflicting data will be added and the analysis and theory must be continuously revised. Indeed, the key-list and chart that the lawyer used in preparing for trial must be finally reviewed and revised in light of the evidence actually admitted and excluded during the course of the trial in order to prepare for closing argument. The utility of the key-list and chart, in that context, is that it makes it possible for the lawyer to see immediately the effect of the evidence unexpectedly admitted or excluded on the theory of the case as previously developed and charted.

The final step should produce a product that accounts for all the significant relevant data that are available; precisely and clearly identifies the logical organisation and inferences necessary to relate that data to the ultimate propositions in issue. In the aggregate, it establishes and makes available for critical review the lawyer's theory of the case and in practice it provides the foundation for preparing and executing the next task in the law job undertaken.

Notes and questions on *Umilian*

How would a student apply the procedures suggested in 'A note on the uses and limitations of Wigmore's Chart Method' in analysing and in constructing a chart analysis of *Commonwealth v Umilian*? To the extent the resulting analysis differs from that reflected in Wigmore's chart, are the differences significant? What can be said that would explain these differences? The purpose of the following notes and questions is to provide a partial response to these issues and the wherewithal to enable students to pursue them further.

A preliminary application of the method

Step 1.   Clarifying standpoint   Any contemporary analysis of the facts reported in the court's opinion must be from the standpoint of a historian. Wigmore prepared his analysis from that standpoint and apparently had two objectives – to provide a demonstration of the method and, perhaps, to determine whether the appellate court was correct in concluding that the evidence, as it reported it, was sufficient to support the verdict and judgment that Umilian was guilty of murder in the first degree. In order to create a fair comparison, the same purposes have been adopted here. There is a third objective implicit in the exercise and the nature of our role as students of Wigmore. The contemporary analysis is post-Wigmore as well as post-*Umilian*, and its purpose is also to appraise Wigmore and his application of the method.

Step 2   Formulating the potential ultimate probandum or probanda   The Massachusetts statute in effect at the turn of the century provided that:

> Murder committed with deliberately premeditated malice aforethought, or ... with extreme atrocity or cruelty, is murder in the first degree.

(Mass. Gen. Stat., ch 160, §1 (1855)). 'Murder not appearing to be in the first degree is murder in the second degree': ibid, §2. Murder in the first degree was punishable by death; in the second, by life imprisonment. Massachusetts accepted the common law definition of murder as 'the unlawful killing of a human being with malice aforethought': 29 CJ Homicide, §59 (1922); see also *Commonwealth v Webster* 59 Mass (5 Cush) 295 (Mass 1850); *Commonwealth v Phelps* 209 Mass 396, 95 NE 868 (1911). In Massachusetts, the significant language was 'deliberately premeditated' because, as in most jurisdictions, malice aforethought could be inferred from the 'unlawfully killing'. The Massachusetts Supreme Court viewed the statutory language 'deliberately premeditated' as requiring that the murder be ' "thought upon, resolved upon beforehand, and not done suddenly", although no particular length of time is required': 29 CJ Homicide, §96, citing *Commonwealth v Tucker* 189 Mass 457, 76 NE 127 (1905).

Accepting this as a fair statement of the controlling legal principles, the potential ultimate probandum might be framed as:

(1)(a) Jedrusik ('J') was dead and
   (b) J's death resulted from the unlawful act of another, and
   (c) it was Umilian ('U') who committed the unlawful act that caused J's death, and
   (d) U committed that act either
   (e) with deliberately premeditated malice aforethought, or
   (f) with extreme atrocity or cruelty.

Step 3   Formulating the potential penultimate probanda   The ultimate probandum might be broken down in the first instance into the following propositions as possible penultimate probanda:

(2) J was dead.
(3) J's death resulted from the unlawful act of another.
(4) It was U who committed the unlawful act that resulted in J's death.
(5) U acted with deliberately premeditated malice aforethought or with extreme atrocity or cruelty in committing the act that caused J's death.
(6) U acted with deliberately premeditated malice aforethought.
(7) U acted with extreme atrocity or cruelty.
(8) U acted with extreme atrocity.
(9) U acted with extreme cruelty.

The logical relationships among these propositions might be provisionally charted as follows:

Chart U-1

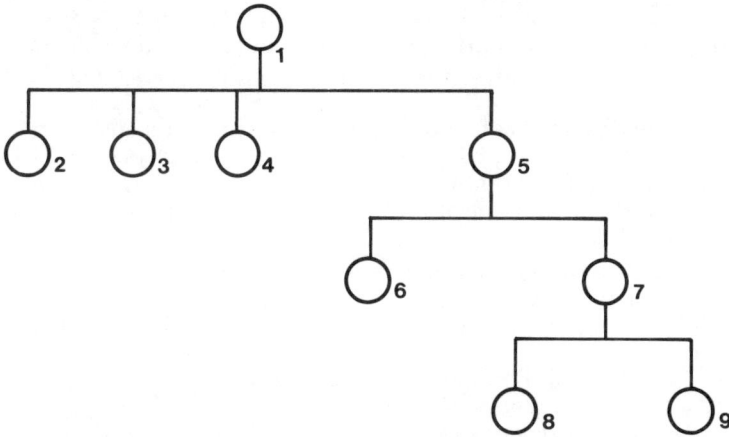

Step 4 Formulating the provisional theories and the strategic ultimate and penultimate probanda The analysis required to formulate the possible ultimate and penultimate probanda for *Umilian* would not differ significantly had the standpoint been that of trial or appellate counsel for Umilian as opposed to that of a historian. The analysis necessary to settle upon a provisional theory and the strategic ultimate and penultimate probanda differs significantly when the standpoint is that of a student analysing a decided case with only those facts provided in the appellate court's opinion. The differences deserve some comment here because they were not recognised or appreciated by Wigmore in his own work.

Limiting the data available to that reported in an appellate opinion imposes a major limitation on the analysis. Those performing the analysis can only analyse that which the court chose to report in its opinion; they cannot check it for accuracy or completeness. It may be that Umilian's counsel raised issues in addition to those the court chose to address, and it may be that the court had either confirming or conflicting evidence that it omitted from its report. Absent research into the record or other historical sources, those who analyse a case on the basis of an appellate opinion must ordinarily analyse it on its own terms.

In *Umilian*, only two claims were reported to have been brought before the Massachusetts Supreme Court – that the evidence was insufficient to warrant the finding that Umilian was the murderer and that the evidence was not sufficient to find that it was murder in the first degree. (Reporter's note, p 103.) The court's opinion suggests that there was no dispute over whether the body found was that of Jedrusik or whether J died as the result of an unlawful act: 'On 10 April 1900, his [J's] headless, mutilated body was found....' (p 103) The opinion provides no data against which these inferences can be challenged. Thus, for purposes of this analysis, propositions 2 and 3 are not strategically important. The opinion does not indicate whether the court upheld the conclusion that it was murder in the first degree on the grounds that the evidence was sufficient to show that Umilian's acts were 'deliberately premeditated' (P7) or were committed with 'extreme atrocity (P8) or cruelty (P9)'. Because the judgment was affirmed, the reported facts should demonstrate that at least one of these conditions was satisfied on the evidence. For that reason, these provisional penultimate probanda remain open for analysis.

This provisional analysis suggests that counsel for Umilian adopted a theory of the case on appeal that the evidence was insufficient to show that 'It was U that committed the unlawful act that caused J's death' (P4) and was insufficient to show that the act was deliberately premeditated or committed with extreme atrocity or cruelty (P5). Because the data for analysis is limited to that contained in the court's opinion, a central question for the historian becomes 'did the court adequately justify its conclusion rejecting Umilian's claims?'

Against this background, propositions 4 through 8 remain strategically important. The court's opinion indicates its theory and thereby gives the structure of its argument. Given the standpoint of the analysis, additional propositions take on provisional strategic importance. From the opinion, they may be framed as follows:

(10) U was the only person who had an opportunity to murder J.

(11) U 'had ample opportunity to commit the murder'.

(12) '[N]o other person had an opportunity to do it [murder J] without discovery.'

(13) U had an established and existing motive to kill J.

(14) U was angry at J because J had tried to prevent and had delayed U's marriage to the Keith's maid.

(15) That anger was still present on 31 December 1899.

(16) U had knowledge that J was dead between the date of J's disappearance and the date on which his body was discovered and his actions indicated a guilty state of mind concerning that knowledge.

(17) U had knowledge that J was dead between the date of J's disappearance [12/31/99] and the date on which his body was discovered [4/10/00].

(18) U's actions between 12/31/99 and 4/10/00 indicated a guilty state of mind with respect to J.

Accepting these propositions provisionally as defining the theory upon which the appellate court affirmed the conviction, the chart might be provisionally expanded as set out in Chart U-2 below:

Chart U-2

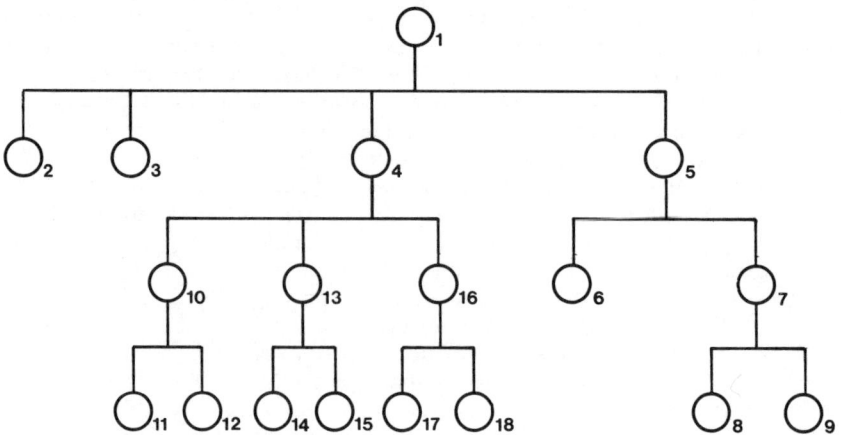

The first four steps in the method establish a provisional framework for completing the analysis. Compiling the key-list would require a sentence-by-sentence analysis of the court's opinion and some judgments concerning how the reported facts were supported in the record – by testimonial assertions or by physical evidence. Each of the propositions so culled would require further analysis to determine how it might be related to one or more of the propositions developed in the provisional theory and to articulate the intermediate propositions necessary to establish the relationship. This process would also require that possible explanatory propositions, not foreclosed by the reported facts, be identified and articulated.

The final steps, preparing the chart and completing the analysis, are likely to be reflexive. The analysis of the reported data may support relevant inferences that were not identified in the provisional theory and probably would require that some of the inferences that were identified be reframed to make the nature of arguments from data to inference clearer. That is an exercise we commend to the student in view of the further notes and questions that follow.

Wigmore as Wigmorean

The first four steps in the Anderson-Twining methodology produced a logical structure that differs significantly from that developed in Wigmore's chart. In our view, these are differences of substance rather than merely of form. In point of fact, Wigmore's key-lists and charts, such as those for *Umilian*, have persuaded us that Wigmore did not fully appreciate the real functions that the chart method of analysis might serve. We develop these differences and their importance here and later set out some speculations on why Wigmore was not a very good Wigmorean.

Wigmore's analysis explicitly addresses only one of the penultimate probanda – that it was Umilian who committed the acts that killed Jedrusik. In the structure of his argument, each of six propositions would independently support the court's conclusion, if it were supported by sufficient evidence:

(a)   1   *Design* to kill J.
(b)   8   Revengeful murderous *emotion* towards J.
(c) 26   U's *opportunity* in time and place was almost exclusive.
(d) 33   U had an uneasy *consciousness of guilt* about J's disappearance.
(e) 47   U knew that J was dead, though others did not.
(f) 51   *Data of slayer* on J's body were of a person having free and intimate access to horse barn of Keith.

It seems apparent, however, that these conditions are not independent and are not of the same order. For example, design and revengeful emotions are clearly related. If Umilian had an established motive based upon revenge, that fact would also tend to support an inference that he had formed a design to kill Jedrusik. So too, the data indicating that the slayer had access and familiarity with Keith's barn is related to the proposition that Umilian had opportunity and that that opportunity was almost exclusive. Similarly, an inference that Umilian knew Jedrusik was dead combines with an inference that Umilian had an uneasy consciousness of guilt about Jedrusik's disappearance to support the further inference that consciousness of guilt stemmed from Umilian's knowledge that he had killed Jedrusik.

Wigmore's failure to identify and articulate the relationships among these propositions makes it difficult to understand what conclusion he intended. Moreover, it conceals support for the theory that apparently satisfied the court. For example, in Wigmore's view, the evidence strongly supported the conclusion that the data of slayer on Jedrusik's body were of a person having free intimate access to the Keith horse barn (P51). At the same time, he viewed the evidence as insufficient to determine whether Umilian had an almost exclusive opportunity (P26). The two are clearly related, and propositions listed as supporting Proposition 51 include one that would also support Proposition 26 – 'No other person but U had at that time such access [to the barn]' (P55). In point of fact, Wigmore appears not to have articulated a theory of the case that could be tested.

Many of the flaws in Wigmore's analysis could be cured by a more rigorous analysis at each step. That analysis would be likely to suggest that a crucial fact in dispute was the date of the murder. If the murder occurred on 31 December 1899, the remaining evidence seems clearly sufficient to support the jury's verdict. If the evidence as to date was unsatisfactory, then the sufficiency of the evidence is far less clear. Neither Wigmore nor the court focus upon this fact. An interesting evidence problem, in this view, would have been whether it was permissible for the jury to draw a negative inference that Jedrusik was killed by Umilian based upon an inference that Umilian was lying when he said Jedrusik left the farm to go Granby on December 31 and did not return.

Exercises

(1) Review *Commonwealth v Umilian* again. Complete the chart by working through Steps 5 and 6. Step 7: What revisions should be made to push the analysis to its limits?

(2) Adopt the standpoint of the lawyer for *Umilian* preparing to defend him at trial. Assume the statement of facts in the court's decision had been submitted to you in a solicitor's brief or an associate's memorandum – well in advance of trial.

   (a) Revise the foregoing chart analysis from this new standpoint.
   (b) Based upon that analysis, what additional questions would you want investigated before the case proceeds to trial?
   (c) What theory of the case would you seek to present on behalf of *Umilian*? What *themes* would you emphasise?
   (d) The priest was presumably a significant prosecution witness. What difference would it make to your case if you discovered that under the law of your jurisdiction most of the priest's testimony could be excluded by the assertion of a priest-penitent privilege? Assuming this privilege was not available, what questions would you plan to ask the priest on cross-examination and why?
   (e) Who are the principal witnesses for the defence? Which propositions on your key-list would be introduced through which witnesses? In what order would you call these witnesses to assure that the defence story was presented in a coherent and dramatically effective manner? Assuming that Umilian will take the stand, 'script' the anticipated direct examination? What will the prosecution ask on cross-examination?

A concluding note

Analysing evidence is required at all stages of a 'case', from the initial client interview or the first report of a crime through a post-trial or post-appeal evaluation of the result. Logical principles are clearly necessary at every stage. Wigmore claimed the principles and his chart method of analysis were as useful for the advocate at the investigative and pre-trial stages as they were for the evaluation at the post-trial stages. We are convinced he was correct, but we believe he failed to recognise fully the significance of the differences in standpoint. We intended this note in part to illustrate these differences and illustrate their importance, but we have intentionally focused our illustrations and comments upon a single standpoint: that of the lawyer preparing for trial after the investigation has been substantially completed. We conclude by trying to set its use from that standpoint in the broader context of the lawyer's job in preparing for trial.

In the final stages of trial preparation, the lawyer typically knows with some precision the evidential data available to support his or her client's case and that available to opposing counsel. Assuming that the controlling legal principles are clear (or that the court has declared the 'law for this case'), the lawyer also has a largely fixed ultimate probandum. But Wigmore was misleading to the extent he implies that this universe of available data constitutes that upon which the trier-of-fact will base its decision. The contending lawyers in the first instance will select from this universe data which they will seek to present or exclude and will then determine how they will be presented and organised.

From this perspective, the lawyers' pre-trial chart is an adjustable instrument. Having charted the possibilities, the challenge becomes: How can I maximise the probability that the trier-of-fact will accept my (or reject my opponent's) ultimate probandum as proven (or not proven). And the tools for this job go beyond logic: Will the rules of admissibility preclude my introducing (or enable me to prevent my opponent from introducing) otherwise relevant data? How can I organise my evidence, prepare my questions, and present my evidence in a way that will enhance the trier's perception of the 'logic' of my position and reveal the flaws in the 'logic' of the opponent's argument? And here the advocate's need for forensic skills in the traditional trial tasks is apparent: the arts of direct and cross-examination, making effective objections and legal arguments, presenting effective opening and closing arguments, the use of demonstrative aids, theatrical skills – all involved, all art; none appear in the chart.

But analysis is a necessary condition to effective use of these other trial skills. The possibility foreseen can be dealt with; the possibility unforeseen can spell disaster. And the chart method serves two functions. It requires the student to engage in a systematic, demanding and rigorous analysis of the evidence to determine the possibilities of a case. It thus creates at least an awareness of what can be done for every case and some skill in the doing. It also may serve (and has served) the same function for the practitioner confronted with a particular problem.

It should be clear from the foregoing account that none of the stages of the recommended procedure for applying the chart method involves a purely mechanical application of firm rules. Rather there is at each stage a need for the exercise of judgment, choice, and skill, with only a few general precepts to serve as guides. In this context, the main value of the method is twofold. First, it suggests a way of structuring and organising a complex argument – the strategic aspect. Secondly, it provides a technique for meticulous, sometimes microscopic, analysis of important aspects of the evidence. Wigmore's science quite properly does not provide a precise formula for deciding questions of importance – eg, for deciding what is 'the jugular' according to the conventional wisdom of practitioners; that is a matter for individual judgment in the particular circumstances of each case.

Thus Wigmore's method is a tool which has its uses and its limitations. Unless the limitations are understood, it is likely to be misused by enthusiasts and to be the subject of unwarranted criticism by those less enamoured. It does not purport to solve all problems of handling evidence. For example, it does not purport to resolve questions of materiality or admissibility nor to be applicable to arguments about questions of law. It provides a method for approaching an actual or potential mass of evidence in a disciplined way, but it does not prescribe the result. Nor does it provide a detailed account of the different kinds of logical relationship between a factum probans and its immediate probandum. It does not address such matters as conjunction and convergence. No two masters of the method are likely to produce identical key-lists or charts for the same case. The method provides a way of ordering material, but not for solving problems. It lays a foundation for analysis, but does not typically give much guidance as to the best method of presentation. Few courts, for example, are likely to accept or welcome Wigmorean charts at trials. Above all the method does not purport to eliminate the human element in any of the stages of the process of handling and analysing evidence.

NOTES

1 Wigmore's treatment of probabilities is neither very clear nor very extensive, but he is reasonably recognisable as a Baconian whose views are in general compatible with those of more sophisticated contemporary theorists of the same kind, such as Jonathan Cohen. It is a weakness of Wigmore's approach that he wrote as if his were the only possible views of rationality, of induction and of probabilities and that he did not even consider the possibility of alternative theories.

2 For a further discussion and critique, see W Twining *Theories of Evidence: Bentham and Wigmore* (1985).

3 The concept of 'theory of the case' and related concepts are developed in *Analysis of Evidence* p 89 ff and pp 194–195.

4 Role becomes more important when we try to use the method to do or to evaluate the job done by persons such as the historian or the economist. For evaluation, the method itself may be a most useful tool to identify hidden biases.

5 Doubters should consult *Watson v Kotler* 264 A 2d 141 (DC Ct App 1970).

IV SAMPLE INFERENCE CHARTS

Some simple modes of charting (source: Schum, 1987)

Figure 1. Elements of a single chain of reasoning

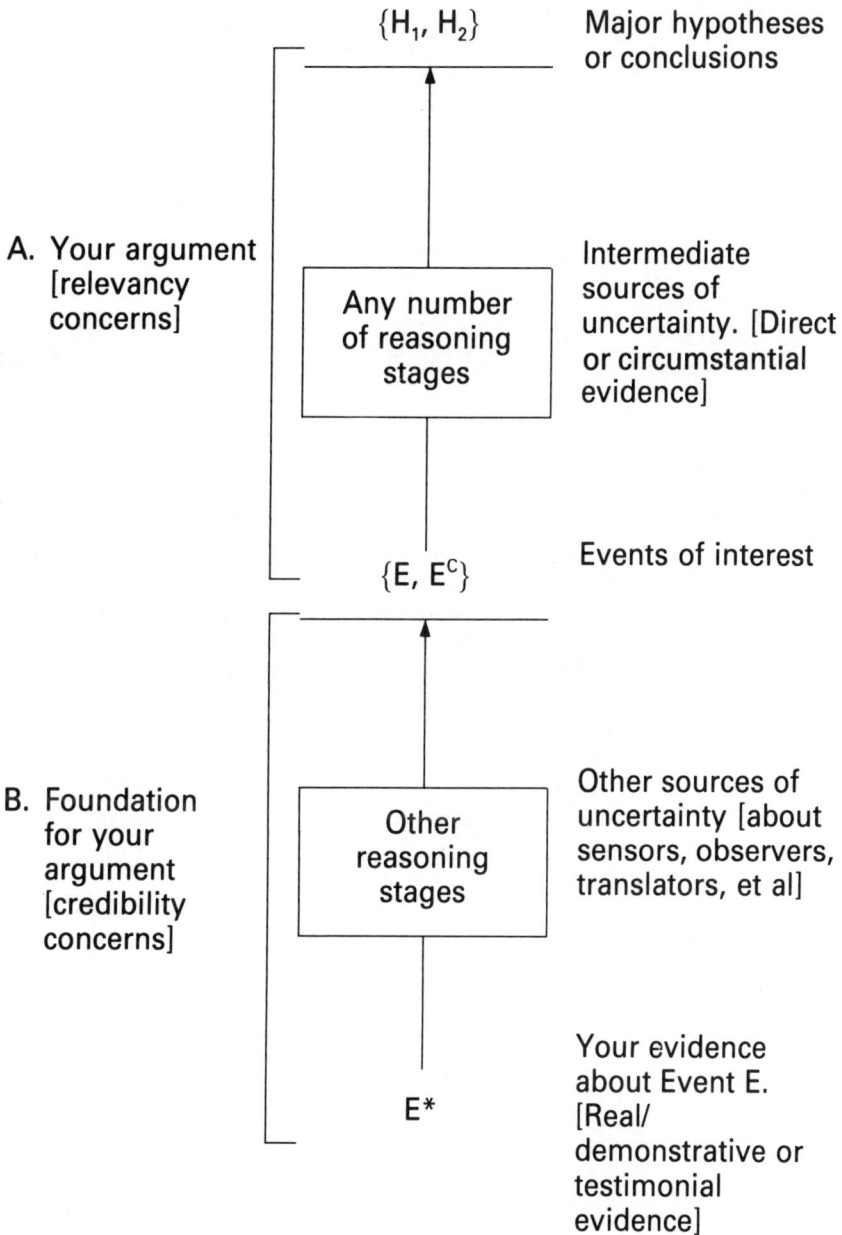

{H₁, H₂} — Major hypotheses or conclusions

A. Your argument [relevancy concerns]

Any number of reasoning stages — Intermediate sources of uncertainty. [Direct or circumstantial evidence]

{E, Eᶜ} — Events of interest

B. Foundation for your argument [credibility concerns]

Other reasoning stages — Other sources of uncertainty [about sensors, observers, translators, et al]

E* — Your evidence about Event E. [Real/ demonstrative or testimonial evidence]

Figure 2

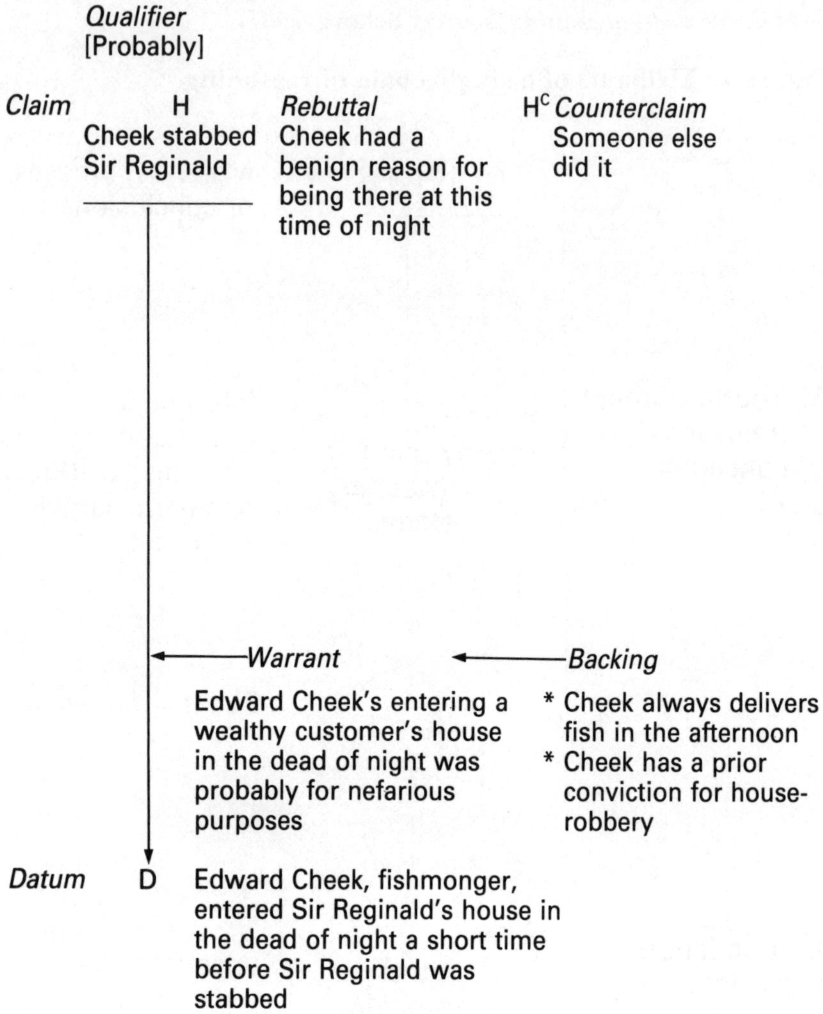

Qualifier
[Probably]

Claim	H	*Rebuttal*	H^c *Counterclaim*
	Cheek stabbed Sir Reginald	Cheek had a benign reason for being there at this time of night	Someone else did it

———*Warrant*   ←———*Backing*

Edward Cheek's entering a   * Cheek always delivers
wealthy customer's house   fish in the afternoon
in the dead of night was   * Cheek has a prior
probably for nefarious   conviction for house-
purposes   robbery

Datum   D   Edward Cheek, fishmonger,
              entered Sir Reginald's house in
              the dead of night a short time
              before Sir Reginald was
              stabbed

Figure 3. Inference upon inference (source: Twining, unpublished)

F fact established by evidence or not disputed   **G** generalization
I inference   **RT** relevant time

F1   Y was murdered in his house at *4.30 pm on 1/1/81* [RT]

Infirmative

1 Y is not dead.
2 The victim was not Y.
3 It was not murder.
4 Location incorrect.
5 Time incorrect.
6 Date incorrect.

F2   Witness (W¹) stated he saw a person with features a.b.c.d. entering Y's house at 4.15 on 1/1/81.   [=RT −15]

Corroborative

1 Another witness (W²) stated F².
2 W¹ an honest witness.
3 W¹ had a good opportunity to see event.
4 Circumstances of W²'s witnessing were favourable.
5 Circumstances of W²'s reporting were favourable.
6 W¹ a competent observer.

Infirmative

1 W is *lying*.
2 W¹ *misperceived*
   eg a. features
        b. location (2's house)
        c. action.
3 W's *memory* faulty.
4 W's description *suggested* to him.
5 W's description of person vague or ambiguous.
6 W's description badly expressed.
7 W's description misrecorded.
8 W's description misrepresented (eg photofit does not fit description).
9 Features of type a often confused with features of type m (G).

I¹   A person with features a.b.c.d. entered Y's house at RT −15.
F3   X has features a.b.c.d.

Infirmative

1 X's features not identical to description.
2 Many people have such features (G).
3 Z is X's double.
4 X has *alibi* for RT −15.
5 X denies entering Y's house.

I²   X entered Y's house at RT −15.

Corroborative

1 X often went to Y's house.
2 X had motive to go to Y's house.
3 X had been invited to go to Y's house at RT.
4 W¹ 'identified' X at identification parade.
5 X admitted to being near Y's house at the RT.

Infirmative

1 X left Y's house at RT −10.

I³   X was in Y's house at RT.

Corroborative

1 X was seen leaving Y's house at RT +30.
2 X's fingerprints in Y's house.

Infirmative

1 Murderer was not in the house at the time of the killing.
2 Y was inaccessible to X within the house (eg locked in his room).
3 X had no weapon.

I⁴   X had opportunity to murder Y.
F4   No one else was in Y's house at the time.

I⁵   X had exclusive opportunity to murder Y.
I⁶   It was X who murdered Y.

Figure 4. Evidence chart for Commonwealth v Umilian (Wigmore)

ISSUE: DID U KILL J　　　　　　　　*Prosecution's case*

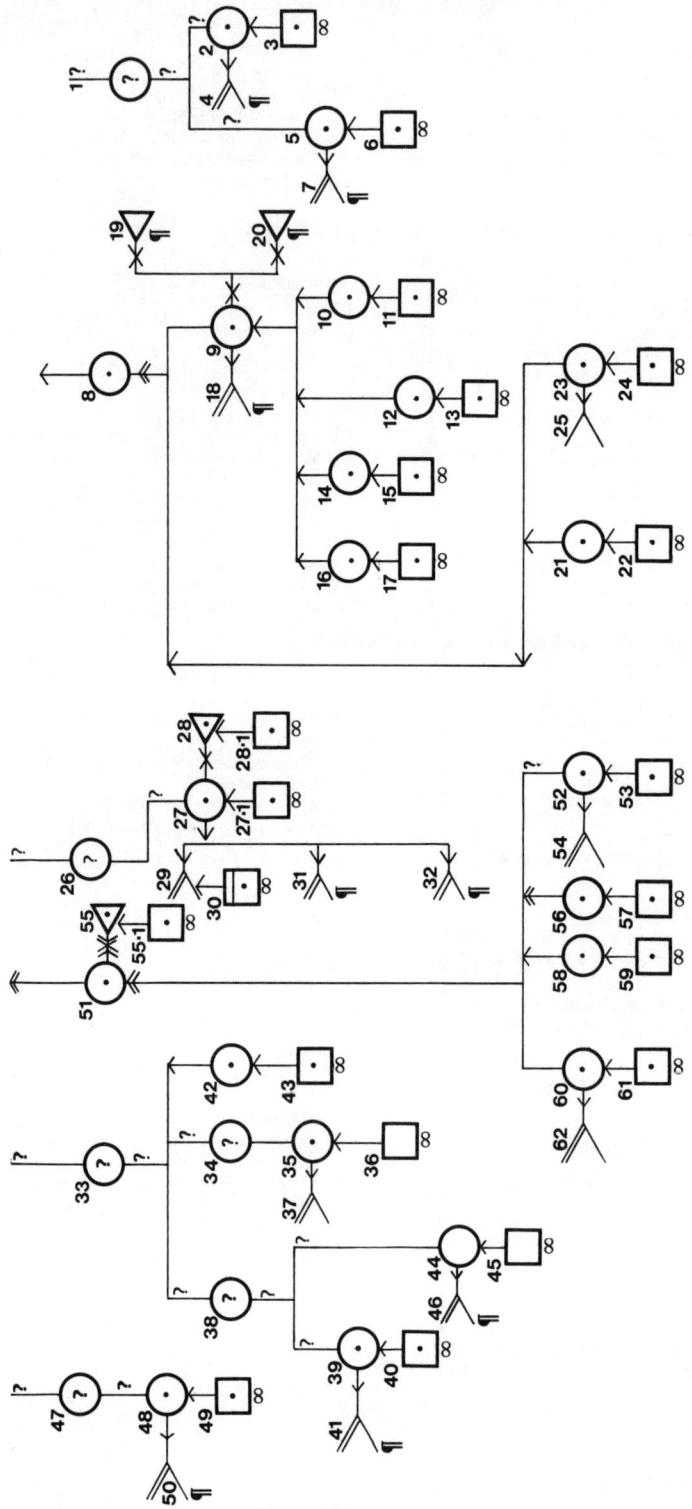

9 Introduction to advocacy

Leo Cussen Institute

The materials which follow are used in a one-day advocacy skills development programme in the Practical Training Course conducted by the Leo Cussen Institute, Melbourne. The Practical Training Course is a post-graduate pre-admission training course and is conducted by the Leo Cussen Institute as an alternative to articles. The Advocacy Programme is aimed at post-graduate students who have had virtually no experience in advocacy except perhaps in university moots.

The skills sought to be developed in this programme are used and expanded on in other topics throughout the course. The advocacy programme includes:

○ Criminal procedure: bail application, plea in mitigation and contested matters.
○ Family law: unopposed dissolution applications and contested applications.
○ Civil litigation: unopposed chambers applications.
○ Advocacy Extension Course: an optional course designed to apply the basic skills to specific problems, eg cross-examination on documents.
○ Interpreters and the law: an optional course in working with interpreters in courts concentrating on difficulties in cross-cultural communication.
○ Practical Trial Programme: intensive simulation of a contested criminal trial in which students prepare a current matter file for presentation to a court and one opposed to members of the Victoria Police undergoing the Prosecutors Training Course. This takes place at the end of the Practical Training Course and participation as an advocate is voluntary although *all* students participate as solicitors, witnesses, court staff etc.

Each student spends a total of six days throughout the seven-month course on advocacy and a further seven days at their option.

In taking a 'building block' approach we have sought to develop the basic skills of advocacy by allowing participants to integrate knowledge and skill in exercises set in differing legal contexts and at different levels of complexity. Throughout the course the materials raise ethical and other practical problems which affect an advocate's conduct.

The programme materials are divided into two parts:

(i) the Course Reference Materials (Part A) which introduce the objectives, overview materials for discussion/analysis with instructors and contain the factual material for the practical exercises; and
(ii) the Practice Papers (Part B) which cover each of the particular skills in depth, discuss applicable principles of law and serve as references throughout the practical training course.

This division reflects a tension in course design between the stress that is placed on discussion/performance/feedback and the need to place the skill of persuasion in the context of substantive legal principles. It follows that the full benefit of the programme cannot be achieved without intensive pre-reading.

The materials are designed by the mentor responsible for topic co-ordination in conjunction with a Consultants' Committee of senior practitioners and judges who are experts in the particular field. The instructors in the Introduction to Advocacy Course are practising barristers of considerable experience and they are assisted in their task by an instructors' manual (general), an instructors' kit (topic specific) and consultation with the topic co-ordinator prior to commencement and during the day.

Some of the applicable curriculum design principles are:

o the need for advance reading and preparation;
o a building block approach from least complex (the persuasion exercises) to more complex (the long case exercise);
o feedback and analysis at each stage of learning;
o videotaped performances for review by the student with feedback by an individual assessor;
o maximum use of discussion/demonstration – practice – feedback cycle;
o instructor student ratio (maximum 1–12);
o peer critique and participation;
o realism in factual material.

We have found that advocacy is popular amongst students and that practising advocates are excellent instructors once they master the principles of feedback and realise its importance in the teaching process.

In conclusion the Introduction to Advocacy course stresses *performance* and in so doing reflects the reality of practice that 'the only way of learning advocacy is on your feet'.

LEO CUSSEN INSTITUTE

PRACTICAL TRAINING COURSE

Introduction to advocacy

TABLE OF CONTENTS

Part A: Instructional materials

Course aims and course summary

A one day course on general principles of advocacy including basic skills of *preparation, listening* and *speech.* Students will be given the opportunity of conducting basic parts of court room procedure such as announcing their appearance, opening a case, examination, cross examination and re-examination of witnesses and making submissions, closing the case and solving ethical problems.

Evaluation

Acquisition of advocacy skills will be tested further in the other advocacy days and in the Crime Current Matter at the end of the course. Instructors will be observing whether students are identifying and observing the skills required in the topic.

Essential acts

Nil.

Essential pre-reading

Important: *All* the following materials must (repeat must) be read prior to commencement. Reading the Practice Papers is vital as they form the basis of class discussion.

Why? It is obvious that the whole of the course materials cannot be covered within one day. These materials relate also to civil litigation, family law, criminal law advocacy and the work for the Crime Current Matter. You should be continually working through them during the whole of your Leo Cussen life.

Resources and references

(a) *Aspects of Cross Examination and Plea Making* (The Honourable Mr Justice Hampel, Leo Cussen Institute publication).
(b) *Pre-trial Criminal Procedure Handbook* (Leo Cussen Institute publication).
(c) *Preparation for Hearing in the Magistrates' Court* (Leo Cussen Institute publication).
(d) *Cross Examination Practice and Procedure – An Australian Perspective* (James L Glasson Legal Books).
(e) Video: 'Ten Commandments of Cross Examination', Irving Younger.
(f) *Advocacy at the Bar* (Keith Evans, Financial Training Publications Ltd).
(g) *New Sentencing Options – Penalties and Sentences Act* (Leo Cussen Institute publication).
(h) Australian Bar News – various.
(i) *Advocacy with Honour* (The Honourable Mr Justice Phillips).
(j) *Criminal Law Advocacy Legal Services* (Tilmouth and Rengelley, Commission of South Australia Publication).
(k) *Plea Making in the Magistrates' Court* (Leo Cussen publication).
(l) *Summary Offences* (Leo Cussen Institute publication).
(m) *The Lawyering Process* (Bellow and Moulton, Foundation Press, 1981).
(n) *Evidence and Advocacy* (Wells, Butterworths).
(o) Australian Law Journal – various.
(p) Law Institute Journal (Vic).

Visits

Students are encouraged in their spare time or on unstructured days to spend some time in the Melbourne Magistrates' Court listening to advocates practice the art of advocacy and in the county court where a complete re-hearing of an appeal from a magistrates' court decision takes place.

Current matter

Later in the course.

Other things

Replaying of your video tape of your advocacy exercise.

Programme

Day 1 of Topic

OBJECTIVES

(1) To understand that advocacy is the art of persuasion and that the basis of all competent advocacy is effective speech.

Preparation

(2) To recall the importance of *thorough* preparation of a case before going to court to appear for a client.

Presentation

(3) *To recall* basic procedures and etiquette in court as important elements in advocacy.
(4) To master principles relating to examination-in-chief.
(5) To develop the skill of cross-examination.
(6) To recall when re-examination is required.
(7) *To develop* professional attitudes to ethical problems as may arise in practice.

Persuasion

(8) *To conduct* simple procedures in a court room as if appearing for a client.

ACTIVITY

9.30–10.15 lecture theatre	Overview Lecture: A lecture by a leading member of the Bar. Students should make notes of the main points made by the lecturer.
10.15–10.30	Morning coffee.
10.30–11.45 lecture theatre	Discussion with instructors on points raised by lecturer and on evidence in chief, cross-examination and the need for preparation. Attention should be paid to and analysis and discussion of the examples extracted in the materials as illustrations of principles.
11.45–12.15 seminar rooms	Exercises in persuasion (Objective 1).
12.15–12.40 seminar rooms	Discussion on the four problems of ethics and arrive at possible solutions (Objective 7).
12.40–1.00 seminar rooms and work stations	5 minute briefing by instructors on what is required in the afternoon exercises, assignment of roles to students followed by 15 minutes preparation by each student at his/her work station. Instructors will be available to the students.
1.00–2.00	Lunch
2.00–2.15 work stations	Further preparation for exercises.
2.15–4.45 seminar rooms	Each student to present before the instructor acting as a magistrate one of the short exercises and one role in the long exercise as prescribed. Students will observe the performance by their fellows and take heed of the comments made by the instructors in relation to techniques and performance of each segment. Each exercise will be video-taped for the student's personal review.

4.45–5.00	A group commentary by the instructor as to perform-
seminar rooms	ance in the exercises.

EVALUATION AND FEEDBACK

Instructors are to observe the level of skill displayed in this first attempt at advocacy and offer helpful advice and guidance.

Attention should be paid to 'Hints on feedback' notes.

Spotlights

General standards – responsibility for the client's case or matter

(1) The client should be told the name and the status of the person responsible for the conduct of the matter on a day-to-day basis and the partner responsible for the overall supervision of the matter.

(2) If the conduct or the overall supervision of the whole or part of the client's matter is transferred to another person in the firm the client should be informed and the reasons should be explained.

(3) The solicitor should advise the client when it is appropriate to instruct counsel. Whenever the client is to attend a hearing at which he is to be represented, he should be told the name of the solicitor or counsel who it is intended will represent him.

Notes for instructors

Hints on feedback

When looking at a student's performance of an advocacy problem and judging its effectiveness, you may wish to consider four areas in organising your feedback. These are:

(1) *Problem analysis* – How has the student thought through the specific problem in terms of strategy and approach. Has he or she developed goals and purposes, thought through all the facts, and applicable law; selected those most favourable, answered those most devastating, and organised them coherently and well?

(2) *Problem execution* – How does the student execute the plan in the context of this problem? How are the words chosen, questions (or statements) arranged in sequence, evidentiary considerations thought through? What kind of relationships are established in the court room with the judge?

(3) *Verbal habits* – To what extent is the student's plan impaired or enhanced by tone, modulation, volume and mood? Are answers echoed, or are filler words such as 'Well, now ...' used?

(4) *Physical habits* – To what extent is the student's plan impaired or enhanced by gestures, movement, eye contact, and body position?

The delivery of a successful critique demands pre-class preparation, attentive observation during the students' delivery and thoughtful analysis of how to give the feedback.

(1) *Planning* – Before coming to class, it is helpful to prepare the day's problems as if you yourself were to deliver the classroom performances. This will aid you both to understand the student's goal and objectives and to offer specific alternatives in terms of questions and strategies.

(2) *Observation* – To capture the details of the student performance to be discussed and to provide specific examples of the general points they wish to make. Use the checklist to develop a system for recording what you see. Use the critique form provided and make brief notes, conclusions, or even checks to indicate the areas on which you want to comment.

(3) *Delivery* – The effectiveness of any critique can be enhanced by thoughtful and careful delivery. Good critique is usually honest, neutral, supportive, accessible, and tested.

General comments on feedback summary

(1) Obtaining feedback about one's own performance is the most important factor in:

   (a) identifying deficiencies; and
   (b) learning how to improve performance.

(2) The most helpful feedback is:

   (a) descriptive;
   (b) specific;
   (c) related to performance; and
   (d) based on objective criteria of worthy performance.

(3) The most unhelpful feedback is:

   (a) judgemental;
   (b) general;
   (c) impressionistic; and
   (d) subjective and idiosyncratic.

(4) Feedback should be focused on the value it may have to the receiver rather than the value of the 'release' that it provides the person giving the feedback. Procedures for focussing the feedback on the needs of the receiver include:

(a) letting the performer comment on his own performance first; and
(b) letting the performer decide which areas he wants to receive feedback on.

(5) Points (1) and (4) determine whether feedback is constructive or unconstructive.

Advocacy – critique sheet

Case content   COMMENT

announcement of appearance
opening
dealing with any initial mistakes
in the documentation

Presentation of the case

logical progression in performance of task assigned
ability to deal with difficult areas
ability to 'field' questions

Observance of etiquette

General delivery

speed of speech
coherent v disjointed sentences
clear pronounciation
facial expression
um/ers etc
head up/down

Persuasion

variation on tone of voice
communication with judge

LEO CUSSEN INSTITUTE

PRACTICAL TRAINING COURSE

Introduction to advocacy

PART A: INSTRUCTIONAL MATERIALS

Objective 1: Persuasion

Speech

[Perhaps the greatest of all the legal skills]

OBJECTIVE

To understand that the basis of all competent advocacy is effective speech.

Effective speech involves precise, clear and persuasive articulation – the exact opposite to long-winded and pointless speaking.

The client in your office is entitled to clarity of expression. You must speak to those who are on the other side of the case or matter, gracefully and confidently. The Court or Tribunal is entitled to an advocate of whom it may be said at the end 'It was a pleasure to listen to that lawyer'.

The marks of care

Here taken at random are some of the characteristics that may identify an advocate.

 (1) clarity;
 (2) sincerity;
 (3) strength;
 (4) softness;
 (5) timing;
 (6) change of pace;
 (7) word power;
 (8) cogency;
 (9) orderly presentation (coherency);
(10) urgency;
(11) persuasiveness;
(12) poignancy;
(13) humour;
(14) forthrightness;
(15) brevity – succinctness;
(16) gravity;

EXERCISES IN PERSUASION

At the centre of advocacy is the need to communicate with the judge in order to persuade him/her.

Try the following exercises in persuasion:

(1) A single exercise:

    ○ Stand, in two minutes convince the group that blue wallpaper is preferable to green wallpaper.

(2) An exercise with a partner:

    ○ Person A sits on a chair with a piece of paper balanced on his knee. Person B sits opposite. Using only the words 'please put the paper on the other knee' person B must persuade person A to move the paper to the other knee.

(3) Another exercise with a partner:

    ○ As for exercise 2 except that person A may argue at large in attempting to persuade B to move the paper.

Instructors *and* students should participate in these exercises and spend a short time discussing the variations in approach and the reasons why a particular approach was taken.

LEO CUSSEN INSTITUTE

PRACTICAL TRAINING COURSE

Introduction to advocacy

Objective 2: Preparation

OBJECTIVE

To recall the importance of *thorough preparation* of a case before going to court to appear for a client.

Some of the matters which need to be considered in successful advocacy are:

Pre-trial techniques

1 Analysis of what is required to be proved:

    (i) law;
    (ii) facts.

    The very first questions asked in any case are those that lawyers ask of themselves, viz 'Where am I going?' and 'How am I going to get there?'

2 Elements in preparation   an overall investigative plan (extracted from an article by D Ross, QC).

(a) Examine information, presentment, particulars of demand, pleadings, statements, records of interview.
(b) What is the cause of action or charge and what are the elements or ingredients.
(c) Study the relevant *Act*, and any relevant *Regulations* under which the proceedings have been launched, and also whether any common law principles are applicable.
(d) Are further particulars of a charge or statement of claim necessary?
(e) Should any application be made to amend the particulars or pleadings to allege further matters or seek other relief?
(f) How can each element be proved?
(g) What can your witnesses say? Is their evidence admissible?
(h) Are any documents or exhibits involved? Has provision been made for their production? Will they be admitted as evidence?
(i) Does the Evidence Act, or any other Act, or the rules of evidence permit or prevent certain evidence being given, and in what ways?
(j) Should further evidence be given?
(k) At the completion of the plaintiff's or prosecution's case, will a prima facie case have been made out?
(l) What contrary evidence can be expected?
(m) Have you gathered appropriate material to put in cross-examination? What is the most appropriate way of putting it?
(n) Visit any scene involved in the transaction.
(o) What can the witnesses for the other side say?
(p) Attempt to learn the background of the other side's witnesses.
(q) Prepare all the possible evidentiary and legal objections you might encounter.
(r) Consider the matter in its larger context
(s) Think through the case from the perspective of opposing counsel.

The process of assembling such materials serves two purposes:

(a) it sets the legal and factual boundaries of the case;
(b) it allows you to prepare to meet the arguments of the other side.

3 Case construction – some suggestions by Bellow and Moulton adapted from their work *The Lawyering Process*

(a) A noted American teacher Louis Nizer once described the work of an advocate as—

> the task of weaving thousands of threads of disconnected testimony into a cloth of persuasive patterns while at the same time dexterously eliminating those strings which would spoil the design.

(b) An overall investigative plan as set out in para (2) is not definitive nor do the processes listed cease as the case waits in the lists. Indeed some aspects continue until the case is concluded. This process of investigation and case construction involves constant revision and re-consideration.

(c) As Bellow and Moulton observe: within this collection of raw information
your choices and actions will be guided by:

   (i) the client's situation and purposes;
  (ii) the uncontroverted facts of the case; and
 (iii) the rules and institutional requirements which will circumscribe what you can
and cannot do. These will set clear limits on the theories and strategies counsel
can pursue.

Both sides must account for these in their respective case concepts.

The notion of a 'case concept' or a 'theory of the case' is central to proper
preparation. It is best thought of as the position you adopt and the approach
that you take to each piece of evidence that may be presented in the case
whether your client disputes that particular aspect or not. The 'case concept'
that is more persuasive and plausible will carry the day.

(d) Since the object of your preparation is to persuade, it may assist you to
liken the trial process to explaining something to someone.

A person will accept a story or an argument which he finds *coherent,
consistent, credible* and *probable*. It is these criteria that should be considered
at each stage of trial preparation viz.

   (i) instructions;
  (ii) evidence-in-chief;
 (iii) cross-examination;
 (iv) re-examination;
  (v) address.

Those qualities which will persuade an ordinary listener are the very ones
on which a court will rely in assessing your client's case.

(e) The object of the advocate throughout the trial is to present his client's
case by calling witnesses and developing arguments or explanations based
on their testimony. Bellow and Moulton suggest that advocates should
ask themselves *exactly* what answers they want from a witness and arrange
these as propositions from which a predetermined conclusion (the argument or explanation the advocate wishes to advance) may be inferred.

(f) The above-mentioned authors maintain that an important aid in preparation for both examination-in-chief and cross-examination is to have
regard to *sequencing*, ie:

○ the order in which witnesses are called;
○ the order in which topics are dealt with during the course of the witness'
examination or cross-examination (a topic is the matter or matters
which the witness is called to deal with in the course of evidence, eg
evidence of identity (topic 1), evidence of subsequent observations
(topic 2) etc);
○ the order in which questions are asked in relation to each topic (see
para (e) above).

LEO CUSSEN INSTITUTE

PRACTICAL TRAINING COURSE

Introduction to advocacy

Objective 3: Presentation

OBJECTIVE

To grasp procedures and etiquette in the courts.

Introduction

The matter in these notes has been substantially adapted from a book –
Advocacy at the Bar. This excellent work was written by Keith Evans, an English
barrister, and is available in the Leo Cussen Library.

1 (1) *1st thought: Respect for the court*

  (a) Remember the law courts wield *authority* and *power*. This demands
       respect from those who come before it. Respect should not only be
       given it should be seen to be given.
  (b) This does not mean that you have to cringe or toady. It does mean
       that part of your mind must be concerned to maintain that *respect*.

  (2) *2nd thought: Appropriate dress*

  (a) Aim to appear business-like, and well groomed.
  (b) The impression you create does matter. You face enough difficult-
       ies at the outset without alienating your court by scruffy character-
       istics or flashy dressing. Blue jeans would not be acceptable.

  (3) *3rd thought: While on your feet*

  (a) Avoid nonchalance.
  (b) Your face should remain an impassive mask and betray neither joy
       nor despair. You should use facial expressions carefully and then
       only to make a point.
  (c) When you address the court, stand *up* and stand *straight*. Never put
       your hand in your pocket. (Do not lean over the bar table peering
       down at notes, lift them up so that you can read them as you stand
       straight.)
  (d) Remember when anyone is taking the oath, you freeze. Do not
       move, and certainly do not speak until the oath taking is finished.

  (4) *4th thought: Use of correct titles*

  (a) *Judge* – Your Honour.
  (b) *Magistrate* – Your Worship.
  (c) *Master* – Master.

As to all courteous forms of address, the beginner tends to overdo the
use of them. Simply use the titles often enough to indicate you know

they are *the proper form of address*, and in order to indicate your respect for the court, but go easy on them.

(5) *5th thought: The courteous tongue*

Relating to the manners required of you in court:

(a) The indirect request.

> *Examples:*
>
> 'I *wonder* your Worship, if this would be a convenient moment to adjourn?' instead of
>
> 'Would your Worship adjourn at this stage?'

(b) Pleasing the Bench.

You do not just stand up and commence calling witnesses or address-ing the court. It is a matter of courtesy to obtain the assent of the judge/magistrate to whatever you are about to do. The first thing you ever say to a judge/magistrate is:

> '*May it please your Honour/your Worship*' or '*May it please you your Honour/ your Worship*' or '*If it pleases your Honour/your Worship*'.
>
> If you are half-way through a cross-examination when you break for the luncheon adjournment, use one of those form of words when you commence the afternoon proceedings.

(c) It is advisable to thank the presiding judge or magistrate whenever possible.

(d) Another form of indirect request:

> 'Perhaps I could *invite* your Honour/your Worship to turn to p . . . of the transcript/report.'

(e) *Polite usage*: Treat slang and even common abbreviations with infinite care.

(f) *The courteous withdrawal*: If you are the last barrister/solicitor in the court room and the judge/magistrate is still on the bench, do not get up and go until the judge/magistrate has told you to go. You are entitled to rise and ask the judge/magistrate if you might be excused.

2 Some general rules about basic advocacy

(1) *Knowing your audience*   This means learning about the disposition of the bench you appear before. Knowledge of this will come from your own experiences and discussions with your friends in the profession. The psychology of communication and language is important.

(2) *Commanding and maintaining attention – some further thoughts of Keith Evans*

(a) Watch the judge/magistrate.
(b) Try, as intently as you can, not to be boring.
(c) Try not to pitch your voice in a *dreary* or *monotonous* tone.
(d) Try not to speak either too slowly or too fast. Nonetheless, you are entitled to take your time in speaking, so that the important part of your submission will sink in.

(e) Language is not one seamless piece of cloth. It is a patchwork of:

  (i) words;
  (ii) sentences;
  (iii) paragraphs.

It is sewn together with:

  (i) pauses;
  (ii) changes of pace;
  (iii) variations in the tone of voice;
  (iv) and even gestures.

(f) When speaking to the judge/magistrate try to maintain continuity. If you have mislaid a paper or cannot find the note you may need for your next point, simply say, 'Would your Honour/your Worship bear with me for a moment. I need to check on a note I have made.'
(g) Be as kind as you can at all times.

  (i) The tough approach is certainly called for in some situations, but only very rarely.
  (ii) But go gently whenever you can.
  (iii) Try to be nice.
  (iv) Nothing helps more to get the truth out of a witness than a friendly and inquiring approach.
  (v) Try suggesting that the witness may not have got it right.

3 Admonitions

(a) During the course of the trial you must lay the foundation for any comments you intend to make in your address to the jury. You are not allowed to comment on matters which have not been touched upon during the evidence.
(b) Never, when acting as an advocate, give or appear to give evidence yourself.
(c) Never offer your 'opinion', it is not evidence, it is not law and it is not relevant.
(d) Keep your objections to an absolute minimum. If you do take an objection rise to your feet, (whereby your opponent should sit down), be prepared to state your grounds and argue for them.
(e) Be as brief as you reasonably can be. Do not seek to prolong proceedings and if they can be shortened by making formal admissions then do so. However your client's interests must not be compromised by any such action. It is sometimes said that judges/magistrates feel the conflict of duty and impatience. Your client must not be a sacrificial lamb on the altar of the court's timetable.

3 Ethics of advocacy

Advocacy is at base all about straight dealing, and remember a lawyer's reputation is the most precious of all possessions.
See Practice Paper: Phillip J *The Ethics of the Advocate*.

4. The arrival at court

(1) *Announcing appearance*

    (a) To the Clerk of Courts (magistrates' court), Associate (county or Supreme Courts) registrar (Family Court);

        ○ Estimate of duration
        ○ Plea to be entered/issues in dispute
        ○ Number of witnesses it is proposed to call.

    (b) To the court

        ○ When
        ○ How
        ○ Plea through counsel
        ○ Mode of address

           – Court
           – Opposition
           – Witnesses.

(2) *Dealings with client in court*

    (a) When should client stand/sit and where
    (b) Communication with client

        ○ Further instructions
        ○ Client's interruptions while the case is running.

(3) *Applications for witnesses out of court*

All witnesses except the informant/complainant/plaintiff/defendant may be ordered from the court before the case begins.

5 The sequence of events in court

(1) *Who goes first*

    ○ Opening statements – where permissible
    ○ Evidence-in-chief
    ○ Cross-examination
    ○ Re-examination
    ○ The no case submission
    ○ Addresses
    ○ Judgment.

(2) *Objections*

    (i) When
    (ii) How
    (iii) What should be included,
eg, 'If the court please I object on the grounds that the evidence sought to be adduced is hearsay'.

(3) *Admissions*

    (a) When – usually at the beginning of proceedings.

(b) How – by formal admission by counsel or by a Notice to Admit signed by the client.

(4) *Tendering documents/exhibits*

    (a) when;
    (b) how;
    (c) objections to documents/exhibits;
    (d) particular examples:

        ○ photographs;
        ○ plans;
        ○ contracts.

An example of procedure

Your client, Abraham Old is in the witness box, being examined in chief:

[To Clerk of Courts]
Q Mr Old, would you look at this document please. Would you kindly take this document to Mr Old.

[The document is then shown to Mr Old, and he holds it in his hand.]

Q Have you seen this document before?
A Yes.
Q What is it?
A A plan of the intersection of Geelong Road and Droop Street Footscray.
Q Who prepared it?
A I did.
Q Could you kindly mark on the plan [the clerk of Courts is given a pen to hand to the witness] with an 'X' the position of your car after point of impact.

Counsel: Your worship, I tender the plan as marked.

LEO CUSSEN INSTITUTE

PRACTICAL TRAINING COURSE

Introduction to advocacy

Objective 4: Examination-in-chief

OBJECTIVE

To master principles relating to examination-in-chief.

The major aim of examination-in-chief (or leading evidence) is to make use of
the evidence of a 'friendly' witness to link items of information which come out
in the course of the examination into an account of what occurred that
supports the claim made and:

(a) is internally consistent;
(b) is consistent with other evidence;
(c) is consistent with the case concept of the side calling the witness; and
(d) contradicts and discredits adverse factual elements and testimony.

An advocate's role is to guide without leading, whilst retaining control and
keeping the evidence in the correct order. The examiner-in-chief will find that
the major difficulties he faces are in refreshing the memory of a witness who
appears to have forgotten or has at least omitted to give a vital part of his
evidence. There are two possible ways out of this dilemma.

The *first* is to suggest indirectly the forgotten evidence and yet not admin-
ister a leading question.

The *alternative* is to ask the witness to repeat his account of what was said in
the hope (sometimes realised) that on second attempt the omission will be
supplied.

The other major difficulty is the question of weak points in the witness's
testimony. These must be toned down and, perhaps, even glossed over. The
following points may be of assistance in carrying out an examination-in-chief:

(1) Try to make all questions short and clear.
(2) Make your examination complete. Before resuming your seat, be sure that
     the witness has told you everything that he knows that will help your
     cause.
(3) Be courteous to everyone, witness, magistrate or judge, and your
     opponent.
(4) When examining do not, if possible, examine from your notes. Either
     memorise the principal facts which the witness will prove, or make a note
     or two on the margin of your notes which lie on the table before you. It is
     often convenient and useful to have at your disposal a short summary of
     the leading facts.
(5) Above all be calm and good-tempered under all circumstances if you want
     to help your client and maintain your reputation.
(6) In deciding how much detail should be brought out it is best to err on the
     side of completeness, ie if the element sought to be established is what a

witness saw you will need to establish the witness's opportunity for vision, familiarity with the scene, his position etc and *not* merely ask 'What did you see?' This provides a plausible basis for his recollection and serves the ends of establishing internal consistency, coherence and probability.

(7) Try to avoid having the witness repeat himself.
(8) Wherever possible make use of demonstrative material, eg photographs, maps and charts.

Further guidelines – 'Guiding without leading' – extracted from an article by David Ross QC

It is a general rule that a witness shall not be asked leading questions during examination-in-chief. A leading question is one framed in such a way as to suggest the answer.

In practice, leading questions are always allowed:

(a) on formal matters;
(b) to introduce a witness to material questions; and
(c) on matters which have been admitted.

Let us look at a motor accident case where damage to the plaintiff's car, the amount of damage, the identity of the drivers, the date of the accident, and so on are all admitted. As is so frequent, the only issue between the parties was liability – whose fault was the accident.

Examination-in-chief on the plaintiff may be as follows:

These are all leading questions on formal matters:

Is your full name John William Smith?
Yes.
Do you live at 15 Stone Street, Black Rock?
Yes.
And is your occupation blacksmith?
Yes.
On the 8th of May this year were you the owner of a Holden Sedan Registered Number LDF 798?
Yes.
And at 5.30 pm on that day were you driving your car in a southerly direction along Beach Road?
Yes.

These are leading questions on matters which are admitted:

At the intersection of Beach Road and North Road was your car involved in a collision with Mr Wright, the Defendant's car?
Yes, it was.
As a result of that collision, your car was damaged, was it?
That's correct.
Did you later have your car repaired?
I did.
And was the cost of repairs $1,473.00?
Yes.

These are not leading questions and they introduce the witness to the only issue:

As you were driving down Beach Road, was there any traffic going in your direction?
No, none.
And as you approached the intersection where the accident happened, what was the visibility like?
It was good. I could get a clear view of everything.

And so on.

Since this is the first chance a witness has to present his version of the facts it is important that he himself be able to present that version. Let the witness appear to tell his own story. The examination-in-chief rules have the benefit of preventing an advocate from playing too forceful a role at a time when it is vital that the witness makes a good impression on the tribunal.

Retaining control

After a thorough preparation with his witness in private, an advocate should be confident that he knows exactly what the witness will say. Equally important is that the witness knows what the advocate will say during examination-in-chief.

Without this full and thorough preparation, few witnesses will have sufficient confidence to leave the control of the evidence to the advocate. But a witness who is well prepared should know first that all the evidence will come out, and secondly, it will be far more effective if he is cued by his advocate.

A witness, however, may find it extremely difficult to curb natural loquacity or impatience. If he is allowed to give evidence in his own way it will probably lack coherence. He will most likely omit important points. A more real danger is that it will breach the rules of evidence. This may result in a trial being aborted, the case having to be recommenced, and possibly the witness having to pay the costs of the aborted hearing.

If, for instance, in a criminal case, a witness in his evidence refers to an accused's prior convictions, or the fact that he has been in prison, this is ordinarily sufficient to have a jury discharged. In a recent case where a male accused was charged with buggery, one of the prosecution witnesses, a prison officer, referred to the accused as 'she'. The jury was discharged. On re-trial, the same thing happened despite, as I understand it, a warning to the witness from the trial judge. The witness was subsequently fined for contempt of court.

Again, it frequently happens in civil hearings that a witness will let fall that one of the parties is insured. In grave situations, a judge may think that this irrelevancy has prejudiced the fair hearing of the action such as to warrant a fresh trial.

Of course, it is impossible to control every word a witness says in examination-in-chief. But, if the advocate and the witness are well prepared and the advocate retains the necessary control over the giving of evidence, the chance of a *faux pas* is almost eliminated.

Inducing the right order

If evidence-in-chief is to be coherent, it must be given in the right order. The right order can vary in different cases, but in general, it is safest to stick to the order of time. This way, each incident can be covered fully before going on to the next.

Many advocates like to induce the witness to give the briefest general outline of what their evidence will be before it is gone into in detail in order of time. This was the method which was used in the example in 'Guiding without leading'. Most expert evidence is conveniently given in this manner, eg:

(a) the nature of bones;
(b) the nature of fractures; and thence ...
(c) the detailed findings and prognosis of a particular injury.

In a motor accident case, the order of the plaintiff's (complainant's) evidence might be:

(a) How he came to be on the scene.
(b) What he saw and heard before the accident:

    (i) movements of traffic, condition of lights;
    (ii) sound of brakes.

(c) What he saw when the accident happened.
(d) What he saw and heard after the accident.

Chaos is likely to result from the confusion of any two of these areas.

Including everything relevant

Everything material should be given in evidence before moving to the next point. Often a witness will be so familiar with his subject, such as layout of streets, trade jargon and so on, that he may wrongly take for granted that they are so familiar to everyone as to need no explanation. It is then the advocate's function to bring out all of the evidence. Unless this is explained to a witness beforehand, this process may seem to him trivial and unnecessary.

Refreshing one's memory

A witness is allowed to refresh his own memory from a note made at the time of the occurrence or shortly afterwards. Before referring to the note however, a witness should be required to exhaust his memory. One of the reasons why a policeman may make copious notes is to enable him to refresh his memory in court if necessary.

Normally, a policeman will say in the witness box 'May I refer to my notes, Your Honour (Your Worship)? The bench will normally ask counsel for the accused/defendant, 'Is there any objection to the constable refreshing his memory?' The advocate would be wise to reply, 'I would like him to exhaust his memory first, Your Honour; and I would like to inquire when the notes were made.'

It sometimes happens that the policeman has little if any independent recollection of the events and that the notes were largely compiled by a fellow policeman.

Toning down weak points

Munkman says:

> Where there is a weak point in the evidence, the manner of dealing with it may raise a difficult problem of practical judgment. It is the duty of counsel to treat the court with frankness, and certainly not to conceal facts if they are relevant: furthermore, if the point is brought out in cross examination, its effect will be more damaging. As a rule, therefore, the better course is to bring out the point in examination-in-chief, without undue emphasis, and toning it down as far as the facts allow (p 46).

Having a witness declared hostile

A hostile witness has been said to be one 'unwilling if called by a party who cannot ask him leading questions to tell the truth and the whole truth in answer to non-leading questions' (*R v Hayden and Slattery* (1959) VR 102, per Sholl J. See also *R v Lawless* (1974) VR 398).

Section 34 of the Evidence Act 1958 reads:

> A party producing a witness shall not be allowed to impeach his credit by general evidence of bad character; but may contradict him by other evidence, or (in case the witness in the opinion of the court proves adverse) may, by leave of such court prove that he has made at other times a statement inconsistent with his present testimony. But, before such last mentioned proof can be given, the circumstances of the supposed statement sufficient to designate the particular occasion must be mentioned to a witness; and he must be asked whether or not he has made such statement.

It often happens that a witness one calls gives unfavourable evidence. Sometimes a witness will say in court the complete reverse of what he has told you in conference. It is rare, however, that you can have that witness declared hostile because you cannot prove the prior inconsistent statement.

One way around this problem is to have the witnesses you expect to call sign their proofs of evidence, or statements, before you go into court. This should only be done after you are quite satisfied that the statement is an accurate account of what the witness will say. The signing of the statement should be done in the presence of the instructing solicitor who will be able, if necessary, to give evidence that the statement was made and signed.

It is wise to make the application to have a witness declared hostile in the absence of the jury. Let us say that a witness in examination-in-chief has sworn something which completely contradicts what he has said in his signed statement. You will naturally be concerned that the evidence does not continue in this fashion.

When you decide to apply to have a witness declared hostile, you may simply say to the Judge, 'Your Honour, there are some legal matters I would like to raise in the absence of the jury.'

Invariably the judge will direct the jury to retire to the jury room, and when this is done, you will say that you propose to question the witness to have him declared hostile. The judge will allow you then to cross-examine the witness based on his previous statement, in support of your application. The judge's decision on whether the witness is hostile will be founded on his observation of the whole demeanour of the witness as well as his answers to questions. The judge will exercise his discretion in deciding, and then the jury will be recalled.

If a witness is declared hostile, he may be asked leading questions in examination-in-chief, and his prior inconsistent statement may be able to be tendered in evidence.

An advantage of a signed statement is that it can be used to rebut an allegation of recent invention. If, during cross-examination, it is suggested that he has just made up his story, counsel re-examining is entitled to show the witness his signed statement and have it tendered as an exhibit.

An example of evidence-in-chief (leading evidence) – examining your own witness

Christopher Barren is claiming $20,000.00 in the county court at Melbourne for damages sustained by him as a result of his having been allegedly assaulted by Constable Abraham O'Brien.

[**Note** – the point at which leading ceases. Is it at question 10?]

Q1	Is your name Christopher Barren?
A	Yes.
Q2	Do you reside at 1 Paradise Lane, Toorak?
A	Yes.
Q3	Are you a bookmaker by occupation?
A	Yes.
Q4	Were you driving a motor car in Punt Road, Richmond on 19 April at approximately 10.00 pm?
A	Yes.
Q5	Did you observe a police car following you?
A	Yes.
Q6	Did the police car drive up alongside you?
A	Yes.
Q7	Did the driver of the police car indicate to you to pull over?
A	Yes.
Q8	Did a policeman get out of the car, and come up to you?

Objections by defence counsel. Kindly let the witness tell the story himself.
Argument as to whether the stage of contention has yet been reached.
His Honour overrules the objection.

Q9	Please now answer the question.
A	No.
	The policeman did get out and come up to me.
Q10	Did you have in your car as a passenger, your clerk Daniel Murphy?

Objection by defence counsel: Your Honour I would like the witness to give his own evidence, and not distinguished counsel.
His Honour: Perhaps the witness should be asked was there anybody else in his car at the time, and the name of that person, and his relationship to the plaintiff.
Plaintiff's counsel: Very well, your Honour.

Q11	Was there anyone else in your car at the time?
A	Yes.
Q12	What was the name of that person?
A	Daniel Murphy, my bagman.
Q13	Tell us what you mean by bagman.
A	He holds the money for me on the course.
Q14	Did Murphy get out of the car?
A	Yes.

Objection: The question should be asked did Murphy do anything.
Judge to defence counsel: Is there any dispute as to the remaining in or getting out of the car?
Defence counsel: No.
Judge: Well then; I cannot see why you are so objecting.

Q15   Did the defendant ask you any questions?
A   Yes.
Q16   What did he say to you?
A   He asked if I had been drinking.
Q17   Did you say to him that you had not been drinking?

Objection by defence counsel.
His Honour: Yes, please just ask him what he said to the constable.
Plaintiff's counsel: Very well your Honour.

Q18   Well then, let's have it again. What did you say to the defendant?
A   I said 'I have not been drinking'.
Q19   Did he do anything then?

Objection.
Judge: Put the question what happened next.

A   The copper grabbed me.
Q20   Did he take hold of your wrist?

Objection.
Rephrased.

Q21   Where did he grab you?
A   On the wrist.
Q22   Did anything happen after that?
A   Yes, he twisted my wrist back.
Q23   Did anything happen to your wrist?
A   Yes, it was broken.

Objection.
Judge: Do you propose to call medical evidence on this aspect?
Plaintiff's counsel: Yes, your Honour I shall put the matter in another way, your Honour.

Q24   As a result of all this did you attend a doctor?
A   Yes.
Q25   Whom?
A   Dr Thomas Bent.
Q26   Where is his surgery?
A   High Street, Toorak.
Q27   How many attendances did you make on the Doctor?
A   Six.
Q28   Was your wrist in plaster?

Objection.

Q29   Did this doctor do anything to your wrist?
A   Yes, he put it in plaster.
Q30   For how long was your wrist in plaster?
A   Six weeks.

Judge: Do you propose to call Dr Bent?
Counsel: Yes, your Honour.

Q31   You are a bookmaker by occupation/profession?
A   Yes.
Q32   Do you attend racecourse meetings in the course of your work?
A   Yes.
Q33   How often?
A   I attend a Metropolitan race meeting every Saturday of the year.
Q34   How many meetings did you miss, as a result of the wrist injury?
A   16 weekly meetings.
Q35   Do you make income tax returns?
A   Why, do you think I am a bottom of the harbour fellow?

Counsel: Please, just answer the question.

A   Yes.
Q36   Take your income tax return for the year ending 30 June 1986 – what was the income stated after deduction of your business expenses?

Objection: Surely the return should be produced as primary evidence or his accountant who prepared the return called.
Judge to plaintiff's counsel: What do you say on this?
Plaintiff's counsel: The accountant will be called.

Q37   Did you suffer any pain in your wrist as a result of its injury?
A   Yes I did, and still do.
Q38   Any disabilities?
A   Yes, I have to employ two pencillers instead of one, every Saturday. I still can't do any pencilling.
Q39   Are you the plaintiff in this case?
A   Yes.
Q40   Are you claiming $20,000.00 to cover your damage, loss and pain and suffering?
A   Yes.
Q41   Is the defendant Abraham O'Brien in court?
A   Yes, there he is (pointing to him).
Q42   Do you identify him as the person who grabbed your wrist?
A   Yes.

NOTE CAREFULLY

(1) The brevity of most questions.
(2) Instructors should then seek from the students their opinions on this example of evidence-in-chief.

LEO CUSSEN INSTITUTE

PRACTICAL TRAINING COURSE

Introduction to advocacy

Objective 5: Cross-examination

OBJECTIVE

To practise the skill of cross-examination through the use of 'leading' or 'closed' questions.

The cross-examination of witnesses has a number of objects, inter alia:

(1) To destroy or weaken the evidence given against you by the witness (this is on the assumption that the evidence is incorrect or incomplete, but not deliberately false).

   Your aim is to establish inconsistency and improbability. As Bellow and Moulton observe in pursuing these goals you must pay attention to such factors as unity, coherence, emphasis, plausibility and completeness. What the cross-examiner argues through questions and answers, even when cross-examination seeks only to raise doubts, must make sense. The examination must have a purpose – a set of attitudes and ideas that counsel wants the audience to accept. You must know the specific proposition (inference) you want the hearer to draw from the testimony.

(2) As important a decision as determining which questions to ask is deciding what questions *not* to ask. This conscious decision is the hallmark of careful preparation and forethought.

(3) To elicit something in your favour which the witness has not stated.

(4) To discredit the witness by showing that he is unworthy of belief (the evidence here is assumed to be deliberately false).

(5) There is of course the requirement that counsel put his instructions – the Rule in *Browne v Dunne*.

There are of course many and varied manners in which cross-examination may be conducted, among them the hard line, the soft line and the humorous line. The latter should be used sparingly.

It is vital that cross-examination be conducted on all material facts in dispute and one's case should be put to a witness where his evidence conflicts with the evidence that one's own client would give.

When to stop

There are a number of pitfalls in cross-examination, and perhaps the most important of these is the extra question. Only experience will show the criminal advocate when to stop, but perhaps a good guide line is provided by the second pitfall, namely never ask a question unless you know the answer. The following story is extracted from Keith Evans' work *Advocacy at the Bar – A Beginners' Guide*.

A very endearing anecdote was told by a now famous High Court Judge at an Oxford college dinner some years ago. It was a story against himself when, as a very young barrister, he was defending two villains on a charge of attempted burglary. The prosecution said that in the small hours of the morning and in the silent emptiness of a town square a police sergeant had come upon the villains trying to break into the local jeweller's shop. He had approached, so he said in chief, to within twelve feet of where they were trying to pick the lock or whatever. Of course, the cross-examination was an attack on the sergeant, designed to show that it was utterly impossible for anyone, let alone him, to have got so close to the burglars without their noticing his approach. And the questions went something like this:

Q Sergeant, would you be kind enough to tell us how tall you are?
A Six foot three, sir.
Q And no weakling! Would you mind telling us your weight?
A Tip the scales at just under twenty three stone, sir.
Q That night – wearing uniform, were you?
A Yes, sir.
Q Helmet?
A Yes, sir.
Q Greatcoat?
A Tunic, actually, sir.
Q Boots?
A Yes, sir.
Q Regulation issue boots, sergeant?
A Yes, sir.
Q What size were they?
A Size twelve, sir.
Q Yes, I see. Size twelve boots. Studded with hobnails, were they, like the normal regulation issue?
A (Pause) Yes, sir.
Q They had a kind of small horseshoe of metal on each heel?
A Er, yes, sir.
Q And you say that you approached to within twelve feet of these men without their seeming to notice your arrival, sergeant?
A (Pause) ... Yes, sir.
Q In a totally empty square at two in the morning?
Q (Pause) ... Yes, sir.
Q Nobody else around was there?
A No, sir.
Q Normal flagged pavements were there?
A (Pause) ... Yes, sir.
Q I mean, you didn't approach over a lawn or grass of some kind, did you?
A (Pause) No, sir.

(Enough? Impossible in the circumstances to believe that the sergeant could have got up to the villains, who had normal hearing, without being heard? Time to sit down? One question too many coming up.)
Q Well, really, sergeant, can you suggest to the magistrates how you could possibly have got as close as you say you did without being heard by the defendants?
A On my bicycle, sir.

The best way of learning the methods and pitfalls of cross-examination is by sitting in court watching cross-examiners in action. It is a useful practice to sit in court and while the witness is being examined-in-chief, ask one's self how to cross-examine, if engaged in the case.

One question too many – a second example

A young man and woman were charged with robbery in company. The victim had said in evidence-in-chief that he had $140.00 on him, and that before the robbery he was buying drinks for the woman in a hotel bar. Part of the 'probing' cross-examination was as follows:

Q   Where did you have the $140.00?
A   In my wallet.
Q   Did you have any change on you?
A   Yes.
Q   In what pocket did you have your change?
A   In my fob pocket.
Q   And you were paying for the drinks out of that pocket were you?
A   Yes.
Q   Where did you have your wallet?
A   In my back pocket.
Q   You wouldn't have needed to take out your wallet in the hotel, would you?
A   No.

So far so good. The jury could easily have inferred that the accused would not have known of the existence of the $140.00. But, the advocate was too enthusiastic.

Q   So the girl would not have known you had the money?
A   Yes, she did. I told her.

The moral of this illustration is this. Let the court draw its own conclusions and stop when you are satisfied that it can. Beware of forcing the conclusions from the witness. It can easily backfire.

The principal methods – extracted from an article by D Ross QC

The main methods of cross-examination are probing, insinuation, confrontation and undermining.

1 Probing

Probing consists of inquiring thoroughly into the details of the story to discover the flaws. It comprises a number of aspects.

Probing is important to separate a witness's observations from his conclusions. A witness gives evidence of identifying someone, say an accused:
Cross-examination as to identification will probably be:

○ What was the state of the lighting?
○ Where was the witness standing? Why was he there?
○ Where was the accused standing?
○ What was each person doing and for how long?
○ Were there other people in the vicinity?
○ How long was the accused under observation?
○ When was the witness first asked to recall the accused?
○ Did anyone speak to the witness about the identity of the accused?
○ Was the accused previously known to the witness?

It is brutal and gauche to simply suggest to a witness that he is mistaken. It is far better to examine him on his observations. This method lacks significant danger. Its great value is to enable a court to infer that the witness could not have identified the accused from the observations he made.

Cross-examination of this sort is used to force a witness to detail his observations exactly. If the same technique is used with a number of witnesses it often happens that although their original conclusions may have been the same, the observations on which those conclusions are made are quite different. Then a court could easily think that only one, or perhaps none, of the conclusions is correct.

In this sort of probing many advocates lead a witness to state positive facts on which he can be contradicted by unquestionable evidence. This leading is even more telling when it contradicts evidence already given by other witnesses on the same side, which the witness being cross-examined had not heard because he was out of court when it was given.

2 Insinuation

This term is used by Munkman to explain the following methods of cross-examination:

(a) *The limits of the evidence-in-chief.* If the witness, in his evidence-in-chief, has failed to speak to an important point, it is useful to make it clear to the court.

(b) Where damaging facts have been proved in chief, an explanation may be obtained which weakens the damaging inference. In *R v Davidson* (a ruling from which is in [1969] VR 667) the Crown sought to imply that the accused had performed illegal operations because his gynaecological practice at a given time contained a high disproportion of patients who were given a dilatation and curettage. The Crown called an independent gynaecologist to depose to the average number 'D and C's' in a normal practice.
On cross-examination by Jack Lazarus (a criminal lawyer):

> 'But you can sometimes get a run on these things can't you doctor?'
> 'Yes, you can.'

(c) *Weakening an inference*: suggesting other possibilities equally consistent with the facts. This is the main method of shaking expert opinion.

(d) *Other helpful facts which assist the case generally.* Each day in civil cases where injured plaintiffs complain of osteoarthritis as the result of their injuries, advocates for the defendant ask:

> 'But all of us will get arthritis in time won't we doctor?'
> 'Yes, we will.'

(A note of caution for intending defendants' advocates. One doctor regularly says to this question 'Unfortunately yes. God save us.')

(e) *The possibility of mistaken observation.* It is often said that no cross-examiner should ask a question to which he does not know the answer. I cannot agree with this theory; otherwise very few questions indeed would ever be asked. And all the material which is obtained by skillful probing and insinuation would not be gained.
One should not, however, ask a question on a crucial point if one does not know that the answer will be either in one's favour, or else contra-

dicted by other evidence so as to make the witness' evidence unacceptable.

The contradictory evidence must be evidence which is sure to be accepted. Usually this sort of evidence is supplied by documents or by oral evidence of a formal nature, for example, the time of sunset in a case where this may be in doubt.

3 Confrontation

Only where you are satisfied that you can call evidence which will be accepted in complete contradiction to the evidence-in-chief, should one begin a cross-examination by confronting a witness with those matters. Sir Patrick Hastings says that if the advocate does have these materials, he should put them to the witness straight away: 'if you are going to charge a witness with fraud, it is wise that your first question would make that clear. If the witness is dishonest, a violent blow at the outset will very often knock him completely off his carefully prepared pedestal of integrity' (Hastings *Cases in Court* Heineman (1949) p 17). Munkman summarises the best techniques of confrontation.

(a) It should not be used without strong material, preferably facts which the witness cannot deny.
(b) The facts should be put one at a time.
(c) As soon as each fact is put and admitted, all its damaging implications should be drawn out one by one.
(d) If the witness offers lame explanations, he should be pinned down to them precisely.
(e) The other facts are then put in turn, in such a way as to demolish the explanations.
(f) The aim is to force the witness to admit the falsity of story; or to make him tongue-tied; or to involve him in contradictions (pp 76–77).

The three techniques referred to are rarely used separately. The skilled advocate may, for instance, have a document in his possession which has been prepared by the witness. It may be, however, that its effect will be wasted if put to a witness early in cross-examination. The best course then would be to use the methods of probing and insinuation to strengthen the witness's evidence so as to make it stand out in sharper relief in comparison with the document. Then confront him with it.

Remember to order your cross-examination so as not to overlook an important point.

Try to make the last question a withering one. Many good advocates drawing to the end of a cross-examination sit down if they get an answer whose effect they believe cannot be improved upon by more questions.

4 Undermining evidence as to credit

Normally, cross-examination must be relevant to the facts in issue. Cross-examination to show that the witness is not the sort of person whose evidence can be accepted is cross-examination as to credit. 'If by cross-examination as to credit you prove that a man's oath cannot be relied upon and he has sworn that he did not go to Rome on May 1st, you do not therefore prove that he did go to Rome on May 1st; there is simply no evidence on the subject' (Scrutton LJ in *Hobbs v Tinting* (1929) 2 KB 1 at 21).

In criminal cases, if evidence is led of the accused's good character to show that he would not be disposed to commit a crime, then he can be cross-examined on his prior convictions. For the dangers of introducing character as an issue in a criminal case, see *R v Donnini* 1973 VR 67 (and 47 ALJR 69) and Crimes Act 1958, s 339.

Witnesses are not entitled to be called to impugn the credit of another witness. But there are some exceptions, which are well explained in Cross (op cit pp 275 ff below). These exceptions are for proof of particular relevant prior convictions, or to prove that a witness may be biased.

Production of documents and cross-examination on documents

A party served with a notice to produce or any person served with a subpoena is required to produce at the court those documents listed in the notice.

If you suspect that a witness has on his person a document which may be of assistance, the witness can be required to turn out his pockets.

This may be of special value when cross-examining policemen. They are likely to have their notebooks or notes of their evidence with them. If you suspect the evidence, you may take the following line.

(1) Refuse to allow a policeman to refer to his notes to refresh his memory during evidence-in-chief until he has exhausted his memory.

(2) On cross-examination, ask him to produce the notes to you, and his notebook.

You might find when you examine the notebook that important evidence is not contained in it.

The manner of using this material varies considerably. The method of requiring production, however, is simple:

'Do you have your notebook on you?'

'Yes'. (to the bench)

'I ask that it be produced, Your Honour (Worship).'

One rule

'If at a hearing, a party calls for and inspects a document held by his adversary, he is bound to put it in evidence if required to do so, provided the document was not being used to refresh the memory of one of the adversary's witnesses' (*Cross Evidence* (Australian edition, Byrne & Heydon; Butterworths, 1986)). The effect of this rule is as follows: If, during cross-examination, you require a witness to produce a document, you may be required to tender it, that is, place it in the hands of the court as part of your evidence. The fact that the document may contain matters of hearsay or be a self-serving statement is just too bad. It still goes in. Perhaps the document could not have been tendered during evidence-in-chief of a witness because it was a prior consistent statement. And the only way it could be tendered was by you calling for its production, and then being required by your opponent to tender it.

Documents and materials which are tendered are called exhibits. Exhibits tendered by the plaintiff or the prosecution are usually marked in letters, the first exhibit being Exhibit 'A', the second Exhibit 'B', and so on. Exhibits tendered by the defendant or the accused are marked numerically, Exhibit 1, Exhibit 2, and so on.

What objects must be produced?

'If the condition of a material object is among the facts in issue, as where it is alleged that a suit made by a tailor does not fit his customer, or that the defendant's dog is vicious, the object must be produced to the judge.'

LEO CUSSEN INSTITUTE

PRACTICAL TRAINING COURSE

Introduction to advocacy

Cross-examination in action

One illustration of cross-examination*

In *R v Adams*, heard at the (English) Central Criminal Court in March and April 1957 (and referred to in [1957] Crim LR 365 and 773), Mr Geoffrey Lawrence QC appointed for the accused who was charged with murdering a Mrs Morrell. Lawrence cross-examined a prosecution witness, Nurse Stronach. The following points were made in Stronach's evidence-in-chief:

○ she was Mrs Morrell's nurse for 11 days prior to her death on 30 November 1950;
○ over this period the patient grew weaker until on 2 November she was 'semi-conscious and rambling';
○ Stronach and the other nurses administered $\frac{1}{4}$ grain of morphia each night to Mrs Morrell as prescribed by Dr Adams;
○ she had given no other injection;
○ the drugs she administered were kept in a drawer;
○ Dr Adams attended at 11 pm each night and gave Mrs Morrell an injection of a substance he took from his bag;
○ she was unaware of the nature of this substance because Mrs Morrell had asked that she be out of the room each time it was administered.

Lawrence had obtained the contemporaneous nursing records made up to Mrs Morrell's death. These records were contained in notebooks.

The notebooks revealed that:

○ Stronach's first spell of duty was 4–25 June, 1950 and no entry mentioned any visit by the doctor or any injection of morphia;
○ during Stronach's second spell of duty, ie October to November, there *was* mention of her having administered another drug 'Omnopon' to Mrs Morrell;
○ the doctor had only visited twice during this period;
○ on each of these visits the nature of the injection was recorded.

Note in particular that Lawrence alternates the different techniques of cross-examining so as to contradict the witness by the production of the records in a most telling way.

Note too the effectiveness of the 'sequencing' of the subjects about which the cross-examination is conducted and also the 'sequencing' of the questions dealing with each subject.

---

* Extracts from *R v Adams* on pp 286–296 are reproduced with permission of the copyright holder, Mr F. Lovett.

Memory

Mr Lawrence: Miss Stronach, how many patients do you think you have attended since Mrs Morrell died?

A   I could not possibly tell you.

Q1   A very great many?

A   Yes. In private nursing we are in and out constantly.

Q2   You have been constantly nursing other patients during the last six or seven years. Is that right?

A   Yes.

Q3   And from what you told my Lord and the members of the jury this morning, you are relying on your memory of events that happened on one case six or seven years ago?

A   Oh yes.

Patient's condition

Q4   Just tell me a little bit about Mrs Morrell so far as you were able to know about her case at the time you were there. We have been told that she was 81 when she died. You knew that she was an old lady, did not you?

A   Yes.

Q5   Did you know that she had suffered from a stroke?

A   Oh yes.

Q6   Very evident in paralysis down the left side?

A   Yes.

Q7   I believe the technical term for that sort of stroke is a cerebral thrombosis, is not it?

A   Yes, that is correct.

Q8   And she had great variations in her condition, did she not?

A   She had.

Q9   But all the time, whether there were these ups and downs, all the time she was going downhill, was she not?

A   Steadily.

Q10   At the end she was, as you have said, very, very weak?

A   Extremely weak.

Q11   And from time to time she had attacks of great irritability, did she not?

A   Due to her condition.

Q12   And that irritability was shown against the nurses, was it?

A   Yes. Not only the nurses; other people.

Q13   And it was a quite irrational irritability, was it not?

A   It was not a normal irritability.

Q14   When you said 'due to her condition' you mean due to the injury to the arteries of the brain?

A   Not only that.

Q15   Well, that for a start?

A   Yes.

Q16   What else?

A   I should say that it was due a great deal to the amount of drugs she was having.

Discussions with others

Q17   Yes, I thought you were going to say that ... Tell me, after all these years, when were you first asked to remember about Mrs Morrell's case by anybody?

A   About the beginning of September, so far as I can tell you.

Q18   Of last year?

A   Yes.

Q19   That would be September 1956, very nearly six years after you had last attended her?

A   Yes, that is so.

Q20   You were seen again on later occasions by a police officer?

A   Yes.

Q21   How many times?

A   I did not keep account, but several times.

The transcript contains the following questions and answers.

Q22   So that between September and early January you had been interviewed by three police officers; is that right?

A   Yes.

Q23   Did you make a statement on each occasion?

A   Except the last one.

Q24   Have you talked about this case to other nurses – Nurse Randall and Mason-Ellis and Bartlett?

A   Well, we naturally conversed together.

Q25   When I say 'discussed the case with her' do not think I am criticising you at all; I only want to know what happened.

A   Yes.

Q26   Do you mean before you gave your evidence at Eastbourne?

A   Yes.

Q27   And since?

A   No, we want to try and forget it.

Injections

Q28   Yes, I can understand that. Now just a word or two about what you said, so that I can understand it. You say that you used to give Mrs Morrell an injection of a quarter-grain of morphia?

A   Yes, I did say so.

Q29   On Dr Adams' instructions?

A   Yes.

Q30   Are you referring to your period of day duty or night duty, when you say that?

A   Well, night duty.

Q31   Did you ever give her anything else by way of an injection.

A   No, I did not.

Q32   No heroin?

A   No.

Q33   No Omnopon?

A   No, not with me.

Q34   And I understand from what you said that the doctor came in the evening after you had come on duty – this is your spell of night duty – and, you say, gave a further injection?

A   That is so.

Q35   And that is what you still say?

A   I do.

Q36   I am reminded of something that Miss Mason-Ellis said; I just want to ask you about it. When she gave her evidence at Eastbourne: 'I knew what I was injecting but I cannot accurately remember now but whatever I gave was booked in a book and passed on to the next nurse'?

A   Yes, that was quite correct.

Q37   That is quite correct?

A   We wrote down every injection we gave.

Q38   You put down ...?

A   Yes, we kept a report of every injection we gave: this is a usual thing when you are nursing, to keep a report of the injections you give.

Q39   It is the usual thing?

A   Yes, it is the proper thing to do.

Q40   Well, all experienced and trained nurses do it, do they not?

A   Yes, they do.

Q41   And that is what you did?

A   Yes, indeed we did.

Q42   All of you nurses did?

A   Yes, we all did.

Book recording injections

Q43   Was that done after each spell of duty, then, or during the night, or what?

A   Every time we gave an injection we wrote it down in the book; what the injection was, and the time, and signed our name.

Q44   And whatever you wrote in that book would be accurate would it not?

A   Oh yes.

Q45   Because it was done right at that very moment?

A   Yes.

Q46   In the case of these books, I suppose everything that happened of significance in the patient's illness would also go down in the book by the nurse?

A   Yes.

Q47   Not only injections, I suppose, but medicines and all that sort of thing?

A   Yes, that is so.

Q48   Doctor's visits?

A   Well, we would just put down that the doctor visited and the time, usually.

Q49   And as distinct from memory six years later, of course, these reports would be absolutely accurate, would they not ... I mean yours would, at any rate?

A   Oh yes, they would be accurate for each one of us.

Q50   So that if only we had got those reports now we could see the truth of exactly what happened night by night and day by day that you were there, could we not?

A   Yes, but you have our word for it.

Record book produced

Q51   I want you to have a look at that book please. (same handed) Would you look at the day report for the 4 June 1950?

Q52   There is no doubt about it, is there, Miss Stronach, that is the very book of daily and nightly records kept by nurses when you started your first spell of duty in June 1950?

A   Yes, that is so.

The doctor's visits and morphine injections

The transcript contains the following questions and answers.

Mr Lawrence: Now, that is the last night that you did duty on that spell, is it not? If you look ahead you will see, will you not, on the next night Nurse Randall was back again?

A   Yes.

Q53   And you never recorded a visit of the doctor in the evening when you were on duty, did you?

A   No, I did not record it.

Q54   You are not saying, Miss Stronach, are you, that if you, as a trained nurse of years of experience, had given an injection of a quarter-grain in that spell of duty you would not have put it down in the book?

A   No. I should most certainly have put it down.

Q55   As such a trained nurse, you would not have omitted to record the visit by the doctor and an injection given by him if in fact it had taken place while you were on duty, would you?

A   No, I do not think I would have done.

The transcript contains the following questions and answers.

Q56   Now let us go to the next period when you came back. You will find that in the third book I have handed to you, and I think you will find it begins on 12 October. Would you look at the day report? And your first entry on that day is 4.00 pm?

A   It is.

Q57   Now, here you are not on night duty but on day duty and this is only a month before Mrs Morrell died, is it not?

A   Yes.

Q58   When you went back in October there was a very big difference in Mrs Morrell's condition, was there not?

A   Yes.

Q59   She had deteriorated very, very much, had she not?

A   Yes.

Q60   We have seen already you entries for the nights in June. Now let us see what you put in the day only a month before she died: '4.00 pm. Asked for a bedpan. Same not used. Position changed. Patient became restless and picking bedclothes.' Do you see what follows? Is this in your writing: 'Hypo injection omnopon two thirds given at 4.30 pm.'

A   Yes.

Contradiction of witness

Q61   That means that you gave that injection, does it not?

A   It does.

Q62   And it is an injection of omnopon?

A   Yes.

Q63   Now, Miss Stronach, do not think that I am blaming you in any way or criticising you for this ...

A   No.

Q64   ... but do you remember telling me earlier this morning before you saw these contemporary records that you had never given Mrs Morrell any injection except morphia?

A   Well, I believed that to be true.

Q65   Well, this entry shows that your memory was playing you a trick, does it not?

A   Apparently so.

Q66   Obviously so. Miss Stronach, may I ask you to face this squarely. Obviously your memory played you a trick, did it not, when you said you have never injected anything but morphia?

A   Yes. Of course, you have got to remember it is a long time ago for us to remember these things.

Q67   That is exactly what I was suggesting to you, that it was a long time ago and that mistakes of memory can be made. This is one of them, is it not, because this is quite clear, is it not: you would not have entered in the report, this day report, an injection of two thirds omnopon by hypodermic at 4.30 pm unless you had in fact given it?

A   No, I certainly would not have.

The transcript contains the following questions and answers.

Q68   Now will you pay close attention to what follows in your writing on 12 October: '7.30 pm. Visited by Dr Adams. Hypodermic injection morphia gr. $\frac{1}{4}$, heroin gr. $\frac{1}{4}$, omnopon gr. one third.' Is it there in your writing?

A   It is.

Q69   You have there recorded the exact nature and the exact quantities for the injection which was given to Mrs Morrell when the doctor visited, have you not?

A   Yes, I have.

Q70   Otherwise you would not have recorded it?

A   No.

Q71   And you wind up by saying at the end 'General condition very low'. That was true, was it not?

A   Oh, yes.

Q72   Only a month before she died. Now, I think we shall find that after doing that part of the day – Are you not feeling well?

A   It is all right, thank you. Thank you very much.

Q73   After doing that part of the day duty, I want a little further help from you in the book because I think you then turn to night duty?

A   Oh yes, on the 14th.

Q74   Well, so be it. Then we come to the night report of 14th October?

A   Yes.

Q75   Is that in your writing?

A   Yes.

Q76   Your first night report then is for the 14th/15th, beginning 10.20 pm. 'Hypo: Inj: Morphia Gr. $\frac{1}{4}$, Heroin Fr. one third, and Omnopon Gr. one third given by Dr Adams.' You see that?

A   Yes.

Q77   That means at least two things. It means you recorded a visit of the doctor at 10.20 pm doesn't it?

A   Yes.

Q78   And it means you recorded again the nature and quantities of the injection which was given by him in the book?

A   Yes.

Q79   That is exactly the same in nature and quantity as the one which you had previously recorded on your half day duty on 12 October, one quarter Morphia, one third Heroin, and one third Omnopon. Exactly the same isn't it?

A   Yes.

The transcript contains the following questions and answers.

Q80   Now we have been through, Miss Stronach, the whole, I think, of your records made at the time, night after night, or day after day, of your nursing duties for Mrs Morrell, have not we?

A   Yes.

Q81   We have not found a single instance where you gave a hypodermic injection of a quarter of a grain of morphia by itself, have we?

A   No. Seemingly not.

Q82   And I think it is only one or two occasions where you record an evening visit of the doctor, and we find that you record exactly what the injection was that was given, do we not?

A   Yes.

Q83   You were no less conscientious, were you, in your duties in every way in Mrs Morrell's case that you would be in any other case of your many years experience?

A   That is so.

Mrs Morrell's condition

The transcript contains the following questions and answers.

Q84   [You said this morning] that on your very last day she (Mrs Morrell) was in a semi-conscious condition and rambling. Do you remember saying that?

A   I do.

Q85	I have drawn your attention to what you recorded on your last day: 'Mrs Morrell has had a much better day on the whole. Has been more awake and taking interest in things'?
A	That is quite possible.
Q86	That is not the picture of a semi-conscious woman, is it?
A	That was the day before. I wrote no report for November the 2nd.
Q87	What? Well, if you are going to say that, are you trying to be as fair-minded as you can on this?
A	Certainly. What I am trying to point out to you sir, is that a patient can change very quickly.
Q88	Yes, I agree, and that was one of the features of Mrs Morrell's condition, was not it?
A	She most certainly was very different on the day I left, on November the 2nd.
Q89	Well, what do you say? What happened on the morning of the last day and what was she like?
A	Well, to me, during the morning it can only – it is possible for it only to last temporarily: – she was to me only semi-conscious during that morning and she rambled; but as to what she was doing the rest of the day I cannot tell you.
Q90	If in fact she was semi-conscious and rambling, that is a condition which you as a trained nurse would put in the book if you had been responsible for making the entries, would not you?
A	If I had been writing the report.
Q91	Well, just open that book, please, if you will, at the 2nd November 1950, and see what Nurse Mason-Ellis said. There is no question about Miss Mason-Ellis being a trained nurse, is there?
A	None whatever.
Q92	'Day report. 10.30 am. Seen with Dr Bodkin Adams. Drops put in eyes. No injection given. 10.50 twenty minutes later, "Passed urine well". Then ten minutes later at eleven o'clock. Just follow this, please Miss Stronach: '11.00 am. Hot milk with soda water and brandy.' Then see what this semi-conscious woman, this semi-conscious rambling woman, is recorded by the experienced Sister Mason-Ellis as having had for lunch at one o'clock on the day you left. Can you read it?
A	Yes.
Q93	What does it say? Read it to the jury, will you?
A	It says she had partridge, celery, pudding, brandy and soda. But, of course, I must add that would only be very, very small quantities that she would be given; she would not have much of anything.

Fencing

Q94	What is the object of adding that?
A	To let you see that she does not eat a great deal. She would not be eating a lot.
Q95	Did you think I had suggested that she had eaten an enormous meal of partridge and celery?
A	I couldn't say.

Q96   Miss Stronach, how many times did you say you had been interviewed
         by police officers before you went into the witness-box at Eastbourne?
A   Three or four times, I think.
Q97   How long did those interviews last?
A   Oh, sometimes two hours.
Q98   How many hours do you think you spent in the company of police
         officers at these interviews before you ever gave your evidence to begin
         with?
A   I do not know. I haven't thought about it.
Q99   Well, try and think about it now?
A   It might be about six hours altogether, I suppose.
Q100   Let me go back to what I was saying. Do you observe that your
         colleague Sister Mason-Ellis recorded that this semi-conscious
         woman ate, if you like, for lunch that day a small quantity of partridge,
         a small quantity of celery, a small quantity of pudding and a small
         quantity of brandy and soda? Do you see that?
A   Yes.
Q101   You have the greatest respect, have not you, for Sister Mason-Ellis's
         ability and conscientiousness as a trained nurse?
A   I certainly have.
Q102   She would not be likely to put anything down if it was not right, would
         she?
A   Actually she has not put down this. It seems to me that I have written
         it down until a quarter to two, and she came on at 3.20 pm apparently.
Q103   You have written it? You have recorded the lunch of the partridge and
         celery and the pudding?
A   Yes.
Q104   Miss Stronach, let us face this: it is another complete trick of your
         memory to say that on the last day when you left Mrs Morrell was
         either semi-conscious or rambling, is not it, now you see what you
         wrote at the time? (a pause) Is not it?
A   I have nothing to say.

Witness falters

Q105   What?
A   I have nothing to say.
Q106   You have nothing to say?
A   No.
Q107   If you have got nothing to say, just turn back the page and see if you
         can recognise Miss Randall's writing, the previous night nurse. Is that
         Miss Randall's writing?
A   Yes, it is.
Q108   Now, before you came on duty on the morning of the 2nd November
         you would have read what Miss Randall had recorded the night
         before, would not you, in the usual routine way?
A   Yes.
Q109   Do you see what Miss Randall recorded the old lady had had for
         breakfast before you came on duty that last day?
A   Yes.
Q110   Just read it to my Lord and the jury, will you please, so that they can
         hear?

A   'Boiled egg, bread and butter, bramble jelly, 2 cups of tea.'

Q111   Boiled egg, bread and butter, bramble jelly, 2 cups of tea, for break-
       fast, followed by partridge, celery and pudding for lunch. Just look a
       little before the breakfast, will you? Do you see that Nurse Randall has
       written – and what you must have read – 'Slept from 11.20 pm until
       6.45 am. Ease on to back during night. Seems very bright and not
       confused'? Do you see that?

A   Yes.

Q112   Now, would you just look at me, Miss Stronach, please, and listen
       carefully to this question. Having refreshed your memory from records
       made by you and your colleagues at the time, it was obviously quite
       inaccurate to say that Mrs Morrell was semi-conscious and rambling
       on the day you left, was not it?

A   Well, I have always believed that she was as far as my memory was
       concerned.

Witness collapses

Q113   Maybe, but in fact, having looked at those notes written down six
       years ago, with no memory at all, it is quite clear that it was wrong to
       say that she was semi-conscious and rambling, is not it?

A   Apparently so.

   The transcript contains the following questions and answers.

Q114   I must ask you to forgive me, because it is of such a vitally important
       matter, for asking you about something else you said. Do you remem-
       ber, relying on your memory, saying that the doctor usually came in
       about 11.00 pm? That is when you allege that he had given the
       injection about which he had not told you?

A   I did. Coming about then.

Q115   And on those occasions you said she was very dopey and half asleep
       because you had already given her an injection which had made her
       dopey; do you remember that?

A   Yes.

Q116   All that, of course, now turns out to be quite inaccurate on these
       records, does it not?

A   Well, since the day nurse had previously given her injection she would
       be dopey.

Q117   Your evidence is that you gave the injection?

A   Yes, so I understood but I can see now that I did not do so.

Q118   So that was quite wrong. And when you say that the doctor gave the
       injections, we have already had this, that on one or two occasions that
       you recorded his visit you recorded the actual amount and quality of
       his injection; we have got that; what I want to ask you about is this:
       you told the members of the jury at the trial of Dr Adams for mur-
       dering Mrs Morrell that after those injections given by him she was
       very dopey and half asleep. Now will you be good enough to turn to
       your own record of 14 and 15 October, the night report when you were
       the nurse on duty. It is in the last book. Have you found it?

A   Yes.

Q119   This is one of those rare instances where you record the doctor as
       having visited and having given an injection. As 10.20 pm you record

the visit of the doctor and you record the actual injection given: one quarter grain morphia, one third grain herion and one third grain omnopon, you see?

A   Yes.

Q120   After which there was no question of her being at all dopey was there?

A   She was talking a lot.

Q121   But look at it: 'Patient continued talking, asking for drinks after well past midnight.' That is to say, for more than an hour and twenty minutes after the injection she was not dopey but she was talking and asking for drinks; is that right?

A   Yes, but it would not be normal talking, you must understand, in that condition.

Q122   Nobody has suggested before, Miss Stronach, that this old lady on 14 and 15 October, aged 81 and within a few days of her death, having had a stroke and all the rest of it, was normal.

A   Quite.

Q123   And later on in the night she is talking incessantly?

A   Yes.

Q124   Now, you read, before you came on duty that night, the day report of the day before, did you not?

A   Yes, by Miss Mason.

Q125   By Miss Mason. You see this in the middle of that report that the doctor visited between 7.00 pm and 8.00 pm and gave the patient the evening injection. Do you see your experienced colleague has put that down?

A   Yes.

Q126   And at 7.20 pm she has recorded his actual visit?

A   Yes.

Q127   And recorded the actual injection, just as you did?

A   Yes.

Q128   A quarter grain morphia, one third heroin, and one third omnopon you see that?

A   Yes I do.

Q129   Just exactly the same quantity of those drugs in combination as was given at 10.20 pm when the doctor visited again, when you were on duty?

A   Yes, she received the first one at twenty past seven.

Q130   Yes, and do you see after that Nurse Mason has recorded at 8.30 pm, an hour and ten minutes afterwards, that she has been dozing lightly since. Not dopey, dozing lightly? Do you see that:

A   Yes.

Q131   And you found that she was talking so incessantly that during the night at 4.15 in the morning, you yourself gave her another two thirds of omnopon in a hypodermic injection, did you not?

A   I did.

LEO CUSSEN INSTITUTE

PRACTICAL TRAINING COURSE

Introduction to advocacy

Objective 6: Re-examination

OBJECTIVE

To recall when re-examination is required.

The purposes of re-examination are to revive weakened evidence and to adduce fresh evidence arising from cross-examination.
   In either of two cases do not re-examine at all:

o First, when the cross-examination has been ineffective or practically so.
o Secondly, where the cross-examination has been the exact opposite: that is to say, has been so deadly as to hopelessly smash the witness's evidence-in-chief. No amount of patching up will be of any avail where a witness has admitted to the cross-examiner that his evidence was false from beginning to end.

LEO CUSSEN INSTITUTE

PRACTICAL TRAINING COURSE

Introduction to advocacy

Objective 7: Ethical problems

Case studies of attitudes and ethical situations

OBJECTIVE

To develop professional attitudes to ethical problems as may arise in practice.

Successful advocacy is managing your case with competency. Cases are won by preparation done days before.

Ethical problems

1 Keeping in step with legal aid

You act for Edna Johnson in matrimonial proceedings which are coming on for hearing shortly. Mrs Johnson is obtaining assistance from the Legal Aid Commission, and you have been authorised to brief counsel to appear at a brief fee of $150.00. You especially want Mr X of counsel to appear, but he is not willing to accept the brief at less than $200.00. Your client suggests you mark the brief $150.00, and come to a private arrangement with counsel as to the other $50.00.

2 Partners on the spot

Your partner, Keith (who operates from your branch office), tells you that he has refused to act for Mr J because Mr J told Keith that although he committed an offence with which he was charged, he wanted to plead not guilty and give evidence that he was somewhere else at the time. Mr J has now consulted you, Vincent, as head of the firm, and told you he did not commit the offence and wants to give alibi evidence. How will you proceed?

3 A tap on the shoulder

Your witness, who has been outside the court room at the time your client gave evidence, is now in the witness box. It is vital to your case that the evidence this witness gives is identical to your client's evidence. It looks like things might be heading in another direction altogether. Your client taps you on the shoulder and says 'tell him what to say'.

4 Go for the honey jar and forget the vinegar jar?

Every time you get half way through a question on cross-examination the magistrate interrupts with a question/statement of his own, most of which you consider to be irrelevant, wrong at law and designed to give your client a hard time. You can feel yourself losing your temper.

LEO CUSSEN INSTITUTE

PRACTICAL TRAINING COURSE

Introduction to advocacy

Objective 8: Conduct of exercises

Summary

(1) Short exercises: A series of vignettes
(2) Long exercises: A complete case

Notes to instructors and students

OBJECTIVE

To conduct simple procedures in a court room as if appearing for a client.

(1) The exercises which follow in the CRM will be the first occasion at the Institute on which the students have been able to demonstrate their advocacy skills. It may accordingly be expected that mistakes will be made. If a serious error is detected, it is suggested that the instructor stop the student, correct the mistake, and then have the student start again. This would prevent a bad habit from becoming ingrained. If, however, the mistake is not so serious, the student should be allowed to continue uninterrupted, and the mistake corrected either immediately after the student has finished, or after all students have finished.

(2) In the following exercises roles will be allocated to each student by the instructor. In each of the short exercises and within the long exercises, a student will appear as counsel to examine-in-chief or cross-examine witnesses on behalf of the various parties to the action. In each instance the remaining students will play the roles of witnesses. In the long exercise it may be necessary to divide the tasks of examination-in-chief and cross-examination of each witness between students so that each performs a different task.

   The instructor will be the presiding magistrate.

   Each student should spend 15 minutes planning their examination-in-chief or cross-examination.

(3) The instructor will be looking at:

   (a) Your speaking capacity. Voice and utterance are very much a part of advocacy.
   (b) Your capacity to offer coherent sentences as distinct from monosyllabic phrases.
   (c) Your capacity to use to the full each vowel sound – not 'jist' for 'just', not 'gunna' for 'going to'.
   (d) Elimination of exclamations such as 'ah', 'um', 'er' or statements such as 'what I mean is this'.
   (e) Your advocacy skills in the practice exercises in:

      ○ examination-in-chief;

    ○ cross-examination;
    ○ re-examination;
    ○ no case submission.

Short exercises

1 Examination-in-chief

You are appearing for Hector Raaymakers, a carpenter who is suing John Dunn for $200.00 which he says is owing to him for work done on repairing the handrail to Mr Dunn's stairs at his home at 9 Ninian Street Surrey Hills on 19 October, 1984. Accounts were sent to Mr Dunn on 19 November and 19 December 1984 but, as payment was not forthcoming, a summons was issued on 19 January 1985. Lead Mr Raaymaker's evidence.

2 Cross-examination

You act for Mr Dunn in the above example. He says that Raaymakers used inferior quality timber and insufficient glue and nails, and that the stair rail is in worse condition now than it was before the repairs. Cross-examine Mr Raaymakers.

3 Cross-examination

A policeman (Constable Shine) has just given evidence that your client was driving a blue Morris 850 at the time of a particular offence (9 months ago). The car was green, and your client has never owned a blue car. Cross-examine on this point.

4 Re-examination

During cross-examination, the police prosecutor has put to your client that he knew his car was unroadworthy before he drove it. Your client wanted to explain that he was taking it to be repaired, but was not given an opportunity to make his explanation. In addition, the prosecutor put the following question:

   'Were there skid marks on the road?'

The answer was 'Yes', however, your client knows that the skid marks were there the previous day, and had been left by another car. Re-examine on these points.

5 Cross-examination after a plea of guilty

Your client has pleaded guilty to a charge of theft. He gave himself up to the police a day after the event, and made full confessions. All of the stolen goods have been returned. The police informant has given evidence which corresponds with your client's instructions, but has not mentioned the above matters. Cross-examine the informant.

6 No case submission

Your client has been charged with the (fictitious) offence of uttering loud words from a moving vehicle. The elements of this offence, according to section 10 of the Loud Words (Offences) Act 1958 are:

(a) that the vehicle be moving;
(b) that the words be uttered above normal voice level (defined as being 3 decibels);
(c) that the words issue from the vehicle.

The prosecution has omitted to give any evidence as to the decibel level of the utterances. Make a 'no case' submission.

7 Evidence-in-chief – clarification

Your client is the complainant in a debt case. He claims that the defendant bought a television set from him for $500, but although he took delivery, he failed to pay on the due date, which was one week after delivery. Your client has, at your request, 'told his story' but has omitted to mention the television set. Without leading, elicit the missing information.

8 Cross-examination

Using the fact situation in the previous example, assume you act for the defendant. He says, first, that he did in fact pay by cheque (and the cheque has been presented and paid) and secondly, that although he paid on 19 February 1985, delivery was never effected. Cross-examine the complainant.

9 Cross-examination

You are prosecuting James Forsythe in relation to a charge of dangerous driving. He has given sworn evidence that he has been driving for 10 years and has never had a conviction. In fact he has held a licence for 8 years (he is 26 years old) and has had convictions in 1978, 1979 and 1980 all in the Oakleigh Magistrates Court, for speeding, exceeding .05 and making a U turn when unsafe. Cross-examine Mr Forsythe.

10 Evidence-in-chief

A is charged with planting fake bombs in Melbourne schools threatening to destroy or to damage property, and making demands with a threat to injure.

It has been alleged in court that A planted simulated bombs at 10 suburban schools, threatened to knee cap businessmen and public servants and to contaminate the water supply.

A has pleaded guilty.

Lead evidence from A of his state of mind – that he has had an upbringing loaded with violence, that when he was five and living in the United States he was robbed by two black boys armed with a knife and what he thought was a gun – that he had been to a violent school in the poor area of San Francisco, and that his mother used to beat him and tell him he was the worst thing that ever happened to her.

11 Examination-in-chief

Continue the examination-in-chief of A. He wishes to tell the court that as a child he had known violence at home, at school and on the streets; and that he had become a child psychologist so that he could help to stop children growing up in a world like the one he grew up in. His mother died from cancer caused by atomic testing in the United States. He has had a very troubled life, and in his twenties he was on the verge of insanity. He also wishes to tell the court that he committed 'the horrible acts' which have been alleged against him but that he had not committed the crimes associated with those acts. He says he had done these 'terrible things' to bring attention to a nuclear war that would destroy humanity. He agrees the actions were horribly wrong and almost without precedent, but that the threat of nuclear war was now a threat without precedent. He says he is very sorry for the emotional harm he had caused and that he would never have considered using real bombs.

12 Cross-examination

Cross-examine A on the evidence given in exercises 10 and 11.

Long exercise

Landers v Brandon and Zernon

Overview

This case involves a car accident. Ms Landers has sued in negligence and joined Mr Zernon and Mr Brandon as co-defendants. Messrs Zernon and Brandon have both filed defences and each has served a notice for contribution and indemnity on the other. Mr Brandon has sued Mr Zernon for damage to his motor vehicle and Zernon has filed a defence. All matters have been brought on together.

You may assume that:

(a) each person has made a statement to the police and will give evidence in terms of that statement;
(b) each counsel's instructing solicitor has received copies of all statements; and
(c) there are mutual admissions of *quantum*.

The 'pecking order' amongst counsel for the parties has been agreed as first Landers, then Brandon, then Zernon. Counsel for Landers will call Kelly and Pounce as witnesses.

Instructors only

Witness	EIC	XXN on behalf of Zernon	XXN on behalf of Brandon	XXN on behalf of Landers
MS LANDERS (Student A)	L	C	D	—
S/C POUNCE (Student C)	G	H	I	—
MR ZERNON (Student D)	J		K	—
MR BRANDON (Student E)	F	A		B
Students: A B C D E F G H I J K L				

Assign each student a letter.

Statements

A Pounce – Senior Constable of Police, Adran Police Station:

On 5 July last year I attended an accident scene in Adran Road, Nestor, where I spoke with Mr B & Ms L and Ms K. I spoke to Mr Z the following day. Upon arrival I inspected the scene and made the following observations.

(1) Debris from the accident was scattered over a 50m area but from the position it was found and the piles of dirt from under the mudguards of the vehicles I put the point of impact 50m east of the gateway of Z's property and approximately 1.5m south of the centreline of the road.

(2) From Z's driveway there is a clear view for 300m west and 1.5km east.

(3) At the time I arrived the gate to Z's property was pulled to but not locked with the padlock and chain.

(4) Adran Road is a bitumen surface carriageway with provision for one lane of traffic in either direction. There are 1.5m granite shoulders on both sides. It is a 75km zone and while it is a straight road there is a sharp incline rising to the crest of the hill. The crest is 120m west of the gateway with the upward slope beginning 20m west of Z's gateway. Unbroken double white lines commence 50m east of the gateway and continue to a point 50m beyond the crest of the hill.

(5) The road was wet, there was a light rain falling.
There were no signs of skidmarks for vehicles travelling in either direction.

(6) Zernon's car was undamaged.
Lander's car had heavy damage right across the front of the car but particularly on the nearside front corner.
Brandon's car had damage on the driver's side particularly in the area of the rear quarterpanel.

(7) I made a diagram of the collison site.

Mr Zernon – lives at 73 Overclose Road, Adran Retired Cleaner:

Adran Road runs east west and my property is on the southern side.
I am 42 and wear glasses. On 5 July last year I was at my property in Adran

Road, Nestor. There is no house on the property and I grow potatoes on the back part of the block. I had been to the farm to check on their progress. I completed my tasks and drove north along the driveway (150m) to the gate. The driveway runs along the eastern side of the property. I got out, opened the gate and drove though. Then I got out, closed and locked it. When I got out of my hot pink utility the front of it was 1.5m from the bitumen surface of the roadway and was on the gravel verge.

I got in my car and after looking to my right and left I indicated to turn right and began to make my turn. From where I was parked there is a clear view to the left for 150m and then there is a hill. I can see a long way to the right, more than 1km. It is a straight road. There were no cars on my left and there were two or three to my right but a long way down. I had travelled one hundred yards when I heard a car engine very close to me and a red car drew beside me and as it did so, it spun to one side and crashed into an oncoming car. At this time I was travelling at 50km per hour. I continued on about 30m and stopped. I walked back. I gave my name and address to the girl who was driving and to the young man driving the red car. He said to me in the presence of the girl, 'Why did you make the turn in front of me?' I said 'I did not. You were travelling too fast.' I left the scene.

Mr Brandon – lives at 106 Nestor Road, Nestor:

I am 19 and an apprentice panel beater. On 5 July last year I was on my way to work. I was late but wasn't in a hurry although my boss hasn't been too happy because I've been late a lot recently. I was travelling in Adran Road at 70 kmph. It is a 75 km zone. I saw a pink utility travelling down a driveway on my right at high speed. It came straight onto the roadway, crossed the double lines and swung to the right. It did not appear to slow down. When it completed its turn, it was 10m in front of me. I slammed on my brakes causing the car to broadside into an oncoming car. I was on the wrong side of the roadway by this time.

I can remember nothing more of the accident or any conversation I had with anyone. I have been back and believe the accident occurred 20m after the gate the car came out of.

My car was damaged and has been repaired for $2,015.00.

Ms Landers – lives in 14 Oakover Road, Nestor, dental nurse:

On 5 July last year I was on my way to work and was driving my vehicle west along Adran Road at 65 km per hour as I got to the hill I saw a pink utility travelling towards me. Then a red car broadsided round it and collided with my car. The red car was on the wrong side of the road.

Our cars locked and skidded into an embankment and stopped. I was shaken and confused. I can remember speaking to the driver of the red car and another older man. The driver of the red car said something like, 'Where the hell did you come from?' I don't think I heard what the other man said but I'm sure he said something. I got names and addresses and then a policeman came and *spoke* to me. There were people milling about. My car was damaged and was repaired at $3,015.00.

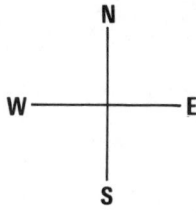

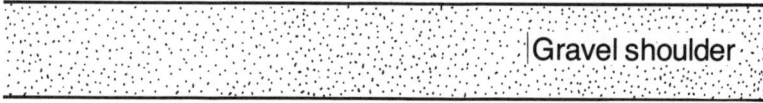

Gravel shoulder

Continuous double lines

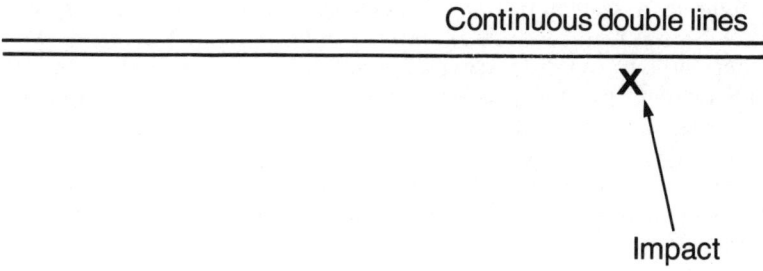

X

Impact

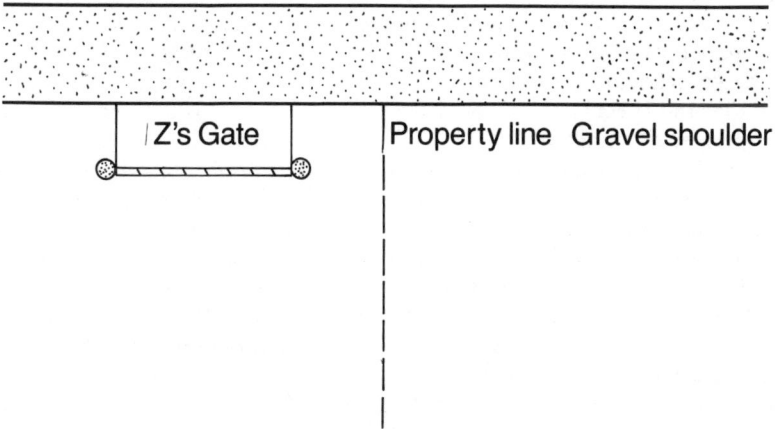

Z's Gate

Property line   Gravel shoulder

10 Skills guides

David Cruickshank

The Skills Guides of the Professional Legal Training Course in British Columbia serve three main functions:

(1) They provide a detailed breakdown of the skill elements that will be taught in a systematic way through the ten week curriculum of the Professional Legal Training Course.
(2) They serve as objective criteria for skill performances; both instructors and learners use them as a checklist to provide detailed feedback by reference to a standard of competent performance.
(3) The same objective criteria are applied to skill performances for assessment of the competence of entry-level lawyers; therefore, they form the basis for a large part of the certification of beginning lawyers in our jurisdiction.

The Guides used for assessment purposes include the writing, drafting, oral submissions, and interviewing and advising guides. The civil trial advocacy guide is used for a two-day mock civil trial conducted before senior lawyers. The lawyers use the guide to give students constructive comments on their performance. The civil trial guides are a matter of record and they are provided to students, but they form no part of formal assessment in the course.

Finally, the specific elements of the Guides are tied to daily lesson plans through specific educational objectives. The educational objectives will be expressed in more detail in each lesson plan. For example, the criteria of using 'legislative sentences' in drafting will be expressed as a more concrete educational objective in a two hour lesson plan. Students will see appropriate examples, will draft their own legislative sentences and will receive comment on their ability to do so. In this way, we try to make sure that skill performances are built up and integrated by moving from less complex to more complex performances. There is an even greater challenge to students through the integration of the guide-oriented skill performance with specific legal transactions. The course is built around a handful of transactions tied to each of these skills. Therefore, in the skill of interviewing, the facts and law that students must deal with in the skill performance are tied to a family law transaction. Therefore, the Guides act as a focal point for connecting skills with substantive and procedural knowledge and issues of professional responsibility.

SKILLS GUIDES

Date:.....................   Completed for: ....
                                  Completed by:..................

Civil trial advocacy guide*

This Guide is designed to assist you in providing detailed, descriptive comments on the strengths and weaknesses of the advocate's performance. Make your comments as specific as possible using examples from the advocate's performance.

The elements of advocacy performance detailed below are grouped under the following headings: Opening Statement, Direct Examination, Cross-Examination, Objections, Re-Examination, Closing Arguments, and General Comments. Check the boxes at the left to indicate whether the advocate demonstrated the relevant elements of performance. Use the space at the right for comments and suggestions for improvement. A space has been provided on the last page for general comments on the advocate's performance.

A OPENING STATEMENT   COMMENTS

[ ] **1** Introduces self, allowing court to note name
[ ] **2** Captures judge's interest at the start
[ ] **3** Succinct overview of case
[ ] **4** Speaks from memory or outline; does not read
[ ] **5** Sets forth client's case clearly and persuasively (not argumentatively)
[ ] **6** Briefly describes issues and intended proof of all matters necessary for client to succeed
[ ] **7** Briefly outlines witnesses to be called and the central evidence they will give
[ ] **8** Does not refer to evidence of doubtful admissibility
[ ] **9** Refers briefly to anticipated conflicting or harmful evidence
[ ] **10** Explains clearly the conclusion judge is being asked to reach
[ ] **11** Speaks at an appropriate rate
[ ] **12** Good pitch and clear diction
[ ] **13** Appropriate language
[ ] **14** Eye contact with the judge
[ ] **15** No distracting behaviour
[ ] **16** Effective use of gesture

B DIRECT EXAMINATION   COMMENTS

[ ]   **1** Avoids leading questions except on intro-
            ductory matters
[ ]   **2** Puts witness at ease
[ ]   **3** Questions are short and understandable
[ ]   **4** Only one question at a time
[ ]   **5** Does not read
[ ]   **6** Organises questions effectively
[ ]   **7** Lays evidentiary foundation for admission
            of exhibits
[ ]   **8** Elicits all the relevant facts
[ ]   **9** Gets witness to explain anticipated damag-
            ing evidence in appropriate manner

C CROSS-EXAMINATION

[ ]   **1** Where appropriate, refrains from cross-
            examining
[ ]   **2** Selects appropriate topics for cross-examin-
            ation
[ ]   **3** Controls direction and pace of cross-exam-
            ination
[ ]   **4** Appropriate language (eg words which
            maximise witness's agreement or disagree-
            ment)
[ ]   **5** Avoids pauses which invite further expla-
            nation from the witness
[ ]   **6** Effectively organises questions to elicit
            information desired
[ ]   **7** Elicits helpful answers from witness where
            possible
[ ]   **8** Alters or abandons line of questioning
            appropriately
[ ]   **9** Develops topics sufficiently but does not
            overkill
      10 Attacks where appropriate, witness's:
[ ]   (a) ability to observe
[ ]   (b) ability to recall what witness observed
[ ]   (c) credibility
[ ]   **11** Does not quarrel with witness
[ ]   **12** Keeps cross-examination as brief as poss-
            ible
[ ]   **13** Starts and ends with strong point
[ ]   **14** Impeaches witness effectively with prior
            inconsistent statements

D OBJECTIONS

[ ]   **1** Objects promptly to improper questions
            and answers
[ ]   **2** Succinctly states legal grounds for objection
[ ]   **3** Does not pursue objection after judge's
            ruling

E RE-EXAMINATION   COMMENTS

[ ]   **1** Re-examines, where appropriate
[ ]   **2** Confines re-examination to appropriate
       scope

F CLOSING ARGUMENT

[ ]   **1** Defines, clearly and simply, the issues
       before the judge
[ ]   **2** Reiterates theme of case
[ ]   **3** Explains how facts and law logically compel
       the conclusion sought
[ ]   **4** Uses exhibits to corroborate or highlight
       main points of argument
[ ]   **5** Positively argues the strengths of own case,
       rather than concentrating on weaknesses of
       opposition's case, where appropriate
[ ]   **6** Answers arguments anticipated or made by
       opposing counsel
[ ]   **7** Eye contact with judge
[ ]   **8** Does not read
[ ]   **9** No distracting behaviour
[ ] **10** Effective use of gestures
[ ] **11** Appropriate language
[ ] **12** Speaks at an appropriate rate and volume
[ ] **13** Good pitch and diction

G GENERAL (use reverse if necessary)

Completed by:..................
Completed for: ....
Date: ....

Writing guide

This guide is designed to help you provide detailed, descriptive comments.
Use the space at the right for comments and suggestions for improvement.

                                                      COMMENTS

[ ] **1** Addresses all relevant facts and legal issues
       appropriately
[ ] **2** Style and format appropriate for intended
       purpose

COMMENTS

3 If advice is given, the advice:

[ ]   (a) realistically addresses client's concerns
      (b) is consistent with the discussion of facts
          and issues
[ ]   (c) helps client make an informed decision
[ ]   (d) protects client's interests

4 Organisation

[ ]   (a) introduction clearly states purpose
[ ]   (b) text is consistent with stated purpose
[ ]   (c) topics are dealt with in a logical sequence
[ ]   (d) appropriate paragraphing
[ ]   (e) conclusion flows logically from text

5 Language

[ ]   (a) correct grammar
[ ]   (b) correct spelling and punctuation
[ ]   (c) precise (except where vagueness is
          intended)
[ ]   (d) concise
      (e) consistent
[ ]   (f) simple sentence structure
[ ]   (g) active rather than passive voice
[ ]   (h) no unnecessary archaic expressions or
          legal jargon
[ ]   (i) language appropriate to the reader

Completed for: . . . .
Completed by:. . . . .
Date: . . . .

Oral submissions guide

This guide is designed to assist you in providing detailed, descriptive comments on the strengths and weaknesses of oral submissions. Use the space at the right for comments and suggestions for improvement.

A CONTENT   COMMENTS

[ ] **1** Introduces self (allowing time for name to be
          noted)
[ ] **2** Explains nature of proceeding or application
          (unless it is obvious)
[ ] **3** States the decision or order sought by client

COMMENTS

[ ] **4** Explains the history of the proceeding (if appropriate)
[ ] **5** States the relevant issues
[ ] **6** In relation to each issue:

[ ]   (a) summarises relevant legal principles and uses relevant legal authorities effectively
[ ]   (b) presents the facts of the case effectively to support client's position

[ ] **7** Effectively summarises to conclude submissions
[ ] **8** Responds appropriately to questions and directions
[ ] **9** Demonstrates thorough understanding of all relevant facts and legal issues

B PRESENTATION

[ ] **1** Uses clear and persuasive language
[ ] **2** Speaks effectively
[ ] **3** Maintains eye contact (does not read notes)
[ ] **4** Is effectively organised

Date: ....   Completed for: ....
Client role:.....................   Completed by:..................

Litigation interviewing and advising guide

This guide is designed to assist you in providing detailed, descriptive comments on the strengths and weaknesses of the interview. Make your comments as specific as possible, focusing on what you hear or observe in the interview rather than on interpretations or inferences you make from what you hear or observe.

A PRELIMINARY PROBLEM IDENTIFICATION   COMMENTS

[ ] **1** Establishes rapport
[ ] **2** Allows client to explain problem in own way, obtaining general description of underlying matter, client's principal concerns, and client's desired solution
[ ] **3** Summarises lawyer's understanding of underlying matter, principal concerns, and desired solution
[ ] **4** Explains what will take place for rest of interview, clarifying lawyer and client roles

B CHRONOLOGICAL OVERVIEW   COMMENTS

   1 Gets client to relate story chronologically,
      using (as applicable):
[ ]   (a) open-ended questions
[ ]   (b) occasional narrow questions for clarifi-
          cation or elaboration
[ ]   (c) repetition to keep client on track

[ ] **2** Avoids chronological gaps
[ ] **3** Avoids sidetracking client with questions for
      details

C THEORY DEVELOPMENT AND VERIFICATION

[ ] **1** Systematically explores potentially relevant
      topics
[ ] **2** Identifies deficiencies in available facts, what
      further facts are required, and methods of
      obtaining those facts
[ ] **3** Uses appropriate questioning techniques to
      motivate and exhaust client's recall of rel-
      evant facts
[ ] **4** Explains legal terms and procedures (where
      necessary to continue fact gathering)
[ ] **5** Avoids premature legal advice

_____

Completed by:....................
Completed for: ....
Date: ....

Drafting guide

This guide is designed to help you provide detailed, descriptive comments on
the strengths and weaknesses of drafting. Use the space at the right for
comments and suggestions for improvement.

                                                      COMMENTS

[ ] **1** Carries out client's instructions
[ ] **2** Protects client's interests
[ ] **3** Addresses all relevant facts and legal issues
      appropriately
[ ] **4** Clearly defines legal rights and obligations
[ ] **5** Demonstrates critical use of precedents
[ ] **6** Meets formal criteria

COMMENTS

7 Organisation

[ ]   (a) material organised in logical categories
[ ]   (b) headings, if appropriate
[ ]   (c) material sequenced logically
[ ]   (d) appropriate paragraphing and sub-para-
          graphing
[ ]   (e) no unnecessary cross-references
[ ]   (f) appropriate format

8 Language

[ ]   (a) correct grammar
[ ]   (b) correct spelling and punctuation
[ ]   (c) precise language (except where vague-
          ness is intended)
[ ]   (d) concise language
[ ]   (e) 'legislative sentences', if appropriate (ie
          meets the 'who', 'what', 'to whom',
          'when', 'where' test)
[ ]   (f) active rather than passive voice
[ ]   (g) present rather than future tense
[ ]   (h) no unnecessary archaic expressions or
          legal jargon

9 Consistency and coherence

[ ]   (a) no internal contradictions or inconsis-
          tencies
[ ]   (b) same word used to mean same thing
[ ]   (c) appropriate definitions
[ ]   (d) defined terms used consistently

Part 3

Studying skills – the future

11 Learning lawyers' skills: research, development and evaluation – the future prospectus

Neil Gold

Learning lawyers' skills: an overview

Learning lawyers' skills directly as a consequence of instructional planning is a relatively new educational activity. For a diverse range of reasons such learning has traditionally been left to be picked up on-the-job through observation, osmosis and practice either under an apprenticeship system or in the early years of licensure. Had it not been for the American Realists, or those who were in some way or another inspired to speak, act or react to their work, and certain specific conditions in the United States of America, we might never have been pushed to the point of current development. Indeed, on the continent, where the realists and American legal culture have had little visible impact in relative terms, the direct teaching of professional skills is largely unknown.[1] It is no accident that the United Kingdom's best known proponent of skills study is a former student and biographer of Karl Llewellyn, co-editor of this volume, William Twining.[2]

Calls for the teaching of legal skills have echoed around the common law world since the Realists' writings in the 1930's.[3] It has been in America within the last twenty years where a critical mass of support for teaching realistically developed in response to the realist call and some very specific local conditions. They included: the debacle of Watergate which involved the actions of many Nixon White House lawyers; United States Supreme Court Chief Justice Burger's loud public complaint about poor advocacy in the courts; Harvard President and former law dean Derek Bok's criticism of traditional advocacy and support for the alternative dispute resolution movement (ADR); the development of social consciousness among certain lawyers and law teachers calling for service to the poor and the skills to support that service; and of course the rich legacy of Frank, Llewellyn, Lasswell and McDougal, the founders and progeny of the American legal realist movement.

In the United States of America, articles of clerkship or pupillage died out with the complete acceptance of three years of study at the university law schools in place of apprenticeship.[4] As a result the universities were left more or less alone to prepare novices for practice. While in recent years interest in post-graduate professional training has grown, few jurisdictions have responded concretely with elaborate, sophisticated and detailed bridge-the-gap courses, as such programmes are known in America. Some recent developments in Washington State and California suggest that the legal profession has become directly interested in skills teaching. Washington now has a ten day mandatory skills course and California is developing major skills assessments and instruction to augment the testing already in place to assess research, analysis and file management skills. Others are likely to follow with various projects now that the American Bar Association has set up a task force on the subject of lawyering skills.

In England, the university and polytechnic communities have flirted with the idea of teaching lawyers' skills, but with a few notable exceptions, including London's South Bank Polytechnic, Birmingham Polytechnic and Warwick University, they have opted for leaving what many there see as pedestrian and practical learnings to the professional stage. Even though there are mandatory professional courses, both post-graduation and pre-licensure, the solicitors' and barristers' branches of the profession were, until very recently, preoccupied in their courses with filling in the substantive and procedural law gaps they perceived had been left by undergraduate law teaching. Perceptions there seem to be shifting, in part due to the Marre Report[5] on the legal profession and its careful listing of lawyers' skills in the section on legal education and training. Too, there was, until recent days, the belief that there was something ineffable about legal skills: not teachable, and learnable only by those with the pre-existing talent. If one was not a natural, one could hardly learn the arts of persuasion, cross-examination, or whatever skill you might identify, through direct instruction. Indeed, calling such learnings identifiable skills seems odd to many still today. However, the Council of Legal Education, which supervises the work of the Inns of Court School of Law on behalf of the Bar of England and Wales, has recommended that the Vocational Course be fundamentally changed to include the direct teaching of relevant barristers' skills. The Law Society has also clearly set its sights on more direct skills teaching. The solicitors' branch of the profession has moved to several fronts. First, they have sought to strengthen apprenticeship through clarifying expectations of both articled clerks and their principals. Secondly, they have added the requirement of compulsory continuing professional education for newcomers to the profession. Thirdly, large City firms have added in-house training officers who are developing wide-ranging programmes. Lastly, the College of Law, an independent body which is an emanation of the Law Society of England and Wales, is revising its one-year mandatory pre-admission vocational court to include more direct teaching of lawyers' skills. In the result, the Law Society has opted for a mixture of on-the-job, institutional and in-house training. These developments, together with wider experimentation, especially in the polytechnics, augur well for lawyers' skills research and development activities in the United Kingdom. The two Nottingham Conferences on Legal Skills and Dispute Resolution in 1986 and 1988 respectively have focused attention on learning lawyers' skills. In December 1989 a third Conference on Negotiation will carry the study further under the joint auspices of the university and the Commonwealth Institute for Legal Education and Training.

In Australia, the abolition of articles in some jurisdictions and reviews of Canadian post-graduate mandatory pre-admission programmes led to the development of a variety of experiments in practical training which sought to blend the acquisition of practical, procedural and substantive knowledge with the practise of practice. There, students work alone or in groups simulating the filling out of forms, the drafting and exchange of letters and other documents, and learn something about advocacy, instruction-taking or negotiation. The tasks of lawyers' work have become central learning focuses, taught with the support of detailed procedural and substantive material disseminated through practice papers. More recently, the College of Law in Sydney and the Leo

Cussen Institute for Continuing Legal Education in Melbourne, the managers of practical training in the states of New South Wales and Victoria respectively, have enhanced or are planning more skills training. Given the recent agreement in Victoria that articles of clerkship should be replaced by a skills and practice course, further changes may be expected there at the behest of the Council of Legal Education. Indeed, each of the Australian states except Western Australia and including the Australian Capital Territory operate courses which have at least minimally been affected by growing skills teaching elsewhere.

Perhaps the boldest and most specifically skills-oriented course developed since British Columbia's Professional Legal Training Programme[6], is located in New Zealand. There the Institute of Professional Legal Studies (IPLS) conducts a thirteen week intensive programme in legal skills. Carefully detailed lesson plans, some of which are excerpted in this collection, have been developed based on experience in Canada, Australia and the United States. In many ways the IPLS course is the current state of the art of lawyers' skills instruction in the Commonwealth.

Canadians, also unsure that the law schools' teachings would adequately cover core areas of practice, developed varied programmes across the ten provinces, occupying from two weeks to eight months instruction. These courses were practical in one sense: they sought to teach the procedures, operations and rules relevant to daily practice activity, but oftentimes not even with the benefit of simulation or practice example or document precedent until relatively recently. But, bordering as it does on the United States, Canada would not be immune from a series of trans-frontier influences: legal realism, the teaching of lawyers' arts and skills, and the legal aid/clinical legal education movements. Today British Columbia's course, though less skills focused than originally conceived, marks the high water mark in the teaching of lawyers' skills in English speaking Canada. Quebec instituted a major shift in its *formation professionelle* with the new programme of skills-based training at *l'Ecole du Barreau*. Ontario has recently committed itself to develop a new sandwich programme which will teach skills and transactions directly and intensively. Nova Scotia and New Brunswick are planning to institute skills-oriented programmes too. Canadian law schools teach appellate advocacy and research and writing skills to all students and interviewing, counselling, negotiation, mediation and trial advocacy as optional courses. With increased skills teaching at the post-graduate pre-admission level, students will undoubtedly press their faculties to increase offerings.

To a lesser extent Malaysia, Singapore and Hong Kong train newcomers to law practice in legal skills. While the professional courses in these countries remain traditionally gap-filling in their orientation, there are clear signs of interest in experimentation and broadening of programme goals. This is perhaps most visible at Hong Kong University where basic skills are given greatest emphasis compared to other Asian common law jurisdictions. Now, the Hong Kong Polytechnic seems poised for action: if local conditions permit they are likely to innovate in the direction of skills-oriented professional preparation.

The earliest professional courses were developed in Africa where conditions were not conducive to apprenticeship. Following the 'Gower Model' recommended by L C B Gower, first Nigeria, and then Uganda, Kenya, Malawi and Zambia adopted pre-admission mandatory practice-oriented courses. These too are predominantly concerned with practical and procedural instruction with relatively less attention given to the direct teaching of lawyers' skills than has been the case elsewhere. Recently, the University of Zimbabwe has opted for a four-year LLB integrating theory and practice with direct teaching of lawyers' skills very much on the instructional agenda. The Norman Manley and Hugh Wooding law schools in Jamaica and Trinidad respectively offer courses with characteristics similar to their African and pre-reform Canadian counterparts.

At the continuing legal education level, skills teaching has achieved equal prominence with other programming. A heavy emphasis on teaching skills is developing in North America, with other continuing legal education providers in Australia and New Zealand following suit. The United Kingdom will not lag far behind.

Developing skills teaching: the legacy of Langdell and analytical positivism

What is perhaps most noteworthy about developments in the United States is that they were generated by thoughtful practitioners (Burger, Frank and others) but were developed educationally by academics (Bellow, Keeton, Binder and so on). In America, unlike anywhere in the Commonwealth, there are, for all intents and purposes, neither practical courses run by the profession nor periods of supervised apprenticeship prior to admission to practice. Absent any mechanism through which the profession might implement its wishes, the nearly two hundred law schools were left with tremendous opportunities for innovation, experimentation and research. Indeed, given the absence of mandatory pre-admission apprenticeship or institution-based learning, the formal organs of the profession are very interested in promoting lawyers' skills teaching in the university law schools. Whether the California and Washington State initiatives, bolstered by the American Bar Association task force, will result in major professional level changes remains to be seen. However, university based diversity is assured. The University of California at Los Angeles and Warwick University law schools jointly sponsored a major conference at Lake Arrowhead in 1986, producing many published papers. A second conference in 1989 continues to support fundamental analysis of lawyers' work and clinical legal education. The Association of American Law Schools Section on Clinical Legal Education has, both on its own and with the American Bar Association Section on Legal Education and Admission to the Bar, sponsored important conferences on teaching skills.

While C C Langdell[7] had initiated the most brilliant change in legal study since its inception, the case method, he simultaneously reinforced law study's illiberal and narrow focus. His 'case' was made up only of the opinion of a trial, or more usually appellate, court. This is a case, with the life taken out of it. Broader conceptions of the 'case' might have included the lawyer's file, the court dossier, transcripts, exhibits, and various other records which attend legal matters. Focussing as he did on the words of judges, Langdell redefined the idea of a 'case' to its narrowest potential.

The positivism which controlled all disciplines took even firmer hold of law which seemed to perceive it had much to gain from the philosophy's reifying force. Abstract rules, with lives of their own, could now be titrated in Langdell's laboratory, the law school library. Legal rules, always the special preserve of lawyers, were now discussed through a special process of legal analysis which has yet, regrettably, to be carefully described as a set of steps or procedures, or even properly scrutinised in the academic literature.

As law study began to develop as a legitimate form of higher education its roots in action were severed. After all, to gain authority within the academy, law needed to be as like other disciplines as possible. In its efforts to join the academy legal scholars missed developing the discipline and scholarly products which would make it welcome there. Legal writing is, of course, varied. Mainstream doctrinal work seems more technical than academic to some critics. The profession's demands, expressed by book publishers' contracts, have resulted in the promotion of practice-oriented works. Law reviews have been the most significant publishers of perspective pieces, though even there work of a fundamental or profound nature is often said to be less typical than in other disciplines. The Arthurs' Report, *Law and Learning*,[8] suggested that Canadian scholars needed to redirect their efforts to fundamental and profound research activities.

The quest for legitimacy carries with it, oftentimes, the forsaking of natural allies and kin, be they in the world of thought or the world of affairs. Law's quest was thus characterised. In the result, history, philosophy, and political theory, among others, were forsaken, as were analyses of the course of legal causes, the workings of the judicial system and study of lawyers' work. Law's implementation of the positivist vision, narrow as it was, could not in the end survive the attacks which would be made on it in the United States, where aspiration, achievement and concern for every person are at the core of constitutional theory and at least some substantial practice. The study of laws as if they were simply value-free, observable data to be unquestionably ingested as information and applied with limited vision or ingenuity was viewed by many as barren, wasteful, untruthful or inhumane.

Learning lawyers' skills: social science, theory and humanism

Nowadays feminist legal theory, critical theory, critical legal studies, sociolegal and empirical work join the realist and neo-realist attacks on the arid, non-human and value-neutral vision of positivism. The law and economics movement has grown and flourished finding favour among a group which might previously have been inclined to positivism. Positivism had stunted the development of law as a discipline. Juridical science was neither a rigorous methodology nor a developing calculus for change. Rather, its narrow compass of cases and statutes left unanalysed the impact of law on persons or society, left under-theorised the role of law in politically complex and globally enmeshed societies, left unimagined the role for law as a means for the achievement of our highest aspirations. Worst, law's positivism separated it from learnings in almost all other disciplines. In a way, law had orphaned itself from an extended family of higher learning. This could not last in a changing world context.

Learning lawyers' skills is one part of the new outreach by law to the world of the social sciences and humanities. Born of concerns for ethical conduct, the doing of good works and the pleas for justice, the direct teaching of lawyers' skills aims, as perhaps no other aspect of learning yet developed in the discipline of law, to match theory with practice, to seek the achievement of social and individual justice through acts likeliest to achieve it, and to re-conceptualise the potential for law to accomplish social good in a time of tremendous challenge from technology, the environment, political strife and the developing interdependency of all nations and all persons.

On a basic level learning legal skills is about competence and client service. Some might say it is simply about efficiency and effectiveness; others would add it is about humanistic values in dealing with persons through inter-viewing, counselling, and negotiation. Also, it is about solving problems through expeditious, merits-oriented, and suited-to-the-needs-of-the-people-and-the-situation mechanisms: traditional advocacy, alternate dispute resol-ution techniques and creativity. Lawyers' skills learning provides means to implement new and old ideologies alike. It is frankly instrumentalist, and it is much more too; for, judged as we are by our deeds and their consequences, legal skills as we practice them, tell more about us than we might wish or appreciate are exposed.

The contributors to this volume have experimented. Their work is testi-mony to this innovation and evidence of critical thought. It also demonstrates the linkage between law work on the one hand, and social science theory and practice on the other. Its aspirations are not only to aid lawyers to be more skilful and therefore more helpful, but also to seek to implement a variety of values inherent in the instructional choices they have made and the theory of action which they have adopted as the content of their skills subject. When negotiators choose Ury and Fisher[9] over other negotiation theorists and students, they make a major value choice for peace, human dignity and respect in a regime which seeks to maximize gain in a principled, merits-based context.

Learning lawyers' skills: the research and development agenda

Few of the teaching plans contained in this work have been 'tested true'. The authors' experience tells them that 'they work' – students perform better after study than they had before it. Most would agree, I think, that more study of the short and long-term effectiveness of such teaching plans must be done. Only carefully structured and planned empirical study can tell us the necessary answers. Is there much point in carrying on without at least some knowledge of what works, what does not, and why? And there is other work too which must be done.

More, richer, deeper, and even more broadly applicable theories of lawyers' practice must be developed. Lawyers' actual work should be watched, described, analysed and generalised. Experts-in-action should be interviewed, video-taped and asked to write about their work.[10] Practice is rich, complex, subtle, varied, personal, challenging and its practitioners must cope with infinite variations of fact, context, culture, personality, aspiration, potential and possibility. The difficulty of practice cannot be underestimated or under-rated. The potential for profound new understandings has never been greater.

Can we induce theory from practice? Can we test theory in practice? Clearly yes. So, where do we go from here?

First, more development and experimentation in the field of lawyers' skills teaching is warranted. Such innovations should be based on (a) evaluation of existing programmes and courses, and (b) fundamental empirical research and subsequent retheorising, analysing all of the pertinent data. Some brief specific descriptions of research and development projects of interest may be helpful.

When the organisers of the then new vocational course in British Columbia took on their task in 1982,[11] they decided to analyse systematically the jobs of lawyers. They sought to describe the functions and tasks of practice in order to provide a basis for discerning whether there were common practical skills which link all legal practice together. This work produced a cluster of some 15 master skills, each of which was made up of elemental skills totalling some 200 sub or microskills. For example: interviewing is a major legal skill. In interviewing, one must be able to question; to question effectively one must be able to use various forms of questions: open, closed, narrow and in a variety of sequences to obtain different types of information from different persons for different purposes. This preliminary research and analysis in British Columbia formed the basis for segmenting skills into their constituent elements, thereby yielding a building block approach to the progress of instruction in legal skills. Course designers were able to build the instruction from an ordering of the master skills into a hierarchy constructed in order of learning dependence. So, just as adding is a basic skill required for all other arithmetic functions, so too, for example is the ability to organise information a prerequisite to being able to communicate either orally or in writing. The skills analysis performed in British Columbia stimulated debate, instructional development and testing, and helped describe the elaborate elements and interconnections in a variety of lawyers' functions. It also demonstrated that these functions were made up of a variety of overlappingly important skills: to return to the skill of questioning, it is a critical skill in each of interviewing, counselling, negotiation, mediation, and advocacy among others. So too do other skills find pervasive application in a number of lawyers' functions.

In England, the Inns of Court School of Law has commissioned Dr Joanna Shapland to study the work of newly called barristers. The simple and obviously important premise is that to prepare new barristers for practice requires a detailed understanding of the actual work done by them, the conditions under which it is done and the specific expectations held of them by their seniors, judicial officers, solicitors and chambers' clerks to name four constituents. Learning lawyers' skills, then, requires knowing what they are and how they are to be employed – their ends, their contexts, as well as their elements.

Some research has been done on what skills are considered most important to effective legal practice. Mostly, this has been based on opinion only. Views of lawyers and judges are accepted as determinative of what constitutes exemplary practice. Recently, a pair of Canadian researchers, Dale Rusnell and Anthony Tobin, sought to identify the elements of excellent practice of counsel on behalf of the Advocates' Society Institute. Once peers and judges had identified the persons thought generally to be exemplary counsel, they were interviewed and asked to describe carefully the detailed elements of their operations. Regrettably, the identified exemplars were unable to describe or elucidate their practice in a manner which revealed their intellectual processes in sufficient detail to make these processes understandable to others. Criteria for decisions were frequently vague and means for identifying issues seemingly automatic or random and not describable by them or those who briefly observed them. However, the research confirmed a basic point that had begun to be lost in the discussions of advocates' performance: the ability critically to analyse, evaluate and develop effective and efficient plans for the accomplishment of goals are root skills of exemplary advocacy. No amount of elegance or eloquence, which had gained prominence as valued advocacy skills, could overcome the well-constructed case from the other side. In the result, the Advocates' Society Institute has embarked upon major continuing legal education for counsel which clearly divides strategic workshops from performance workshops and then carefully interconnects the two to maintain an emphasis on the analytical and planning components.

Nonetheless, the criteria by which excellent performance may be measured are not yet known. Until choices are made about what matters most – results or process – we may never know what leads to excellence.

The three research and development projects briefly described above are illustrative of the kind of activity which must be conducted if we are to learn the nature, function and impact of lawyers' work. And equally importantly, we will struggle much less directedly to improve lawyers' contributions unless we conduct this work on a wide scale. Many disciplines will inform this enterprise: social psychology, sociology, anthropology, education, training, practical reasoning, mathematics and more.

Lawyers' skills: a public issue

Unlike health care, legal services are not considered of such fundamental importance that there should be government support for research. This plainly myopic view undoubtedly has contributed to the inefficient legal system about which everyone complains and to the ineffective legal system which scholars, judges, lawyers and politicians continually denounce. (Though only research could tell us if these complaints and denouncements are truly justified!) Recently there have been studies of the judicial system in New Zealand, the State of Victoria and the provinces of Ontario and British Columbia, Canada. The role of lawyers in the operation of these systems was not carefully analysed. Yet procedural wrangling, inadequate preparation and disruptive conduct are all aspects of counsel's performance which affect the timeliness of operations of the courts, have an impact on public perceptions of the justness of our justice system, and perhaps, most influential when governments consider it, escalate the costs of operating the public apparatus. Lawyer effectiveness and efficiency is not just a private matter for lawyers and their clients to sort out (the market). Nor can it be the sole preserve of professional regulation; for, the public interest is at least the shared concern of professional governing bodies and governments, to the extent that lawyers' conduct affects the performance of public institutions.

Just why governing bodies have not taken seriously the learning of lawyers' skills is at minimum mysterious. A review conducted in British Columbia in 1982 of complaints and suits lodged against lawyers leads to the conclusion that poor communication skills, bad management and an absence of systems were at the root of a preponderance of client grievances against their lawyers. The failure to invest in research and development while spending untold sums on discipline is clearly an example of cure at the expense of prevention.

Absent funding for research and development, legal skills education will continue to develop with the efforts and good will of some about whose intentions are clearly good but whose choices are made on uninformed speculation. Even the gifted amateurs among the developers of new forms of legal education will continue to be unsupported to the extent which might make them knowledgeable, educated, professional educators.

Members of the legal profession will need to contribute finances if informed advances are to be made. As professional 'taxpayers' in support of professional activity they stand to gain the most directly: better service, more quickly and less expensively delivered, ie higher profits with more satisfied clients in the end. If work is easier, less burdensome and more productive, perhaps the membership will see its way clear to supporting, through finances, their personal efforts, and morally, educational research and development activities. Along the way some private foundations and government departments might also see the merit of such research to the public interest and support this much needed activity.

Learning lawyers' skills: the future

Learning lawyers' skills is an enterprise in its infancy. To make a beginning is difficult, but not so challenging as finally disposing of the most critical issues. Tentative step by tentative step, work has been begun. We are now a network of researchers, developers and evaluators of lawyers' skills and instructional programmes. This volume is modest but real evidence of common law world-wide activity. Unrepresented here, but active in this work are Malaysians, Singaporeans, Indians, Carribbeans and Africans. Their task, given local economic conditions, is much more daunting than that in the developed world. As the law schools, pre-service and in-service providers and governing bodies develop links among themselves, and as governments begin to perceive the role of research and development in the amelioration of the judicial process, more innovation and testing are bound to develop. Our next volume, *Learning Lawyers' Skills – The Next Generation*, will bear witness to the products of enhanced research.

NOTES

1 A notable exception is Limburg University, Maastricht, The Netherlands. See J Moust and H Nuy 'Preparing Teachers for a Problem-Based, Student-Centred Law Course' (1987) 5 Journal of Professional Legal Education 16.
2 William Twining *Karl Llewellyn and the Realist Movement* (1973); see also W Twining *The Karl Llewellyn Papers* (1968).
3 Jerome Frank 'Why not a Clinical Law School?' (1933) 81 U Pa L Rev 907.
4 Robert Stevens *Law School Education in America from the 1850's to the 1980's* (1983).
5 *A Time for Change, Report of the Committee on the Future of the Legal Profession*, Chairman: Lady Marre CBE. Presented to the General Council of the Bar and the Council of the Law Society, July 1988, at 153.
6 Neil Gold 'The Professional Legal Training Program: Towards Training for Competence' (1983) 41 Advocate 247; and (1983) 1 The Journal of Professional Legal Education 1.
7 C C Langdell *Cases on Law of Contracts* (1871) at chs V–VII.
8 *Law and Learning: Report to the Social Science and Humanities Research Council of Canada by the Consultative Group on Research and Education in Law*, April 1983.
9 Roger Fisher and William Ury *Getting to Yes: Negotiating Agreements Without Giving In* (1983).
10 Donald A Schon *The Reflective Practitioner: How Professionals Think in Action* (1983); see also D Schon *Educating the Reflective Practitioner* (1987).
11 Gold, n 6 above.

Index